PITT *versus* FOX: FATHER AND SON

PITT *versus* FOX

FATHER & SON

1735-1806

By
ERICH EYCK

Translated by Eric Northcott

OCTAGON BOOKS

A DIVISION OF FARRAR, STRAUS AND GIROUX

New York   1973

THIS BOOK WAS
ORIGINALLY PUBLISHED AS
DIE PITTS UND DIE FOX' VÄTER UND SÖHNE
BY EUGEN RENTSCH VERLAG
OF ZURICH
1946

TRANSLATION FIRST PUBLISHED 1950

Reprinted 1973
by special arrangement with G. Bell & Sons, Ltd.

OCTAGON BOOKS
A DIVISION OF FARRAR, STRAUS & GIROUX, INC.
19 Union Square West
New York, N. Y. 10003

LIBRARY OF CONGRESS CATALOG CARD NUMBER: 72-13742

ISBN 0-374-92673-5

Printed in USA by
Thomson-Shore, Inc.
Dexter, Michigan

CONTENTS

ERRATUM

PAGE 375, line 14 from foot, *for* Westminster Abbey
read St. Paul's Cathedral.

ILLUSTRATIONS

NOTE ON THE TRANSLATION

The courteous help and advice of Dr. Eyck have been of great assistance in preparing this translation, and with his concurrence some corrections have been embodied in the English version.

CHAPTER I

HENRY FOX: BEGINNINGS

ONE day in May, 1744, London society was all agog. The Duke of Richmond's daughter, Lady Caroline Lennox, had eloped with Henry Fox—a commoner! True, the young couple's first call had been made upon an obliging cleric, who had not asked too many questions and had married them off in a trice. This admittedly lessened the scandal, but it did not remove it, for the blood royal flowed in the veins of the Duke of Richmond, though not, of course, wholly unmixed with more common fluid. The Duke could rightly claim the gay and wily Stuart monarch, Charles II, as his grandfather; his grandmother, on the other hand, was no queen but that beautiful French girl, Louise de Kéroualle, later to become Duchess of Portsmouth in reward for her services to the King. Still, the English aristocracy of the eighteenth century were not as a rule over-nice on questions of legitimacy. '*Non - j'aurai - des - maîtresses*', was the answer George II gave to his consort, when Queen Caroline on her death-bed told him to remarry; but with understanding magnanimity she brushed this demur aside with an '*Ah! mon Dieu! cela n'empêche pas.*' Then again, Georgiana, Duchess of Devonshire, whose beauty has been immortalised by Reynolds, shared her house on terms of the closest friendship with Lady Elizabeth Foster, whom she knew to be her husband's mistress and the mother of two children by him. No, the Duke of Richmond's circle did not regard the slight left-handedness of his descent as a slur on his royal birth, and the powerful Duke of Newcastle, who as Secretary of State really had enough on his hands with current international tangles, ran up and down in a great to-do to air his distress at 'this most unfortunate affair', until his colleague, the ever-cheerful and bibulous Lord Carteret, took the wind out of his sails by remarking, 'I thought our fleets or our armies were beat, or Mons betrayed into the hands of the French. At last it came out that Harry Fox was married, which I knew before'.

Henry Fox, the hero of the romantic adventure, was already

a man of some mark in politics: he had a seat in the Commons, and, as a skilful and effective debater, was a figure of considerable influence there. The Fox family, too, had close connections with Charles II, though, indeed, of a much more prosaic kind. Stephen Fox had entered his service at a time when, after the execution of his father, Charles I, he was still a king in exile. The young Charles had entrusted him with the administration of his privy purse, no light task to discharge on behalf of a man who was to pass through all the vicissitudes of a revolutionary period and displayed uncommonly clearly the hereditary Stuart lack of an economic sense. Stephen Fox proved fully equal to this task, and his dependability won him not only the confidence of his master, but also the best of credit with bankers and financiers. That, while holding this office, he had opportunities of amassing a considerable fortune and availed himself of these opportunities to the full, earned him no reproach from any of his contemporaries, nor will anyone who knows the customs of those times find it a cause for censure today.

This Stephen Fox (Sir Stephen from 1665 onwards) married for a second time in 1703. He was then in his seventy-seventh year. In 1704, as he records with naïve pride in his own memoirs, 'to my great surprise as well as the wonder of the world', a son was born who was given his father's name. 'A greater wonder', it is later recorded in the same place, 'happened on the 28th of September, 1705', when twins, a boy and a girl, were born. It is this second son, Henry Fox, with whom this narrative is concerned.

Henry lost his father when he was eleven. Sir Stephen Fox died in 1716, in his ninetieth year, and left a considerable fortune to his children; this enabled them to have the best education that the England of the day could offer. The two boys were sent to Eton, where even then the sons of ruling families used to be given their grounding for life and were prepared for the parts they would one day have to play in the government of their country. Henry Fox also went up to Oxford for two years (1721–1723) but, as history records no academic successes, he probably took his studies no more seriously than did any other scion of the aristocracy. Another traditional element in the education of those of his station was the 'Grand Tour', a round trip of at least one year on the Continent, during which one made a point of visiting Paris in order to acquire polish and finer manners. This part, too, of the prescribed curriculum was duly carried through by the two Fox boys.

They had no need to cast about for a living. Like other young people in the same favoured position they were now faced with the problem of whether or not to enter politics. In the England of that day this was, of course, by no means as weighty a matter as it became some hundred years later. To be a member of the Commons and thus a member of the High Court of Parliament was a social distinction. What was certainly more important still for many people was the prospect it offered of one or several of the countless sinecures, pensions, posts and petty offices which enabled a man 'who belonged' to live at the expense of the state and to provide for his family. In any case getting elected presented no difficulty to a man backed by an influential family or influential friends. For influence meant first and foremost having at one's disposal one or more of the many boroughs in which a few dozen 'free and independent voters' were ready to cast their vote for any man recommended to them by their patron or anyone who would pay them an adequate sum for their trouble.

Of course, to become a member of Parliament meant joining one or other of the two great parties into which England had been divided politically since the seventeenth century—the Whigs or the Tories. Since 1714, when the House of Hanover had occupied the throne of England, the Whigs had indisputably been the dominant party. Their leaders, and in particular the great aristocrats, had been the authors of the Glorious Revolution of 1688 and had expelled James II. It was the Whigs who, by the Act of Settlement of 1701, had ensured the Protestant succession and had secured the Crown of England for the Elector of Hanover. The Tories had always inclined to the Stuarts and their notions of divine right, and, in the closing years of Queen Anne, had endeavoured to open the door again to the Stuart claimant. Since then, it is true, many of them had watered down the wine of their Stuart toasts, but for the ruling Whig party the temptation to represent the Tories as still in sympathy with the banished dynasty and enemies of the reigning house was too strong. Besides, this made it all the easier to keep up the demand that only Whigs should hold offices and positions of favour at court and in the state. At the head of the party in power was Sir Robert Walpole. Few ministers have in their own day been the objects of such violent controversy, attacks and hatred as he. Posterity, it is true, has not acquitted him of all reproach, but it has almost unanimously recognized that to him must go the credit for playing the greatest, perhaps the most decisive, part in the development of England and her political institutions. As a statesman he was certainly no genius, but he possessed in outstanding measure the faculty which distinguishes the statesman from the jobbing politician and the amateur: a grasp of essentials. And for him what did seem essential was to end once and for all the internal disorders from which England had suffered in the seventeenth century and to strengthen and consolidate the new order of things which had existed since 1714. That meant accustoming the English people to a dynasty which had absolutely nothing to recommend it except its adherence to the Protestant faith, and finally obviating a return of the old dynasty with its appeal to ancient, deeply-rooted monarchical doctrines and traditions, the only really damaging objection to it being its Catholicism. When Walpole took over the direction of affairs in 1721, only six years had passed since the Stuart claimant, the son of the exiled James II, had tried to regain the crown by rebellion. When Walpole fell in 1742 it was only three years before the even more dangerous attempt by the Young Pretender, Charles Edward, to thrust from Scotland into the very heart of England. In his intervening twenty-one years of office, Walpole had staked all on keeping the peace for his people, because he was firmly convinced that for a nation as commercially active as the English only a long peace could secure the material and political calm and consolidation which would banish any thought of a fresh revolution.

Constitutionally speaking, the significant fact is that Walpole recognized that the House of Commons was ideally suited to provide a firm foundation for this policy of restoring confidence. The King's influence on policy was still, of course, very strong. Within certain limits all the preceding kings had conducted, or tried to conduct, their own personal policy, and even the Georges regarded the ministers primarily as their servants; the ministers themselves seldom took umbrage at this idea and thus they looked upon the favour of the Crown as their main support.

But it had also been seen that in the long run no policy and no ministry could stand up to the consistent opposition of Parliament, comprising then—as now—the Lords and the Commons. In case of need the Crown could influence the composition of the upper House by the arbitrary creation of peers, a measure to which Queen Anne had resorted only a few years before in order to compel acceptance of the Peace of Utrecht in 1713; an attempt to limit this prerogative of the Crown had been foiled in 1713 by Walpole, who thereby showed unerring political instinct. But the lower House was an elected body representative of the taxpayers. No one understood better than Walpole, who was the foremost finance minister of his age, what that meant. His first concern was always to assure himself of a reliable majority there. In this he was helped above all else by his uncommon gift of persuasive oratory and of expounding the most complicated problems so clearly and intelligibly that even the simplest country squire could follow him. But he was too good a judge of men and too great a cynic to rely on this alone. He knew that a large proportion of the members expected their parliamentary mandate to produce something tangible—either money or honours. He recognized this need by rewarding out of government resources the votes of those who supported the administration. That is why Walpole's political opponents attacked him so violently as the fount of parliamentary corruption, and there is an undeniable flavour of corruption in his system, however much the other side exaggerated it. Few, if any, will share the view of Sir William Harcourt, Gladstone's Chancellor of the Exchequer, who once asked with a smile what possible objection there could be if the clever people paid the foolish people for voting as the clever people thought best. But in fairness it must be remembered that all the things which today hold a party together—organization, programme, press and the like—did not and could not exist at that time. A party was hardly more than a group of powerful gentlemen, who were linked by certain, often rather vague, fundamental views and frequently by family connections as well, and around whom clustered their personal followings. It is in the nature of things that the bond which holds such a party together slackens as the day of their close-knit unity in opposition recedes ; the danger of splitting up into rival personal factions increases corres-

pondingly. The most effective means then known of combating
this tendency was the system which the administration called
'patronage' and those in opposition 'corruption', and this, as
will be seen, had nothing strange about it, whether it was
wielded by Walpole or by the Whig aristocracy.

But whatever one may think about this, the fact remains that
Walpole's policy most effectively enhanced the importance of
the Commons. He was the first leading minister who fully
realized that his place must be in the Commons if he was really
to lead. At that time it was still customary for most of the
members of a ministry to be peers and thus members of the
Lords, and a ministry's prestige partly rested on the high rank
of its noble members. Almost every government had to have a
duke in it, and a commoner was quite definitely an exception.
But this exception often set his heart on not remaining exceptional but on being translated to the Lords with as high a rank
as possible. There are instances enough to be found among
Walpole's predecessors and successors, but he himself was too
astute to sacrifice the basis of his political strength to a social
ambition of this kind. Only when defeated did he consent to be
made Earl of Orford, and when he then met in the Lords the
man who had previously been his keenest political opponent,
he greeted him with the words: 'My Lord Bath, you and I are
now two as insignificant men as any in *England.*'

Equally important in the development of Parliament was the
fact that Walpole laid the foundations of the system which is to
this day the distinctive characteristic of the British constitution
—the Cabinet system. The Cabinet, which in normal times
governs Britain, consists of ministers, mainly, that is to say, of
the heads of the great central departments. It carries the legal
and political responsibility for the policy and administration
of the realm. It is headed by a prime minister whom the rest
are pledged to follow in all important questions; anyone unable
to do this must place his office at the prime minister's disposal.
All members of the Cabinet have a joint responsibility to
Parliament and are linked in solidarity with their colleagues.
These principles by no means obtained in full in Walpole's day,
nor does it follow that he recognized them. In particular, it was
then considered a doubtful privilege for anyone to be known as
the leading or first or prime minister. The man in question

would anxiously disclaim such a title; it was too reminiscent of the Earl of Strafford who had paid on the scaffold for his alleged aspiration to such a post. Nor did ministers in office hesitate either to speak in open debate on controversial questions or even to take different sides when the division was called. But in actual fact Walpole succeeded more and more in making Cabinet decisions, taken under his presidency and decisive influence, the recognized basis of the administration's policy and in having dissentient ministers relieved of their posts by the King. This determining influence of the principal minister was possible only because it was he and not the King who now presided over the sittings of the Cabinet; Queen Anne had presided but the change of dynasty affected this decisive point. George I was a man of fifty-four when he ascended the English throne. One might think that he would have employed the preceding years in preparing himself for this post, which had appeared an almost certain prospect for more than a decade. But this would argue a frame of mind utterly remote from George's. Strange as it may seem, he looked on his elevation to the throne of Britain not as a rare piece of good fortune but as an inconvenient and burdensome dispensation of Providence which he could not well avoid because, when all was said and done, one simply did not refuse a crown. How much more comfortable was his position as Elector of Hanover than as King of England! As Elector he was a German prince, that is, a man whose word was law within the often admittedly narrow confines of his own country, and one before whom everyone bowed low. Even if these German principalities were mostly far too small to conduct an independent foreign policy, the uninhibited consciousness of divine right enjoyed by the reigning prince flourished all the more freely within the country. Not that they had all been hardened despots. Many were in a greater or less degree benevolent fathers to their people, but in their own eyes they were all of them an end in themselves and one which their country had to serve. In the same way it was, to them, quite natural that every citizen in the land should accept with complete submission all their decrees and decisions without venturing to measure them by the yardstick of a subject's limited comprehension.

How different was the lot of the King in Britain! There one

found mighty, wealthy aristocrats who, even if they did observe the forms of court etiquette, let it be seen in no uncertain manner that in pride and consciousness of their own worth they yielded place to no king, that, indeed, they had deposed one king and set another in his place. There the King could not impose taxes at his own sweet will, but Parliament had to sanction every single penny raised, even the Civil List for the personal needs of the King and his family. There the King could not simply promulgate a new law by decree, but a bill had to make its way—often a dangerous and painful way—through both Houses; worse still, even the common people sometimes made their voice heard. Pamphlets, the authors of which were mostly untraceable, kept criticising in a way which was often disrespectful, and the Lord Mayor and Aldermen of the City of London spoke with a plainness and boldness which no respectable merchant in Hanover would have allowed himself to use. What charms could such a position hold for a German prince? Yet, again, it could not be denied that a king was something rather grander than a mere elector. This consideration weighed all the more heavily since in 1701 the Elector of Brandenburg had, by imperial consent, risen to be King of Prussia. The worst of this was that the reigning King of Prussia, Frederick William I, was George's son-in-law. Had not another German prince, the Elector Augustus of Saxony, won himself a crown, if only that of Poland? And should a Hanoverian, then, refuse the crown of England? Above all, as King of England, he was still Elector of Hanover, where he could always recuperate from the vexations and inconveniences of the part he had to play in England.

When George I set foot on English soil in 1714, he did not even known enough of the native tongue to make himself understood by his ministers. With Walpole, who had learned a respectable amount of Latin at Eton, he could at least converse in the tongue of the ancient Romans, even if in not altogether classical Latin. How could a king like this be expected to preside over an English council of ministers, who in any case were taken up with questions with which George I was far too lazy to familiarize himself? He relinquished this task, quite without envy, to Walpole, whom he could confidently count upon to raise the money he needed for himself and for his German favourites and mistresses. Still less did he allow himself to become tied to England by such political tasks. Whenever possible he went off to Hanover, which he sighted with the feelings of a boy who goes home for the holidays from an unpleasant school.

A king like this was obviously not quite the man to win a warm corner in the hearts of his new subjects. What they heard of his family life—of the luckless wife doomed to expiate a love-affair with lifelong imprisonment, and of the son with whom he kept up a constant and embittered quarrel—was also hardly calculated to increase his popularity.

At the time when the two Fox brothers were turning over the idea of going into Parliament, this son, George II, had already ascended the throne which he was to occupy for more than thirty years (1727-1760). This second George, too, felt himself to be a Hanoverian in exile over here and he fled to his native land as often as he could. Still worse in the eyes of the English politicians and the English people, he was at pains to exploit his dual position to favour his electorate at the expense of his kingdom. This was a particularly serious matter in an age of international tangles which involved both countries, and not always in the same way. Countless political crises sprang from the resulting complications. The gulf which these political difficulties opened up between the English and their King was not bridged by any personal merits in the sovereign. George II has had the misfortune to come down to posterity delineated by a most intimate acquaintance. There lived at his court a man who knew how to wield a pen and committed to his journal, with a malice equal to his relish, his experiences there—this was John, Lord Hervey. Courtiers have at times the faculty of seeing the weaknesses of their lords and masters more clearly than their good qualities and of recouping themselves for having to pay much in the punctilio of court ceremonial by putting down very different coin in their confidential journals, when the glitter and burden of the day are laid aside. Hervey is an outstanding instance of this, and his portrait of George certainly does not err on the side of flattery. But the picture he paints of his patroness, Queen Caroline, shows that he can render justice and give praise. Both portraits are so vivid that no one who has read Hervey's memoirs can forget them. One can almost sense

B

the atmosphere of leaden *ennui* which the heavy, morose King spread about him, till it became a torture, borne by his much more intelligent Queen with exemplary patience every evening on which His Majesty honoured her with his presence. One can hardly blame her if she heaved a sigh of relief when he took a mistress with whom he spent at least a part of these interminable evenings. To be sure Hervey dipped his pen in gall when he described his King; but he has on the whole recorded the facts faithfully, and in consequence one may accept his portrait of George II in essentials, especially as it shows many traits typical of German princes of that day and many qualities natural to a thick-headed Guelph.

One feature of the family life of the House of Hanover became particularly important in English politics: the constantly-recurring antipathy, and even hatred, between father and son, between king and heir. With George II and his son, Prince Frederick, this is particularly marked, and Hervey, who had a private feud with the prince, was at pains to see that posterity should be well informed, in the most minute and unsparing detail, about this family conflict. Without question the prince was a stupid and worthless youth, but there is no satisfactory explanation of the almost pathological hatred with which not only his father but also his mother regarded him. Queen Caroline did not blush to tell her intimates frankly that she wished this son of hers would 'sink to hell'.

By virtue of the special nature of the English constitution, the opposition between King and heir now had a singular political effect: the heir to the throne became more or less a party leader. As has already been emphasized, the personal influence of the King on the composition of the administration was still very great—at least, in a negative sense. Aversion felt by the sovereign for any particular member of Parliament kept him— perhaps for ever, and in any case for many years—out of every office of importance. What was such a man to do if he were ambitious and did not wish to be banished for life to the opposition with the sweets of office untasted? The first thought to occur to him was that even kings do not live for ever, and that one day a new Pharaoh would rule in Egypt. Now if there also existed open opposition between the ruling and the future monarch, an alignment suggested itself. Whoever had nothing

to hope from St. James's, where the King resided, looked the
more eagerly to Leicester House, where the Prince of Wales
held court. Here everyone who was at odds with Walpole and
was working for his overthrow could be sure of a friendly reception and a sympathetic ear. But Walpole had a whole host
of such enemies, not merely from among the Tories, whom he
excluded on principle from all offices of state and at court, but
also from among the Whigs. For he could make no use in his
Cabinet of independent men with views of their own; a fact
which throws into relief how much the composition of the
ministry was decided by personal intolerance and by purely
material considerations of uniformity.

§

This short sketch may give some idea of the state of political
and party life at the time when the Fox brothers were about to
make up their minds to enter Parliament. They first had to
decide on a party, and, if this decision turned out in favour of
the Whigs, on one of the Whig groups which were striving for
supremacy.

Family tradition seemed to indicate the Tory party; their
father had made his name and fortune as a faithful servant of
Charles II and had to the end of his days cherished the memory
of the 'martyr' Charles I. But were such traditions to determine
the careers of ambitious young men who were not anxious to
eat the stale bread of opposition all their days? By good fortune
they struck up friendships in the decisive years with influential
members of the court party, particularly Lord Hervey, the
diarist. Hervey was a faithful henchman of Walpole, to whom
he was particularly valuable by virtue of his confidential
friendship with the Queen. The worldly-wise courtier gained
great influence over the Fox brothers, who were about ten
years younger than he, and it was probably not over-difficult
for him to convince them that they could entrust their frail bark
to no more experienced pilot than the statesman then in power.

Finding a suitable constituency presented no difficulties if
one had the support of this minister, who swayed ministerial
and court influence. Even if one were defeated at the polls, it
was not too difficult to *corriger la fortune*, for could not the
majority in Parliament which supported the ministry pro-

nounce the election of one's opponent null and void? So little concerned over the result was Henry Fox that he did not even return to England for the General Election of 1734, showing a preference for the company of an interesting young woman in Paris and Nice. Offsetting this, his brother Stephen stood for two seats. In one case he was returned but in the other he was defeated. But Parliament annulled this latter return and declared Stephen the legally elected representative. The other seat thus fell vacant, and in the circumstances nothing could be more natural than for the electorate to repose its confidence in Henry Fox in place of his brother Stephen. The returning officer was bought over by Walpole and this decided the matter.

And thus on February 28th, 1735, Henry Fox took his seat in the Commons as member for Hindon in Wiltshire.

Ten days before, on February 18th, 1735, a by-election had taken place in the borough of Old Sarum. This borough consisted of a few acres of arable land on which no living soul dwelt: but since in the grey mists of antiquity a small town had once stood there, its right to parliamentary representation still obtained. The electoral roll was not overwhelming; it totalled precisely seven. Those who wished to fulfil their civic duty and cast their vote had to be conveyed by the interested candidate to the poll, that is, to a tent which the returning officer brought with him. Of course, the votes were in the hands of a member of the oligarchy, the purchaser of the seat, which was doubly attractive because of these convenient facts. In this case his name was Thomas Pitt, and the man whom his loyal retainers, obedient to his behest, returned to the Commons was his brother, the twenty-seven year old Cornet of Horse, William Pitt.

Thus met, on the very threshold of their political careers, the two men who for more than a quarter of a century were to be constant rivals, intermittent allies and finally the most bitter opponents.

CHAPTER II

WILLIAM PITT:
ANCESTRY AND BEGINNINGS

WILLIAM PITT was as far removed as Henry Fox from being a scion of the rich and established nobility which formed the core of the Whig oligarchy. His great-grandfather was a simple country parson, rich only in children. With his grandfather Thomas, known as Governor Pitt, a young contemporary of Sir Stephen Fox, the family comes for the first time into the full light of history. Of course, if by a governor one pictures a man who has risen by his own exertions to a position of eminence in the service of king and state, thus achieving an honourable old age, then one would gain a most erroneous impression of Thomas Pitt. He was a strong man and an adventurer who had made himself so troublesome to the powers that be, that they had hit upon the oft-proven expedient of winning him over to their side and to the path of virtue by the offer of a high position in their own service. The scene of his adventures and successes was India, to which he first went in 1674 as a youth of about twenty. It was in the days of the East India Company which owned a number of factories there and controlled them under the authority of the English Crown. Its most valuable asset was its monopoly of overseas trade with India, which English sovereigns since the days of Elizabeth had granted it time and again. Monopolies were never popular in England, and so the seafarers and merchants who, in defiance of the Company's charter, went to India and carried on illicit trade there, were for the most part looked on by the public with the same indulgence as are smugglers in some coastal village which profits by their illegalities. For years Thomas Pitt was one of these interlopers, and one of the most formidable, because he was most energetic, courageous, intelligent and skilful. So little did this illicit activity damage his reputation that when, in 1683, he returned home for several years, he contrived to be elected for Parliament, although, it is true, for a borough which he had pocketed for cash, the very same Old Sarum in which his grandson's political career began. Even if the grandfather achieved nothing of note in politics, this very fact shows how astute he was. He not only knew that to possess land in England was a good investment for the capital he had acquired in India; he also realised how advantageous it was for a man of his unusual way of life to secure good political connections. He was a fervent Whig, and the Whigs had emerged decisively victorious from the revolution of 1688.

Some years later, after Pitt had once more shown in India what a dangerous competitor he could be, the political threat to the Company's situation was such that they decided to enlist in their ranks this man, who knew every trick of the trade and, moreover, sat in Parliament as a member of the party in office. And thus it was that in July, 1698, he was able to land in Madras as Governor of their two main forts on the Coromandel Coast. Nor were the expectations placed in him disappointed. The energy and ingenuity, with which he had once made himself so formidable to the Company, he now applied just as ruthlessly and successfully against their competitors. Letters of his which have survived show that he had his own methods of dealing with those who ventured to cross his path.

The post of an East Indian governor was, even by the standards of those days, a high and important one. It is, therefore, surprising at first glance that his emoluments were a meagre three hundred pounds a year. But this is very easily explained. No one, least of all the Company, expected their officials to live on their salaries. The financial value of their posts lay much more in the chance which they afforded of carrying on business on one's own account. Of course the real plums fell to His Excellency the Governor, and if his name was Thomas Pitt, one could rely on his making the most of the crop.

One of these transactions of his has become famous and has made him famous, too. He managed to acquire a diamond of fabulous size and value for twenty-five thousand pounds in a way which, by the standards of the day, was not scandalous. For fifteen years his main concern was first to bring this diamond to Europe (his son had to take it, concealed in the sole of his shoe), and then to sell it. It was not until 1717 that he managed to dispose of this 'Pitt Diamond' to the Regent of France for one hundred and thirty-three thousand pounds; and although part of this enormous price was never paid, it was none the less a good stroke of business.

When Governor Pitt returned home from the East in 1710, he was a rich man who bought castles and estates, a man who—in his own right, as it were—could sit in Parliament. His children could marry into proud, noble families; one daughter became the wife of Earl Stanhope, who is numbered among the most successful of England's foreign ministers, and, up to the time of his death in 1721, the real leader of the administration, as Walpole later became. But apart from this the Governor did not find his family a great source of happiness. Discord and strife reigned almost uninterruptedly. When in India he had sent home many extremely outspoken letters, in which he most sharply condemned first one member of the family and then another—not omitting his wife, whom he describes, quite simply, as 'mad'. After his return, quarrels and conflicts never really ceased. He had grown used to the methods of an Oriental despot in the East and they suited his mode of life, but they were hardly calculated to manage and hold together an English family. Gout, the hereditary disease of the Pitts, increased his natural irritability to a condition which at times became morbid; not infrequently his manner gave rise to the suspicion that he was not quite right in the head. Many observers surmised even then that he bequeathed to his descendants a certain tendency to insanity.

At all events, he was thoroughly dissatisfied with his children. He despised his eldest son Robert as a weakling; and when this Robert betrayed a sympathy for the Tories he roused the full wrath of his father, who remained an out-and-out Whig throughout his life.

Only one member of his family gave him any pleasure, and this was William Pitt, the younger son of Robert, whom he so heartily despised. In the child the Governor discovered a chip of the old block. He was no milksop like his father. His manner and bearing showed that he had a will of his own and he evinced an intelligence which gladdened the heart of the old man of action. When he went to Eton, his grandfather took him out as often as possible in order to enjoy a few days or hours in his company. 'He is a hopeful lad', he said of him, 'and doubt not but he will answer yours and all his friends' expectation'.

He lived long enough to see his grandson grow up to be a young man of eighteen before death brought him, in 1726, the peace which he had never known in life. In the same year William Pitt left Eton which he had attended together with his brother Thomas, his senior by three years. At Eton he had an excellent classical education; in particular, he was able, even as an old man, to quote with effect and understanding from the classics. But he was not happy at Eton; indeed, he later declared that any boy there who was at all sensitive was cowed for life. Possibly this impression can be explained by the fact that the gout, which plagued him even then, kept him from any active part in the games and sports which were so important at the school. But what proved most useful for his future career were the friendships he made there with other boys from influential families, such as the brothers Richard and George Grenville and George Lyttelton; these were to be of great significance in the years which followed.

From Eton, William Pitt went up to Oxford. In his very first year there he lost his father, who survived the Governor by only a year. This last year of his father's life was racked by disputes, now chronic among the Pitts, centring on the family and the estate. The bulk of the father's fortune passed to the elder son, and William had to make shift with a modest annuity of one hundred pounds left him by his grandfather, added to which was a yearly income of about the same amount from his father's estate. Fortunately, the relations between the two brothers were so good at the time that Thomas gave him the money needed to complete his education.

Little is heard of the mother. She came from the noble Villiers family, which produced many extravagant characters. There were seven children of the marriage and several of these were abnormal, not to say deranged. Lord Shelburne, who was for a time intimately connected with William Pitt in later life, states that a high degree of insanity was present in the family. It is perhaps a not unjust assumption that predispositions on the maternal side combined with the tendency inherited from Governor Pitt to produce this unhealthy result. The mother survived the father by only a few years. She died in France in 1736, whither she had retired after the customary squabbles over the estate.

William remained at Oxford for only a year. The climate was bad for his gout. But with the help of his brother he was able to go on and spend about a year at the University of Utrecht, where numerous young Englishmen were then studying. It is not known whether he ever intended following a learned profession. At all events, his life took quite a different turn when, shortly after his return to England in February 1731, he became a cavalry officer.

How did he come to do this? In eighteenth-century England —and even up to the time of Gladstone's reform in 1872—the post of an officer was not one to which the King summoned those who had shown their suitability for it in a course of training. It was a post which the aspirant purchased, usually from the previous holder, or, in the case of a vacancy on the establishment, from the man to whom the regiment belonged. The cavalry regiment which young Pitt entered was the Second (or King's Own) Regiment of Horse under Lord Cobham. Cobham seems to have facilitated Pitt's entry by waiving the customary fee of one thousand pounds. This Lord Cobham, who thus became Pitt's patron at an important point in his career, was not only an outstanding officer who had won his laurels in Marlborough's campaigns, but also an ambitious politician who had attracted notice. A member of the nobility and a Temple, he was related to Pitt's friends, the Grenville brothers and Lord Lyttelton, in whose company and at whose country seats Pitt spent much of his time after his return from Utrecht. Besides this, Pitt was connected with Lyttelton by his brother Thomas's marriage with Lyttelton's sister. The focus of this whole circle was at Stowe, which Cobham had restored with great magnificence. Young Pitt was introduced here by his friends and the lord of the manor took a liking to him. If he did open up an army career to him, the young man's military usefulness appears to have been of less moment than his political parts. The purely military duties of an officer in peace-time were not over-exacting, nor did they entail a great expenditure of time. If, as he later boasted, Pitt during his time as an officer really studied all the military manuals he could lay hands on, he must have done this not in the fulfilment of his duties, but of his own accord. His military service did not keep him from an extensive social round away from his garrison nor from a six

months' trip which took him to France and Switzerland in 1733.
Thus he contrived, somewhat belatedly, to make his 'Grand
Tour', and he gained knowledge of an important area of the
Continent and of the French language. Both served him in good
stead later. Among the geographical impressions which he re-
ceived, the sight of the junction of the Rhône and the Saône at
Lyons must be mentioned, because to this he owes one of his
most celebrated flights of oratory.

In this year a warm and mutual attachment kept him in close
touch with his sister Ann, who was four years younger than he,
and probably the only one of his brothers and sisters who was
intimate with him for any length of time. This attachment
found expression in an animated correspondence, the brother's
share in which has survived. This has an especial value in
throwing light on his personality, for the letters are not yet
couched in the stilted and unnatural style he adopted later,
which renders most of the letters he wrote in his prime unread-
able. Here he reveals himself as he was by nature: lively, sensitive and at time humorous. He is frankly concerned about his
sister's health, teases her about the admirers who pay their
addresses to her and describes graphically the roistering and
carousals of his comrades. Several of the letters are written in
French, and testify to his earnest exertions to master the language. In reading these youthful letters to Ann, one feels it to be
doubly painful that even this family bond did not remain intact
throughout his life but was one day severed abruptly.

In 1734, Pitt returned to England and his political career
began at once. Lord Cobham, who had made him an officer,
also guided his political footsteps. But these now lay along the
path of opposition. Cobham, it was true, was just as much a
Whig as Walpole, but at the time he was bitterly at odds with
him. The minister had introduced an Excise Bill in 1733; under
this, tobacco and wine were to be made to yield revenue more
readily by means of an excise duty than they could by customs
control in the face of widespread smuggling which was hard to
combat. This eminently reasonable project ran up against a
demagogic opposition, which unscrupulously whipped up the
deeply-rooted objection of the people to any form of excise. In
the lower House, none the less, Walpole managed to retain his
majority. But he was under no illusions about popular opposi-

tion and was far too astute a politician not to realise that such strong popular feeling must be taken into account, even if, thanks to the existing system of representation, it did not find full expression in Parliament. So he withdrew his bill amid the triumphant cries of the opposition. But he was determined to show that no one might defy him with impunity, and so he prevailed on the King to dismiss the leaders of the resistance from those offices which they held in the state and at court. Among those who had raised their voices loudest in the controversy had been Cobham. He had an official post, though not in the civil administration but in the army. But this did not protect him from Walpole's resolve to make an example of him. He was dismissed and relieved of the command of his regiment.

Cobham was the last man to take this lying down, and he possessed influence and contacts enough to make himself a thorn in the minister's side. He formed his ambitious young kinsfolk into a political clique which was dubbed 'The Cobham Cousinhood'. Pitt, along with his friends, was enrolled in this cousinhood. Cobham must have recognized early on that his young Cornet of Horse possessed talents which could be admirably employed in a ruthless opposition campaign. A seat was to hand. To what end other than this had the shrewd Governor acquired, some decades before, the rottenest of all boroughs, Old Sarum?

And thus it was that in February, 1735, Cornet William Pitt was able to take the stage on which he was one day to become the principal actor.

CHAPTER III

PARLIAMENTARY APPRENTICESHIP.
WALPOLE'S FALL. CARTERET

WHAT sort of place was this House of Commons, which Fox and Pitt entered almost simultaneously in February 1735? That it had much about it which today appears odd is shown by the very fact that an officer on the active list like Pitt could take his seat there. The dual rôle of an officer sworn to unconditional obedience to the King and of a parliamentarian independently maintaining his own opinions, even, it might be, against the King's ministers, was nothing outrageous in those days, although Cobham's fate had just shown what cheerless consequences it could have. The opposition tried, on the basis of this experience, to raise to the dignity of law the principle that officers should be irremoveable. But this notion was so obviously misconceived that when it was brought forward it met with a resounding defeat. If one were to measure the Parliament of the eighteenth century by the standards of the democratic assembly of the twentieth, one would meet nothing but anomalies and absurdities at every turn. But no one who thinks historically will expect it to have been a popular representative body in which the voice of all sections of the people could be heard. It was an aristocratic assembly, in which the influential circles wielding a decisive influence at that time were more or less represented and gained a hearing.

There was always a strong group of country landowners, members for the counties in which they had their seats and their estates. This class was particularly important because it was primarily in its hands that the administration of the countryside lay. These squires were most of them Tories with Jacobite sympathies, supporters of the Established Church, and opponents of the new-fangled principles of religious toleration and of the Nonconformists, who in their eyes were the very worst type of Whig. But although Walpole was well aware of all this, he took care not to interfere over-much in their control of local government. He had to his very fingertips too sensitive a feeling for politics to misuse the Whigs' parliamentary majority by kindling fresh conflicts which would have plunged the country into renewed disorder. These country members did not constitute a party of their own, but were an independent element and respected as such by both the ministry and the opposition.

Another element, independent to some extent, was represented by members for large towns, led by the City of London, men from the world of commerce and finance who took up the cudgels for the economic and political interests of their own circles. But the number of such independent constituencies was very small; it was out of all proportion to their real importance. The electoral distribution of seats had been static for decades and had in no way kept pace with developments; the quicker these moved, the wider grew the gap.

The lion's share of the seats fell to those provincial towns and small market towns, scattered all over the country, which had received the right of parliamentary representation far back in the past and had preserved it ever since without diminution 'as of right'. The personal qualifications for voting in these constituencies were as varied as they were numerous, but were almost everywhere restricted to a small, at times microscopic, number of people. The smaller the electoral roll, the easier it was to control it, and thus most of the narrower of these constituencies were 'pocket boroughs', that is to say, boroughs which were virtually in the pockets of either the government or of rich landlords; they were looked upon as personal property and might be disposed of, just like any other property, by way of sale or hire. In the government constituencies certain officials, notably Customs and tax officials, formed the backbone of the electorate; they, of course, had to vote as ordered from above.

In such a setting, parliamentary anarchy would inevitably have developed had not two important circumstances worked against it. One was the close solidarity of most of the influential families, based not only on manifold personal relations but also on common, if somewhat vague, political convictions. The other was their working agreement with the Crown and ministry, an agreement born of the interests which both sides had in common. Such a system, based primarily on personal contacts, could only last any length of time if men could be found who would constantly re-knit these strands and deliberately make it their business to keep the system running. During the reign of George II, the Duke of Newcastle (one of the Pelhams) was the connecting link. The Duke was a very rich man and owned considerable landed property. In the neighbourhood of his estates he had, from the very outset, a predominating influence, so that the election of his candidates there was a foregone conclusion. But his ambition aimed higher: he wanted to extend his ministerial influence over the greater part of the country and to this end he not only devoted indefatigable pains—testified to by his almost endless correspondence—but he also sacrificed to it a considerable part of his fortune. Of course he did nothing by halves: voters were bought, patrons were won over by titles and offices, privileges and benefices were bestowed only with party interests in view, dependent voters and even electoral officials were given orders; and similar methods were used to keep the elected members in hand. Small wonder that every Cato in the opposition pilloried the Duke as the father of corruption. But however true this may be, it is also true that he never enriched himself, that one of his opponents said emphatically, on his death, that his hands had always been clean and that he left public life a much poorer man than he entered it, although he was a minister almost without a break for nearly forty years from 1724 to 1762.

Newcastle has been very unfavourably judged by his contemporaries and by historians. Macaulay, in particular, in his *Essays,* has sketched with his inimitable art a portrait of him as vivid as it is unfriendly, in which the Duke cuts an almost comic figure. Now admittedly no one can consider Newcastle a great statesman, but he was not so completely insignificant as this. His letters—a historical source of the first order—often disclose extremely intelligent arguments which testify to clear political vision. But what he manifestly lacked were character, personality and decision. There is in these often interminable letters a constant nervous indecision, a lamentation over real or imagined slights and a suspicious mistrust of anyone who smelt in the least like a rival.

These defects would probably have made him an impossible person in the long run if he had not had a friend who was always ready to advise him with calm discernment and statesmanlike insight. This was the Lord Chancellor, Lord Hardwicke. The career of this outstanding lawyer is an instance of how, even in the aristocratic England of the eighteenth century, a particular talent opened the way to the greatest offices of state and to the highest dignities. Philip Yorke was the son of a middle-class provincial attorney. He himself became an attorney in London and gained an unusually high reputation even as a young man. Newcastle recognized his political and parliamentary usefulness and procured him a seat in the Commons. Yorke never forgot this. Throughout his whole life he remained loyal to Newcastle, and, what was perhaps more difficult, he bore with his weaknesses. Within a short time he became, in 1720, when barely thirty, Solicitor-General, that is, one of the two law officers on whose advice the ministry relied in all legal questions. From there he made rapid progress up the ladder until in 1733 he became Lord Chief Justice, and, as Lord Hardwicke, a member of the upper House. With his appointment as Lord Chancellor in 1737, he reached the topmost rung of legal ambition. For the Lord Chancellor is not only the chief judge in the land but also presides over the upper House, where he sits on the Woolsack. But, in contrast to the Speaker of the Commons, who is condemned to dignified silence, the Lord Chancellor intervenes frequently, and with the full authority of his high office, in the debates of the House of Lords, and is even, at times, the most important government spokesman there. A man of moderate but firm political views, a Whig who clung to the traditions of the Glorious Revolution and the House of Hanover, he not only wielded considerable influence in the Lords, but was looked upon by the King as his most reliable counsellor in times of difficulty.

Neither Newcastle nor Hardwicke sat in the lower House. But here the administration had no need of further helpers so long as Walpole remained. In the debate on the Excise Bill he had already shown that no one could strike the right note in that House as well as he. Near him on the government bench sat the Army Paymaster, Henry Pelham, a younger brother of Newcastle, an unobtrusive, practical man, who faithfully supported his chief and was well liked in the government party. Henry Fox, too, enrolled in this party. During his early years in the House he was not prominent as a speaker, but Hervey saw to it that his abilities and his loyalty to the government did not pass unnoticed by the leading minister. It was a time when Walpole could make use of every able recruit, for the opposition was indefatigable in its attempts to overthrow him. The punishment he had meted out to his opponents after the defeat of the Excise Bill had strengthened the ranks of the opposition with many gifted and dangerous men.

In the Commons at the head of this opposition stood Sir William Pulteney, one of the Whigs who had offended and rebuffed Walpole and had waged an uninterrupted war to the death against him ever since, with the ultimate hope of one day being able to step into his shoes. His contemporaries praise him as an outstanding parliament man and his speeches as incomparable masterpieces. How correct this judgment is cannot be assessed by posterity as his speeches have not survived.

At that time there was not even moderately reliable parliamentary reporting. This was not through lack of interest on the part of the public but because of a legal obstacle. Whoever reported speeches made in Parliament infringed its 'privilege' and ran the risk of imprisonment for 'an indignity' to the House. Nothing could be in sharper contrast to the outlook of some modern member of Parliament, whose ambition it is to see himself quoted as often and as fully as possible in the newspapers. Of course, this paradoxical 'privilege' has a historical explanation. In the early days of Parliament, and particularly of its struggles with the Crown, members had to be protected from persecution by the King on account of their speeches. To this end, they were granted the privilege of barring all and sundry from attending their deliberations or reporting on them without permission. A characteristic and anachronistic survival of this privilege is the continuing right of any member to 'spy strangers' and thus have the galleries cleared. Gradually this antiquated right went out of use, but during the recent war secret sessions were still introduced by the Leader of the House rising and solemnly declaring: 'I spy strangers'.

What is today only a curiosity was in the eighteenth century a most serious and controversial question, about which a few more words may be said. Gradually the ban on reporting was circumvented when some newspapers published reports on 'Debates in the Senate of Lilliput' or similar mysterious bodies, in which the speakers' names were so paraphrased or hinted at that every informed reader knew at once who was meant. But the speeches which here appeared in print were often at least as much the product of the reporter as of the supposed speaker. Dr. Johnson, who battled his way through some lean years with journalistic hackwork of this kind, confesses that he himself composed most of the speeches on the basis of a few notes communicated to him by others.

Thus one of the most important sources for a knowledge of parliamentary activity of that day is lacking. This is partly off-set by the accounts given in contemporary memoirs and in the letters which politicians wrote to their friends in the country or abroad. To them, animated parliamentary proceedings were just as interesting as the latest society scandal or details of the squabbles between His Majesty and the Prince of Wales. In the front rank stands the greatest English letter-writer of the eighteenth century, Horace Walpole, youngest son of the minister, who himself sat in the lower House from 1741 to 1767. Horace spoke very seldom, but took notes of what he heard with all the more assiduity in order to assuage his friends' thirst for information or to collect material for his memoirs. To him we owe much of what we know of Pitt's most important speeches.

Thus the English parliamentarian of that epoch was unable to make any speech with an eye to an outside audience. Only in exceptional cases could he count on his words echoing among the people, and it is a feather in Pitt's cap that he none the less succeeded in catching the public's eye. But even if speeches in Parliament had to dispense with any propagandist effects, in the House itself they were all the more important. Since party ties were so much looser than today, far more members' votes depended on which side could convince them of the merits of its case. Indeed, even those members who were more or less closely bound to the administration still required it to put forward its arguments in an intelligible and convincing manner, and threatened rebellion if this were not done. Parliament was by no means so corrupt that ministers could have relied on monetary arguments alone.

Pulteney—to return to our account of the Commons—recognised that as things were, the opposition must needs use other means to win over public opinion. He found them in broadsheets and pamphlets, composed under his direction by

c

hired writers, which attacked Walpole with the weapons of wit and satire. In this he had no scruples over collaborating with an avowed Tory, whom he could regard as an ally because this man hated Walpole even more than he did. The Tory in question was Lord Bolingbroke, part author of the Peace of Utrecht and the focus of the bitterest attacks from the Whigs of his day. He had been allowed to return home from exile, where he had for a time worked in the service of the Stuarts, but Walpole made it impossible for him to take any active part in politics. All the more busily did he ply his extraordinarily skilful pen. He had the reputation not only of having been the best parliamentary orator of his day but also of standing in the forefront of political writers. He had reconciled himself to the Hanoverian succession, but the destruction of the rule of the Whig aristocracy was the mainspring of all his thoughts and writings. He saw an increase in the power of the Crown as a means of achieving this end. 'The Idea of a Patriot King' was the imposing phrase which he put on the title-page of his most important work. He himself considered its contents so dangerous that at first he did not dare to publish it. It did not exert its influence until the following reign, when George II had given place to his grandson, George III. It is perhaps no mere chance that the name which the men of the opposition gave themselves suggested the title of Bolingbroke's work. They styled themselves 'The Patriots'. They were able to claim Frederick, Prince of Wales, as their patron and fellow worker; he felt that his mission was one day to play the rôle of the 'Patriot King'. William Pitt, too, joined the ranks of these patriots at the same time as other young followers of Cobham, who were called the 'Boy Patriots'.

Frederick gave Pitt his first opportunity to come into the limelight as a parliamentary orator. In 1736, Frederick married a German princess, Augusta of Saxe-Gotha. The bitter enmity prevailing between him and his parents was common knowledge, and the ministry in consequence deferred to the King's wishes by not bringing up this domestic matter for debate in Parliament. The opposition was all the more aware that here was a golden opportunity to embarrass the ministry. Pulteney moved an address of congratulation and Pitt addressed the House on the motion. With as much ingenuity as malice he contrived to intersperse his speech, under a show of deepest loyalty, with pointed remarks which must have flicked the King on the raw. With almost diabolical skill his speech was so worded that in public no one could say a word against it, but that in private everyone recognised its true import. The King raged and Pitt was famous. But George had other means besides parliamentary discussion of paying back a personal attack. Was he calmly to accept such provocation from a young officer of his army? At the end of the session Pitt was relieved of his commission. When later Walpole was violently attacked by a member for this persecution, he answered roundly: '. . . If ever any officer of the army, because the King refused to comply with some very unreasonable demand, should resolve to oppose in everything the measures of the government, I should think any man a most pitiful minister if he should be afraid of advising His Majesty to cashier such an officer.' So far, so good. But the only logical solution would have been to pronounce that in law the post of an officer was incompatible with that of a member. Walpole, however, could not take this course because he could not dispense with military patronage in rewarding members who were loyal to the government. He left his example as a 'legacy to all future ministers' and they acted upon it. Again and again one will meet officers and admirals who are at the same time members of the House.

Disciplinary action is two-edged. If on the one hand it helps the government to spread fear and respect, on the other it invests its victims with the halo of martyrdom. Thanks to his misfortune, Pitt enjoyed an unusual popularity and found great favour in the ranks of the opposition. Against this, however, the loss of his pay hit him rather hard. But this too was made up to him in the following year when the Prince, who in the meantime had become completely estranged from his family, gave him a post in his household.

These disputes in the royal family were also the means of giving Henry Fox the opportunity of proving his loyalty to the ministry. George had granted his son a yearly allowance of £50,000, with which Frederick was far from satisfied. He wanted at least £100,000, the sum which had been granted to his father as Prince of Wales by George I. Beyond this, the Prince complained that there was no fixed provision for the payment of his allowance, but that it depended on his father's goodwill. Once more the opposition saw an admirable means of embarrassing the government, and its leaders arranged with the Prince that they would raise the matter in Parliament. By way of preparation, influential members were sounded as to the attitude they would adopt. Thus it was that the Fox brothers were among those consulted, a sign that they were already of some consequence in Parliament. But they were not at all inclined to play the opposition's game. On the contrary, Henry Fox at once told his friend, Lord Hervey, the confidant of the Queen and Walpole, what was afoot. Hervey, of course, was not slow in bringing this to the ear of his patroness, who was at first quite unwilling to believe her son capable of such a move. Walpole had no such doubts, and at once took counter-measures which in fact only narrowly averted the overthrow of the ministry. Pitt, who had been the Prince's adviser in this matter, came out on his side when he spoke in the Commons debate, and this still further strengthened the aversion which the King felt for Pitt.

Fox, on the other hand, was soon able to bask in the first rays of government approbation. Hervey was indefatigable in commending his two young friends to Walpole. Finally he so far overcame the latter's initial resistance that Henry was appointed Surveyor-General, a post which, while it carried no political influence, brought in an income of £1,100. But that was enough to satisfy his appetite for the moment. Walpole, too, might well be content to have secured the constant support of a speaker who was listened to with interest in Parliament, because he both found compelling arguments and was able to advance them deftly and logically. This minister with so many enemies was well able to use such assistance, since at the end of 1737, by the death of Queen Caroline, he had lost his most important and reliable supporter at court. Besides, a storm now blew up which threatened the very foundations of his policy. So far he had always succeeded in keeping his country at peace. This had been by no means easy, since disputes and wars had been breaking out almost uninterruptedly on the Continent, and, in particular, England's ally Austria was invoking her aid. It is characteristic of Walpole that during the War of the Polish Succession he justified his policy of peace to the Queen with the words: 'Madam, there are fifty thousand men slain this year in Europe, and not one Englishman.' Such words redound to Walpole's credit as a politician and above all as a man, even if one cannot forget, on the other hand, that such a policy of safety-first must inevitably mean that England's alliances grew looser and that she slipped into a position of isolation.

This would perhaps not have been so serious a matter had Walpole succeeded in carrying his peace policy through to the end, and in avoiding military conflicts. But the opposition were bent upon thwarting this policy and fanning into flame England's differences with other countries. It was with Spain that such differences were most acute. Britain had substantial commercial relations with the Spanish colonies in South America. These were regulated by the Assiento Treaty between the two powers, but each complained that the other was constantly infringing it. The Spaniards maintained that the English were resorting to every kind of sly ruse to extend their trade far beyond the treaty limits. The English maintained that the Spaniards were abusing in an arbitrary and brutal manner their right of search of foreign ships. Probably both complaints were justified: the English seafarers who sailed to the West Indies were most of them adventurers, whose respect for international treaties was in inverse proportion to their greed for gain, and the Spanish *guarda costas* did not concern themselves unduly over nice distinctions between permitted goods and contraband.

Walpole sought to remove these difficulties by negotiations with the Spanish government, with which he even succeeded in arranging a treaty early in 1739. But the opposition did what so many oppositions have done before and since then in the face of a peace-loving government: they denounced its policy as weak-kneed, and whipped up national passions. A great clamour went up at the real and alleged maltreatment meted out by the Spaniards to captured British seamen. The greatest outcry was that occasioned by the tale of woe of a certain Captain Jenkins, who declared that the Spaniards had cut off one of his ears, which he produced wrapped in cotton. To this day it is debatable whether this atrocity story was merely an invention of the gallant captain, and whether, if someone had only taken the trouble to lift up his wig, the ear would have been found in its natural place. But this idea occurred to no one when Jenkins concluded his story with the moving words: 'I recommended my soul to God and my cause to my country.' 'Jenkins' ear' became the slogan of all those who urged war with Spain.

In Parliament Pitt was one of those who called most loudly to arms. In ringing, fiery words he called for defence of the nation's honour against the arrogance of Spain. 'Is this any longer a nation?' he thundered. 'Or what is an English Parliament, if with more ships in your harbours than in all the navies of Europe, with above two millions of people in your American colonies, you will bear to hear of the expediency of receiving from Spain an insecure, unsatisfactory, dishonourable convention?' The tall, commanding figure, the eye flashing with anger and the powerful voice all lent particular emphasis to these words. The opposition cheered, the Prince of Wales applauded from the gallery and even government supporters conceded that it was a brilliant speech. The best debaters were put up against him, not the least of whom was Henry Fox, and once again the parliamentary majority remained behind Walpole.

But in the long run he had to bow to the storm, especially as not only the King but also members of his own Cabinet, such as Newcastle, inclined to war. Against his better judgment he agreed in October, 1739, to a declaration of war on Spain. Morally as well as politically it would now have been the right course for him to retire, but the King would not hear of this and Walpole let himself be persuaded to remain. This was neither to his own advantage nor to that of his cause. He was not the man to prosecute a war with all his might, particularly if he considered it in his heart of hearts unjustified and calamitous. When the Londoners noisily celebrated an initial success, he made the bitter pun: 'They now *ring* the bells, but they will soon *wring* their hands.'

But neither Walpole nor Pitt nor the jubilant Londoners could foresee that nearly nine long and difficult years would pass before the bells of peace could ring again. Only with the Peace of Aix-la-Chapelle (30th April, 1748) did hostilities cease, having in the meantime involved nearly all Europe and convulsed the pattern of its boundaries.

It was no surprise to Walpole that in her struggle with England Spain got help from France. Since the War of the Spanish

Succession the throne in Madrid had been occupied by a
Bourbon, a scion of the French royal house, and even if a union
of the two states under one crown was forbidden by the Peace
of Utrecht, no treaty in the world could prevent the close
family connections of the two royal houses from finding expression in alliances and a similarity of policy. But that these
transactions would give rise to an almost Europe-wide confla-
gration sprang from circumstances which even a far-sighted
statesman could not calculate in advance. In one and the
same year, 1740, Frederick William I of Prussia died in May,
and the Austrian Emperor Charles VI, in October. The throne
in Berlin was occupied by the twenty-eight-year-old Frederick
II and that in Vienna by the twenty-three-year-old Maria
Theresa.

The Emperor Charles had made it his life's work to guarantee
the undisturbed succession of his daughter against all conceivable dangers. His 'Pragmatic Sanction' welded all the lands
of his crown into one indivisible whole which was to pass to her
intact. First he had had her acknowledged by the representative
bodies of all the countries he ruled, and then, by negotiations
lasting for years and involving many sacrifices, he had induced
the states of Europe to recognise and ensure her succession. Not
only had the German Empire consented to this, but in company
with many others Prussia, France and England had agreed to it
as well. If that fundamental principle of international law,
'treaties must be kept' (*pacta sunt servanda*) had possessed the
least binding force, then Charles could have departed this life in
the serene consciousness that the inviolability of the Hapsburg
realms and the undisturbed succession of his daughter were
assured.

But for the young King of Prussia treaties were merely scraps
of paper, by which one felt bound only when reasons of state
made it politic. Of more importance to him than the treaties
which his father had signed were the army of eighty thousand
men, and the army fund of ten million thalers, which had been
left to him. The death of the Emperor and the succession of a
young princess appeared to him a challenge from destiny to
wield these instruments of military power so as to extend his
own domains. And so, before the fateful year 1740 was out, he
stood with an army at his back on the territory of the Austrian

province of Silesia, which bordered his country and therefore seemed to him the most suitable area for grafting on to it. Not only was the whole framework of the Pragmatic Sanction shaken to its foundations, but there also began for Europe, and in particular for the old Holy Roman Empire, an era of wars which lasted, with some interruptions, for almost twenty-five years, until closed by the peace of Hubertsburg in 1763.

In this era the groupings of states changed like colours in a kaleidoscope. The period is the despair of all historians because it is impossible to reduce these fluctuations of policy in the chancelleries of Europe to an intelligible system. Only two sets of states remain consistently opposed to each other. One, of course, is Prussia against Austria, and the other, England against France. The antagonism between England and France dates from at least the time of Louis XIV and William III. But Walpole had striven, successfully for a time, to replace it by an amicable understanding. However, since the war with Spain, this had all gone by the board. France, like Britain, had guaranteed the Pragmatic Sanction. But after the King of Prussia had set a bad example, and had actually—at the battle of Mollwitz —gained a military success, even the French court, which had for generations looked upon the court of Vienna as its Continental rival, no longer hesitated to make an alliance with Frederick, so as not to miss the prospective spoliation of the Hapsburg inheritance. In consequence, England, who had at first sought to mediate between Vienna and Berlin, now ranged herself on the side of the Hapsburgs. In addition to antagonism towards France, the notion of fulfilling a treaty obligation also prompted this action, especially as the court of Vienna had been regarded as an ally ever since the days of Marlborough and Prince Eugene. At least it can be said that, whatever the attitude of English politicians, the English people were inspired with a certain enthusiasm for the young Queen of Hungary, who had been the victim of a treacherous attack.

But the situation was complicated still further by the fact that the King of England was also Elector of Hanover. One cannot perhaps blame George if the interests of his electorate, which was exposed to attack from both Prussia and France, were of as much concern to him as those of his kingdom. But public opinion in England must have felt it to be a slap in the face when it learned that the very man, who, as King of England, had promised Maria Theresa help against France, had simultaneously concluded, in his capacity as Elector of Hanover, a treaty of neutrality with the self-same court of France; and he had, moreover, undertaken by the terms of this treaty to cast his vote at the imperial election for the Bavarian Elector Charles, at that time Maria Theresa's enemy, whom Prussia and France sponsored as a rival candidate to her husband, Francis of Lorraine. Even apart from this, the English had long suspected that they were being exploited, particularly financially, in the interests of Hanover. Indeed, this mistrust of Hanover was probably the opposition's trump card. Of course, the storm now raged round Walpole's head, although he had had nothing to do with concluding the treaty. But since then he had made the best of a bad job and had perforce given it his approval, in contrast to Newcastle, who foresaw the fateful consequences. These were all the more serious since the results of the General Election of 1741 had already whittled down Walpole's majority considerably.

Throughout the whole war Pitt had attacked the minister most sharply and had searchingly criticised his policy. Pitt's bearing was for the most part extremely impressive, and the opposition already regarded this man, who sounded the patriotic note with consummate mastery, as one of their most effective spokesmen. Walpole acknowledged his significance and the danger he represented by repeatedly replying to him in person. A characteristic phrase in such a reply has come down to us: 'A patriot, Sir! Why patriots spring up like mushrooms! I could raise fifty of them within the four-and-twenty hours . . . It is but refusing to gratify an unreasonable or an insolent demand, and up starts a patriot.' True, no one could reproach Pitt with having asked for anything for himself; but Walpole was not alone in suspecting that his patriotic zeal would take another turn if the government consented to assuage his burning ambition. At all events his speeches at this period show that considerations of party politics outweighed purely objective factors.

As long as the old Parliament was in being, Walpole could rely on his solid majority. Pitt, in alliance with the Prince of Wales, had contributed powerfully to the setback the ministry suffered in the election. In the new Parliament which assembled in December, 1741, it was soon apparent that the wind was blowing from another quarter. The government party and the opposition were almost evenly balanced, and when Walpole was defeated in the division over a disputed election, he saw that his day was done and acted accordingly. On February 9th, 1742, he consented to be created Earl of Orford by the King and was thus transferred from the Commons to the Lords. This was an open confession that he could no longer maintain his position in the post which by political conviction he felt to be the only one for him. A few days later he relinquished all his offices.

Did this mean that the golden age of political purity and incorruptibility had now arrived? Only too quickly was it seen that the defects of English politics had deeper roots than the craving for power of a minister capable of wielding it. If the members of the opposition had imagined that their hour had now come, then a bitter disillusionment was in store for most of them. If they had hitherto profited by the fact that the ministry was not at one with itself, they now laboured under the disadvantage that most of Walpole's colleagues, notably Newcastle and Hardwicke, calmly remained in office after his overthrow. Thus only a few places fell vacant, and to these the King summoned only such men as he could tolerate personally and whom the defeated minister recommended. For he still set more store by Walpole's advice than anyone else's. He offered Pulteney the leadership of the new government. But the latter at once committed several blunders which very quickly terminated his political career. On the one hand, he felt that, in the interests of his popularity, he ought to set an example of unselfishness by declining to lead the government and being content with a seat in the Cabinet. On the other, he himself destroyed his popularity by letting himself be persuaded to accept his own elevation from the Commons as Earl of Bath. In this he showed that his flair for politics lagged sadly behind Walpole's. More successful was the former leader of the opposition in the Lords, Lord Carteret, who took over the post of Secretary of State and now became the real director of the government's policy, particularly its foreign policy. He had already occupied this position with success under George I, to whom he had made himself almost indispensable through being the only one of his ministers who could talk to him in German.

Carteret was a gifted man of unusually wide culture, who could enjoy among his books all the hours not taken up with his political duties. He was as completely at home with the Greek and Latin classics as only a real classical scholar is today. Even in his last hours, when his powers were flickering low, he quoted to a subordinate who asked if he might show him the text of the Peace of Paris, which had just arrived, the lines of Homer in which Sarpedon extols the duty of standing fast in battle and the death-struggle. One might half envy an age in which active statesmen had such tastes, if one did not also know that Carteret paid almost equal tribute to a vice of that same age, the bottle. Even during Cabinet meetings he would frequently fortify himself with one or more bottles of Burgundy, and no one could then foresee whether wine would give wings to his soaring genius or would cripple its flight. As unusual as his personality was his conception of the duties of an English statesman. In an age when the thoughts of most ministers revolved round patronage, Carteret exclaimed, 'What is it to me, who is a judge or who a bishop? It is my business to make kings and emperors and to maintain the balance of Europe.' In saying this he might well be conscious that he knew more about European politics than any other English, and every other foreign, statesman. But for all his brilliant qualities, Carteret lacked one ability indispensable to a constitutional minister, that of collaborating with his colleagues on a basis of confidence and equality. Speedily as his talents and capacity brought him to the fore, just as rapidly did he undermine his own position by the inconsiderate and highhanded actions with which he gave offence to the other members of the Cabinet.

Pitt was among the opposition leaders who had been passed over in the reconstruction of the ministry. Walpole's influence was still strong enough to exclude him and other members of the Cobham group, the Grenvilles and the Lytteltons. Apart from this, the King saw in him a personal enemy who had insulted him. Pitt soon resolved to continue to make himself awkward by opposition. The new men had been given office on condition they did not persecute the vanquished Walpole any further. To this very end Pitt now directed his energies. He was one of the members who put through a measure for the setting-up of a committee to investigate the irregularities laid at Walpole's door. On this occasion Fox showed that, although he had retained his office, he was still loyal to his old leader. He vigorously opposed the motion, in a speech which touched particularly on the accusation that Walpole had used public funds to influence elections and to bribe members. With astonishing frankness he claimed that 'men of fortune and understanding' had an exclusive title to political influence. It was not, he said, for the 'giddy' and 'tumultuous' mob to raise their voices. Today such talk sounds the very acme of irresponsibility, but most eighteenth-century politicians were secretly of this opinion, even if not everyone voiced the sentiment so frankly.

Although the committee of investigation was composed almost exclusively of enemies of Walpole, it did not succeed in bringing anything very damaging to light, because the officials who had worked under the defeated minister could not be induced to make any disclosures. Pitt was highly indignant at this negative result. It was only with difficulty that he became reconciled to the impossibility of bringing Walpole to book for his real or alleged transgressions. But as the years went by he came to realise that this statesman, once so hotly attacked, had also possessed a greatness of his own and his own good points; indeed, that in many questions in which he himself had most vehemently assailed him, Walpole had pursued the right policy. In 1751, when Walpole was no longer alive, Pitt had grace enough openly to admit that, as far as the right of the Spaniards to search English vessels was concerned, Walpole's view had been correct and his own had been mistaken. Some years later he went so far as to praise Walpole, who, as he told his friends, had died at peace with him.

Of Carteret, too, Pitt spoke with high esteem in later years and candidly recognised his statesmanlike abilities. But as long as he was principal minister he had no sharper or more spiteful critic than Pitt. It must be admitted that Carteret's policy, for all its brilliance, also had its seamy side, which aroused the resentment not only of the parliamentary opposition but also of his own colleagues, and this finally led to his fall. True, he was at first successful in giving a fresh impetus to the conduct of the war. His greatest success was in inducing Frederick of

Prussia to make peace with Maria Theresa, the preliminaries being settled at Breslau in June, 1742. The Peace of Berlin which followed gave Frederick what he had entered the war for, Silesia. For this prize he was ready to leave his ally France in the lurch, as he had already done in the secret agreement of Kleinschellendorf, which he had concluded with Austria in October, 1741, and had broken again in December. In November, 1742, Carteret even succeeded in arranging the Treaty of Westminster between Prussia and Great Britain, by which both parties mutually guaranteed each other's possessions. The withdrawal of Prussia from the war weakened France and strengthened her most important opponent, England. Carteret would have liked to turn this to account by overpowering France by an attack from the Continent. But where could he raise the necessary soldiers? England's own army was insignificant. There was no general military service and there still prevailed a rooted mistrust—most determined among the Tories—of standing armies. The English tradition was to fight their wars with mercenaries hired from small foreign powers. Now the electorate of Hanover had an army of sixteen thousand well-trained soldiers. The Hanoverian treaty of neutrality had expired and, since the danger of French or Prussian aggression was over, was not renewed. But George now declared that his electorate could no longer bear the burden of such an army and that he must disband it. So all that remained for the Cabinet to do was take it into English pay.

From a military viewpoint this policy was probably quite sound. In 1743 the army, in which the Hanoverian contingent played an important part, was able to defeat even the French army on German soil at Dettingen and under the personal leadership of the King, who may not have displayed any particular talents as a general but certainly showed dauntless courage. Whatever might be said for the Hanoverian mercenaries as a military factor, however, they were politically a millstone round the government's neck. The Hanoverians were distinctly unpopular in England, and their maintenance at the expense of the British taxpayer was, in the opposition's view, proof positive that England was being exploited in the interests of Hanover.

None expressed this opinion more sharply and more explosively than Pitt. Like an avenging angel he raged in the Commons against Hanover, against this King who could put his electorate before his kingdom and his Hanoverian troops before his English officers and men, and against the ministers who were kow-towing to the throne and betraying their own country. He declared that England had been degraded to 'a province to a despicable electorate'. The King had, he said, ignored his English officers and listened only to his Hanoverian generals. He even attempted by subtle mockery to question the King's personal courage, of which George was very proud. But the heaviest weight of the invective, of which Pitt was a past master, was brought to bear on Carteret. 'A Hanover-troop-minister', he called him, 'a flagitious task-master', whose only party was the sixteen thousand Hanoverians. He attacked Carteret's dominance in the Cabinet, stigmatising him with the dreaded name of 'sole minister'; he referred to his well-known propensity for the bottle by reproaching him with having renounced the British nation after bemusing himself with the potion of which poets relate that whoever enjoys it forgets his own country. A pity that Carteret could not reply to him, for as a speaker he had no need to fear comparison even with a Pitt. But he sat in the upper House and so could not meet him face to face.

Success did not attend Pitt's philippics. The majority, in which once again Henry Fox was prominent as a speaker, rallied to the ministry's support. The pay of the Hanoverian troops did, it is true, finally vanish from the English budget, but only after the subsidies for Austria had been increased by a corresponding amount, out of which they were thenceforth paid by Maria Theresa. *Plus ça change, plus c'est la même chose.* The one practical success which Pitt's invective did achieve was to increase the King's dislike of him to hatred. But how did Pitt expect to reach the goal of his ambition when George, with true Guelph obstinacy, kept the door of the Cabinet shut to him? On this occasion even the Prince of Wales was displeased with Pitt, who still had to learn that anger is a bad counsellor and that the uproarious applause of a factious opposition can be bought too dearly.

None the less, Carteret's sun was setting. The goals of his foreign alliances grew steadily more remote; he paid less and less consideration to his colleagues, attempting to confront them with *faits accomplis*. Such behaviour can be excused, if at all, only in a man who is successful. And for the absence of success Carteret had first and foremost to thank Frederick of Prussia, who again showed that he remained bound by no treaty if his interests beckoned another way. In the Peace of Breslau he had undertaken to give no further help to the opponents of Maria Theresa. In consequence, Carteret might have been forgiven for confidently believing that Frederick, with whom he had, moreover, concluded the Treaty of Westminster, had finally retired from the war. Perhaps he had gone too far in his reliance upon this when, in the Treaty of Worms, which he concluded in September with the courts of Vienna and Turin, he made no mention at all of the Treaty of Breslau. From this Frederick concluded, suspiciously, that the allies meant to take Silesia from him again after first conquering France. Not only was this suspicion completely groundless, but Frederick's own minister, von Podewils, gave as his opinion 'on his oath and his conscience' that the treaty contained nothing hostile. But Frederick was quick to measure other people's corn by his own bushel, and so he concluded a new treaty of alliance with France and invaded Bohemia in August, 1744. The effect of this behaviour on his contemporaries can be seen from one of Hardwicke's letters, written some years later. In it he speaks of the rooted animosity of the King of Prussia towards the House of Austria, of his incurable jealousy and dread of their vengeance which, as he well knew, he had fully deserved, and of his abandoned perfidy and falseness.

Whatever one might think of it, Frederick's act of aggression was the downfall of Carteret's whole system. The malcontent ministers—Newcastle, his brother Henry Pelham, who now presided over the ministry as First Lord of the Treasury, Hardwicke, the Lord Chancellor, and others—now laid the categorical choice before the King: Carteret or us. Personally, George preferred Carteret to the rest of his ministers put together, but on the advice of Walpole, who though a dying man mustered his remaining strength to come to London for this purpose, he decided in favour of the Pelhams, and Carteret had to resign.

Pitt might be well pleased at this turn of events. Pelham, who always preferred compromise to a struggle, had already been in contact with his group, in which the old intriguer Bolingbroke seems to have acted as intermediary. Pelham now took the opportunity of recasting the government on a broader basis— this was called the 'Broad Bottom Administration' in the political jargon of the day—and of installing a number of Pitt's closest friends in office. For Pitt himself he could do nothing because the King, who, in any case, had been offended by the forced dismissal of Carteret, nourished too strong an antipathy towards the man who had ridiculed Hanover. Pitt himself seems to have recognised this obstacle at the time. He had at this period, by a freak of fortune, reached a situation which allowed him to sit back and watch developments.

On October 18th, 1744, the once powerful Sarah, Duchess of Marlborough, died at the great age of 84. Memories of a day that had long passed stirred again at this name. Who among those then living still recalled the beautiful young lady-in-waiting, who almost seventy years before had married Colonel John Churchill, subsequently England's greatest general and Duke of Marlborough? Like a legend long faded into silence sounded the tales of her sway over Queen Anne, which ended only with her dramatic fall from favour. The great military hero had now been dead for more than twenty years, but the Duchess had lived on, energetic, imperious and quarrelsome as she had always been. She would not have thought life worth living had she been unable to hate someone with all her heart. In her declining years she bestowed her particular abhorrence on Walpole, who, she believed, had imposed, upon her in some question of taxes; besides, he had taken away her privilege of walking in the King's garden. Whoever picked a quarrel with this man was her friend, and the fulminations which Pitt had hurled at him were as music in her ears. In gratitude she bequeathed him a legacy of £10,000 in her will and even left him the reversion of a share in her huge fortune, although this latter was, in fact, never realised. She expressly stated her motive for this bounty in the words: '. . . upon account of his merit in the noble defence he has made for the support of the laws of England, and to prevent the ruin of his country.'

Ten thousand pounds; this was a considerable fortune for a man who had hitherto had to manage on £300 a year. It suddenly made him independent. He could now give up his position in the Prince's household, which would have fettered him politically, seeing that he had brought himself into opposition to the Prince by his campaign against Carteret, although, as things turned out, Frederick preserved his personal goodwill towards him. The legacy of the old Duchess also allowed Pitt to live in a style which more nearly matched his grandiose tastes. But he was never thrifty and, although his income increased considerably later on, he constantly ran into debt.

It must be said that Pitt never really attained full enjoyment of life. In the course of this year, 1744, he experienced for the first time one of those severe attacks of gout which from that time forth frequently recurred and finally became a factor in English history. That he suffered very severely from gout is unquestionable. But it is also worthy of note that he used it as a means of heightening the effect of his presence in the House. When he rose, swathed in woollen bandages and leaning on crutches, he seemed the living embodiment of a patriotism which even the most agonising sufferings could not hinder in the discharge of its duty, nor did he refrain from giving point to this in words of pathos. Woe to the opponent who then ventured to interrupt the flow of his eloquence by an interjection! He was at once shattered by cries of anger and obloquy, the effect of which was multiplied by the visible apparatus of the sick-room.

§

The year 1744 also marks an epoch in Henry Fox's life. It is the year of his romantic elopement with Lady Caroline Lennox, with which this narrative began. Both the Fox brothers had for years been on friendly terms with the family of the Duke of Richmond. It may have been in 1743 that the twenty-year-old eldest daughter of the Duke won the heart of the thirty-eight-year-old Henry, and it was not long before she returned his love. The ducal parents sought to check the course of destiny. But when they showed signs of removing their daughter from London for several months, the lovers cut the Gordian knot by running away and getting married. At first the Duke and Duchess could not forgive their daughter for taking this step. Neither she nor their son-in-law were allowed inside her parents' house. But after a few years milder counsels prevailed. They saw how Fox was gaining an increasing reputation and

D

finally—despite the Duke's opposition—became Secretary at War. They could no longer hide from themselves that here was a son-in-law of whom even a Duke need not be ashamed. And so when, in 1748, their eldest grandchild was born, natural feelings overcame injured pride and they took the first step towards a reconciliation. Thenceforth peace and friendship prevailed, and the Duke in particular became more and more impressed by his son-in-law. For, in his domestic life, Henry Fox evinced qualities with which those who knew him as a public figure would hardly have credited him. He was, and remained to the end of his days, a loving and tender husband, who lavished upon his 'Lady Caroline' unending care and adoration.

Towards his children he showed a love which had only one great fault—that it was not tempered by some little strictness and firmness. This man, who pursued his aims in political life with ruthless energy, was at home as clay in the hands of his children, particularly his favourite, his second son, Charles James, whose career was later to disclose all too clearly the fateful effects of this paternal weakness.

CHAPTER IV

PAYMASTER PITT AND
SECRETARY FOX

THE war was not going well for Britain in 1744 and 1745. Her army was defeated at Fontenoy by the French, brilliantly led by the Maréchal de Saxe, and the Dutch barrier towns, which played a great part in British policy at that time, fell to him one after the other. The successes of the French had one redeeming feature for England: Frederick of Prussia, concerned lest they should now become too powerful, turned his back on them in characteristic fashion and made peace, first with England and then with Austria.

Now at least the administration no longer had to fear Pitt's fulminating attacks in Parliament. He, moreover, showed in the clearest possible manner that his opposition had ceased with the fall of Carteret. The Cabinet manoeuvre already mentioned, by which the Hanoverian mercenaries were transferred to Maria Theresa and her subsidies correspondingly increased, was raised in the Commons. Of course, the opposition speakers pointed out that, as far as the British taxpayer was concerned, this was robbing Peter to pay Paul. However, they caught a Tartar in Pitt. He rose in patriotic wrath, and demonstrated with all his fire that this expedient was necessary in the national interest and was widely different from Carteret's policy. Who could possibly object if the Queen of Hungary hired these Hanoverians? 'God forbid . . .' he added, 'that those unfortunate troops should by our votes be proscribed at every court in Europe.' It was a most effective speech, which completely silenced the opposition and showed the Pelhams unmistakably how valuable and important it was to attach this man permanently to their interest. Many, of course, found the speech quite irreconcilable with Pitt's earlier ones, but had to admit the courage with which he openly braved such comparisons.

If Pitt in these and similar speeches struck the patriotic note and called for unity, he soon had the chance of showing that he was in earnest. Walpole's constant fear was realised in 1745:

43

the Stuarts, taking advantage of England's difficulties abroad, made a further attempt to win back their crown. On July 26th, 1745, Prince Charles Edward, the Young Pretender, landed in Scotland, routed the weak royal forces which had been sent against him, and in November stood on English soil. The way to London seemed open. If the French managed to land troops a catastrophe was to be feared. In this crisis Pitt gave all the backing he could to every measure taken by the administration to defend the Crown, and he opposed all attempts to divert Parliament's attention to other matters, even to those which in other times would have had his support.

The Pelhams now made serious efforts to get Pitt into the ministry. In November and December, 1745, there were repeated negotiations in which Pitt formulated his conditions. The difficulties lay in differences of opinion on the conduct of the war. The situation had, it is true, been somewhat alleviated by the agreement already reached between Prussia on the one side and England and Austria on the other; but Pitt demanded concentration on naval warfare and a more drastic whittling down of land warfare than the ministry was prepared to countenance or the King would ever accept. So at first the negotiations broke down, but not for long. Pitt felt that he had the ability to grasp the nettle of this war which had been dragging on for so many years and to bring it safely to an end. He wished to become Secretary at War. And so, in February, 1746, he gave the ministers to understand that he would raise no further difficulties and was ready to join their ranks. Newcastle seized on this opportunity and within a short time an agreement was arrived at. There were to be several ministerial changes and Pitt was to be appointed Secretary at War.

But when Newcastle laid this plan before the King, he met with inflexible resistance. George was willing to approve all the other changes, but Pitt, the man who had mocked and insulted him and his electorate—him he would by no means stomach. He saw in the demand nothing less than a fresh personal affront. Apart from this, he had not forgotten that it had been the Pelhams who had forced him to part company with Carteret, whom he had found so congenial. (Carteret had since become Earl of Granville.) Walpole was no longer there to give good advice and restrain him from imprudent actions, having died in the preceding year. Instead George now took counsel with Walpole's erstwhile opponent, Lord Bath, formerly Sir William Pulteney, who not only confirmed him in his resistance but declared it to be against his royal honour to allow his ministers to impose their will on him. George would not have been a German ruler if he had not enthusiastically concurred in these sentiments.

The Pelhams, and even Pitt, seem to have been quite reconciled to the mere fact of this refusal. But when George, on the strength of the support promised by Lord Bath, heaped reproaches on them, Newcastle and the other Secretary of State, Lord Harrington, asked to be relieved of their posts. This the King granted forthwith and summoned Lord Bath and his friend, Granville. But something now occurred for which George had not bargained, something unprecedented in British constitutional history: all the ministers expressed their intention to retire together. For days they thronged almost to the King's door to surrender their white staffs or other badges of office. In the end he was reduced to the extremity of apprehensively keeping his door shut to everyone who looked like a minister bent on resigning. In the meantime Bath and Granville tried to form a ministry. But no one was willing to embark in their leaky vessel. After two days the crisis had melted away. Bath had to bring back his Seals as Secretary of State with a sigh and confess that he had promised more than he could fulfil. But Granville said, with a laugh, 'Upon my soul I knew nothing of it. I was sitting quietly by my own fireside reading . . . Demosthenes; the King sends to me to take the Seals. I . . . was amazed at it. But, like a dutiful subject of the Crown, I obeyed.' Then, though he owned it was mad, he added he would do it again tomorrow! Typical of a Carteret and typical of the eighteenth century. No one seems to have taken it amiss in the long run.

After this fiasco nothing remained for George but to swallow his Guelph pride and his Guelph obstinacy, and to ask his old ministers to take on their offices once again. It was 'an event which will appear to posterity more surprising than anything that has happened', wrote Lord Chancellor Hardwicke. In fact posterity can here see emerging a principle which, despite many setbacks, was later to triumph completely, that of a united parliamentary ministry which could make even the sovereign respect its political standpoint and sacrifice his favourites to it. But there is one respect in which the position of the Pelham ministry in 1746 contrasts fundamentally with that of a modern Cabinet—the idea of going into opposition if dismissed was still far from its thoughts. Hardwicke, who had a long, frank discussion with him when the crisis was over, solemnly assured the King that 'as long as he lived he would never enter into a formed opposition to any administration.' In this he was obviously voicing not only his own real views but also those of most of his colleagues. Clearly opposition was hardly befitting in any man whom the King had once honoured with his confidence. There was still an insufficiently sharp distinction between the King and his ministers for opposition to be considered as directed only against the ministers, and not against the sovereign.

This singular turn of events considerably strengthened the ministers' position. When they again proposed Pitt to the King, the only concession he could get from them was that they would content themselves with Pitt's being given a subordinate post. He first received an Irish sinecure (22nd February, 1746) and two months later the more important, but still subsidiary, office of Paymaster-General to the Forces. The Paymaster-General was not a member of the Cabinet, but sat on the Privy Council which still had a comparatively formal existence. Every new member of the Privy Council had to swear an oath before the King. And so George was compelled to bring himself to receive in person the man who had so grievously insulted him. He is said to have shed tears when Pitt knelt before him to take the oath. But how was he to know that one day the most glorious events of his reign would be linked with this man's name?

The post of Secretary at War, which the King refused to Pitt, fell to Fox in May, 1746. True, he was not fired with the same burning passion as his rival to use this post to infuse a new spirit and a new vigour into the prosecution of the war. Fox merely looked upon it as an office much like any other, only as it entailed more work it was a less agreeable one.

Meanwhile the Stuart rising had collapsed. In April, 1746, Charles Edward was routed at Culloden and was forced to roam the wilds of Scotland as a fugitive, protected from his pursuers by nothing but the romantic loyalty of the Scottish clansmen and by Flora Macdonald, who won immortal fame as his rescuer. The victor of Culloden was the Duke of Cumberland, George's younger son, on whom his parents lavished all the love and favour which they denied to his elder brother, Frederick Prince of Wales. Despite his youth Cumberland had been made Commander-in-Chief of the British forces on the Continent, where he had proved an unlucky, if gallant, general. All the greater was the rejoicing over his victory at Culloden. But after this success he felt it to be his duty to complete the punishment of the rebels, and the cruelty with which he did this earned him the name of the Butcher. Much as the English had trembled before the wild horde from the north in the days of its triumph, they found just as little to their taste this bloody retribution which mainly fell on humble cottagers and shepherds for the sole reason that, faithful to local custom, they had followed the chief of their clan wherever he led them. A salutary consequence of this abortive rising was that this anachronistic clan system was now abolished by legislation, mostly initiated by Hardwicke, which was the first real step towards the evolution of modern Scotland. The Stuart cause was now dead, and never again was the banner of revolt unfurled. Charles Edward, who for a few months had shone in the brightest light of heroism, ended his days in obloquy and oblivion as a drunkard.

§

The post of Paymaster-General ranked far lower than those of the Secretaries of State, the Lord Chancellor, the Lord President of the Privy Council, the Chancellor of the Exchequer and, of course, the First Lord of the Treasury, who exercised many functions today performed by the Prime Minister. But in one respect it possessed a most tempting advantage over all these glittering offices: it very quickly made its holder a rich man. Even the salary was quite considerable, about £4,000 a year. But this was not all it yielded, nor even the main part of it. The Paymaster was by tradition treated less as a salaried official than as a state banker. The monies voted for the army were paid to him, and they remained in his hands until he was called upon to make disbursements from them for army needs. In the meantime he could make use of them on his own account. Still more lucrative were the subsidies which were paid to England's allies in time of war. On these the Paymaster could get a commission of one-half per cent. If he left office, the auditing of his accounts lasted several years and until this was concluded he was allowed to keep any unexpended sums in his own pocket for his own use. A Paymaster had to be a most unenterprising business man indeed if under this system he could not retire a very rich man.

All former Paymaster-Generals, without scruple and without occasioning the least offence to anyone, had exploited these advantages. But there was one exception. Henry Pelham had contented himself with his salary, although his passion for gambling cost him a lot of money. When Pitt took over the office he consulted Pelham and at once decided to follow his example. But whereas Pelham had exercised his abnegation in silence, Pitt at once proclaimed his own from the roof-tops. He always had an eye to the broad masses of the people, whose favour he courted because his keen political sense told him that here he could find independent support, if need be against court or parliamentary intrigues. What could more effectively strengthen his popularity, particularly with the City merchants, than so tangible a proof of his selfless patriotism? As things turned out he completely achieved his purpose in the twinkling of an eye. The English people contrasted him sharply with the typical politicians of the day and made a very warm place for him in their hearts. This affection towards him was, of course, not without its consequences, as the future was to show. The people demanded that their hero should remain true to the picture they had formed of him.

No one expected the holder of such a lucrative office to work himself to death in it, and so the Paymaster-General could rely on his well-trained subordinates with a mind at rest, although this does not mean that Pitt did not take his duties seriously. But in this office he achieved nothing of which history need take especial note.

The position of Secretary at War which had fallen to Fox entailed more work and responsibility, even if it embraced only a part of the functions of a modern War Office. It can be said of Fox, too, that he took his duties seriously. A character sketch drawn of him at the time by Horace Walpole lays particular stress on this. 'In the affairs of his office', it runs, 'he is as minute and as full of application as if he were always to remain in the same post, and as exact and knowing as if he had always been in it'. For Fox the most important advantage which the post carried was that it brought him into close relations with the Commander-in-Chief, Cumberland, for this worthy was to play a significant rôle in the political groupings of the years to follow.

With the entry of Pitt and Fox, the administration had the most effective parliamentary fighters on its own side. Fox's strength lay in a profusion of clear, convincing and logically-ordered arguments, as well as in the influence which he knew how to manipulate in personal discussion with members, although he could not yet support it with the decisive argument of patronage; for Pelham, as head of the government, had reserved this for himself. Pitt, on the other hand, was the man who joined battle with the foe in stormy debates. In this he had to wrestle with many difficulties which he had brought upon himself by his earlier aggressive and excessive opposition. His mere transition from the opposition to the government benches had brought him under the suspicion of many, and numerous pamphleteers exercised their wit over this change of front; one even conjured up the spirit of the dead Duchess of Marlborough to brand the renegade. His position was most delicate when, shortly after he took office, the Hanoverian mercenaries were once again a subject of debate. The Pelham administration now asked for the very thing which Carteret had earlier demanded, pay for eighteen thousand Hanoverians. That Pitt voted for the measure is understandable, in view of the office he held. But he was not content with simply voting. He also spoke energetically in favour of the motion before a House which still vividly remembered how, with flail and bludgeon, he had rained down blows on Carteret for making the same demand. Small wonder that one of Carteret's friends sprang to his feet, and in a caustic speech remorselessly reminded him of all the contradictions in which he had enmeshed himself. Pitt could not say much in reply, but neither does he seem to have felt very crushed. Complete consistency was not one of his ideals. Perhaps, too, he knew how quickly the world forgets, and that a man of the strength with which he credited himself is powerful enough to disregard the words he uttered the day before yesterday.

Questions like that of the Hanoverian troops were deprived of their topical significance when the war, which had gradually lost all reason for continuance, neared its end in October, 1748, the month of the Peace of Aix-la-Chapelle. It was a peace of which neither party could be proud. There was, at bottom, no victor and no vanquished. France and Britain reciprocally restored their conquests to each other, and merely gained an oppressive burden of debt as a reminder of the long years of war. The question over which England had originally plunged into war with Spain, the right of the Spaniards to search English ships, was not even mentioned in the treaty.

Maria Theresa had, it is true, the satisfaction of seeing her husband Francis on the imperial throne, but she had neither won back Silesia nor received any compensation for it. Besides, Austria's stock had fallen sharply in the estimation of her English ally. The longer they continued, the less had her military achievements fulfilled expectations, and they were inversely related to her pretensions and obstinacy in the peace negotiations. On the other hand, far-sighted people could not blink the fact that the importance of Prussia had increased extraordinarily despite all objections—however well-founded—to the political tactics of its King. Hardwicke, the very Lord Chancellor who in 1747 had so sharply condemned Frederick's bad faith, writes in July, 1748, to his friend Newcastle: 'You know I am a hearty friend to the old system [the alliance with the Hapsburgs against France] . . . But, notwithstanding that, I see, and we all have felt, the lameness of the old system without Prussia. It has been the great maim and weakness of the whole alliance . . . If you gain Prussia, the confederacy will be restored and made whole, and become a real strength; if you do not, it will still continue lame and weak, and much in the power of France . . . But the right measure seems . . . to be to have, even now, such an alliance always in view . . .' But Frederick had already made his choice from among English politicians. His envoy in London had commended Pitt to him as 'the greatest orator in the House of Commons . . . a man universally beloved by the nation.' To this the King replied: '. . . Mr. Pitt has the feelings of a true Englishman. You are therefore to compliment him from me, and inform him that I wish his views were generally held. England and Prussia would then be closely united, a thing impossible as long as England is directed according to the special interests of Hanover.'

Thus the alignments of the Seven Years' War were already casting their shadows before. One obstacle, of course, was the deep aversion which George II felt for his Prussian nephew. He called him 'a mischievous rascal, a bad friend, a bad ally, a bad relation and a bad neighbour, in fact the most dangerous and evil-disposed prince in Europe'. And yet a few years later the day was to come when, as allies, they were to face a world in arms.

The British administration devoted the years immediately following the conclusion of peace to restoring the country's shattered strength, and particularly its crippled finances. In this sphere, Pelham, who emulated his preceptor Walpole, undeniably earned high credit. Pitt supported him to the utmost of his powers, even if he opposed him in detail over a reduction in naval strength which seemed to be too sweeping. At that time he so far enjoyed the confidence of the two Pelham brothers as to be able to mediate when differences broke out between them; these disputes were more often due to the Duke's petty jealousies than to any material divergences of opinion.

He also supported them in 1755, when they proposed to introduce a measure to emancipate British Jews. In recognition of their patriotic activities during the war and the Stuart rebellion, the Pelhams brought in a bill to sanction their naturalization. The bill went through Parliament. But a section of the clergy and those of the merchants who feared increased commercial rivalry, raised such an outcry against the bill that the ministry felt compelled, in view of the General Election of 1756, to repeal the Naturalization Act. Here too Pitt supported the ministry and voiced unequivocally his disapproval of this narrow-minded agitation. '. . . Religion', he said 'has really nothing to do in the dispute . . . The spirit they [the public] are at present possessed with is not a true Christian spirit'.

But when the agitators went so far as to try to deprive Jews in the colonies of the British nationality they had already possessed for a decade, he called upon the House in words of fire—and with success—to resist this move.

A still greater stir was caused in 1753 by a bill drafted by the Lord Chancellor to regulate the formalities to be observed in contracting marriages. It was intended to remove the scandalous abuses which had crept in, thanks to the previous laxity of the system. Unscrupulous, grasping clerics made a very lucrative business out of marrying, for a cash payment of the fees, any couple, even if they were minors or intoxicated, who applied to them. Hardwicke demanded public and repeated calling of the banns, public registers kept by the clergy of the established Church and, in the case of minors, the consent of the parents. Later generations regard all this as self-evident, but in the eighteenth century it appeared to many as an encroachment on personal freedom, an interference by the state in people's most private affairs. The arguments hurled against the measure both in and out of Parliament can today only be called scurrilous.

Henry Fox appointed himself leader of this opposition. He had contracted his own marriage in a way which this bill would make illegal, and that marriage was the joy of his life. He therefore felt that he was fighting for the happiness and the rights of all lovers by attacking the Clandestine Marriage Bill with untiring vehemence. A scene at the third reading shows the ready wit and vitality which he displayed. He declared that the bill had been completely altered during the deliberations upon it and, as a visible proof of this, he waved before the eyes of the members a copy of the original draft in which all amendments had been entered in red ink. Murray, the Solicitor-General, who sponsored the bill, and who had had many a skirmish with Fox, called across to him: 'How bloody it looks!' Whereupon Fox, quick as lightning, answered in words like Macbeth's: 'Yes, but you cannot say I did it', and, passing on to 'Julius Caesar', continued, paraphrasing Mark Antony:

> *'Look what a rent the learned Casca made:*
> *Through this the well-beloved Brutus stabbed!'*

As a parliamentary battle of words this was prime sport, and Fox won fresh laurels as a debater. But by a disastrous error he allowed himself, in the heat of the argument, to be led into making a violent and unjust personal attack on the author of the bill, Hardwicke. Attacks on the legal profession are a favourite device for winning popular applause, and Fox, who shared this notion, launched out on an onslaught of this kind to the great diversion of the House. But to concentrate them upon the head of the profession, the Lord Chancellor himself, was a serious mistake. Fox did not shrink from comparing him to a giant spider, a notion which Hogarth used in composing a caricature of Hardwicke. This was made even worse by the fact that Fox, as Secretary at War, and Hardwicke, as Lord Chancellor, sat in the same ministry. Even if the modern doctrine of joint responsibility as between the members of a Cabinet did not then obtain, it was already expected that their objective differences of opinion would be composed objectively among themselves. Fox himself quickly sensed what a signal error he had made and in his final speech he retracted his personal remarks with a burst of apologies and encomiums. Of course, this only made matters worse and did not save him from a *coup de grâce* delivered by the Chancellor in the Lords, which reached a climax in the words: 'I despise the invective and I despise the retraction.'

Fox, usually so cool and calculating, had this time let himself go completely astray in the heat of battle. Already there were whispers of his impending dismissal. Things did not reach this pass, however, for not only did his parliamentary influence make him too valuable to the Pelhams but he also had the support of his patron Cumberland. However, the King told him plainly that he was in the wrong, and less than a year passed before he learned how much harm he had done himself by incurring Hardwicke's enmity.

§

Home politics underwent a far-reaching change as a result of the sudden death of the Prince of Wales in the spring of 1751. This brought about the collapse of all the political combinations at which he had worked so busily with an eye to his coming accession to power. Those politicians who did not enjoy the favour of the reigning monarch now had no one left upon whom to place their hopes. For the Prince's son, who now became heir apparent, was a mere boy of thirteen. In consequence Cumberland's importance increased. He had his own party in which Fox was prominent. The Pelhams, on the other hand, resisted his influence as they saw in him the danger that military power might gain the upper hand over civil power. Pitt and his group were on their side. Although Pitt's relations with the Prince of Wales had no longer been good of latter years, his death was a loss for him none the less. For he did not want to remain

Paymaster-General for ever; he hoped to become Secretary at War or Secretary of State, and the personal antipathy of the King still stood in the way of any such promotion.

§

The years between the Peace of Aix-la-Chapelle and the death of Henry Pelham in 1754 form one of the quietest periods in Pitt's public life. In his private life, he was almost yearly impaired in health by severe attacks of gout, which sometimes plagued him for months at a stretch and compelled him to visit such fashionable spas of the day as Bath and Tunbridge Wells. When he became Paymaster-General he was thirty-eight years old and still unmarried. Until then he had lived with his sister Ann, who had been so close to him in his youth. Now he suddenly and abruptly broke up the home. The exact reason for this rupture are not known, but possibly it can be explained by the temperament of brother and sister. They were too much alike to get on together for any length of time: they were as like as 'deux gouttes de feu' says Horace Walpole. Possibly too, the tendency to insanity, which they inherited from their forbears, was already showing itself. It emerged plainly a few years later in Ann. She never forgot the abrupt breach and her brother's part in it, and she gave him much cause for annoyance in later years. From the letters which are still preserved it can be concluded that neither was an easy person to live with. But here and there in William's letters a more human and understanding note is struck; they show that he did not lack knowledge of himself, and that some remnant of the old brotherly affection still survived in him despite all their disagreements. This often haughty and imperious man appears a tender, almost a humble person, when he writes to Ann: 'I have infirmities of temper, blemishes and faults, if you please, of nature without end; but the Eye that can't be deceived must judge between us, whether that friendship, which was my very existence for so many years, could ever have received the least flaw, but from umbrages and causes which the quickest sensibility and tenderest jealousy of friendship alone at first suggested.'

William was never on terms of close intimacy with his other brothers and sisters. He was so estranged from his brother Thomas that, in 1747, he had to give up the Old Sarum con-

stituency which the latter controlled and change over to a
government seat placed at his disposal by Newcastle. Indeed,
in his zeal on behalf of his irreplaceable parliamentary champion the Duke had gone to the length of appearing in person at
the polls, and taking a seat beside the returning officer in order
to intimidate any voter who appeared likely to kick against the
pricks. No wonder that, during these years, Pitt showed no
interest in the fair conduct of elections. Thomas died abroad in
1761, a ruined and embittered man, deeply in debt. He left a
son of the same name who was later created Lord Camelford.
With this nephew Pitt kept up for years an active correspondence
in which he gave the young man hints about his education and
on how to make his way in the world, advice on his reading and
the like, all of which do the writer much credit as a man. But
the curse which hovers over all the family relationships of the
Pitts seems also to have affected the pleasant intercourse
between these two; in the manuscript left by Camelford his
famous uncle appears in a far from agreeable light.

At this time Pitt's relations with his friends were happier than
those with his family. He was, of course, no longer a penniless
young man needing support, the man who had considered it a
favour to be received as a guest at the country seats of the great.
He now possessed his own country seat where he could indulge
his passion for building and for laying out gardens. He seems to
have enjoyed a certain reputation for this; indeed, his friends
took his advice when they planned their own gardens and, after
the fashion of the time, set them off with antique temples and
statues.

His closest and most important friends were the Grenville
brothers. The eldest, Richard, soon after the death of his uncle
Lord Cobham had inherited the exalted title of Earl Temple.
This public recognition of his prominence accorded with his
nature. He had a very great—one can safely say an exaggerated
—idea of his own importance. He considered himself not only,
in accordance with his professed faith in the Whig programme,
as a champion of his country's freedom, which to a certain
extent he was, but also a statesman with a flair for leadership.
Among his good qualities may be reckoned his generosity and
readiness to give financial help, which stood even Pitt in good
stead in critical times. His younger brother George sat in the

Commons and enjoyed considerable prestige there. In 1744 the Pelhams, in broadening the basis of their administration, had summoned him to an office of secondary importance. He was a man of parts and took his parliamentary duties very seriously. He would have become Speaker had he not allowed himself to be thrust into a ministerial career. Yet a third brother, James, sat in Parliament. He was particularly attached to Pitt. Pitt became still more closely linked with the Grenville brothers when he married their only sister, Hester, in the autumn of 1754. Pitt was then forty-six and Hester was already thirty-three. They had, of course, known each other for a long time although no sign of mutual attachment had shown itself. Her brothers are said to have been very surprised when they heard of the betrothal but they gladly gave their consent, and Pitt thanked Temple in a fulsome letter. How he came to fall suddenly in love with a girl who had been so near him for so long is nowhere related. But the depth of his affection cannot be doubted. It emerges clearly from the letters written during his engagement, even if it flaunts itself in a stilted and highly ornamental style. The intense suffering which had undermined his health does not seem to have deterred Hester. On the contrary, the thought of being able to look after him had attracted her. She shouldered the burden of his constantly-recurring illness with devotion and self-sacrifice. She was a woman of neither outstanding beauty nor unusual intellect. But Pitt was fully content for the whole of his life with the choice he had made, and one cannot doubt that he had every reason to be so. To him she was a loving and solicitous wife and to his children a tender and conscientious guide and mother.

It goes without saying that Pitt's social position advanced still further through this relationship by marriage with one of the leading families of the nobility. And there came a time when he could make good use of such support.

CHAPTER V

PELHAM'S DEATH TO
THE SEVEN YEARS' WAR

B EFORE this transformation of Pitt's life was complete,
another change had occurred in public life which brought
to an end the calm of the immediately preceding years.
On March 6th, 1754, Henry Pelham died quite suddenly in his
fifty-ninth year. He had, it is true, been no great statesman.
But he had fulfilled the task which had fallen to him to the
general satisfaction; he had kept his country at peace, strengthened her finances, introduced much-needed reforms, discreetly
guided Parliament without any serious storms into quiet
waters, and inspired in the now ageing King a confidence
which was expressed in the words he uttered on learning of
Pelham's death: 'I shall now have no more peace.'

The very question as to who should be Pelham's successor
and head of the administration could not fail to stir up contention and intrigues. Every carefully controlled ambition now
surged impetuously into the light of day. The most impetuous
of them all was Henry Fox's. He had been able to regard himself as Pelham's most important supporter in the Commons, and
thus believed he was his natural successor. But instead of relying
on his well-founded claims and preserving a dignified reserve,
he flung himself into nervous, over-precipitate activity, which
ruined any chances he might have had. Pelham had drawn his
last breath at eight o'clock in the morning, and in the early
hours of the day Fox was already scurrying from door to door
to canvass support. One of the first people he tried to see was
the man whose competition he most feared: Pitt. But Pitt was
out of town. Then, thinking that the Lord Chancellor would
have the last word in the reorganisation of the Cabinet, Fox
wrote him, in one day, no fewer than three messages of abject
apology. How he must now have regretted his rash, unfair
attacks on Hardwicke during the debates on the Clandestine
Marriage Bill!

The news of Pelham's death reached Pitt at Bath, where he

had been taking the cure for some months. So far it had done him no good, and just at this critical juncture he was so ill that a journey to London was out of the question. Of course he too was hoping that his day had dawned: surely at long last the King would be prepared to overlook the insults heaped on him in the impetuosity of youth? For years Pitt had been a doughty champion of the government, punctiliously careful not to give any offence. He at once reached for his pen to confide his thoughts to his friends in London, the Grenvilles and the Lytteltons. For the common good he advocated carrying on the King's Government in peace and quiet for the rest of his life and also—and this is noteworthy—strengthening the hand of the Princess of Wales as far as possible against the moment when the King, who was over seventy, should die. Most characteristic of the age is this obvious effort not only to serve the reigning monarch, but also to take good care to keep in with his successor. The heir to the throne was by now a boy of sixteen. His upbringing had been put in the hands of his mother; she it was who would have decisive influence over him were he to ascend the throne while still young and immature. However, support for the Princess also meant opposition to Cumberland, her rival in the royal family, who was Fox's patron. Yet in his first letter Pitt wrote of Fox as the person most likely to be considered for the Exchequer.

Pelham had held this office along with that of First Lord of the Treasury—or prime minister in modern parlance. The two offices could only continue to be combined if the new leader of the ministry sat in the Commons, of which the Chancellor of the Exchequer had to be a member. George entrusted the reorganisation of the government to Hardwicke, in whose considered shrewdness he had justified confidence, but he told him at the outset that he expected no person who had flown in his face would be proposed to him. This of course was aimed at Pitt. On the other hand, the King was at first quite agreeable to Fox's appointment, evidently on the recommendation of Cumberland. One cannot blame Hardwicke if he was not exactly overjoyed at the prospect of having placed over him the very man who had just recently made such a violent and personal attack upon him. But his opposition was also made on grounds of policy. Behind Fox he saw the figure of his patron, the Duke of Cumberland. Now the Duke was Commander-in-Chief of the army, and for this reason Hardwicke feared that, if Fox were put at the head of the ministry and of the lower House, he would combine in his own person three sorts of power—financial, parliamentary and military. This ran counter to all precedent and particularly to Whig principles. In the days of Cromwell the English had discovered just what was meant by a military régime, and they had learned one lesson which they had never forgotten—that in all circumstances the military must be subordinate to the civil power.

So the Chancellor then tried—and with success—to win over both King and Cabinet to the view that Newcastle, who had been a Secretary of State for thirty years, should lead the government. This left two offices vacant: a Secretary of State and a Chancellor of the Exchequer were needed, and both had to be found from among the members of the Commons. Legge, a staunch Whig, went to the Exchequer. The real competition was for the Secretary's post, and the only serious candidates were Pitt and Fox. Pitt was a sick man and at Bath, but from there he directed the campaign which his friends in London, particularly Sir George Lyttelton, were carrying on for him and his circle. Above all he urged them to proceed with reserve; there was to be no threat of opposition in the event of a refusal. Apart from the private letters he wrote, he addressed a communication to Lyttelton which was really for the eye of the Lord Chancellor. Hardwicke did not fail to recognise either Pitt's importance or his shortcomings, and he certainly preferred him to his rival. As he assured Pitt on his honour, he took the greatest pains to talk the King round. He explained how necessary Pitt was to ensure a good majority in the Commons— a thing which George also desired. This must be fortified, he told him, 'not only by numbers, but by weight and abilities'; in other words, only a man of Pitt's great qualities could take under his wing the government majority, left a mere fledgling by Pelham's death. Newcastle, too, if Hardwicke can be believed, supported these efforts, though presumably with rather less enthusiasm.

For the Duke was now suffering from that incurable malady —jealousy of everyone who seemed likely to challenge his power and influence. He was, moreover, well aware that he was by no means so firmly established in the King's favour that he could risk making himself even more unpopular by vigorously supporting a man whom the King could not stomach. As it turned out, George remained obdurate. Pitt's friends—yes, they might earn advancement, but Pitt himself—never! So Hardwicke had to be content with the promotion of Lyttelton and George Grenville, and to confess his failure to Pitt in as tactful and friendly a letter as he could compose.

Now only the question of Fox remained. He was to receive the Seals of the Secretary for the Southern Department, the lesser of the two Secretaries of State as they then existed. This did not particularly appeal to Fox, who had never been interested in foreign affairs, but what made it attractive was the leadership of the Commons which was to be linked with it. The man who negotiated with him on Newcastle's behalf had expressly promised him this, but when he saw Newcastle himself, he had a most unpleasant surprise. The new head of the administration did, it is true, confirm that he would get the leadership of the Commons, but not the control of the secret service money. Worse still, this was to remain a secret even to the leader-designate of the lower House. Characteristically Fox replied that, if he was kept in ignorance of that, 'he should not know how to talk to members of Parliament, when some might have received *gratifications*, others not.' The inner workings of Hogarthian parliamentary life are here revealed in all their unlovely nakedness. Of course, Fox did not question for a moment the necessity of gratifications to hold together a majority in Parliament, but he felt that the force of oratory and capacity for political leadership which he knew himself to possess were equally necessary. The Duke, on the other hand, who had controlled the party organisation for so many years, persuaded himself that he could manage by using gratifications alone, and thought that he would only be sure of staying in office for as long as he kept them entirely in his own hands. He felt this all the more keenly as a fresh general election was looming up. Neither would budge. After a little hesitation, Fox, on the advice of his friends, refused the post of Secretary of State, which had lost all its charms for him, and remained Secretary at War. Newcastle ranged further afield and gave the Seals, together with the official leadership of the Commons, to Sir

Thomas Robinson who, though a seasoned diplomat, was completely without parliamentary experience or talents.

Pitt was grievously disappointed and mortified by this turn
of events. He would in any event have agreed to serve under
Fox, whose ability and achievements in the House he acknowledged, rivals though they were. But a parliamentary nonentity
like Robinson, with not one tenth of his own talent—this was
too much! In his letters to Newcastle and Hardwicke, where the
formal phrases can only half conceal his indignation, he complained of the King's inflexible dislike of him which was barring
his way to any office of importance for ever, and hinted that
nothing remained for him but retirement from political life.
Rather more frankly he wrote to his friend Lyttelton: 'I am
unwilling[1] to sit there [in Parliament] and be ready to be called
out into action when the Duke of Newcastle's personal interests
might require, or Government should deign to employ me as an
instrument.' His pride was deeply wounded and in his heart of
hearts he could not forgive Newcastle for not making a Cabinet
issue of his promotion. From now on his animosity towards the
Duke grew stronger and stronger. Nevertheless, he agreed to
represent a constituency which Newcastle had placed at his
disposal in the new Parliament; indeed, he thanked him for it
in terms of extravagant respect. In general the Duke could be
more than satisfied with the results of the elections: they gave
him a bigger majority than ever. With this support he believed
that he could look forward to a quiet session.

How very wrong he was! It is true that Pitt's letters to Newcastle and the Chancellor had disclaimed any thought of
opposition, and, as he did not give up his post as Paymaster,
the ministers felt that they could rely on this assurance. But in
reality he was determined to repeat the tactics which he had
used once before at the outset of his career. Whom could the
government put up to counter him in debate so long as Fox, too,
remained sulking in his tent? For Fox had soon come to regret
refusing the Seals, particularly as many of his friends had told
him that he had made a mistake. Soon Newcastle and Hardwicke were disturbed by the long and frequent discussions between the two malcontents. The Lord Chancellor wrote to his

[1] The word Pitt actually wrote was 'willing' (Lord Rosebery, p. 338 and
footnote), but the sense shows clearly that he intended to write 'unwilling'.

friend in October, 1754, that it seemed as though 'fire and water should agree.' His suspicions were well founded. Pitt and Fox had sunk their mutual differences to make common cause against the man by whom each felt he had been deceived.

Pitt fired the first shot, and it was one which reverberated. In November, shortly after Pitt's wedding, the Commons were considering the question of a contested election. This always happened after a general election, and in view of the huge government majority no one bothered greatly whether an odd election here and there was annulled. The fact, too, that the member whose election was contested defended himself in a humorous speech was nothing out of the ordinary, and the House followed his witty sallies with complacent amusement. In times past Pitt himself had dealt with an attack in just this way. However, *autres temps, autres moeurs*. He was on his feet at once, and at his very first words a general silence compact of uneasiness and expectancy descended on the House. With the austerity of a Cato and the pathos of a prophet he reproved the members for their frivolous hilarity in debating a question in which the dignity, nay more, the constitutional position of the House was at stake. And then, growing more and more heated with moral indignation, he fired his shot at Newcastle. If the Whigs, he exclaimed, did not unite 'to defend their attacked and expiring liberty', then 'you will degenerate into a little assembly, serving no other purpose than to register the arbitrary edicts of *one* too powerful *subject*.'

So thundered His Majesty's Paymaster-General against the First Lord of His Majesty's Treasury in the very Parliament where he had to thank the First Lord for his seat! And the game went on. Fox gaily joined in. Poor Robinson was goaded by the two matadors in turn and made to look a fool.

Obviously things could not go on like this. One of the two mischief-makers had to be won over by promotion, and in the circumstances it is hardly surprising that the choice fell upon Fox, although Newcastle and Hardwicke secretly inclined to Pitt. The King arranged for Fox to be asked what he wanted. Fox first submitted his answer to Pitt for approval, trying as far as possible to fall in with his objections and wishes. Fox also intimated to the King, through Hardwicke, that he would be no party to any plans directed against Pitt. When this was conveyed to the King, he broke in at once with the words: 'And I assure you [Fox] has done himself no good by it.' George was for dismissing Pitt there and then, but on the advice of the wary Chancellor he gave up this idea. Fox was given a seat in the Cabinet, and undertook to support the government's policy on all occasions in the Commons, without becoming its leader.

Pitt had no reason to resent Fox's conduct, for Fox had agreed every step with him in advance. It is certain that neither ever looked upon their alliance as anything more than a tactical expedient. They can scarcely have considered joining forces to form a ministry which would exclude Newcastle and thus drive the majority of the Whigs into opposition. Such a tactical alliance could only last as long as the two partners were both in the same boat, yet at first they kept up their friendly contact. However, at the beginning of May, 1755, Pitt suddenly broke off the friendship. All connections between them were at an end, he declared in the hearing of a third party. In a private conversation with Fox he was quite courteous towards him and assured him of continuing feelings of personal friendship, in contrast to Newcastle whom he roundly repudiated. But on the point at issue he was like granite. 'Yet', said Fox, 'are we on incompatible lines?' Whereupon Pitt returned the enigmatic answer: 'Not on incompatible, but on *convergent.*'

How can this abrupt break be explained? Nothing had happened immediately prior to this which could have given Pitt cause for complaint against Fox. Nor did Pitt himself ever assert that it had. But he could not help contrasting his own wholly unsatisfactory position with that of his more fortunate rival. For was not Fox not only a member of the Cabinet but also of the Regency Council, which governed England, while George, in the face of all the remonstrances of his ministers, once more dallied in his beloved Hanover? If Pitt were casting about for a way out of the impasse, he had not far to look before lighting on that member of the royal family whose importance he had already emphasised so strongly in his first letter after Pelham's death: the widow of the Prince of Wales and mother of the future King. Pitt knew, of course, that the Princess hated Cumberland and that her hatred also extended to Fox, whom she regarded as one of his most able lieutenants. He was by now convinced that he might expect nothing but snubs from the

King for ever and a day. If he were ever to get on, he must turn resolutely towards the rising sun.

In the Princess's household at Leicester House Lord Bute was now the man who mattered. Bute was a Scot, a nephew of the Duke of Argyll, who headed the Whig hierarchy in Scotland. But Bute's own political views lay in a different direction. He had already enjoyed the favour of the late Prince of Wales, and had been at one with him in his efforts to exalt the power of the Crown and break up the parties, especially, of course, the Whigs. After Frederick's death he was the avowed favourite and influential adviser of his widow. Contemporaries, King and people alike, explained this favour very simply as being due to a love affair between the pair of them. This view won all the more credence as Bute was a man with an imposing presence and a very winning manner. Whether it is correct must be doubted; at all events no sort of proof of it has ever come to light.

To all appearances, it was Bute who brought together Pitt and the Princess of Wales. This would not have been difficult, for the advantages to both parties were only too patent. Could the Princess make a better acquisition than the most popular orator in Parliament, whose incisive words could reduce even the boldest opponent to silence and round whom the lesser men of the Leicester House party might rally? There would be no lack of opportunity for active opposition: the tangled skein of foreign policy saw to that.

For months dark clouds had been gathering overhead. The peace which England and France had patched up at Aix-la-Chapelle was hardly more than an armistice, and in distant parts of the world not even that. In North America, in particular, where British and French colonists were cheek by jowl, skirmishes had never really ceased. In 1754 open hostilities broke out and blood was shed. Both countries were feeling keenly enough the after-effects of the long years of war and sought to avoid a fresh outbreak. However, both felt in honour bound to take up arms to help their compatriots on the far side of the Atlantic. And so gradually there arose a war which by international law was no war at all, because both sides fought shy of a formal declaration. Newcastle here followed the policy, justified in itself, of making as little fuss as possible about the military operations which were deemed necessary, so as not to force France into a declaration of war. But Fox, the Secretary at War, and Cumberland, the Commander-in-Chief, who were both pressing for war, cut clean across this policy—to quote but one instance—by publishing in the official gazette news of an expedition which should have remained secret.

This was the dilemma of British policy: should she concentrate all her strength upon a war at sea and in the colonies, in which she could rely on the superiority of her fleet, or should she open a war on two fronts against France, and stop her from concentrating her strength for a colonial war by attacking on the Continent? The most resolute advocate of the continental policy was, of course, the King. He was thinking of the dangers which a war with France might bring to his electorate. Nor were these dangers by any means imaginary; they were, in reality, greater even than George knew. As early as 1755 the King of Prussia was urging the French to hurl their troops against the electorate the moment the British declared war. 'C'est le moyen le plus sûr', he told the French Ambassador, 'de faire chanter ce ——!' The dash stands for a word which Frederick applied to his dear uncle, a term so vigorous that the pen of the well-bred Frenchman recoiled from setting it down. The martial ardour of the nephew cooled somewhat, however, when the French made the staggering reply that his proposal was an excellent one, but that they assumed that their esteemed Prussian ally would carry out the operation himself.

But, quite apart from all question of Hanover, there was much to be said from Britain's point of view for this war on two fronts—only it called for the acquisition of allies on the Continent. From her old allies, Austria and Holland, little could be expected. As has been seen, Prussia was not worth sounding diplomatically at this time. And so if allies with trained soldiers were to be gained, there was nothing for it but the traditional bait of subsidies. In 1755 George concluded a treaty with the Landgrave of Hesse-Cassel, who, for a payment of some £300,000 in good English money, turned over to him 12,000 of his well-beloved subjects. Of far greater significance was the conclusion of a subsidy agreement with Russia in September of the same year. By this, the Czarina Elizabeth undertook to place no less than 55,000 men at the disposal of Britain or of one of her allies (*scilicet* Hanover) for defence purposes. She did not, it is true, do this on the cheap. For every year of peace £100,000 sterling was to be paid and for every year of war half a million pounds. But was not the money well invested if Britain used it to buy the help of a great power in the war which was imminent? Newcastle had every reason to count these agreements as a political triumph, provided that he could get Parliament to endorse them.

Throughout the whole of the summer of 1755 the principal ministers had bargained with Pitt to dissuade him from his opposition and win him over to their side. After Pitt's personal attack, Newcastle had had no dealings with him and had left the initiative to Hardwicke. Pitt had some objections to the subsidy treaties, but the Chancellor did not consider them insurmountable, provided that Pitt's personal demands could be met. However, Pitt showed how far he had fallen back into the habits of his early years in opposition by adopting the old anti-Hanoverian tone. He admitted that Hanover ran the risk of occupation by the French or the Prussians if England and France should come to blows, but that did not move him. Hanover, he blithely suggested, could be compensated after the war for any tribulations it had endured. Of course, he could not have had a moment's doubt that so singular a policy would never win the King's approval.

As matters stood, it is not surprising that the negotiations broke down. Even a long personal interview which Newcastle had with Pitt had no result. Pitt was completely courteous but firm in his refusal. His attitude had, if anything, stiffened. He let it be clearly understood that only his appointment as both Secretary of State and leader of the Commons could satisfy him. This was precisely Newcastle's sensitive point. He had no doubt that in this position a man like Pitt would usurp the power of the ministry and completely displace him. The best course would be to resign at once. Of course, he did not seriously consider doing this and so he was left with the cold comfort that Pitt, backed to the hilt by Leicester House, would offer dangerous opposition to his plans.

Once again that left no one but Fox. In the meantime he, too, had put up his price. A seat in the Cabinet was no longer enough for him. He knew, as well as Newcastle did, the difficulties with which the subsidy treaties menaced the Duke, and so he let it be known that he had serious objections to them. Newcastle took the hint and asked him for an interview. In the event it proved easier to reach agreement with Fox. However he demanded a visible mark of personal favour from the King, that is to say, some post which would single him out as the man who enjoyed the King's particular confidence. As things stood, this could only be the position of Secretary of State, combined with the leadership of the Commons. The Duke hummed and hawed; he was so very unwilling to give up the least fraction of his power. But what else could he do? Experience had shown the manifest absurdity of his bright idea of managing without a leading minister in the Commons and buttressing himself up with patronage alone. Besides, the King, influenced by Cumberland, approved of Fox's promotion. And so Fox's wishes were met. The official announcement was delayed for a little because, under the existing constitution, this would entail a by-election and Fox could not be spared at the opening of Parliament. But he obtained the definite assurance that the announcement would be made as soon as the parliamentary situation permitted. Robinson vanished in the débâcle.

Cumberland was jubilant and the Princess of Wales was beside herself with rage. She felt that she had not merely been personally insulted, but also deceived. And, of course, it was upon the hapless Newcastle that the vials of her wrath descended.

Nothing was left for Pitt but open opposition. In the middle of November the new session began. In the customary way, Parliament opened its deliberations with an address in answer to the Speech from the Throne. This had referred to the threatened conflict with France, not, of course, without stressing His Majesty's love of peace and the purely defensive nature of his attitude, but it had, none the less, used strong language about the enemy across the Channel. The Address, which was also drafted by the ministers, replied in the same vein. The debate, which touched on all outstanding questions of foreign and domestic policy, had already lasted more than ten hours when Pitt began speaking at one o'clock in the morning, and went on to hold the House in tense silence for more than an hour and a half. Once again, the text has not survived, but the effect which the speech produced on its hearers is known. In particular Horace Walpole, who—whatever one may think of his politics

—possessed the eyes and ears of a cultivated and aesthetically trained observer, was for the rest of his life completely enthralled by this eloquence, pouring out like a torrent hitherto long dammed up and combining wit and humour with animation and fine language. 'Pitt surpassed himself', he wrote to a friend, while still freshly under its spell, 'and then I need not tell you that he surpassed Cicero and Demosthenes.' A speaker's success depends on his delivery, and that was certainly true on this occasion, so posterity may spare itself the labour of analysing and criticising the few sentences of the speech which have been preserved. The peroration was once again a personal attack. where one must bear in mind the whole histrionic artistry of the speaker if one is to appreciate its sensational effect to the full. After Pitt had painted in bold strokes the insignificance and unimportance of his own office, he confessed his inability to solve the riddle why certain sentences in the Address sounded as if they were the work of some hand which had not touched the rest. 'Yes', he cried, clapping his hand to his forehead as if sudden light had broken in upon him, 'I too am inspired now! It strikes me! I remember at Lyons to have been carried to see the conflux of the Rhône and the Saône; this, a gentle, feeble, languid stream and, though languid, of no depth—the other a boisterous and impetuous torrent—but they meet at last; and long,' he added, with biting irony, 'may they continue united to the comfort of each other, and to the glory, honour and security of this nation!'

The feeble and languid stream was a gibe at Newcastle, as everybody saw at once. But 'Who is the Rhône?' Fox asked Pitt after the debate. When he would have brushed this question aside as unfair, Fox pressed him further with the sweetish-sour jest, 'Why, as you have said so much that I did not desire to hear, you may tell me one thing that I would hear.'

To swallow this affront Newcastle would have had to be even slower and more inept than Pitt had depicted him. No one can have been surpised when within a few days Pitt was dismissed. Some of his friends, such as his brother-in-law, George Grenville, were shown the door along with him. It is characteristic that Bute was one of the first to whom the members out of office reported their punishment, and that it was Bute who sent George Grenville a letter of condolence in reply, saying,' 'tis

glorious to suffer in such a cause and with such companions.'
Pitt and his followers were supported by the national prejudice
against Hanover. Bute had still to discover how this same
national prejudice could turn against the Scots, and then he
found suffering less glorious.

A man who lived in the style of Pitt and was, moreover,
married to a woman of good family, found it a heavy blow to
lose the high salary of his office. But Temple at once sprang into
the breach by advancing his brother-in-law and political ally
an annuity of £1,000 until better times came. Pitt and Hester
were both deeply touched by this princely generosity, and expressed their thanks by writing letters in terms of unsurpassable
extravagance. 'I am more yours than my own . . .' wrote Pitt on
22nd November, 1755. 'I equally love and revere the kindest of
brothers and noblest of men.' This will sound a little strange to
those who know that the warmly-prized friendship of the
comrades-in-arms was one day to end in contention and mutual
reproaches. The last crisis had already cost Pitt one of his former
allies, George Lyttelton, who had agreed to become Chancellor
of the Exchequer.

On the very day of his dismissal Pitt had his first serious
brush with Fox, who had meanwhile received the seals of office
as Secretary of State. Pitt exposed a chink in his own armour
when, in his fury, he described the negotiations of the preceding
summer in a way which suggested that the Seals had been offered
to him but that he had declined them. Naturally Fox took him
up on the point, and he found himself forced to explain away
his words. Thenceforth they crossed swords almost daily; since
Fox possessed not only a compact majority and high office, but
also a cooler temperament and a reasoned case to defend, Pitt
usually came off second best, however brilliant his phrases and
however fulminating his invective. At all events Fox fully discharged the task he had taken over; he piloted all the ministry's
bills through the House. The subsidy treaties—even that with
Russia—which had been so hotly contested, were passed with a
two to one majority.

But this same Russian treaty was destined never to come into
force, although that by no means implies that it was of no
importance. On the contrary, its consequences were more far-
reaching than those of many other treaties binding two great

powers for a long term of years. It set in motion what has become world-famous in history as 'le renversement des alliances'.

'By this measure is not Prussia thrown into the power of France?' Pitt had thundered during the last debate on the Russian treaty. 'What can he [Frederick] answer, if France proposes to march an army into Germany? If he refuses to join them, will they not threaten to leave him at the mercy of the Russians?' This time Pitt proved a bad prophet. The treaty had exactly the opposite effect.

It has already been seen how, as early as the spring of 1755, Frederick of Prussia had tried to set the French on Hanover. At that time he was obviously in the French camp, but he had never envisaged his alliance with France as meaning that he should himself make sacrifices on her behalf. If the French refused to play his game, it was still further from his thoughts to play theirs. The old Franco-Prussian treaty of alliance was on the verge of expiring, and he had still been unable to make up his mind to renew it. His unwillingness to commit himself prematurely increased when he heard of the negotiations in train between Russia and England. As these hung fire or progressed, so his attitude towards the French veered this way and that. An attempt to upset the negotiations, by letting it be known in London that the appearance of Russian troops in Germany would compel him to plunge into the war, failed. When, however, he learned of the final conclusion and ratification of the treaty, his one desire was to reach a settlement with England; he breathed again when the British Government officially informed his Ambassador of the agreement, assuring him not only that it was purely defensive in aim but also that George II was prepared to forge a still closer link with Prussia. Lord Hyndford, a former British Ambassador in Berlin, had already said years before that Frederick was more in fear of Russia than he was of God. If it came to a fresh war with Austria, a Russian attack in his rear might prove fatal. But if England had the Russian bear on a chain, as Frederick put it, he must himself enter into an alliance with England so that she might not turn the bear loose on him. Whether he hoped to avoid a European war altogether in this way, or whether on the contrary he intended to secure his rear for a fresh war with Austria is here beside the point. Suffice it to say that he very promptly and very gladly welcomed the British initiative, and on January 16th, 1756, only a few weeks after Pitt had uttered his prophecies of disaster, a convention between Britain and Prussia was signed at Westminster.

The convention mentions the hostilities which had broken out in America and the possibility of their spreading to Europe. In this event, both kings pledged themselves not to allow their forces to march through each other's territory and to restrain their respective allies from so doing. But if a foreign power caused troops to enter Germany, the signatories would oppose them with their concerted strength. George had thereby ensured that his electorate would be protected by the Prussian army. In the event of war Frederick would be able to count upon English subsidies amounting to £670,000 each year.

Frederick completely miscalculated the consequences of this treaty. It opened the way for his most formidable diplomatic opponent, Count Kaunitz, the Austrian Chancellor, to realise his ambitious scheme of a triple alliance between Austria, France and Russia. The 'old system' by which England and Austria were grouped against France was not only abandoned but inverted. On May 1st, 1756, a defensive treaty between the courts of Vienna and Paris was concluded at Versailles. On May 18th Great Britain declared war on France. On August 29th, 1756, Frederick invaded Saxony, thus beginning what is known as the Seven Years' War, which only ended in February, 1763, with the Peace of Hubertsburg. In this war England ranged herself alongside Frederick as an ally on the basis of the Convention of Westminster until November 3rd, 1762, when she signed peace preliminaries with France at Fontainebleau.

§

The Convention of Westminster was laid before Parliament on May 14th, 1756, that is, a few days before England's declaration of war. Pitt, who had waged an untiring and relentless war of words on the ministry throughout the session, looked on this convention, which soon afterwards was to become the cornerstone of his superb war leadership, with the eyes of a member in opposition. He branded it as a charter for the favoured treatment of Hanover, which he had so hotly opposed. He accused the government of buying this treaty at the cost of British rights.

He would not have signed it even if he had been given the five great offices of state held by the men who had put their signature to it. How fortunate it was for him that the times very soon became too critical, and he himself too indispensable, for his opponents to divert themselves by casting in his teeth when in power his speeches made in opposition.

§

England's declaration of war was occasioned by the French attack on the island of Minorca, which lies in the Mediterranean off the coast of Spain. Since the War of the Spanish Succession it had belonged to Britain, and was one of the most treasured possessions of the English and a symbol of their predominance in the Mediterranean. Pitt touched a tender spot when he uttered sombre prophecies in Parliament of its impending loss. Of course the ministry had sent a naval force, under the command of Admiral Byng, into the Mediterranean to relieve Minorca. But since they agreed with the popular view in fearing that the French might attempt a landing on the coast of England itself, they felt that they ought to keep the bulk of the English fleet in home waters. Byng proved quite unequal to his task. He was afraid his forces would prove inadequate, and turned back to Gibraltar without having ventured to try conclusions with the French. As a result the English garrison on the island could not hold out and capitulated at the end of June.

The news of this defeat aroused indescribable alarm and indignation. The British nation had been flicked on the raw. The army might be beaten by the French in a battle on land: that had occurred often enough and was not taken too tragically, for in the eyes of the English the army was only an auxiliary arm, and they knew that its strength was not to be compared with that of a great power on the Continent. But the fleet—that was quite another thing! Every Englishman felt it was a national concern; nay more, it was the pride of the nation. The English were used to fighting their land battles, in part at least, with foreign mercenaries. But the fleet was manned by the country's own sons and, even if they had most of them been driven together by brutal press-gang methods, they were still expected to give proof of their British courage and tenacity in the hour of danger, and this expectation was rarely disappointed. But now a

British fleet had turned tail before the enemy without a fight, leaving him the spoils of victory. This was the crowning humiliation. Of course a scapegoat had to be found. Who was the chief culprit? Byng, who had avoided battle, or the ministry which, he maintained, had not given him enough ships? The less the masses knew of these questions, the more passionate did their accusations become. Byng, of course, was haled before a court-martial. But the chance of turning popular feeling against the ministry was far too tempting a one for the opposition to miss. Parliament did not sit in the summer; but city corporations sent in petitions demanding strict investigation and accusing the administration of negligence. The City of London, where Pitt was especially popular, was in the van.

Newcastle, painfully aware of his low prestige with the public, reviewed with some concern the forces he could muster for a struggle against Pitt and the opposition when Parliament reassembled in the autumn. A serious loss was already threatening him. The Attorney-General, Murray, a clever Scot, and, according to the Lord Chancellor, the most outstanding lawyer in the country, was demanding the recently vacant post of Lord Chief Justice, to which the Attorney-General had a traditional claim. This meant his leaving the lower House, and it was there that he had been of the utmost value to Newcastle, because he had the Duke's full confidence and was a match for Pitt in eloquence and experience. But in one respect, let it be said, he was far from being Pitt's equal: in the courage, the passion even, to face his opponent in the fray. He disliked the rough and tumble of parliamentary conflict and far preferred the repose and dignity of the Bench, to which he knew he had been born and upon which he did in fact, as Lord Mansfield, become one of England's greatest and most constructive judges. So it was all to no purpose that Newcastle made him the most extravagant offers—naturally without any regard to the country's finances— to retain him in the lower House.

A second and even more grievous blow fell in October: Fox resigned. In the spring session he had again led the Commons with complete success. His parliamentary reputation had, if that were possible, grown even greater. But it was otherwise with his work as Secretary of State. Foreign policy was not at all in his line, and the more he had to concern himself with it officially

F

the less did he feel that he was in the right place. Lord Granville roused no answering echo in his breast when he called out to him: 'I want to instil a nobler ambition into you, to make you knock the heads of the kings of Europe together, and jumble something out of it which may be of service to this country.' His position in the ministry was precarious. He mistrusted its leader, Newcastle, who returned the compliment. Newcastle suspected that Fox aspired to his position, and Fox suspected Newcastle of setting the King against him. Probably both were right.

The situation was complicated still further by one of the quarrels in the royal family which are so characteristic of the period. In this year, 1756, the young Prince of Wales completed his eighteenth year and thus came of age. The King was anxious to grasp this opportunity of withdrawing him from his mother's· influence, and of setting him up with a household of his own away from her. The Prince and his mother not only contrived to avoid this but also came forward with the demand that Bute should be appointed Groom of the Stole to the Prince. The King, who shared the common view that Bute was the Princess's lover, was indignant at this demand, behind which he scented an opposition manoeuvre; his dislike for Pitt was only heightened by it. It was not until October that he complied with the Princess's wish. In the handling of this delicate matter Newcastle and Fox had once again not seen eye to eye.

To crown all these vexations there now broke the storm unleashed by the fall of Minorca. Was Fox to defy it alone in the Commons? He could vividly imagine how Pitt would thunder and whip up passions. And for whose sake was he to bring this torture on himself? For the head of a government whom he mistrusted and despised, and for a king who was not his friend. The prospect held few attractions for him. At first he had the idea of offering his post to Pitt. Then came one of the eternal squabbles with Newcastle over some favour to be bestowed on one of his friends, and on the 13th October, suddenly resolved, he threw up his office.

This was still some weeks before Parliament was due to reassemble. Newcastle and the King had, therefore, every reason to be angry with Fox for choosing this particular moment to resign. How could the gap possibly be filled at such short notice? Only one man possessed the necessary qualities, and that was the man to whom the King and the Duke had the strongest possible objections: Pitt. In his parliamentary philippics he had made the Duke look ridiculous by comparing him to a child driving a go-cart, containing an old king and his family, close to the edge of a precipice. He had touched the King on a very tender spot by calling Hanover a province not even marked on the map, adding, with a metaphor which miscarried, that 'he ardently wished to break those fetters, which chained us, like Prometheus, to that barren rock.'

What a humiliation for the Duke to have to propose this very man, this malicious fellow Pitt, to the King as Fox's successor! At first George resisted. 'But Mr. Pitt won't do my German business,' he objected. When Newcastle returned to the charge at the next audience, the King raised another difficulty: 'Suppose Pitt will not serve with you?' 'Then, Sir, I must go', answered the Duke, whereupon the King consoled him with the words, 'My Lord, I know your faults, but I know also your integrity and zeal for *me*.'

The King's surmise proved well-founded. The first condition which Pitt made when the Lord Chancellor broached the matter with him was Newcastle's resignation. For the rest, his programme was a mixture of fundamentals and trivialities; but that was not where its real significance lay. What really was important was Pitt's consciousness of his own mission, summed up in his famous words to the Duke of Devonshire: 'My Lord, I am sure I can save this country, and nobody else can.'

Braced by this self-confidence Pitt took a step which he had always avoided before: he called on the King's mistress, Lady Yarmouth. This lady, a former Frau Wallmoden whom George had brought over with him from Hanover, had gradually become a national institution. Ministers and politicians with something on their minds which they wished the King to hear made a point of visiting the room in the Royal palace 'below stairs', where the lady lived and listened with kindly understanding to the hopes and grievances of her visitors. The England of the eighteenth century thought none the worse of anyone who took this path. Only the King grumbled if someone else had gone 'below stairs'. 'Mr. Pitt shall not go to *that channel* any more', he said to Lord Hardwicke. '*She* does not meddle and shall not meddle.' The Lord Chancellor had to exert all the diplomacy he could muster in giving Pitt to understand that the negative reply which he brought him from the King referred not only to his official proposals but also to those transmitted through Lady Yarmouth, although this channel could not be named in so many words.

Yet this royal refusal could not alter the course of events. Newcastle bowed to the inevitable and resigned. The King had then to find a new First Lord of the Treasury, and he chose Fox. Whatever he held against him, he still found Fox more congenial than Pitt, the confidant of the Princess of Wales and of Leicester House. Fox had already started to pull every string he could in order to gain admittance to the Treasury, but what good would the help of all the big-wigs in the land do him if they did not include Pitt? And so Fox went to see him, significantly enough at Leicester House itself. There, at the head of the stairs, they held a long conversation which naturally excited lively curiosity among the onlookers. 'Mr. Pitt exceeding grave . . . They did not seem to part amicably.' The observation was correct. Pitt told Fox bluntly that he refused to sit in a Cabinet with him. Not even Cumberland's intervention could shift him from this standpoint, which had probably been agreed with Bute and the Princess.

The comings and goings went on for a few days longer. Finally Pitt consented to modify his conditions slightly. The Duke of Devonshire, one of the leaders of the Whig aristocracy, was now prepared to lead the ministry if Pitt became Secretary of State. On this basis a new government came into being in the last few days before the opening of Parliament.

Newcastle and Fox were dropped. Hardwicke followed his old friend, and resigned from the office of Lord Chancellor which he had held for nearly twenty years.

Pitt might well think that he had now reached a goal worthy of his gifts and his ambition, and for the first time in his life he was able to direct his country's policy. He had made his way ruthlessly and at times unscrupulously, but his success was due above all else to his personality, the forcefulness and incontestable superiority of which impressed all who saw him in the turmoil of parliamentary battle between the opposition and the followers of the government. To this personality his opponents now paid the highest tribute conceivable by recognising William Pitt as the one man who was indispensable in the hour of need.

CHAPTER VI

SECRETARY PITT AND
PAYMASTER FOX

THE fourth of December, 1756, the day when Pitt kissed hands upon receiving from the King the seals of office as Secretary of State for the Southern Department, marks the beginning of the most important period—both personally and historically—in his life. It is now that he rises to the leadership of his country in a world war and takes his place among the immortals.

When he took office things were black enough. But it was, basically, a situation typical of Britain in the opening stages of any great war. Unprepared or ill-prepared, she first suffers grievous defeats which she sustains with exasperation but with unbroken spirit; then she gradually marshals her strength until she deploys a power as surprising to herself as to her enemies and her friends. On this occasion the initial difficulties were all the greater as she had not one but two wars in prospect. She had to reckon on a war with France in which most other powers would be either neutral or friendly to England. But, three months after the declaration of war between France and England, the surprise attack made by Frederick of Prussia on Saxony, which ran counter to the intentions of the Convention of Westminster, set all Europe ablaze, and France became the nucleus of a coalition of three great powers. On the other hand, this grouping produced an unexpectedly close alliance between Britain and the French coalition's real opponent, Frederick, who as ruler of Prussia could not only fling a first-rate, hard-hitting army into the balance, but was also in himself a priceless military asset, as he was a brilliant general of outstanding intelligence. So far Frederick had been victorious. Not only had he conquered Saxony and forced her army to capitulate, but he had also defeated, though not decisively, an Austrian army at Lobositz. But how long would he be able to stand up to a coalition whose forces were far superior to his own on any objective reckoning?

If events abroad were serious, Pitt's position at home was hardly satisfactory either. He was generally looked upon as the head of the government although he was not officially at the helm. But no one saw the Duke of Devonshire, who had taken over at the Treasury, as anything more than a figurehead concealing Pitt, who, as everyone knew, had in fact formed the ministry according to his own wishes. But it was in this very matter that Pitt had already shown himself not really as strong as he and others had imagined. He had been completely unable to fill all the key posts with men who enjoyed his confidence. His own adherents were far too few in number: they hardly amounted to more than his brothers-in-law. Temple, whose interests, of course, claimed first consideration, was given the Admiralty, around which the storm of public abuse had raged with especial violence at the time of the Minorca fiasco. His brother, George Grenville, became Treasurer of the Navy; and he actually did know something about figures and finance. But many of the other posts had to be filled with adherents of other groups, followers of Fox for example. As his colleague in the Northern Department—the more important office of the two— Pitt had to defer to the King's wishes and accept Lord Holderness, who had occupied it hitherto. Only Newcastle and his friends were still excluded on principle.

These, however, were still by far the most important section of the Whigs. Newcastle's following did not fall off, although he had now lost his office and, along with it, much of his power to give jobs—a sign that his influence rested on a more lasting foundation than patronage alone. The Tories, it is true, placed themselves at Pitt's disposal as parliamentary reinforcements. Some of them were, in any case, his followers, like Beckford, the member for the City of London, who later became Lord Mayor. Other Tories now saw their first opportunity of effacing the disrepute which had hitherto barred them from all offices and high dignities. In any case there were now no Stuarts left, no cause, that is, claiming their loyalty in opposition to the House of Hanover. But there were too few of them to be able to offset any defection by Newcastle's following.

In these circumstances it was for Pitt both wise and expedient not to provoke the Duke unnecessarily. An effective war-cry against the late government had been the demand for a parliamentary committee to investigate the Minorca expedition. Of course the new government had to meet this demand. But when Hardwicke, who had a particular axe to grind (his son-in-law, Lord Anson, had at the time been First Lord of the Admiralty), visited Pitt shortly after he had taken office, the minister assured him that he had no great love of recriminations and intimated that he would display no particular zeal in this direction. As things turned out, the investigation itself brought nothing particularly damning to light. Nor was this mere parliamentary shadow-boxing, for some months later Pitt agreed to Anson's return to the Admiralty.

It was only to be expected that the negative result of the investigation was a sore disappointment to Byng's friends. The more blame heaped on the retiring ministry, the greater the whitewashing of the Admiral. He had been found guilty by a court-martial on January 27th, 1757, of dereliction of duty in the face of the enemy. By the wording of the Act under which he was tried, the court had been compelled to condemn him to death; but they had unanimously recommended him to the King's clemency, as in their view the punishment was disproportionately severe. But popular sentiment clamoured for Byng's death. In the Commons, of which he was a member, his friends made strenuous efforts on his behalf, and Pitt was compelled to make his own position clear. He declared himself *for* the granting of a pardon. This does him credit, for he must have known that he was thereby jeopardising his popularity. But it was all to no purpose. The King was determined to make an example, and when Pitt emphatically represented to him that feeling in Parliament favoured a pardon, George replied, with a promptness and perspicacity surprising for him: 'Sir, *you* have taught me to look for the sense of my subjects in another place than in the House of Commons.' So Byng had to go to his death, and Voltaire, who had also made efforts to obtain a pardon for him, immortalized the tragedy in one of his best-known epigrams: 'Dans ce pays-ci,' he writes in *Candide*, 'il est bon de tuer de temps en temps un amiral, *pour encourager les autres.*'

Of course, this episode is a relatively trifling issue beside Pitt's measures for winning the war. In some points of policy he was forced to tread the path of his predecessors. It was quite out of the question for Pitt, the responsible statesman, to denounce the Convention of Westminster, a course which Pitt, the opposition speaker, had urged. Quite the contrary in fact: he now had to work at strengthening the bonds which linked England with her one effectual ally. Opposition speakers might thunder against subsidy treaties, but the Secretary of State laid before Parliament a demand for £200,000 for the King of Prussia, and supported the setting up of an army of observation in Germany to consist of 36,000 Hanoverians and 24,000 Hessians. His speech lost nothing in energy and vigour by his knowledge that every member present could cast in his teeth arguments which he had advanced on precisely the opposite side. It was left to Fox to remind him that he had previously called the German treaties a millstone round England's neck. The overwhelming majority paid as little heed as Pitt to such inconsistencies. They admired the way in which the new Secretary of State was able to expound his policy and relate it to its wider context, and they approved his demand. Frederick was jubilant at this success, and had his especial thanks conveyed to Pitt through the British Minister to Prussia. Pitt reciprocated with a letter, in which he goes into complacent ecstasies over 'the infinite condescension and gracious goodness of His Prussian Majesty.' This, however, did not prevent Frederick, when Pitt was put out of office a few months later, from voicing the hope that England would now at last find more active, serious statesmen than Pitt and the Pelhams. But even if Pitt did many things which his predecessors had done, or would have done in his place, there can be no doubt that he brought a new note and a new spirit into the conduct of the war. The Speech from the Throne itself which opened Parliament was a product of his pen, and used a more vigorous and martial language: it was a call to the people to realise the gravity of the hour, and the magnitude of the task. It stressed the dangers looming up in America and announced the formation of a national militia. The nation must realise that everything depended on its own exertions, and that it was not enough to hire foreign mercenaries for the defence of England. To fill the gap left by the return of the German troops Pitt raised a few Highland regiments, a bold step when one recalls that only a decade earlier the Highlanders had rebelled against the Royal House, turning their eyes to France for aid. But the step proved to be justified. Pitt pursued a similar policy of confidence towards the American colonists. He shipped fresh forces overseas and encouraged the Americans to supplement the exertions of the mother country by their own, so as to make possible an offensive against the French, who had scored some resounding successes in the opening months of the war.

The other front on which the British and the French were disputing the mastery of a continent was in the East Indies. Here, too, the British cause had suffered severe setbacks. Calcutta had fallen into the hands of a nawab who was allied with the French, and the English captives had met a ghastly fate in the 'Black Hole'. Happily nothing of these grim happenings was yet known at home, and before the news arrived, the young Robert Clive, at the head of the small East India Company force, had smashed the power of the Nawab and defeated the French in the decisive and brilliant engagement of Plassey (June, 1757).

Pitt applied himself vigorously to devising plans for an offensive war against France on all fronts. Even his malady, which repeatedly kept him in his bed, could neither damp his ardour nor interrupt his work. But he was not to carry his plans into effect at once. For on April 6th, 1757, he was dismissed.

In his heart of hearts the King had never become reconciled to Pitt's elevation to office. Stern necessity alone had driven him to appoint this obnoxious man, and he longed for nothing better than to discard him as soon as the emergency had passed. Pitt's personal bearing can scarcely have given him grounds for complaint. Whenever he was received in audience by the King —and, on account of his illness, this did not occur on more than six occasions—he was at pains to adopt a most respectful tone and demeanour. No courtier who had danced attendance all his days in His Majesty's antechamber could excel this man who, in Parliament, played the rôle of a tribune of the people. But he had one failing. He would make—as George himself complained—long speeches at the King, very fine in their way, no doubt, but ranging far beyond the royal horizon. This alone might not have proved insurmountable had not Pitt also possessed a brother-in-law who was a constant source of extreme exasperation to George. Temple, as First Lord of the Admiralty, frequently had to deal with the King in person; on these occasions he displayed so undisguisedly his inordinately high opinion of his own importance that the King never failed to work himself into a fury. He called Temple's manner nothing short of insolent and in particular he could not forget the tone in which he had attempted to hector him into granting a pardon for Byng. But worst of all, the new ministers were in the counsels of Leicester House. Was George to see his own daughter-in-law on the throne in his own life-time? These apprehensions were constantly conjured up and kept alive by his son, the Duke of Cumberland; and the Duke's agent, Fox, was indefatigable in making plans for a new ministry to expel and replace Pitt's. But all these plans foundered on some reef or other, especially as Newcastle and his friends refused to be drawn in.

But other circumstances were at work to force a decision. The army which had been raised in Germany to fight the French, to protect Hanover and to lighten Prussia's tasks, needed an English Commander-in-Chief. Frederick wanted Cumberland appointed to this post, because, as the King of England's son, he was the most likely to maintain authority over the various contingents which made up the army. The Duke himself had little relish for this, partly because he was profoundly pessimistic about the military position of this army and his prospects of winning fame as a general at its head, and partly because he feared that his dear sister-in-law, the Princess of Wales, might take advantage of his absence to become complete mistress of the situation. To guard against this he demanded that Pitt should be dismissed. The King was only too ready to assent. He first had the pleasure of sending Temple about his business, hoping that Pitt would answer this affront with his own resignation. But Pitt, never one to make matters in any way easier for his adversaries, remained. On the following day he, too, received his dismissal.

But once again George was to learn that in a constitutional state it is easier to cut short the life of a ministry than to conjure up a new one out of thin air. He was first to discover that he had employed the most effective means of restoring the full lustre of Pitt's popularity, which had been somewhat tarnished by his attitude in the Byng affair. Now that Pitt had been overthrown by a court party, he once again became the great patriot belauded by his fellow-countrymen. In the forefront came the city corporations. They demonstrated against the court by making Pitt a freeman of their cities, and by solemnly presenting him with the freedoms in golden caskets. 'For some weeks', to quote Horace Walpole, 'it rained gold boxes.'

But, more important than this, the country urgently needed a government, particularly in the middle of a war which posed the gravest problems. It is almost incredible that at such a time Britain was without a regular administration for nearly three months. Of course, negotiations were going on all the time for the formation of a new Cabinet. At first it looked as if Fox had got his chance again. The King turned to him, and a number of the leading aristocrats were prepared to throw in their lot with his. But Newcastle was astute enough to follow the advice of his friend Hardwicke, and, for all the King's bluster, to remain stubborn. Soon after Pitt's overthrow the former Lord Chancellor had already summed up the problem in these terms: 'No solid plan of administration can be made for him [the King] by anybody, that will give him ease and comfort for the remainder of his days, . . . but such a one as may, if possible, unite the whole royal family and bring *the succession* to support and give quiet to *the possession*.' In other words the politicians who took over the national destinies at this difficult juncture must feel assured that they would not be turned out of office by a new Pharaoh if the old one should suddenly end his days. In short, no ministry could subsist unless it enjoyed the backing of Leicester House.

But Leicester House meant William Pitt. This was made very plain when Hardwicke, sued for help by a despairing monarch, finally undertook to form a new ministry. Pitt attended the conference to which he was then invited accompanied by Bute, who held a watching brief for his royal employers, so that he could agree in their name to any eventual compact. After many difficulties the new coalition came into being. It comprised both the Newcastle group and that of Pitt and his friends. The Duke returned to the place at the head of the Treasury which he had vacated nine months earlier, and Pitt once again became Secretary of State for the Southern Department.

It was the best combination possible in the circumstances. For the rest of his life it did, in fact, provide the King with a stable administration which could rely on a compact majority in Parliament. This majority looked to Newcastle rather than Pitt as its leader, but as the Duke left the military and political conduct of the war in Pitt's hands this was certain to be animated by his spirit. Pitt's decisive importance in this sphere received such overwhelming recognition that his influence extended far beyond the official round of his duties. The exact limits of responsibility were at the time still drawn somewhat primitively, followed no logical pattern, and were, like so much else in England, a product not of reasoned reflection but of historical evolution. There were not, as there are today, a Home Secretary and a Foreign Secretary, but two Secretaries of State, competent to act in both fields, whose responsibility for foreign policy was divided geographically. It is obvious that such a system could work on only one of two conditions: either both Secretaries had to be of one mind in all important questions, a pre-established harmony which is of course extremely rare, or one of them would have to take his cue from the other. This had already emerged in Newcastle's day, when the Duke had laid himself open to the charge of despotism because in the long run he could never work in harmony with any colleague who wanted to follow a policy of his own. During Pitt's term of office it was even more implicitly understood that he would demand the unconditional acquiescence of his colleagues and treat departmental demarcations as if they did not exist. In time of war there was simply no other alternative. Pitt's dictatorial manner in no wise smoothed the path of co-operation for his colleagues. But, grudging or cheerful, to a man they all recognised his mastery in everything touching the conduct of the war and they nearly always deferred to his wishes. Only the financing of the war he did not regard as his affair. He gladly left this to Newcastle and the Chancellor of the Exchequer, who often enough groaned under the burden.

Pitt had successfully brought about Temple's return to the Cabinet. But he had at least made one concession to the King in appointing Temple Keeper of the Privy Seal, which meant that he would come but rarely into personal contact with George. His other brother-in-law, George Grenville, once more became Treasurer of the Navy. By common consent Hardwicke was co-opted to attend all Cabinet meetings, but he declined to return to the Woolsack.

But what of Henry Fox? What was the outcome of all his activity? Neither of the two groups in the coalition wooed his aid. But, on the other hand, neither wished to drive him into the arms of the opposition by snubbing him too openly. He was, and remained, a formidable parliamentary debater and he possessed powerful friends in both Houses. And so both groups were prepared to meet one of the King's wishes by installing Fox in an office which the King had promised him but which was, on the other hand, not important enough to admit of his influencing policy. This post was that of Paymaster-General to the Forces, which Pitt had occupied until 1755. But whereas Pitt had regarded it only as a stepping-stone to greater things, his former rival had now reached the point where he welcomed it as a haven of refuge from the storms of higher politics. He was now fifty-two, at an age, that is, when ambition has not as a rule finally expired. What can have made him thus prematurely resigned? It is not unjust to assume that, after his failure on this occasion to secure a leading position, he doubted whether such a post would ever again come his way. The days of the old King seemed to be numbered, and in his heir's entourage Fox's name was anathema. His patron, Cumberland, had not shown himself strong enough to try conclusions with the heir apparent; he was, moreover, still remembered by many as the 'Butcher of Culloden' and laboured under widespread unpopularity. This odium extended to Fox himself, who had friends in Parliament, but none among the people. All contemporary reports leave absolutely no doubt on this point. But it is not easy to see how this unpopularity had arisen. Newcastle and his friends reproached Fox for leaving them in the lurch in October, 1756, but this can hardly have been the reason underlying the popular dislike of him. He had, after all, only waged political warfare with weapons in common use among his opponents.

By becoming Paymaster Fox had let himself be thrust into a political blind alley. But, to offset this, the post held one especial attraction for him. It dangled before him the prospect of amassing a large fortune in a few years. Of course, if he intended to follow the example of Pelham and Pitt and accept nothing beyond his official salary, then the question would not arise. But was he bound to do this? Their practice had not been regularised by any statute or legal ruling; it was looked upon by experts as a mere eccentricity on the part of these two gentlemen and not binding on their successors. Fox did not feel himself bound in any way. He thought of the huge sums which had to pass through the Paymaster's hands in time of war, and of the enormous subsidies on which the customary one half per cent commission would run into thousands of pounds annually—for one could count on the war's lasting a few years longer. Provided he went no further than his predecessors—that is, except Pelham and Pitt—his conscience would not prick him in the least. He was only acting in accordance with the spirit of the age, not found in England alone, in looking on his high office as a milch cow which would keep him supplied with butter. It was the accepted thing for a successful politician to provide his children with sinecures which would spare them the distressing necessity of earning their daily bread by their own exertions. In this tradition Fox, too, had made provision for his sons. He had three, the second of whom, Charles James, was his particular favourite. It also went without saying that he desired his wife to live in a style befitting a duke's daughter. For years he had occupied one of the most magnificent properties to be found near London, Holland House, destined to become the centre of Whig society in the first half of the nineteenth century. When Henry Fox's grandson, the third Lord Holland, was in residence here, it was a meeting place for every person of consequence in the political and intellectual life of England. Here it was that the young Macaulay made his debut in society, and amazed everyone by the sheer inexhaustibility of his knowledge and the infallibility of his memory.

One can well understand the head-shakings of Fox's contemporaries. By resigning he had admitted, in their eyes, that his inveterate rival Pitt was the better man, thus giving up the race for lost. That Fox regarded the plight of his country as a good opportunity to line his own pocket, while the other bent all his energies to leading her to victory, was the only criterion by which the two could be compared. The higher Pitt's fame mounted, the lower Fox sank in public esteem.

§

It was on June 26th, 1757, that Pitt received the Seals a second time from the hands of George II. On October 25th,

1760, the King died at the age of seventy-seven. In the intervening three years Pitt, with the consent of his colleagues, the King, Parliament and the people, ruled Britain as Secretary of State and led her in war against France and her allies. It was a war waged in almost every part of the world as then known, on all the seas and oceans, on the banks of the Weser as well as of the St. Lawrence, in the West Indies as in the East Indies. A man who could run such a war, who could send out armies and fleets for its battles and brief their generals and admirals, must needs have a head for world strategy. The situation called for a man of fiery spirit which would not flinch from the heaviest responsibilities, which would endure the inevitable defeats and setbacks with unshakeable confidence and exploit successes with unremitting energy. He needed the capacity to expound to Parliament and the people the broad conceptions underlying his policy, and to steel their resolve to accept sacrifices and hold out at all costs. Pitt achieved all this, and the massive success which came his way was no mere gift from the hand of providence, but the result of hard work and of a well-considered, purposeful policy. The commanders of the English armies and navies, who gained brilliant victories, well knew how much they owed the Secretary of State; none left his office without feeling that Pitt had inspired him with fresh courage and had communicated his own resolution to him. And each knew that the Secretary had prepared and organised everything that could humanly be foreseen to ensure success and concentrate forces at the point where they could most decisively make their weight felt. The people, who had been plunged into gloom by the initial failures, awaited the outcome with limitless confidence since Pitt had taken over. As if by a miracle feeling veered round completely under the influence of his energy and personality.

Not all Pitt's plans were successful or decisive. His repeated attempts at landing troops on the French coast, even if they had come off, would hardly have borne the fruit he hoped. But this is of little consequence beside the ideas he conceived on the grand scale and applied with success.

He now fully appreciated the importance of the German theatre of operations. Here, as he saw, France might be so attacked and kept busy that she could be prevented from concentrating her full strength on the war at sea and in the colonies, and might exhaust herself in countless battles and campaigns. France was much more densely populated than Britain. She had eighteen to twenty million inhabitants as against the six to eight million in the British Isles. But England disposed of far greater economic and financial resources, and could therefore hold out longer if the worst came to the worst.

But in Germany England's only ally of any consequence, Frederick of Prussia, had to be supported. A few days after Pitt had taken office news reached England of Frederick's heavy defeat at Kolin. This merely spurred Pitt to greater efforts. But on the heels of this followed a second catastrophe in Western Germany, and one which this time had to be put down to Britain's account. Cumberland had found his gloomy forebodings borne out: neither his generalship nor the weight of his forces was any match for the French and he was driven back ver deeper into Hanover. In the end he felt justifiably compelled to capitulate on September 8th, 1757, at Kloster-Zeven, thus putting paid to any further part in the war as far as his army was concerned.

Politically the worst of it was that Cumberland could point to instructions and discretionary powers which the King had given behind his ministers' backs. It was the old story—the clash of British and Hanoverian interests and George's anxiety for his threatened electorate. The ministers to a man set their faces against him, and declared that the United Kingdom was not bound by the Convention of Kloster-Zeven. The aged king was alarmed and shifted his ground, trying to unload all responsibility on to his son, whom he heaped with the bitterest reproaches when he returned. As a result Cumberland surrendered all his offices—a very fortunate result, too, since Prince Ferdinand of Brunswick now took command of the army operating in Western Germany and proved a capable and successful general. The ticklish question of the binding force of the Convention luckily never became acute, because the French themselves infringed it, and thus allowed the British ministers to regard it as null and void.

Pitt had no reason to like Cumberland, who had brought about his overthrow in the spring. But he was above hitting a man when he was down. On Pitt, too, the King tried out his old trick: the blame, he said, was entirely his son's. He went further: never had he given him any orders to come to terms. But Pitt replied, in icy tones: 'But *full powers*, Sir; very full powers!'

The military consequences of the capitulation were more than offset by Frederick's brilliant victory over the French at Rossbach (November 5th, 1757). This was followed a few weeks later, on the fifth of December, by his equally great victory over the Austrians at Leuthen. The King of Prussia was now the most popular man in England—after Pitt. Even inns were named after him—always a sure sign of particularly wide popularity. Pitt sought to intensify the enthusiasm for Frederick by holding him up as the champion of the Protestant cause against the Catholic powers—a rôle eminently unsuitable for this sceptical king, who used religion and creeds as so many butts for his wit. Frederick returned the compliment by writing of Pitt: 'England has long been in labour, . . . but at last she has brought forth a man.'

But for all this, Germany was, of course, only a secondary theatre of war in Pitt's eyes. The war at sea and in the colonies had always to be to the fore. His aim was to strip France of her colonies, particularly those in North America, by powerful military operations, and at the same time to use England's superior naval strength to blockade her. He was the ultimate authority for all these movements by sea and land. Thanks to his own military training, which, though brief, he had supplemented by the widest possible reading on the subject, he understood enough of the art of war not only to put his finger on the strategically correct points of attack but also to provide systematically for expeditionary requirements. It is not surprising that it took some time for the military machine which he had built up to reach its full momentum and for his work to produce results. And so 1758 brought many setbacks as well as some appreciable successes. The greatest of these, in the eyes of the English, was the capture of the French fort of Louisbourg on the Ile Royale, which lay opposite the mouth of the St. Lawrence and thus commanded the entrance to the Canadian mainland. Pitt made a further thrust along the path thus opened up in 1759, which both for him and for Britain became 'annus mirabilis'. The key position on the St. Lawrence was the town of Quebec, which was defended by the crack French general,

G

Montcalm. Pitt now turned his eyes to Quebec, convinced that with its fall French power in Canada would receive its death-blow. Its conquest called for a joint attack by sea and land, and he prepared this combined operation with the greatest energy and deliberation. But what perhaps tipped the balance was his decision to put the venture into the hands of a general only thirty-three years old in whom, with unfailing insight, he had discerned the qualities of a successful soldier. This was James Wolfe, who had already displayed his courage and resolution at the taking of Louisbourg. He fulfilled Pitt's expectations in full measure. The storming of the Heights of Abraham, which covered Quebec, on September 13th, 1759, was a stroke of masterly strategy and intrepid determination. On the next day Quebec fell; but among the dead were Wolfe and Montcalm.. This day sealed the fate of Canada, and with it the fate of France as a colonial power in North America.

This was the crown and summit of success in a year in which Britain tasted victory on all fronts. At sea her fleets showed all their old superiority, and in every engagement trounced the French so soundly that they could bring no influence to bear on the further course of the war; the danger, feared by so many for so long, of an invasion of the British Isles had passed into the limbo of forgotten things. In the West Indies the island of Guadeloupe—important as the richest sugar-producing area and the assembly-point for French privateers—was conquered. In Germany Ferdinand of Brunswick defeated the French on August 1st at the battle of Minden. It must be admitted that one considerable liability stood in the debit column: the heavy defeat of Frederick the Great a few days later at Kunersdorf, from which he never fully recovered.

Frederick was far too much of a sceptic to be under any illusions about the switching of the main military effort which was going inexorably forward. He no longer had the resources for large offensive campaigns and, once put on the defensive, was finally forced, despite an odd success or two, to succumb to the combined superiority of his enemies. Three months before his defeat at Kunersdorf he had already opened his heart to Mitchell, the British Minister to Prussia. He made no bones about confessing his need for peace as soon as possible; the British ministers, he said, must set the ball rolling. 'But', he went on, 'can your ministers make a peace? Are things yet in that situation? . . . I hope I shall not be forgot.' Adding immediately, 'No, I am in no danger. Mr. Pitt is an honest man, and firm; my interests are safe in his hands.' Frederick had every reason to talk in this vein, and no less reason to ensure that Pitt should learn how flatteringly he thought of him. Pitt missed no opportunity of underlining his resolve never to conclude a peace which did not, at the same time, fully safeguard the interests of England's Prussian ally. He expressed his true conviction when he said, in the letter of thanks which he wrote to Mitchell, '. . . *no Peace of Utrecht* will again stain the annals of England.' As a good Whig he could never forgive Queen Anne's Tory government for having purchased peace after the War of the Spanish Succession at the expense of her allies.

But did not this situation threaten to arise again? One can hardly expect a whole nation to practise continuously the same unselfishness to which enlightened statesmen may sometimes attain. The longer the war dragged on, the stronger the Englishman's desire for peace was bound to grow, and the more his country's military successes accumulated, the more easy it must seem to get a peace to satisfy England's interests. Were the people to go on kicking their heels year after year, waiting for such a peace, merely because their Prussian ally had no prospect of seeing his own interests satisfied? As long as Frederick had been providing the English newspapers with news of victories it had been quite another story, but that time had now passed; even if fresh Prussian victories came along at Liegnitz and Torgau in 1760 they hardly seemed likely to bring Frederick any nearer to his goal.

And then in October, 1760, George II died. The old gentleman had at last, by degrees, convinced himself that his nephew Frederick, to whose character and policy he had so many objections, was his only ally worthy of the name, and he had rejoiced over his victories, for all the world as if Prussia had not been the dubious and dangerous neighbour of his electorate. He had also discovered by degrees that this Mr. Pitt, the sight of whom had once made him shed tears of vexation, was not only an exceedingly correct minister, overflowing with protestations of devotion, but a very successful one, too. The speeches which the Secretary of State delivered to him at his audiences he understood as little as he had done three years earlier, but since the measures justified in these harangues were usually crowned with great success, he had no need to trouble his old head overmuch to fathom their meaning. When, years before, Newcastle had proposed Pitt's appointment, the King had demurred: 'Mr. Pitt won't do my German business for me.' And now he had done it for him, and so brilliantly that he need have no further qualms about the safety of his electorate. Pitt, too, was well content with the old gentleman, who gave him a free hand in all essential matters. Later he praised him, after his death, as being frank and just, so that one always knew where one stood with him. In this tribute there was an obvious criticism of the King who had meanwhile taken George's place on the throne of England.

CHAPTER VII

THE NEW KING

GEORGE III was only twenty-three years old when he took up his heavy task of being the ruler of the British Empire. His natural abilities were slight—at the age of eleven he still could not read properly—and any seeds of promise in him had been parched and stunted by a faulty education. He had lost his father at the age of twelve, and the two people responsible for his education were his mother and Lord Bute. From his father, Prince Frederick, he can hardly have learned anything worth knowing. His mother had grown up as Princess of Saxe-Gotha, that is in the atmosphere of a German provincial court, where the title 'Serenissimus' bore witness to the theory of divine right. She never really emerged from this atmosphere. British constitutional monarchy was, in her eyes, not a higher stage of evolution but a step down from that real, absolute monarchy so brilliantly personified in the German system of electorates. Certainly she cannot be blamed for not liking the moral atmosphere at her father-in-law's court and in the houses of many English aristocrats, nor for being at pains to remove her son from such influences. But the means she adopted had serious consequences. To spare the prince any influence which might possibly be harmful, she cut him off from every influence, severed all his connections with the outer world, indeed with life itself, and left him to grow up in the narrow confines of her own household.

Bute was at her side and shared her ideas; and Bute contrived to fill the young prince with an idolatrous self-esteem, but lacked every single quality which the mentor of the future head of a constitutional state needed. The late Prince of Wales had once summed him up neatly by saying he would make an excellent ambassador in any court where there was nothing to do. At all events he combined violent ambition with a touchy lack of real self-confidence, overweening pride in his judgments of others with a horror of responsibility. He taught his pupil to look with contempt on all English politicians, and to think of himself as the chosen saviour of a nation supposedly threatened by the gravest dangers. It has been disputed whether George was brought up on the theories which Bolingbroke developed in his pamphlet, 'The Idea of a Patriot King'. But one may doubt whether he ever really possessed the intellectual maturity even to read and weigh up such a work. In any case this makes little difference, as he was brought up on the theory of the divine right of kings, which his mother had absorbed at the court of a petty German princeling. What else could she mean when she constantly exhorted him: 'George, be a king'? On top of this came Bute's personal aversion to the politicians of the day, who, in his opinion, had underrated and slighted him.

The fruits of such an upbringing are well shown in a letter which the Prince, hardly out of leading-strings and remote from all contact with practical politics and politicians, wrote to Bute in May, 1760. '. . . I look on the majority of politicians as intent on their own private interests instead of that of the public.' There is only one way out, he adds: Bute must take the Treasury himself—and Bute's health was the only thing which really interested the future king.

This condemnation of George's embraced Pitt; indeed, no politician was attacked with such venom as he was. George called him 'the most ungrateful and . . . most dishonourable of men', 'the blackest of hearts', and other pleasant things of the same sort. And yet only a few years before Pitt had been in the inner councils of Leicester House. Bute had supported him when he was negotiating with Newcastle and Hardwicke about his return to the Cabinet, and in the years which followed he had kept up an intimate, friendly correspondence with him. It is obvious that differences must have arisen after that. Pitt had clearly not shown himself as amenable to the wishes of Bute and the Prince as they had both expected and demanded of him. In August, 1759, Bute sent Pitt a letter in which he complained of his refusal to meet the Prince's wishes and—while protesting his entire goodwill and readiness to mediate—disclaimed responsibility for the consequences. The task of keeping on good terms with both King and heir at the same time was obviously more difficult than Pitt had earlier imagined, and if, in case of a conflict, he ranged himself on the side of the ruler of the day he only acted as the situation demanded and his own official status required. But one may surmise that the high and mighty tone which he had got used to in his unique position was hardly calculated to make his refusal to meet the Prince's wishes any easier to swallow. Under the influence of Bute the Prince saw Pitt as a man who owed his rise to the Princess of Wales and to his 'dearest friend', but, now that he had his foot on the summit, spurned the hand which had helped him to reach it. Thence it is that there springs his resolve 'never . . . to see him [Pitt] in any future ministry.' The fact that this man had rendered the most distinguished services to the country evidently counted for nothing in the eyes of this King-to-be, who believed himself called to his position by divine providence, to champion the common good as against the self-seeking of the politicans.

And now this callow youth becomes King. In British eyes he had one signal virtue lacking in all his forbears: they had been born and bred in Germany, but he in Britain. He played this trump card skilfully in his first public statement in the famous sentence: 'I glory in the name of Briton.' Still, those Englishmen who were infected with a hatred of the Scots and mistrusted Bute as a Scot, took exception to a term which was obviously chosen to include the Scots along with the English. But more important than such sentiments was the new King's attitude to the problems of the day, particularly to the war. And there George's first declaration to the Privy Council contained words which must have shown Pitt that at least *his* days of harmonious co-operation with the Crown were numbered. Whilst no mention at all was here made of England's allies, the war was described as 'bloody and expensive'. Pitt was furious at this one-sided description, and insisted that 'bloody' should be expunged and replaced by 'just and necessary'.

Even the old Duke of Newcastle was soon to discover that a new day had dawned. At his first audience, the King referred him to Bute who, he said, knew his views exactly and would expound them to him in more detail. It took no special per-spicacity to recognize that henceforth Bute would put his own ideas into the King's mouth and that, as Pitt promptly said, he would be 'the [prime] minister behind the curtain.' Hardwicke, who sized up the whole situation very clearly, gave his friend Newcastle the one really sensible piece of advice—to use the change of sovereigns as a chance to retire into private life. At first the Duke tried to act on this, but when the King urged him not to deprive the Crown of his services and experience at this critical moment, and promised him his confidence and effective support, he weakened, more especially as the leaders of the Whig oligarchy and the City financiers were pressing him to remain at the Treasury. Yet for the Duke this was an unhappy step. The King did not dream of keeping his promise, which he had never intended seriously. For George and Bute the Duke was a mere pawn in the game which they were playing with him and with Pitt. Their aim was gradually to bring Bute to the head of the ministry, and then to conclude a peace which neither Pitt nor Newcastle could support. These two statesmen working together were strong enough to spoil the game which the King and his favourite were playing. So it was necessary to set them off, one against the other, until they had been disposed of singly.

Unfortunately Pitt so conducted the peace negotiations as to play into his opponents' hands. These negotiations had begun in the spring of 1760, before the new King's accession. In France the Duc de Choiseul had come to the fore. He was a favourite of Louis XV's mistress, Madame de Pompadour, but for all that a man of independent views who had a policy of his own. He had come to think that prolonging the war was beyond France's capacity, already severely impaired, nor did he believe that such a course would gain his country any successes sufficient to justify the outlay. At his instigation a peace congress was decided on, but never met. Private negotiations between France and Britain came to grief over Pitt's demand that Prussia should be included; this the French could not accept.

After the change of sovereign in England, on November 7th, 1760, four days after the battle of Torgau, Frederick of Prussia wrote a letter to Pitt in his own hand frankly describing the difficulty of his position. Despite the victory he had just won, in view of the prodigious superiority of his enemies he saw no prospect of defeating them decisively, of humbling their pride and frustrating their ambitions. The letter overflowed with compliments to Pitt, 'a true Roman' in whom he placed his entire confidence. Pitt showed the letter to Newcastle, not without blushing at this fulsome praise from the King. But the Duke was quite delighted to read in this royal missive Frederick's unequivocal plea that Pitt should find some way of bringing this ruinous war to a glorious end. As the minister who bore the increasingly heavy burden of financing the war, Newcastle had particular cause to welcome any prospect of ending it.

Thus he was well satisfied when Pitt explained to him in concrete terms the concessions which England would have to make to get a settlement. But that Pitt was also well aware of the political difficulties facing him at home since the accession of the new King is shown by his remark to the Duke: 'Formerly, my Lord, if I had not had an opportunity to see the King, if you told me you would answer for the King's consent, that was enough; I was satisfied. Where is that satisfaction to be had now?' There was now only one man who had the King's ear, his favourite Bute, whom he called his dearest friend. Bute now had a seat in the Cabinet: the key position which he thus occupied had sooner or later to be recognized by giving him some important office. In March he became Secretary of State for the Northern Department. The King had contrived so to arrange matters that the proposal was formally made by Newcastle while Pitt was confronted with the *fait accompli*. Pitt had every reason to regard this as a slight, if he had wished; but he accepted it without demur, probably because even he considered that this promotion simply reflected the progress of events.

So far Bute had given Pitt no cause to regard him as an enemy of his policy. Perhaps he also thought a step forward had been taken, as by assuming important office officially Bute took on a share of the responsibility, while he himself, thanks to his superior professional skill and personality, could confidently count on retaining control in the face of a tyro like his new colleague.

As it happened, peace negotiations between England and France did start up. Pitt, in whose hands they were once again placed, now had an understanding with Frederick by which he was prepared to agree that Prussia should not be invited, but he was determined vigorously to safeguard her interests within the framework of the negotiations. Both parties appointed a peace envoy who called on the minister of the other power. Pitt's delegate to Choiseul was Hans Stanley, while de Bussy came to London on Choiseul's behalf.

The French minister was under no illusions about having to

cede to Britain a large part of the colonial territory which she had conquered in the course of the war. He proposed as a basis for the talks the formula of 'uti possidetis'; that is, that the position reached on certain fixed dates by the military operations of both parties should form a starting point for the negotiations. Then each party would exchange any part of its conquests which seemed dispensable or less important for corresponding gains made by the other side. But whereas Choiseul proposed the earliest dates feasible, Pitt wanted to defer fixing them until the last possible moment, because he counted on England's registering in the meantime fresh gains for which he had already paved the way, thus giving him more valuable counters with which to play at compensation. This expectation proved well-founded. In June, 1761, English naval and land forces captured the island of Belle-Ile off the south coast of Brittany, west of the Loire estuary. In July came the news of the occupation of the French island of Dominica in the West Indies and—biggest prize of all—of Pondicherry on the coast of India. Pondicherry was the centre of the local French possessions, and its conquest by Clive in January, 1761, marked the end of French power there and finally decided which of the two great powers should control the richest of all the colonial territories. This appreciably strengthened England's prospects in the peace negotiations.

But the real stumbling-block was a question which at first blush appears trifling compared with the great territorial changes which were at stake. This was the right of the French to fish off the coast of Newfoundland. Britain had taken Newfoundland itself from the French under the Peace of Utrecht, but France had retained fishing rights along a large stretch of the coast-line. The island itself was only thinly populated, but in the fishing season the coast swarmed with vessels which reaped a rich harvest there. Fish was much sought after, especially in the Catholic countries of Europe, where it was the only dish allowed on Fridays and during fasts. Choiseul clung to these fishing rights with remarkable tenacity: he would, he confided to Stanley, be stoned in the streets of Paris if he let them go. But Pitt was equally set on depriving France of any share in the fisheries. In April, 1761, he told Newcastle that if he ever signed a peace which did not secure Britain's exclusive rights, he would be sorry that he had ever recovered the use of his right hand which had recently been crippled by gout. Apart from economic reasons he was also prompted by the consideration that the French would seize this opportunity to train seamen to man their warships. Most of the other members of the administration were unwilling to let the chance of peace slip through their fingers for this point alone, and the sagacious Hardwicke represented to Pitt that monopolies like this would arouse the hostility of the other European powers, particularly Spain. But it was impossible to get Pitt to budge an inch until it was too late and Choiseul had ceased to desire peace.

This was largely due to the tone which Pitt had adopted during the negotiations. He always spoke like a conqueror who held all the trump cards and was certain of being able to bend his opponent to his will. Hardwicke wrote with some concern to his friend Newcastle about a note of Pitt's, saying it was 'in a very haughty and dictatorial style, more strongly so than any which I remember to have seen of Louis XIV in the height of his glory and presumption.' But all attempts by Pitt's colleagues to induce him to become more conciliatory foundered on his obstinacy; he even declared in advance, on occasion, when he had a draft to lay before the Cabinet, that he would not allow his notes to be cobbled. He was quite unmoved by the yearning for peace understandably felt by large sections of the nation, a yearning to which many of his colleagues were not altogether indifferent. Pitt, too, certainly desired peace, but only on condition that it was made in the way he thought best so as to fulfil the expectations which he himself had stirred up in the people.

During the negotiations the threat of an extension of the war, if an early end were not made to it, had appeared. Spain, with whom Pitt had cultivated good relations in the opening years of the war, had gradually become restive. She had all kinds of complaints to make about England's conduct of the war at sea, which was inevitably ruthless in those ruthless days. More than this, a new King, Carlos III, had ascended the throne in Madrid in 1759; he was a confirmed anglophobe who thought the right moment had now come to wipe out an old score. To this end he trod the path of his predecessors, and came to an understanding and an alliance with his Bourbon neighbour Louis XV. And so Choiseul could glimpse the prospect of a new family compact on the lines of those of 1733 and 1743, and he lost no time in fostering it by taking up Spain's complaints in his negotiations with England.

Pitt was highly indignant when, on July 23rd, the French plenipotentiary handed him a note in which the Spanish complaints and demands were set out at length. He flatly challenged France's right to come forward as the advocate of the demands of another power with which England was at peace, and even, technically, in some sort of alliance. The moment for handing him this note, too, was very ill chosen, for news had just reached London of the conquest of Dominica and Pondicherry as well as of a success—though not a decisive one—achieved by Ferdinand Brunswick in western Germany. In these circumstances Pitt was able to prevail on the majority of the Cabinet to reject the French note out of hand, but the tone in which he did so was once again so brusque that Choiseul could label it 'impératif et peu fait pour la négociation.'

After this exchange of notes further negotiations were futile, even though they did drag on for some weeks longer. Truth to tell Pitt was mainly responsible for the breakdown. He set his face against any retreat, although he realized full well the possibility, or rather the probability, that if the war went on Spain would come in on the side of France. These two states had, in fact, concluded their third family compact on August 15th, 1761, and agreed on a secret clause by which, on May 1st 1762, Spain would declare war on England if peace had not been made by then. These details were not known to Pitt, but he had enough information to form a rough picture of the plans of both courts. Even then the British secret service employed fairly successful methods. In particular, it was able to lay its hands on the correspondence of foreign diplomats (in this case, that of the Spanish ambassadors in London and Paris) and also, when necessary, to decipher it.

Armed with this intelligence, Pitt now demanded that the government's reply to the failure of the negotiations should be a declaration of war on Spain. This war was in any case bound to come, he argued, and it would be a crowning ineptitude of foreign policy to leave Spain the choice of the date. He particularly stressed that the vessels which every year brought Spain the silver mined in her American colonies had not yet reached port. If there was any delay in declaring war, these ships would be snugly anchored in Cadiz harbour, and Spain would then be incomparably better equipped for war.

One can hardly blame the other ministers for being flabbergasted at this proposal. They had wanted peace, and in this the country was undoubtedly with them, but instead they were now to present it with another war. The war which Pitt proposed was avowedly preventive, and any preventive war arouses misgivings which Bismarck has summed up in the classic formula that no one should presume himself able to look at the cards held by Providence. But, unlike his colleagues, Pitt had a low opinion of Spain's strength and believed with good reason that he would soon be able to dispose of her in a war for which he was already preparing.

At the Cabinet meeting of September 21st Pitt's only supporter was Temple, whose manner and tone was eminently suited to intensify and sharpen differences. The other ministers at least managed to secure a postponement of the decision until further reports should come in from Stanley in Paris.

Bute belonged to this majority. Hitherto he had sided with Pitt when differences of opinion arose. His one wish was to lay the foundation of the King's popularity by showing him to his expectant people as a peace-maker. The more favourable the peace and the more it met the demands of the people, or at least of influential circles among them, the greater the popularity of George III. For example, the monopoly of the American fisheries was one of the City's pet projects, and, to avoid dropping behind, Bute had had to make common cause with Pitt over this. He had backed Pitt to obtain a favourable peace, and now this hope had vanished. Instead, Pitt was now expecting his sovereign, who desired peace above all else, to declare war once again. So far it had been in Bute's best interests to keep Pitt on his side so that the King might draw the greatest profit from his popularity. But if Pitt resigned because he could not obtain a fresh declaration of war, then his popularity—or so Bute thought—would not survive his withdrawal into private life. So, immediately after the stormy Cabinet meeting, he approached Newcastle, who had opposed Pitt, and told him 'that the thing was over; that, after what had passed, Mr. Pitt and my Lord Temple could not stay' in the ministry. Newcastle asserted that he was by no means anxious to see

Pitt go: everything possible must be done to keep him. Bute answered off-handedly: 'Impossible.' They then considered who should succeed him. He went on to offer Newcastle and Devonshire, who was of the same mind, a firm alliance; from now on, he said, they must stand together. Hardwicke had been unable to attend the meeting because his wife had died a few days before.

The die was cast on October 2nd. Ten ministers, this time with Hardwicke and the peers responsible for the army and navy among them, appeared at the meeting. Pitt now raised the issue categorically: an immediate decision to declare war on Spain or else his resignation. When he saw that he could not bring the majority round to his way of thinking, he summed up his views in a hard-hitting farewell speech which sounded almost like a proclamation. He had been called to office, he said, by his sovereign and, he might say, in some degree by the voice of the people, at a time when others had abdicated the service of the State. There was hardly one expedition which he had proposed that had not been treated beforehand as chimerical and ridiculous. It was called *his* war and it had been a successful one. And now he knew the little interest he had either in Council or Parliament. Then, after recapitulating his reasons for a declaration of war, he came to the very root of his apologia: that in his station and situation he was responsible, and would not continue without having the direction. He added: 'I will be responsible for nothing that I do not direct.' (A century later the young Bismarck could write: 'I will play the tune in the way which I think is best, or play none at all.').

These words were spoken with the pride and self-confidence of a man who could boast of feats that had astounded the world, who respected the joint responsibility of the Cabinet only as long as it was in harmony with his will and his ideas. Neither side could retreat, and so, on October 5th, Pitt handed the King a request to be relieved of his post.

George received the departing statesman very graciously, but made not the slightest effort to retain him. But when he requested Pitt to name his own reward for his long and successful services, this man—who had just hurled at his colleagues his own proud '*Here stand I, I can no other*—' was so moved by this royal condescension that he burst into tears.

§

Even if it cannot be said that Pitt was brought down by Bute's intrigues, it is a safe assumption that the King and his favourite were cock-a-hoop at his removal. They had advanced a good step nearer their goal of raising the power of the Crown above that of all the politicians. Their only concern now was lest Pitt might go into opposition. The events of the last decade had made clear to even the most purblind observer how dangerous Pitt could be in this rôle, and the reception which his resignation met with among the people, and particularly in the City, showed plainly that his popularity had only been strengthened. And so at all costs care had to be taken that Pitt should feel himself hampered in offering opposition to the King, and the surest way to do this was to place him under an obligation by conferring favours on him. This does not imply that George and Bute failed to recognize at the same time what just claims the successful war leader could make on his royal master's gratitude, but expediency was nevertheless uppermost in their thoughts. With this in mind Bute, in a letter dated October 6th, offered Pitt the choice of two high, well-paid offices. One was to be Governor of Canada with the unusually generous salary of £5,000 a year. Bute probably thought that if he induced Pitt to accept this he would secure the advantage of removing this formidable man far from London and Westminster for a considerable time. Pitt, however, declined both proposals in a letter in which he positively revelled in protestations of devotion and gratitude; a few crumbs from the feast were even dropped on Bute's plate. But this refusal was by no means final. Pitt gave, rather, an unmistakable hint that he would gladly accept a reward for those who were dearer to him than his own self. This indication was not hard to interpret; and so Bute replied at once that the King had decided to bestow on Lady Hester Pitt a peerage in her own right. Thus Pitt's family received the desired social advancement and Pitt could retain his seat in the Commons. Hester became Baroness Chatham. A family thus taken into the bosom of the nobility must, of course, be maintained at state expense, and so Pitt received for himself and his two children an annual pension of £3,000.

In itself such a payment was nothing extravagant by the

standards of those or of later days. On the contrary, it was quite the usual thing for a state to reward leading statesmen and generals after a successful war. For example, it seemed right and proper that, after the victories of 1866 and 1870, Bismarck should receive state grants and become the rich squire of Varzin and Friedrichsruh. And so, at first blush, it seems hardly credible that by accepting these rewards Pitt fell into deep disfavour with the people, and that the announcement, which George and Bute at once issued, was met by an indignant outcry. From the peak of popularity, which Pitt had reached with his resignation, he at once plunged into the uttermost depths of odium. Never had the Tarpeian rock seemed so close to the Capitol. Pamphlets in which Pitt was remorselessly pilloried, and his doings dragged in the dust, mounted in fluttering piles in the bookshops. The London coffee-houses re-echoed with execrations of the man who had been bought by the court. In the City he was burned in effigy by a mob. Why so ugly a reception of a perfectly natural act? Pitt had departed sharply from the ideal picture which the nation—not without his encouragement—had formed of him. In him they had seen selflessness personified, the one statesman who spurned wealth and honours with the contempt and simplicity of an Aristides, the tribune of the people who was conscious of the antithesis between himself and the selfish aristocracy. There was no place here for Baronesses of Chatham and fat pensions. To live up to such an ideal Pitt would have needed the austerity of a Spinoza. And how far removed he was from that! But could it well be otherwise? Men of lofty deeds are of a different clay from the philosophic sages of the world of ideas.

A particularly piquant side-light is afforded by the attitude of Ann, once Pitt's favourite sister. Unhappy for all her gifts and unable to cope with life, she had, shortly after the succession of George III, asked her exalted brother to procure her a state pension. Like some proud Roman who would never sue for a favour, Pitt had refused. She thereupon went to Bute, who was all compliance. When she informed her brother of this success, he wrote her a frigid letter of congratulation in which he expressed his displeasure at seeing the name of Pitt in a pensions list, and requested her to make it clear to all that he had had no part in the matter. And then, only ten months later, the name of

LADY SARAH LENNOX, CHARLES FOX
AND LADY SUSAN FOX-STRANGWAYS

Pitt appeared on the list for a second time, only now it was William himself who was accepting the favour. Ann at once sat down and copied out his wounding letter in order to return it to the sender with a mere change of inscription; this was a revenge after her own heart. Luckily some understanding friends were able to dissuade her from sending off the letter.

Pitt was quite taken aback by the storm which so suddenly raged round his head. He was not the man to suffer in silence, and he hit on the expedient of a letter to his most influential friend in the City, Alderman William Beckford. Here he declared bluntly that the measures to be taken in regard to Spain had led to differences of opinion with his colleagues, of which he gave a most subjective account; he had resigned, he said, because he was in the minority. He repeated that he would not be responsible for measures which he might not direct himself. The favours which the King had bestowed on him he described as 'unsolicited'. Pitt's colleagues might complain that he was revealing Cabinet secrets without authority, but in the circles for which it was intended the letter had the desired effect. The old enthusiasm revived and the City's representatives came out enthusiastically for Pitt and an energetic prosecution of the war.

It almost seemed as if the fallen minister would go into opposition in spite of everything. At Beckford's request he and Temple attended the official Guildhall banquet given in the King's honour. The brothers-in-law were received with a deafening ovation while the royal pair was passed by almost unnoticed. Still more pointed was a demonstration against Bute, staged by Beckford. On the way to the Guildhall his coach was set upon by the crowd who raised shouts of 'Damn all Scotch rogues!' and 'No Bute!' But Bute must have had some premonition of this, for he had taken the precaution of having a guard of bruisers who got the better of his assailants. All this went far beyond Pitt's intentions, and he later regretted ever having accepted the invitation. He had by no means decided on opposition; quite the reverse—he wanted to keep the way back to power open. To do this he had to avoid frittering away the King's favour beyond recall, the more so as he could not now rely on any party connections—not that he wished to do so. In the party sense he was now a lone figure. Only Temple had resigned along with him, as had a younger brother in a minor

H

post, James Grenville. On the other hand, the far more important brother, George Grenville, had not only remained in office but was a member of the Cabinet and leader of the Commons. Although Temple had previously assured him that his resignation was a purely personal matter and in no way obliged his brothers to follow suit, he resented George's attitude so much that he broke off all further relations with him. Thus another member of the old 'Cobham Cousinhood' had left the ranks. Temple was almost the only one of the group who clung fast to Pitt, although it would perhaps have been to Pitt's advantage if he had broken with Temple without more ado.

Within the ministry George Grenville associated with Bute, who treated him as a personal friend; it must, of course, be remembered that their connection dated from the time when Grenville, together with Pitt and the other members of his circle, had flocked to Leicester House. But Bute's plans went further. He wanted Grenville as a support against Newcastle and his friends. True, he had offered Hardwicke a post, but only in the expectation, which was fully realized, that he would refuse it. Immediately after Pitt's fall the old Duke noticed countless signs that the hunt was now in full cry after him. That he voted against Pitt in the critical meetings can hardly be held against him, for he had objective grounds for doing so, but this did not alter the fact that without Pitt he was too weak to resist the machinations of a Bute.

CHAPTER VIII

HENRY FOX:
TRIUMPH AND DISASTER

WHILE Pitt led his country in war against France, Fox sat in the Paymaster's chair, gathering in the millions voted by Parliament and seeing to it that these were used to pay the troops punctually and provide them with rations and munitions. Through his hands passed the huge subsidies which the British taxpayer grumblingly disgorged for the King's allies, and he, far from grumbling, pocketed the commission which the bad old custom assigned as a perquisite to His Majesty's Paymaster-General. Not that Fox ever failed in his duty in these difficult years; but he made money while Pitt made world history. This was the only light in which his contemporaries could see it and this was the yardstick by which they had to measure him. He also appeared in his place in the House, though he intervened but rarely in debate. None the less, he was still accounted a man to be reckoned with.

Fox had nothing particularly favourable to look for from the change of sovereigns. His patron was Cumberland, the man best hated at Leicester House. Even as a boy young George had heard nothing but ill of his uncle, whom he credited with the most sinister designs. Fox, of course, as Cumberland's right-hand man in Parliament, figured in an equally murky light, and in the edifying discourses with which Bute regaled George about the turpitude of British politicians, Fox in particular was held up as an awful example.

Cumberland and Fox were, therefore, most agreeably surprised when the young King received them courteously and genially, although the Duke could not rid himself of the suspicion that this was mere play-acting. But Fox let himself be misled by these auspicious omens and he blurted out to George a wish which had obsessed him for years: a peerage for his wife, Lady Caroline. She was, after all, a duke's daughter and ought to be made a countess at the very least. But he met with defeat: George declined the gambit.

Refusals like this merely spurred Fox on to try his luck in some other way. The entrée to the King lay through Bute, and so Bute must be won over. Fox employed as go-between a young nobleman who had recently begun to make his mark and was destined to become one of the most controversial figures of his day—William, Lord Fitzmaurice, or, as he became shortly after, on his father's death, the Earl of Shelburne, the style by which he is known to history. He later rose to the dignity of Marquis of Lansdowne and fathered a family which played a distinguished part in nineteenth-century history.

Shelburne was on terms of intimacy with Bute, and became acquainted with Fox. In February, 1761, he engineered several conferences at which Fox recited his aspirations to Bute. These were only partially granted; he obtained nothing more than the promise that they would be realized within the ensuing twelve-month, but this was enough to dispose him to help the King's favourite. Bute reckoned with the likelihood that he would need support in the Commons to carry out his plans, and Fox, with his adaptability, skill in debate and influence in the House, seemed to him the very man for the job, for he was no friend of either Newcastle or Pitt and could therefore in all probability be used against them both.

Yet it almost seemed as if Fox would open up quite another connection with George, and one which would gain him favour and influence with far more immediacy.

The Duke of Richmond, whose daughter, Caroline, Fox had carried off and married in 1744, had in 1745 become the father of another daughter, Sarah. After her parents' death this Lady Sarah Lennox lived with her sister at Holland House. As a duke's daughter she was of course received at court, where she got to know young Prince George. He, a bashful young man of twenty-one and not yet independent, confessed in a letter to his 'dearest friend', Bute, that the fair sex was beginning to disturb him. In the winter of 1759-60, before his accession, that is, more confidences followed by letter: he avowed his love for Sarah Lennox and described her enchantments in halting phrases. His dearest wish, he declared, was to see her at his side on the throne. But he added, characteristically, that if Bute should frown on this plan he would place his happiness in the other's hands. '. . . If I must either lose my friend or my love, I will give up the latter, for I esteem your friendship above every earthly joy.' The upshot may be imagined. George's mother, the Princess of Wales, and Bute, his mentor, could hardly have hit on anything less suited to their plans than a link by marriage with one of the families of an aristocracy whose power they were bent on destroying. If there were anything at all which could make such a union more horrifying still it was the thought that it might assist Fox, their arch-enemy's confidant, to far-reaching influence. And so it is quite understandable that Bute, wagging an admonitory forefinger, should leave his young charge under no illusions that never in any circumstances might he marry into an English family, but that he must look for his queen in the pages of the 'Berlin Almanack', which listed in a form convenient for reference the German courts, great and small, together with the marriageable princesses. It is equally understandable that George should meekly obey and bury his nose in the Almanack, even though he declared that he would not marry until 'the old man', meaning his grandfather, was dead.

But when he had become king and once again saw Sarah Lennox, now a girl of sixteen—all his good resolutions went by the board. Sarah must indeed have been a bewitching creature; that old cynic, Horace Walpole, waxes quite enthusiastic when he describes her appearance in private theatricals at Holland House. A charming study by Reynolds shows her on the balcony of Holland House in the company of her nephew, Charles Fox, and his cousin, Susan Fox-Strangways. Young George now went over to a direct wooing, but this made no powerful impression on the young thing, whose head was full of some other love affair at the time. Fox, of course, saw things in quite another light. If he, a plain commoner, could marry a duke's daughter, why should a duke's daughter not marry the King? There were no legal obstacles. The principle which the court lawyers of the German princes had salvaged from the Middle Ages, that a king's consort must be his equal in rank, did not exist in England. Fox tried to incline his young sister-in-law to the royal suit. The malicious tongues of London society declared that on his advice the young beauty allowed herself to be seen daily in becoming rustic dress, gardening in the grounds of Holland House, at the hours when the King normally came by on his ride.

But while court society already saw Sarah Lennox as the

future queen, Bute and his patrons led the docile George back
to the Berlin Almanack, and at last he discovered in Mecklen-
burg-Strelitz a princess whom he agreed to take, although, as
he said with a sigh, she was no beauty; but to make up for this
she fulfilled one stipulation he had made in advance: she had
neither intellectual pretensions nor political leanings. Well,
that was George's own private affair when all was said and done.
But it was far from befitting a king that, even when negotiations
were under way with the Strelitz court, he continued to lay
siege to Sarah and to profess his love for her.

On July 8th, 1761, Fox attended a formal session of the Privy
Council and here he heard the news from the King's own lips:
George had decided to marry 'Miss Charlotte of Mecklenburg'
as Fox called her. Now at least he could form some impression
of the good faith and sincerity of this king who felt that he had a
mission to lead his people out of vice into the paths of virtue.
But the jilted young beauty's heart was not broken; the letter in
which she told a friend of her indignation at the deception
practised on her is as refreshing in its unvarnished naturalness
as it is questionable in its spelling. In the later years of her long
and eventful life she never once mourned the vanished crown,
but called the 22nd of September, 1761, the day on which
George and another woman were crowned, the happiest of her
whole life.

§

The coronation festivities had only interrupted for a few
short days the ministerial crisis brought on by Pitt's differences
with his colleagues. Bute knew that Pitt's days were numbered
and was casting about for someone to replace him. Of all the
possible candidates, Fox had certainly still the greatest parliamentary talent, and so it is not surprising that Bute should
mention his name when talking things over with the Duke of
Newcastle. But the Duke's former confidential secretary summed
up the situation and the actors in the drama in one telling
phrase: to appoint Fox would be 'going from the most popular
man to the most unpopular man in England.' Hardwicke, who
passed on this observation to Newcastle, wholeheartedly concurred in it, although, as he wrote, his personal resentment
against Fox had been laid asleep and buried these many years.

But Fox was not only unpopular with the people; he was unpopular with the King as well. In dealing with George Grenville, Bute based his request that Grenville should decline the Speaker's chair which he had been offered and lead the ministerial party in the Commons, on the argument that only in this way could Grenville protect the King from the risk of having to take orders from Fox. When Grenville had complied, Bute warned him that he should never mention Fox to the King, who was bitterly incensed with him.

And yet only one short year was to pass before Fox was leader of the Commons with Cabinet rank, George having urged him to obey this summons. Political developments had made him indispensable.

In January, 1762, war broke out with Spain, just as Pitt had prophesied. In the same month a still more significant event occurred: the Czarina Elizabeth died and the half-mad Peter III succeeded her. A fervent admirer of Frederick of Prussia, Peter promptly concluded not only a peace but also an alliance with him. And thus, within a short time, the number of England's enemies had increased and that of Prussia's had been reduced by a very formidable power. Bute was now all the keener to reach an early settlement, and felt all the less impelled to throw away favourable opportunities for England for the sake of Prussia. It is possible that by a just assessment of the feeling prevailing in England Frederick could have saved the alliance. His London representatives urged this upon him, but all they got for their pains was a brusque reprimand from their master, who had a sufficiently low opinion of his ambassador, von Knyphausen, to cast in his teeth the utterly baseless suspicion that he had been bribed by Bute. But how could one expect an autocrat like this, who listened to the grievances of his own people only when it suited his plans, to attach any importance to the murmurings of an allied nation? The latest turn to his fortunes, favourable beyond his wildest dreams, far from strengthening his readiness for peace, only increased his lust of conquest. The British ministers saw this clearly enough from the brief letter which Frederick wrote in answer to George's request to set out his ideas and plans at length; had they any remaining doubts on the subject, these had been dispelled by a letter from Frederick to his London ambassador, made available to them by their secret service. For there they could read that his Prussian majesty considered them as lunatics only fit for Bedlam. 'I have already seen so much of that offensive style in the intercepted letters from his Prussian Majesty . . .' wrote Hardwicke to Newcastle, 'that nothing of that nature surprises me . . . But I have been long convinced that this Prince has done himself much more harm by his pen than ever he has done himself good by it, notwithstanding his excessive vanity of writing.'

All the same, neither Hardwicke nor Newcastle was prepared to drop Prussia completely. This, the former Lord Chancellor wrote, could not be done 'consistently with the King's honour.' But George himself and his advisers thought quite differently. This cleavage of opinion was finally settled when the question of the continuance of the Prussian subsidies came up. When Bute brought about their cancellation Newcastle resigned and Hardwicke, loyal to the last, now retired into private life for good (May, 1762).

George and Bute could not but rejoice at this turn of events. Not only could Bute now take over the leadership of the ministry—a step for which both had been panting—but now, too, the axe was really laid to the tree of Whig supremacy, the felling of which was their supreme purpose. For all the contempt they felt for the old Duke personally, they did not fail to appreciate his importance in holding the party together. At the farewell audience, George offered him a reward for his long services. But Newcastle was well aware of what he owed to his place in history. He declined all rewards in dignified words, contenting himself with the knowledge that he had sacrificed a considerable part of his private fortune to the cause into which he had put his heart and soul. If his private fortune had suffered by his loyalty, it was his pleasure, his glory and his pride, he told the young king, who had already learned in the nursery to look down with virtuous contempt on all English politicians.

The Cabinet was now so far purged of any possibly refractory elements that Bute was able to take the nearest road to peace with France. He sent the Duke of Bedford to Paris to conduct negotiations, the very minister, that is, who had always most vigorously pressed Pitt to make peace. Of course, matters did not pass off entirely without difficulties and clashes. Bute's eagerness for peace at any price was so unbridled that he found

himself in the paradoxical position of not welcoming, but de-
ploring, British successes, because they compelled him to raise
his demands for compensation. And there was certainly no lack
of such successes in 1762, particularly where Spain was concerned. She tasted defeat on all fronts. The heaviest blow was
the occupation of Havana by British forces in August, and it was
precisely this which caused Bute the greatest embarrassment.
Before the news reached London he thought he had peace in his
pocket. But the other ministers, George Grenville in particular,
insisted that some compensation should be given for the return
of Havana. When even the King's personal intervention failed
to move Grenville, Bute did, it is true, concede the point, but
he determined to find someone more pliable and less scrupulous
to replace this stubborn leader of the Commons, who was, moreover, asking to be shown the inner workings of parliamentary
patronage. The most glittering peace with France was worth
nothing to him if Parliament, particularly the Commons, refused to endorse it.

No one could foretell how the House would vote; the grouping
of the parties was far too complex for that. How many of those
who had been elected with Newcastle's help would still take his
line after his fall from power? How many, on the other hand,
would join the ranks of the few avowed followers of Bute now
that he wielded influence and patronage? How many would be
carried away by Pitt's eloquence if he should decide to speak
against the peace? The experiences of the last decade had
shown one thing: the case of the administration and of the
peace must be advocated in the House itself by a man capable of
speaking compellingly, or at least persuasively, by a man who
could, if necessary, take on Pitt.

At the time when his difficulties were piling up, Bute had
angled for a rapprochement with Newcastle, but the old Duke,
on the advice of Hardwicke and Cumberland, had brushed
aside these overtures, much as he still hankered for the outward
splendour and influence of a ministerial post. Bute now believed that if he was to obtain the support he needed then
Henry Fox was his only hope.

Their relations had been good ever since, in April, 1762,
Fox's heart's desire had been realized by the elevation of his
wife to the rank of Baroness Holland. Hers was, it is true, a later

creation than the Baroness of Chatham's, but Fox had reason to hope that if he minded his p's and q's some further advancement might be achieved.

They were on common ground to the extent that Fox urgently desired an end to the war and was not disposed to quibble over the conditions on which peace was made. True, he was aware of Bute's unpopularity but he put this down to the fact that he was a Scot. Fox's explanation of the widespread dislike of the Scots can be made to bear a more general application: 'Every man', he wrote, 'has at some time or other found a Scotchman in his way, and everybody has therefore damned the Scotch.'

The greatest obstacle to an understanding with Bute lay in Fox's long and intimate connection with Cumberland. The old feud between the two branches of the royal family had not diminished. Bute and Cumberland were at daggers drawn. For this reason the Duke had latterly drawn closer to Newcastle, whom Bute had supplanted. Hence an alliance with Bute meant, for Fox, breaking with Cumberland. He had repeated conferences and correspondence with Cumberland, and was forced to conclude that the latter would never forgive him if he took such a step. At the beginning of October while in the country, he received an urgent summons from Bute to come to London. On October 6th George told Fox with a wealth of flattery, either personally or by the mouth of Bute, that he needed someone in Grenville's place who could lead the Commons and defend his (George's) liberty. Only one man, he said, was capable of this, and that man was Henry Fox. The King was to make him a Secretary of State; this Fox, however, promptly refused. To lead the Commons, he replied, would make such demands on him that in his declining health he could not take on the duties of the other post as well. He was not averse from leading the Commons, but he gave a frank warning that his own unpopularity would only heighten Bute's.

Before Fox finally decided to accept the appointment, he paid one more visit to his old patron. But Cumberland was unyielding. When Fox finally asked him whether this meant the end of their long years of collaboration, the Duke merely 'replied very coolly that his doors were always open to everybody . . .' None the less, Fox could not bring himself to decline the offer. On October 13th he kissed hands on his appointment as 'a Cabinet Councillor and His Majesty's Minister in the House of Commons.'

George was at pains to see that Fox got the impression that by taking over this office he would be rendering him the greatest service, and one for which he could ever after count on his royal gratitude. Nor, apparently, did these entreaties fail to find their mark. But how differently Fox would have viewed the King's intentions had he known that George justified his appointment to Grenville in the words 'we must call in bad men to govern bad men.' Young and immature as George was, he had nothing to learn in the art of dissimulation.

Fox would quite certainly have hesitated to accept if he had heard what Bute was saying about the same time to the man he was replacing. George Grenville was quite rightly surprised and indignant when, on October 11th, Bute notified him, with the customary protestations of warmest friendship, that in the interest of 'the best of kings' he must surrender the seals and the leadership of the Commons, and offered him the Admiralty instead. To break down Grenville's resistance to this proposal, he as good as promised him the succession to his own post at the Treasury, that is, at the head of the ministry; he himself, he declared, was tired of this office, to which he did not feel equal, and only his regard for the King, who had been a broken man on hearing of his intention to resign, had prevailed on him to continue in office until peace should be concluded. Had Fox learned of this, he would have been quite clear in his own mind that he was to be used as a mere makeshift for a few highly critical months, only to be cast aside as soon as the crisis was over.

Fox's appointment caused a sensation in political circles. Hardwicke's view was that Bute had now decided 'to support himself by *power* only', and he prophesied that power placed in such hands would rouse the greatest possible popular resentment. At first it did not seem so. The journalists and pamphleteers, who ordinarily leaped at any chance of pulling Fox to pieces, remained discreetly silent, to Fox's own surprise; even the City was quiet. Obviously the longing for peace was so strong among the people that they wanted to give a chance to the man on whose skill and ruthlessness they were counting to bring them safely to port. Immediately on his appointment Fox set about gathering his old friends round him. But he experienced

some bitter disappointments. He offered Cumberland command
of the army, but the offer was contemptuously rejected. Devonshire, a personal friend of years' standing, deplored in an outspoken letter Fox's connection with so hated a man as Bute, a
connection which could only harm the King.

Devonshire was to be the first to discover that the war of
annihilation against the Whigs had started. As Lord Chamber-
lain he belonged to the Cabinet but had not attended its
meetings since Newcastle's resignation. At this point he cried
off once again from 'attending a meeting on some pretext or
other. George, now that he had won over that 'bad man' Fox,
felt strong enough to give full rein to his royal displeasure without counting the consequences. On the morning of October
28th he met Devonshire and Newcastle both on the way to
London, and his suspicious nature led him to conclude that they
were going to meet and hatch some conspiracy against him.
When later that day Devonshire was announced at the Palace,
George sent him word by a page that he would not see him,
whereupon Devonshire sent back an enquiry by the same route,
asking with whom he should leave his wand of office. Soon
afterwards George struck Devonshire's name out of the Council
Book.

These were rebuffs which no king had ever ventured to give
a powerful peer since the Glorious Revolution. And this peer
was the head of one of the famous Whig families which had set
up the Hanoverian dynasty. No one now could fail to see that the
King felt himself quit of his debt of gratitude, and that he was
severing the bond which had linked the dynasty with the Whig
aristocracy and the Whig party for half a century. Obviously all
that now remained for the Whigs was to go into opposition. But
this was so foreign to all their traditions that it is not surprising
that a representative of these traditions, like Hardwicke, could
not bring himself to do it. However they were all fully aware
that there was no possible hope of effective opposition without
Pitt.

After leaving the ministry, Pitt had remained rather aloof.
In the winter session of 1761 he had defended his policy in a
speech of some length in which he had coined the oft-quoted
maxim: 'America had been conquered in Germany.' But he
had refrained on principle from any attack on the administra-

tion. Oddly enough, he was now forced on the defensive. A whole series of speakers attacked him, one of the most vigorous being a newcomer to the House, Colonel Barré, a gallant officer of Huguenot extraction, who had distinguished himself at Quebec as Wolfe's Adjutant-General and now surprised the House with his almost classical gift of oratory. Barré, later to become one of Pitt's most faithful followers, on this occasion called him a chameleon who 'had turned to the colour of the ground upon which he stood,' 'a dangerous, profligate and abandoned minister, who had thrust himself into the Closet upon the shoulders of a deluded people.' Charles Yorke, the Attorney-General and one of Hardwicke's sons, rose to make an effective defence of the memory of George II which Barré had impugned. No one spoke in Pitt's defence.

Pitt's subsequent bearing in the House also showed moderation and an endeavour to avoid open conflict with the court. Indeed, in a speech in May, 1762, when Newcastle's fall was imminent, Pitt specifically attacked the party system and claimed credit for having helped to break it down. True, he also attacked at the same time those who, under cover of the anti-party watchword, really meant to replace one party by another, which, in fact, was the intention of George and Bute, who wanted to build up a new Tory party which would rally unconditionally round the throne.

After this the prospects of an alliance between Pitt and the Whigs were not rosy should they decide to go into opposition. The only question was, whether their various objections to the peace concluded by Bute would prove to have enough in common to bring them together.

On November 3rd, 1762, peace preliminaries between England, France and Spain were signed in Paris. It was natural that this peace should prove more favourable to Britain after all her great successes in the war; it only remained to be seen whether her representatives had fully succeeded in obtaining all the advantages to which these successes entitled them. To be sure, England might well be gratified that France surrendered the whole of Canada and, as far as the East Indies were concerned, was forced back into the position she had occupied in 1749, having, that is, to yield pride of place to Britain. The restoration of Minorca, too, which had fallen in 1756, was well

calculated to satisfy national sentiment in England. But in
checking the list of conquests which England restored to France
and Spain with these countries' achievements in the war, one
could hardly blink the fact that they had done disproportionately
well out of the transaction. In the matter of the fishing rights
along the Newfoundland coast Britain had made considerable
concessions and had even handed over a few small islands to the
French. As for Prussia, France did, it is true, agree to evacuate
the territory she had conquered on Prussian soil, but not to
restore it to Frederick, so that in theory there was a possibility
of its occupation by Austrian forces. In practice, however, this
danger was obviated by separate agreements. Anyone who could
look behind the scenes could, of course, understand Bute's
showing no particular zeal for Frederick's interests, for he knew
that Frederick had constantly intrigued against him and had,
in particular, tried to bring him down by carefully cultivating
the Prussian connection with Pitt. If Bute held Frederick in
lower esteem as an ally than did his eulogists in the City, he
could at least quote chapter and verse for so doing. None the
less, Bute's policy was shortsighted and pernicious. It is largely
responsible for the estrangement which kept England and
Prussia apart for two decades and caused England considerable
harm. Political amateur that he was, Bute failed to grasp that
even the foibles of a powerful prince are political factors which
one cannot disregard with impunity.

The peace, then, offered grounds enough for attack. What
was unfortunate from the opposition's point of view was that
these grounds were varied, some coming under fire from the
Whigs and others from Pitt. Hardwicke prophesied that Pitt
and Temple would 'declaim and flame' against the peace as a
whole but would lay their chief stress on points upon which he
and his friends could not agree with them. In spite of this, with
goodwill on both sides it would doubtless have been possible to
organize a united opposition front and, for instance, to concentrate on the treatment of England's ally, Prussia, about which
Pitt and the Whigs were of one mind. After all, much of the
secret of mature parliamentary campaigning lies in overcoming
internal differences by working for a common aim. But this
spirit of give and take was lacking.

True, Pitt still professed to be a Whig. He had, he maintained, always represented the principles of the Whigs and the revolution, and would remain true to them for the rest of his days. But he was further than ever from realizing that to make specific principles prevail one must work with those of like mind. His whole nature was averse to being incorporated in a party, for at times incorporation necessarily meant subordination. This was now even less possible for him than before, since, as Secretary of State, he had grown accustomed to seeing others defer to his will and his point of view. Just as he was unwilling to belong to any administration 'without having the direction', so too he was unfitted for membership of a party in which others also wanted a share in the direction. These others were Newcastle and his friends, and he could not forget that they had left him in the lurch a year before; for it was thus that he looked on the difference of opinion which had led to his resignation. Was he to lead an opposition campaign against Bute, which, if successful, Newcastle would survive to reappear in a new administration, even though he himself would be certain of a key post in it?

But did he in any case desire such a success? An opposition triumph with the political situation as it then was would have meant forcing on an unwilling king an administration which would oust his 'dearest friend' and in which he would see nothing but personal enemies. It was this very thing that Pitt wanted to avoid. '. . . He had felt inexpressible anxieties at holding office against the goodwill of the Crown', he told one of Newcastle's emissaries who negotiated with him about future collaboration. This was the root of the matter. Pitt did not conceal the fact that he considered the favouritism which George had introduced pernicious and Bute himself totally unsuited to lead the nation. But—he declined to bring about his fall by parliamentary means. Constitutionally, this was a step backward compared with the attitude of the Pelhams in 1746, when they had forced George II to dismiss Bath and Granville and to summon Pitt to office. But a transition period has now been reached, in which constitutional principles only gradually develop without being recognized in theory, let alone consistently followed. Profound study of a constitutional problem is the last thing one can expect of a Pitt. His cogitations were far less complex and far more personal. He believed that sooner or later George III would have to come back to him, just as had happened with

George II, and that, if summoned at the royal pleasure, he would himself be able to form an administration in which he alone, free of all party ties, would carry weight.

Of course, it cannot be overlooked that the Whigs, too, lacked much of what went to make a powerful opposition, particularly an inner unity and a readiness to make personal sacrifices to political conviction.

Fox was the very man not only to justify the peace to the House and to become the brains of the government party, but also to make it brutally plain to every member that the horn of plenty would be shaken only over those who voted for the court and that the bread of opposition would be very bitter. From the moment that he took over the conduct of the King's business in the Commons, he was firmly resolved to show that it was in safe hands. He had himself warned the King of his unpopularity. But once George had brushed this consideration aside, Fox was quite unconcerned whether, in fulfilling the task he had taken on, he increased or lessened his unpopularity. He now had but one aim: success. He was there to put through the acceptance of the peace preliminaries in the Commons, and put them through he would by hook or by crook. It is doubtful whether there was ever any serious risk of defeat. The people's hunger for peace was undeniable, and the responsibility of rejecting a settlement already drawn up was so heavy that few members could really have mustered enough courage to do it.

But Fox was determined to leave nothing to chance or even to probability. At the moment when the peace was laid before the House he had to be absolutely sure of its going through. There were two means of ensuring this: patronage and intimidation. This time there was, of course, no question that the First Lord of the Treasury should withhold the administration of patronage from the Leader of the House. What he had refused to George Grenville, Bute now conceded unconditionally to his successor. With Fox he felt sure that neither moral nor political scruples could make him swerve from his course. And as things turned out Fox made the most energetic and unscrupulous use of the power at his disposal. Everyone venal was bought up. Horace Walpole relates that a shop was publicly opened at the Pay Office, where votes were sold quite openly, over the counter, so to speak. The figures Walpole gives have recently been sub-

HENRY FOX

jected to expert criticism, and certainly Walpole is not a chronicler on whom one can place unhesitating reliance, but the picture he paints is true enough in its general outline.

Fox did nothing by halves. He and Bute also bestowed or promised titles and sinecures wherever this appeared necessary to clinch the outcome. When the parliamentary battle was joined Fox was confident of victory. Sixty votes were the most he gave the opposition. When the Whigs met at Newcastle's house to work out a plan of campaign, none could escape the impression that defeat was inevitable.

None the less Newcastle and Hardwicke ventured to oppose the peace preliminaries in the Lords. But there they encountered so great a desire for peace that no one even forced a division. In the Commons Pitt, of course, was the main focus of interest. It had been doubtful whether he would attend the House at all, for he had once more been laid low by a severe attack of gout. He made a telling display of his poor state of health with the aid of that now familiar theatrical apparatus of his when he appeared in the Commons on December 9th to join in the debate. But there can be no doubt that he was really ill and it was only by a supreme effort that he undertook the strain of a long speech. This lacked the old fire, and the impression which his words normally made was missing on this occasion. Besides this, his speech was inordinately long, lasting more than three and a half hours. This in itself shows that it was taken up with detailed criticism, which never secures a great effect. Even when he justified his own policy point by point, this can hardly have possessed the charm of novelty. He rose to greater heights when he tore to shreds the clauses relating to Prussia. He condemned the desertion of the King of Prussia and went so far as to call him the most magnanimous ally that England had ever had. 'Insidious, tricking, base and treacherous' were the epithets he applied to the administration's conduct.

All this can hardly have been music in the ears of Fox and Bute; but they could disregard it if only Pitt did not vote against the treaty. For them, the vote, and not the speeches leading up to it, was the crux of the matter. And here they had a pleasant surprise. Immediately after speaking Pitt left the House, so that Fox, who spoke in reply, was able to content himself with a few sentences. But Pitt did not even return for the division! That, of

I

course, took the heart out of his opposition—but in this way he escaped the persecution which fell upon the dissentients and he kept the way to the King open. Of course, Pitt was not the only prudent member. Of Hardwicke's three sons who sat in the Commons, two were absent from the division and the third voted with the administration. Fox won the day, a little more than sixty rallying to the diehard banner.

These now experienced an unexampled punishment, or, one might perhaps more accurately say, a campaign of revenge. Fox dealt with the losers as if they had been a hostile army whose defeat must be sealed by ruthless and untiring pursuit. They were the King's enemies and must be so punished as to cripple their power for ever. Since their influence rested largely on the patronage and protection they could afford, it was necessary at the same time to strike at all those who enjoyed this patronage and protection. It was natural that Newcastle and other power-ful peers should be stripped of their dignities, such as the Lord Lieutenancies of their counties. One might even concede the need to purge the key offices of all those who had risen thanks to Newcastle and his friends, for, after all, there was no fixed tenure of office to protect them from such arbitrary action. But Fox set to work with a thoroughness which knew no bounds, unexampled even in ages of the most naked despotism. The case of every official, down to those in the most subordinate posts, was investigated to see whether he did not by some chance owe his position to a Whig peer; if this was proved to be so, he was hounded out of office, even if he had given a generation's service in his post and had never mixed in politics. Newcastle's letters are full of his distress at the fate of these lesser men whose only offence was that they had once enjoyed his protection. If Fox had previously been unpopular, he was now loathed. But he wrote to Bute with cynical pride: '. . . I don't care how much I am hated, if I can say to myself, I did His Majesty such honest and essential service.' Cumberland, with whom he had worked closely for so many years, shook his head and remarked that he had been grossly deceived in Fox; he had always thought him good-natured, but he was now showing himself vindictive and inhuman.

Of course, Fox was not the only offender. These persecutions would not have been possible without the approval and active support of Bute and the King. But a distinction must be drawn. Bute and George wanted to smash the Whig party once and for all in order to leave only one party in the field, namely, the one which would follow the King and do his bidding.

This was what the Princess of Wales meant when, after the peace had been approved, she exclaimed triumphantly: 'Now my son *is* King of England.' Since, in the eyes of George and Bute, a party was nothing more than a conspiracy for reciprocal favouritism and the exploitation of the country, they thought they would deal the system a mortal blow if they demonstrated that party allegiance only brought personal losses in its train. That a party was built on ideals which lived on, even if they had at times been sunk in oblivion, was a conception quite outside their range of vision. George and Bute, none the less, had a political goal in view. But Fox thought only of the immediate problem and of the ministry of the day to which he belonged, that ministry which he wished to build up solidly on the one foundation he now believed in—naked power.

But it was the biter bit. While Fox was visiting misfortune on hundreds of innocent and harmless men and braving the hatred of a nation in order to anchor the Bute ministry firmly, Bute was thinking only of how he could shed the oppressive burden of office as quickly as possible. For the noble lord was, for all his vanity, a pitiful weakling. He, who had never administered an office of state before his pupil's accession, now discovered that there was more in it than he had dreamed of, or had ever lectured about to his prince in the seclusion of Leicester House. He did not feel equal to the responsibility which such an office entailed. It depressed and appalled him. He was conscious of a mounting hatred towards him. The London mob pelted his coach with mud whenever they discovered him out driving. The powerful City merchants on whose goodwill his post at the Treasury depended turned their backs on him when he attended a Guildhall banquet. The gentry refused to drink the health of the First Lord of the Treasury at one of their convivial gatherings. The newspapers were waging a bitter campaign against him. Bute had certainly conceived the lot of the peacemaker as something quite different from this. If this was how things went on the morrow of a great political triumph, what dangers would menace him if he ever met with failure? And how could he well avoid failures when every day brought him in his official capacity fresh problems quite beyond his ability to handle? An amateurish attempt to bring in a new tax aroused lively opposition, led in the Commons by Pitt and in the Lords by Hardwicke. No, there was only one way out for him, retreat into private life, sweetened, perhaps, by some lucrative office at court. Not, of course, that he wished to relinquish political influence altogether. He was sure of having his pupil's ear, and would not his words have far more effect if, instead of proceeding from the mouth of Bute the Scot, they came from the King of England?

Since October, 1762, George had known that Bute wanted to retire once the peace was safely gathered in. He had struggled to avert it with prayers and entreaties. But when on February 10th 1763, the peace was at last signed and sealed (the Peace of Hubertsburg between Frederick the Great and his enemies followed on February 15th) Bute told the King that his resolve was now firmly fixed, and George had to endure a loss which seemed to him quite unbearable and irreparable, however much Bute might strive to persuade him that the political situation was now so simple that even a child could cope with it.

Fox knew nothing of all this until the beginning of 1763. He lived in the belief that he had accomplished his task to the complete satisfaction of Bute and the King and that now the reward which he had stipulated was awaiting him. The principal element of this reward was a peerage. This would mean the end of his membership of the Commons and, of course, of his leadership there as well. But this suited him very well. He had looked on the leadership of the Commons during this historic session as the keystone of his political career. After this he wanted to retire to the peace and dignity of the Lords, 'The world forgetting, by the world forgot.' He was anxious, moreover, to live more of a family life and to spend at leisure the rich income which his post as Paymaster would continue to drop into his lap. He was completely taken aback by Bute's decision to retire, and he went to the greatest pains to dissuade him. On March 11th he handed Bute a memorandum containing a detailed plan for the reorganisation of his ministry. It is a very remarkable document. It reveals Fox as a good judge of men, possessing a keen eye for the weaknesses but also for the abilities of his colleagues. Equally characteristic is the absence from it of any broader political vision. His one guiding principle was expediency. This took him to the extreme of recommending even the selection of judges with an eye to political considerations, and he raised the question whether Hardwicke's sons should be deprived of their posts.

Bute's surprising answer to this proposal was an offer to let Fox take over the Treasury from him. This is doubly surprising when one reads the letters which George wrote to Bute at this time. They reveal not the faintest trace of gratitude for the services which Fox had undeniably rendered him. On the contrary, George calls him the most unprincipled of all politicians, and one whom he could never trust. He now went so far as to assert that it was only with the greatest repugnance that he had approved his appointment in the preceding October, and criticised Fox's system of corruption, the fruits of which he had most readily garnered, with virtuous abhorrence. Fox's memorandum of March 11th strengthened still more the distaste he felt for him, but—he declared himself agreeable to the proposed new appointment; it seemed, he said, inevitable but he would 'feel rejoiced whenever I can see a glimmering hope of getting quit of him.' A highly agreeable fate would have awaited Fox if he had accepted Bute's offer! But he had his wife to thank for being spared such a fate. She feared that in his state of health so exacting an office would be the very worst thing for him, and her urgent entreaties overcame the promptings of his ambition.

But Fox now suddenly learned, to his consternation, that it was generally assumed that, upon his imminent departure from the Commons, he would also give up the Pay Office. Young Shelburne, who had acted as go-between in the Fox-Bute negotiations was responsible for this. He had concluded from remarks which Fox had made on occasion that he was prepared to do so, and had reported Fox to Bute in such a way that the latter assumed Shelburne was transmitting Fox's definite consent. To Bute this was most satisfactory, since he could use this coveted post to reward a protégé or woo a follower. But neither Bute nor Shelburne had ever considered it necessary to acquaint Fox with this understanding, although they could easily have done so often enough. One cannot blame Fox for considering himself deceived by Shelburne, whom he had hitherto regarded as his friend. Horace Walpole records that Bute attempted to pacify Fox by talking of a 'pious fraud.' Fox is said to have replied: 'I can see the fraud plainly enough, but where is the piety?' If it is not true it is a neat enough story. It is quite possible that any such sinister intention was far from Shelburne's thoughts. One can explain this comedy of errors by the fact that he was too young to handle such knotty negotiations and that he lacked the necessary clarity of expression, as is shown by his ponderous and often obscure letters. But it is not surprising that these squabbles, which, of course, at once set all political tongues a-wagging, earned him the reputation of being an intriguer. He suffered from this reputation for the whole of his life and it was not without its effect on the course of history.

What was Fox to do now? For him the worst of it was that Bute had informed the King of his imminent resignation and George was naturally elated at the news. For a day or two Fox toyed with the idea of getting up on his hind legs and threatening to remain in the Commons, where he could make himself very much of a nuisance to the administration. But what would then happen to his peerage? He had counted on becoming a viscount but had to rest content with a lesser title. And so he entered the Lords as Baron Holland. But he stayed—at least for a few years—in charge of the Pay Office.

His political rôle was played out. Never again was a political post entrusted to him. He did not even succeed in achieving a higher rank in the peerage, on which his ambition had now concentrated. He was a spent force and was treated as such; in particular, many of those to whom he had shown favour and who had paid him homage now turned their backs on him. He, who in the closing years of his political career had reckoned only with the baser qualities of his fellow-men, was shaken to the core by the measure of ingratitude he now encountered. In order to enjoy and exercise power for a few months he had stooped to become the creature of a monarch who despised him; he had persecuted and injured old friends, and incurred the odium of high and low. Could the title of Baron Holland solace him for this? Luckily he had the faculty of finding comfort and happiness at his own fireside and of forgetting all his vexations in his pride in the gifts of his son Charles, who was now growing up.

CHAPTER IX

GRENVILLE, WILKES AND
THE STAMP ACT

BUTE had arranged for George Grenville, Pitt's brother-in-law and Temple's brother, to succeed him; at the same time Grenville became Chancellor of the Exchequer. As has been mentioned, Bute had offered him the reversion of this office as early as October, 1762. In the meantime, the feud between Grenville and Pitt had become so embittered that Grenville inevitably appeared even more strongly a natural successor in the eyes of this peer who was once more going behind the curtain. Not only had the two brothers-in-law openly crossed swords in the House; Pitt had so far forgotten all their former friendship and thrown discretion to the winds as to make Grenville an object of ridicule. Bute knew that such wounds are slow to heal, and that Grenville would be all the more constrained to seek support from the King and his parliamentary janissaries, who now bore the party label of 'The King's Friends'.

George Grenville was a man of great parts and not inconsiderable capacities, and above all one who always tackled his political work in deadly earnest. He would bury himself in a problem until he believed that he had found its solution, to which he then clung with a characteristic tenacity. Just as he lacked flexibility, so also did he lack imagination. In his speeches in the House, as in private conversation, he displayed wearisome prolixity and didactic pedantry, nor could he change his tune even in the presence of the King.

In peaceful times he might have been the very man to administer a high office of state with painstaking efficiency. But he had not the gift of leading the country in days when party passions ran high, and problems of a new kind and of an import which could scarcely be grasped were coming to the surface. He had been barely two weeks in office before his administration was involved in a controversy which began with a highly-seasoned newspaper article and ended in a great constitutional conflict.

These squabbles centred round John Wilkes, at that time member for Aylesbury. For years afterwards Wilkes' name was the battle-cry of all Englishmen who still clung passionately to the old ideals of freedom, and yet seldom has there been a man less fitted to be idealized. He was a profligate and a spendthrift who ran through his wife's fortune, and then showed his gratitude by treating her badly. In the Hell-Fire Club, in which the most rip-roaring roués and blasphemous sinners of London society foregathered, he could always outbid his boon companions in folly and daring. But the man had the qualities of his defects. He was fearless and utterly free from hypocrisy; he never made himself out to be better than he was. He had an inexhaustible wit and the gift of scintillating conversation, important accomplishments in circles which set so much store by piquant and lively table-talk. For this reason he was sought after by everybody, regardless of party, and even the cross-grained Dr. Johnson, who declared that the Devil had been the first Whig and had written a pamphlet against Wilkes, was entranced when he met him at a friend's dinner-table. In political and journalistic campaigning Wilkes was a master tactician, who could unerringly expose his opponent's weak points and had the knack of using the weapons which would do him the most damage. There is an anecdote, equally typical of Wilkes and the society of his day, which illustrates the point. An article, published anonymously by Wilkes, gave offence to a peer, who angrily asked him whether he had written it. Wilkes curtly refused to answer him. A duel with pistols was the inevitable result. After the first exchange of shots, with neither party wounded, Wilkes said that he now admitted he had written the article. His lordship was satisfied and 'he then desired that we might now be good friends, and retire to the inn to drink a bottle of claret together . . .' And thus what had begun as a duel to the death ended in a convivial drinking bout. Wilkes' full account of the affair is a miniature literary masterpiece.

Politically Wilkes was one of the followers of Pitt and Temple. He was on terms of particularly close intimacy with Temple, who helped him not only with the ready money he constantly needed but also with his journalistic venture, the *North Briton*. Wilkes had chosen this title for his paper as a sly dig at Bute, that much-hated Scot, and the paper lived up to its name. Even

Temple at times felt constrained to warn Wilkes not to get too deeply involved in this vulgar Scot-baiting.

Today the *North Briton* would probably moulder in the same oblivion as the other mushroom newspapers which for a time fed London's appetite for scandal and controversy, had not the forty-fifth issue caused the widest political repercussions and thus achieved immortality. It contained a criticism of the Speech from the Throne with which George III had prorogued Parliament on April 19th, 1763. In this speech the conclusion of peace was, of course, tricked out in the most glowing colours as a blessing for the country; and Wilkes, who as a follower of Pitt condemned the peace, had made a most violent attack on the ministers for putting lies into the King's sacred mouth. In itself, the article was no worse than a hundred other current political squibs. In any other paper it would probably have caused no stir at that time, and in the nineteenth century any law officer of the crown would have deemed it harmless. It began by establishing that constitutionally a speech from the throne was to be regarded as an announcement by the ministers, not by the King, and it went on to heap praise and flattery on the King himself. But all to no avail; George looked upon the article as a personal affront. The Secretaries of State, Lord Egremont and Lord Halifax, laid it before the Attorney-General, Hardwicke's son Charles Yorke, who pronounced it a seditious libel. Thereupon Halifax issued a *general* warrant against the authors and printers of No. 45 of the *North Briton*, not against specifically named persons, for, as was then the practice, the *North Briton* appeared quite anonymously, without mention of its author or printer. On the basis of this warrant government agents broke into Wilkes' rooms and confiscated all his papers, after he and about fifty others had been haled before the Secretaries of State, who sent him to the Tower.

Politically and legally the ministers had done the most stupid thing possible. Instead of letting a 'less tenable performance of a day'—to use a phrase of Bismarck's—pass by with the day which saw its birth, they had magnified the article into a matter of the gravest national concern over which everyone had to take sides with the most passionate intensity. Where freedom, particularly that of the press, is concerned, the English are very touchy, and this freedom seemed in danger if a man who had openly voiced what thousands were thinking could be locked up merely because his views ran counter to those of the court. Not only did the mob grow heated for 'Wilkes and Liberty', but aristocrats of the bluest blood, with the prime minister's brother, Temple, at their head, also came out in favour of the victim. Still worse, Wilkes was a member of Parliament and as such enjoyed the privilege of protection from arrest, except on the grounds of felony or treason. But the worst thing of all was the general warrant. Was an Englishman, already—as things were then viewed—protected from arbitrary arrest by the terms of Magna Carta, to be deprived of his freedom by a warrant in which his name was not mentioned and which had been issued not by a magistrate but by a secretary of state, that is, by a politician in office? And all this had happened to a man who, as the whole world was now to learn, was a fighter of the first order, an expert in handling the weapons offered him by the common law of England. Wilkes waged this war of words with so much dexterity, wit and courage that his letters and manifestoes, which were of course at once published, brought the laugh on to his own side. Even today when the dust of two centuries has settled on the controversy, they still divert the reader. But in court, too, Wilkes conducted his campaign with complete success, thanks to Pratt, the Chief Justice of Common Pleas, and Pitt's friend and legal adviser. Pratt pronounced Wilkes' arrest a breach of privilege amid a storm of applause from the onlookers, who escorted the released man in a triumphal procession from Westminster Hall to his house. Pratt later pronounced general warrants illegal, whereupon all those subjected to wrongful arrest successfully sued their captors for damages. After years of litigation Wilkes succeeded in getting £4,000 in damages awarded against Halifax. The good, solid citizens of the London jury were only too willing to show by their verdict how much they abhorred the arbitrary actions of the ministers. The London mob gave vent to its feelings with even more violence, to quote but one instance, by publicly burning Bute in effigy.

And so the opposition had a most welcome and popular stalking-horse for a vigorous campaign against the administration. But it was still very difficult to get Pitt and the Whigs to work together in harness. True, Pitt now realized that in the long run he could not remain a solitary figure and he took pains to explain away his earlier utterances against all party bonds. He also had long and confidential conversations with Newcastle which showed that he sincerely desired an honourable understanding. But not only did his attitude towards many points raised by the Wilkes affair differ from that of the other wing of the opposition; there was also a personal matter which made it hard to reach an understanding. Pitt wanted Pratt, whose attitude had his unstinted approval, to be made Lord Chancellor. But Charles Yorke, who, as Hardwicke's son, was the pet candidate of the Whigs, had also set his heart on the office.

George, on the other hand, was now highly dissatisfied with his ministers. Although he himself had encouraged them to attack Wilkes, it did not suit him to have them suffer one defeat after another in the process. Besides he found them too independent in many matters. He and Bute had intended that Grenville should always consider himself as a tool of the fallen favourite and act on his directions. But Grenville was not the man to display this kind of 'gratitude'. Worst of all, the didactic pedant in Grenville got terribly on George's nerves. He could not for the life of him bear either the long lectures which Grenville read him or the recitation of his arguments in remorseless detail. He is said to have exclaimed in his distraction that he would rather see the devil in his Closet than Mr. Grenville.

The King would have liked to stiffen the administration with men of authority and standing. So he had Hardwicke sounded, but at once withdrew into his shell when Hardwicke said that he would only come in if his friends came in too. For in no circumstances would George have any dealings with a party. He wanted an administration in which he could play off one minister against another. There would be an end to this if the ministers were held together by party ties. Any solidarity among the ministers would deprive him of what he called his 'independency'. If in these circumstances nothing could be done with the old Whig party, perhaps something could be arranged with Pitt. Bute in particular, who was once more in close and constant touch with George and on whom George still relied in tight corners, urged this course upon him. The relations between Bute and Pitt had now, with the passing of the years, been through every conceivable phase. But when Bute sent word to Pitt that he wished to discuss matters of the highest importance with him, Pitt did not hold back. In an interview lasting three hours they talked at length and apparently without reserve. Pitt did not refrain from criticizing the administration, and he also made it clear that he would not come in alone, or merely with Temple, but that Newcastle and his friends must join him too. And so Bute must have seen that if Pitt came into the administration, George would have to abandon the personal policy he had embarked on a few months before. None the less, Bute asked Pitt to go in person to lay his plan before George and even undertook to get him an invitation to the Palace.

This duly arrived, and on Saturday, 28th August, Pitt had an audience lasting three hours in Buckingham House, then known as 'The Queen's House'. At this audience George gave Pitt the impression that he fully agreed with his proposals, and he even went so far as to ask him to draw up a list of his candidates for office. In the end he postponed further discussion until the Monday. So sanguine was Pitt that he asked Newcastle and Devonshire, as well as Hardwicke, to come to London as quickly as possible. But when he again saw the King on the Monday, the wind was blowing from quite another quarter. True, George at first let it appear that he was still in earnest, but after discussing a few personal questions he suddenly declared: '. . . I see this won't do. My honour is concerned . . .' He did not tell Pitt why this should be, nor did he ever make it clear subsequently. It was obviously only a phrase he used in order to extricate himself, and one which his old tutor had most probably whispered in his ear. Pitt always maintained that it was a complete mystery to him why the negotiations had broken down, and what reasons George could have had for changing his mind so completely between Saturday and Monday. One can only guess that George and Bute, when they talked things over on the Sunday, came to see that an administration uniting Pitt with the heads of the Whig party would be strong enough to display a will of its own which would not bow even to the King's. Thus George's worst fears would have come true.

What else could the King now do but go back to Grenville? *He* had been completely staggered, and not a little uneasy, when he visited the Palace on the Saturday and there outside the King's door came upon his dear brother-in-law's sedan chair, which everyone in London could recognize a hundred yards off by the 'boot' in which the ailing statesman lodged his gouty foot. Grenville remembered better than the King the solemn assurances with which His Majesty had pledged him unswerving loyalty and support at the time when he took office. One cannot blame Grenville if he now demanded guarantees before undertaking to continue in office. These could only lie in the complete destruction of Bute's influence, and Grenville demanded that Bute should leave the capital. In vain might George protest at being asked such a thing when he had already done so much for his ministers. Grenville now knew what value to place on all His Majesty's fine words.

But when Grenville was once again safely in the saddle, he showed that the last few months had taught him nothing. The campaign against Wilkes went on, but this time in Parliament, where the ministers were on firmer ground than before judges and juries. When Parliament reassembled in November, the ministers easily carried a motion in the Commons which condemned the *North Briton* as a false, scandalous and seditious libel, fit only to be burned in public by the common hangman. Carrying out the terms of the motion was, of course, not quite so easy. A public burning meant that there would be spectators. If their sympathies were on the side of the persecutor, then everything would pass off smoothly. But if they were on the side of the persecuted, then anything might happen, for there was no police force in eighteenth-century London, and to call in the military might easily lead to bloodshed. When the hangman was about to cast the *North Briton* into the flames in front of the Royal Exchange, the mob snatched the paper from his hands and threw in the fire in its place a jack-boot, a popular, punning symbol for Bute, and the respectable City merchants who were watching the show from their windows and balconies clapped their hands in enthusiastic applause.

Wilkes' popularity had been still more enhanced by a mean trick which the ministers had played on him. He had had printed on a private press for friends who shared his tastes a dozen copies of a daring, obscene satirical poem called 'An Essay on Woman', which he may well have composed himself and had in any case provided with spicy annotations. One of the copies had, by some rather dubious means, fallen into the hands of the Secretary of State, Lord Sandwich, whose own private life gave him of all people the least right to raise his hands in pious horror. He had been just as much at home in the Hell-Fire Club as Wilkes. Sandwich had the effrontery to recite in the Lords this essay obviously not intended for publication, in order to brand Wilkes as a corrupter of good morals and unworthy of the honour of being a member of Parliament. At this, the administration set to work with all the means at its disposal to expel Wilkes from the Commons and thus strip him of his dangerous privilege. The situation was aggravated by the fact that Wilkes was severely wounded in a duel which bore all the marks of an attempt on his life, and finally fled to France to escape persecution.

For weeks the most violent disputes over Wilkes raged in Parliament, and in the course of them the most important constitutional questions came up for decision. Pitt, too, took a lively part in these disputes. Not, perhaps, out of any sympathy with Wilkes and the *North Briton*! Quite the contrary; he attached great importance to expressing as emphatically as possible his detestation of Wilkes' pamphleteering. True, Pitt was fully justified in detesting the way Wilkes had played the demagogue and exploited the English dislike of the Scots, but his indignation at the supposed insult to the King seems heavily exaggerated. One cannot dismiss out of hand the explanation that he was striving to keep alive the favourable impression which he believed he had made on George at his last audience. But irreproachably clear and vigorous was his intervention on behalf of the threatened rights of a member of Parliament and the freedom of the citizen, now menaced by general warrants. In this last point his position was particularly delicate, since he himself had issued warrants as Secretary of State. But a war produces exceptional situations and obliges an administration to take exceptional measures to meet them. Today this is everywhere recognized and everywhere customary. At that time such distinctions were as yet not acknowledged, and Pitt was therefore thrown back on rather artificial arguments and distinctions in order to square his present theory with his former practice. But of one thing there is no doubt: the spirit which he championed in these constitutional struggles was the real old Whig spirit and showed that he was justified in professing 'revolutionary principles'.

However the strength of this stand was counteracted by the assiduity with which he declined any party allegiance and emphasized his own isolation. Against the ranks of the administration, banded together and linked by internal and external means, only a compact opposition could have had any prospect of success. That such a success was not impossible was shown when the administration's majority in isolated divisions fell to as low as about ten. If Pitt had taken the opposition in hand firmly and consistently, then this dwindling majority could in the end have been changed into a minority. But neither by nature nor conviction was he the man to do this, however much his eloquence and his popularity seemed to mark him out for the task. He was intolerant of opinions which differed from his own. The opposition had received a valuable reinforcement: Charles Yorke, as distinguished as a parliamentary debater as he was outstanding as a lawyer, had thrown up the office of Attorney-General before the session began. But Pitt by no means rejoiced over this. To be sure, in many important legal questions Yorke did not see eye to eye with Pratt, whom Pitt followed, and Pitt then intensified such differences of opinion by the mordancy with which he attacked Yorke. In any event the administration finally had its own way and Wilkes was expelled from the Commons. Some years went by before he returned home, when he at once became the focus of political attention again.

In the autumn of 1764, when the battle over Wilkes had already been over for some months and Hardwicke had meanwhile died (March 6th, 1764), Newcastle, now an old man yet still working to build up a united opposition party, ventured on a fresh approach to Pitt. But he received a most discouraging response. In his stiffest and most pompous style Pitt stressed his unwillingness to give up 'the free condition of a man standing *single*, and daring to appeal to his country at large, upon the soundness of his principles and the rectitude of his conduct.' In support of this attitude he claimed among other things that his war policy had not been defended in Parliament, which is too far-fetched to sound convincing. The true explanation of his change of front since the summer of the preceding year lies in his increased realization of his own importance. The Whigs had—had they not?—declared often and plainly enough that without him no move against the administration would have

any prospect of success and that everything depended on his
co-operation; and then, in those audiences at the end of August,
the King had, as he understood it, hinted that he would at any
time welcome him as a leading minister, and that the party was
nothing but a burden, which he dragged along behind him, and
a stumbling-block on the path to his goal. And so Pitt had
grown more and more convinced that to attain political influence
he needed no party and that a party would only prove a hind-
rance in reaching his personal objectives.

And so there was no hope of any kind of effective opposition
to the King and his ministers. And yet at that moment the state
was nearing a crisis in which the unity of the realm was at stake
and a vigilant opposition was an indispensable necessity. The
curtain was going up on the first act of the secession of the North
American colonies.

§

On the credit side of Grenville's administration might be
reckoned the zeal and expert knowledge with which he applied
himself to ordering the national finances and nursing them back
to health. Seven years of war can play havoc with the finances
of even the strongest nation and saddle its citizens with an
almost unbearable burden, particularly when the war leader
cares so little for the cost as Pitt. The national debt (funded and
unfunded) had mounted from seventy-two million pounds to
one hundred and thirty-two million, a heavy load for a country
with exports of the order of fifteen million pounds a year, and
with a population of no more than eight millions. In these
circumstances Grenville's policy of retrenchment was basically
sound, even if it sometimes led him into being a little cheese-
paring and practising false economies.

In times of financial stress Chancellors of the Exchequer are
prone to cast about for new sources of revenue, and so it was
natural for Grenville to cock a reflective eye at England's North
American colonies, to see whether they could not perhaps do
something to lighten the imperial load. He had this all the more
at heart since the war, the source of all the financial difficulties,
had been very largely conducted in defence of these colonies.
England's American colonists on no account wished to become
French subjects, a fate which would have threatened them if

England's army had been worsted in Canada. Their other, and more formidable, foes were the Red Indians and against these too they had to call on the mother country for armed assistance. And so Grenville could put forward some quite solid arguments for his plan.

British North America consisted of thirteen colonies, extending along the Atlantic coast between Canada and Louisiana, once French and now Spanish. Each colony had its own constitution with a separate representative assembly, which fixed the taxes to be raised. Each was accustomed to regard itself as self-contained, and not as a component part of the American colonies as a whole.

Active trading linked most of the colonies with the mother country. In accordance with the outlook of the age, this trade was governed by the principles of mercantilism, which ensured the mother country a monopoly of trade and an exclusive market in her colonies. The Americans were bound to ship their most important products, such as cotton, tobacco and sugar, solely to Britain. Industries which might compete with those in the home country were forbidden them. On the other hand to a large extent the colonies enjoyed a monopoly of the English market for their products. At bottom the Americans had very little to complain about in this sytem, under which their economy and their population expanded. If the regulations were ever too oppressive they were sidestepped in the simplest way possible— by non-compliance. There was a lot of smuggling and as a rule the authorities were content to wink at what they could not prevent. After all, some three thousand miles separated them from their American colonies.

This great distance, however, now had far more serious consequences. Travel between the home country and the colonies was negligible. Small wonder, when with a favourable wind it took at least six weeks to cross the Atlantic, and, without one, three months or more. Not one of the English statesmen in whose hands lay decisions of policy affecting America had ever set foot on American soil. The despatches which the King's governors sent to his ministers were frequently anything but unbiassed sources of information. The colonies had, of course, their own agents in London, including so important a figure as Benjamin Franklin, representing Pennsylvania. But their words

K

seldom carried weight with the men in power. A few Americans and West Indians sat in Parliament, as well as several English merchants, who knew America from doing business there. But one could not look for over-much sympathy with the hard-working, plain-living and democratically-minded Americans in those English aristocrats who for the most part looked upon the rents from their tenants and state salaries, pensions and sinecures as the only sources of income compatible with their station.

Grenville cannot be accused of taking lightly the serious step of imposing a tax on the Americans. He laid his plans before the agents for the colonies before submitting them to Parliament, and he could claim in his own defence that Franklin, who proposed that the money should be voted by the colonies' representative assemblies, said in answer to his question that he did not know whether the colonies would be able to agree among themselves over the sum to be raised. As finance minister Grenville was, therefore, fully entitled to lay before Parliament his Stamp Act, which made all legal documents liable to stamp duty. The financial burden thus imposed on the colonies was not excessive. No more than £100,000 a year was expected from it, and this sum was to be applied to paying and victualling troops who would be stationed in the colonies for the defence of the Americans.

Technically all this may well appear quite convincing. But, as Catherine of Russia once said to Diderot, laws are written on human skin, and in politics there are, to use one of Bismarck's phrases, *imponderabilia*: these cannot be inferred from statistics or documents—the statesman must have his own sixth sense for them. Walpole had possessed this sixth sense; when someone suggested taxing America he had retorted, 'I have old England set against me, and do you think I will have New England likewise?' Grenville had no such flair, as his handling of the *North Briton* affair had already shown. Over and above this weakness, the zeal with which he attacked the study of American finances proved to be a real misfortune. A paradox, coined in later years by one of his subordinates, contains much truth. 'Mr. Grenville,' this man said, 'lost America because he read the American despatches, which his predecessors had never done.' And so, all unsuspecting, he stumbled into a conflict in which there was infinitely more at stake than the £100,000 which he intended to raise in America. Things were no better in Parliament. No more than 40 votes were cast against the bill in the Commons. Only Colonel Barré, who could claim to know the Americans better from first-hand observation than the other members did, raised his voice in warning and called the Americans 'sons of liberty'. The gallant colonel, who had won his first parliamentary laurels by a vehement attack on Pitt, had in the meantime become his faithful follower. Pitt himself was absent from the House; once again gout had seized upon him. But even if it had not, it is hardly likely that he would have made an appearance. By then he had been staying away for almost a year. On March 22nd, 1765, the Act, which had the King's full approval, received the royal assent. It was to come into force that November.

But a storm at once blew up in the colonies which far exceeded all expectations. Nor did it spring from purely imaginary causes. What greatly contributed to its violence was that the administration tried at the same time to enforce the existing laws even more stringently and to suppress smuggling; presumably the mob which maltreated customs officials in Boston was not chiefly impelled by constitutional considerations. But what proved of decisive importance was that the leading American lawyers unearthed a constitutional formula which was taken up by the representative assemblies of the colonies, as it offered a basis for common action by all the colonies. Hitherto each colony had thought only of itself, but now for the first time they felt they had a common cause against the mother country. The formula, which Patrick Henry first proclaimed in the Virginia assembly, was that the representative assembly of a colony alone had the right to impose taxes and other burdens on that colony. This is the doctrine epitomized in the celebrated phrase 'No taxation without representation'; it challenged the authority of the Parliament of England, which had hitherto passed laws for the whole empire without hesitation, to raise taxes from the Americans because they were not represented there. This doctrine became the common slogan of the Americans. For now, for the first time, the majority of the colonies were agreed on a single policy. It was an act of the greatest significance when in October, 1763, representatives of no fewer than nine colonies met in New York to support the Virginia resolution and agree upon a joint declaration of their grievances and demands. It was the first step towards closing the colonial ranks in opposition to the mother country. This was all the more momentous since an important element had vanished which had linked the English colonists in America with Britain. Hitherto they had considered the home country as their natural, indispensable support and protection against French expansion. But since the French had been driven out of Canada and the Union Jack flew over Quebec this ghost had been laid, and with it the need for close connection with the ruler of the waves.

The enforcement of the Stamp Act in North America ran up against insurmountable obstacles. But the Americans did not merely confine themselves to passive resistance; they went over to a counter-attack. The import of English goods was boycotted. A trade which brought Great Britain gross receipts of two millions sterling every year was gravely threatened. The English merchants suddenly saw that their very livelihood was at stake if Grenville's policy were to be pursued.

But it was far from George's thoughts to reproach Grenville in the slightest for his treatment of the colonies. On the contrary, Grenville here seemed to him a champion of the rights of the Crown against dissident subjects. It was a far more trivial mistake which unseated the minister.

Early in 1765 George III showed the first signs of the madness which recurred later and in the end completely overpowered him. For some days he was obviously incapable of ruling, and when he had recovered he could not escape the need to provide against the eventuality of another attack or of his dying before his eldest son, then three years old, came of age. A regency bill had to be agreed upon with Parliament. This had its own particular difficulties by reason of the rivalry between George's mother, the Princess of Wales, and his oldest male relative, Cumberland. In his draft of the bill Grenville was clumsy enough to offend the Princess deeply and to give his political opponents the chance of putting him publicly in the wrong. The King could not forgive him for this, and it was only the question of finding an acceptable substitute which stood between Grenville and his dismissal. George turned to his uncle, the Duke of Cumberland, and asked him to procure a man to free him from Grenville's intolerable tyranny. Apparently on

Bute's advice George empowered the Duke to negotiate with Pitt and his brother-in-law and ally, Lord Temple.

On May 19th, 1765, his Grace went in person with a military escort to Pitt's country seat at Hayes to conclude the negotiations, already well developed by intermediaries.

This indeed was something which had never been seen before! It gives some idea of the special, more, the unique position which Pitt occupied not only in the eyes of the people but also of the court. He had now been out of office for four years, a sick man, who very seldom came to the House to speak. But this had not impaired his prestige. He was still the one statesman who could help even if all the others proved broken reeds, and the senior prince of the royal house had no need to regard it as a condescension to visit Pitt in person and ask him to become a minister.

In the preliminary talks Pitt had made a series of conditions which were feasible in themselves, even if they did entail a change in the direction which His Majesty's administration had taken of recent years. Perhaps the most sweeping departure he made was in foreign policy: he demanded an alliance with Prussia. This shows that he wanted to pick up the threads from the point at which he had left office; but with Frederick as hostile and suspicious as he was, these prospects had only a very faint chance of being realized.

But it was not over these conditions that the negotiations came to nothing. Several causes seemed to have conspired to bring about their breakdown. Pitt took exception to various other persons who were to come into the ministry with him, particularly Lord Northumberland, a relative of Bute's. Temple, who had also appeared at the Hayes conference, was even more uncompromising in his refusal. He thought that he had not been shown a consideration which matched his pretensions and his inflated idea of his own importance. Another factor seems to have been that just about this time Temple was in the middle of patching things up with his brother, George Grenville, and a reconciliation between them did in fact come about in May; they had both held aloof ever since Temple had left the ministry in company with Pitt. This burying of differences extended to their brother-in-law, Pitt, as well, to the great joy of Hester, who had, of course, suffered from this family feud. But Pitt made

it clear to Grenville from the very outset that this resoldering of
old family bonds did not affect their political differences; for
this reason he asked him to avoid talking politics at family
reunions.

Now that the negotiations with Pitt had broken down,
George was thrown back on Grenville and the former ministers.
Naturally, they made new conditions which, just as naturally,
provoked him against them still more. But without making any
bones about it he met one of their demands—removing Lord
Holland from the Pay Office. In this the ministers were
prompted by Holland's friendship with Bute. Where was the
use, they were able to urge, of removing Bute from court if his
friend stayed in office, a friend who knew all the ins and outs of
parliamentary and political life a hundred times better than
Bute, and who could handle men so much more adroitly than he?

Since he had ceased to be a political force, Holland had for
the most part kept in the background and had been away doing
a great deal of travelling on the Continent. From time to time
he was attacked by the yearning to plunge once more into
active politics, but, as he found no encouragement anywhere,
these led to nothing. He still followed the progress of his former
rival with the most critical interest. When in August, 1763, Pitt
had these sensational audiences of the King, Holland spitefully
said that he had known from the outset that Pitt's 'demands
were, however he should word them, crown or sceptre.' But he
would not have been heartbroken if Pitt or anyone else had
brought George Grenville down. For his hostility towards
Grenville had grown even stronger; he held against him his
ingratitude towards Bute, whom he counted as his friend and
whose theories he still accepted without question. But, in his
heart of hearts, Holland knew that his sun had set and that he
would never again play an active part in politics. His physical
powers were waning and his health very unsettled. If only the
King would be gracious enough to promote him from Baron to
Earl, then he would have been well satisfied with his lot. But
even this trifling favour was denied him.

He really only remained in office to put in order his highly
complicated accounts, dating back to the war years. He had
conducted so many private transactions with the public monies
entrusted to him that a new Paymaster would hardly ever have

found his way through the maze. But he was too old a hand to delude himself that things could go on like this for ever and a day. Sooner or later the time would come when the leading minister would need the post to instal some politically valuable colleague in it. And so, after he had swallowed his first transport of anger, he took his dismissal with philosophic calm, finding comfort in the adage: 'To live at ease is the sure method to live long.' The means to live at ease his years in office had procured him in abundant measure.

Contemporaries cannot have shown any undue interest in the disappearance of the once so controversial figure of Henry Fox from the scene. The world of politics was more engrossed with the question of how long George Grenville would hold his ground in the face of the unconcealed hostility of the King. This was now so great that George even went to the trouble of sounding Pitt once more, through Cumberland, in mid-June and of receiving him twice in audience on the 19th and 22nd of that month.

This time Pitt seemed inclined to accept and the King was disposed to agree to all his conditions. Among these, curiously enough, was a more conciliatory policy towards the American colonies. But once again Temple upset the applecart even though on this occasion the Treasury, that is the formal position of prime minister, was offered to him. What were his reasons for refusing? He told his brother George that they were twofold. First there was 'the difficulty there would be to form a proper plan to carry on the public business in the House of Commons'; by this he meant that there the administration would be dependent on Pitt alone, who, however, in consequence of his poor health, would not be able to undertake any continuous parliamentary activity. Secondly, Temple referred to other 'reasons of a tender and delicate nature' which he would not even reveal to his brother. From Temple's character it has been concluded that the real reason was that, bursting with the consciousness of his own importance, he was no longer willing to play second fiddle to his brother-in-law. However this may be, Pitt did not feel equal to the task without Temple's co-operation; perhaps, too, he had cause to fear that Temple, now reunited with George Grenville, would offer him dangerous opposition. He therefore declined, and even a request written in the King's own hand could not make him change his mind.

CHAPTER X

THE ROCKINGHAM MINISTRY

IF George was unwilling to bow to Grenville, only one way out was left: a Whig ministry. True, this was the exact opposite of his supreme aim—to smash the Whig party; but his plight was desperate and in his heart he may well have found comfort in the thought that, at no very distant date, he could rid himself of this ministry also if it made too independent a showing. Once again Cumberland was his go-between, and this time a very willing one, convinced as he was that the country's salvation lay in an administration built from the best elements in the Whig party. Newcastle, of course, could not be left out, but the old gentleman was perfectly content with the sinecure office of Lord Privy Seal, in which post he could place his years of experience at the Cabinet's disposal. The leadership of the ministry had to be entrusted to a man of the younger generation. He belonged to a group of politicians who felt that of recent years those inside the Whig party had lost sight of its principles in their scramble for jobs and state favours, and who wanted to base their political careers on loyalty to principles and personal integrity. This group looked to the thirty-five-year-old Marquis of Rockingham, a very wealthy owner of large estates, as its leader. It was Rockingham who headed the new administration.

True, he fell a long way short of being a born leader in politics. His was no strong, let alone inspiring, personality. He had never before occupied a high office of state. The gift of oratory was denied him; an almost unconquerable shyness prevented him from taking part in parliamentary business as frequently or as effectively as his position seemed to demand. Only occasionally, when provoked by unjust attacks, was he able to come out of his shell and surprise the Lords with a spirited defence of his policy. It was, too, hardly conducive to his public effectiveness that, as the owner of large stables, he took a passionate interest in the turf and on occasion allowed a debate in the House to take second place to a race at Newmarket. But he was a man of character and inspired confidence. People knew that he would stick to his principles and resign sooner than go against them. It had been noted how he had repeatedly shown the King that court favour or the splendour of office left him completely cold if his political principles or his loyalty to political friends were at stake. The men who clustered round him knew and appreciated his reliability, and in consequence they took his advice even on occasions when they had originally held a different opinion. He gave notable proofs of that most difficult art of the party leader—bringing together a number of independent spirits and inducing them to act in concert—and this at a time which was thoroughly unfavourable to his party. As soon as he took office he showed an open mind and a knowledge of men by appointing a young and impecunious writer of Irish extraction as his private secretary and political adviser and keeping him on despite the suspicion cast upon him. For this young man was Edmund Burke, destined to become the spiritual leader of the Whig party and one of England's greatest political writers.

The Rockingham ministry held office for little more than a year—from July 1765 to August 1766. But not only did it open up a political career to Burke, which in itself would suffice to make it memorable: it also carried two political measures which redound to its lasting credit—it repealed Grenville's Stamp Act and had general warrants declared illegal.

The ministry had to approach the question of American taxation very gingerly. A few months after it came to power, news came from across the seas that the colonists were putting up much stronger resistance than had been expected to the Stamp Act, and hard on the heels of this followed complaints from English merchants of the heavy losses they had already suffered, and the still heavier ones which would threaten them if nothing was done to placate the Americans. But the administration could be in no doubt that every step it retraced would meet with the strongest opposition in Parliament as well as at court. It felt its position to be weak. The majority in both Houses seemed to depend on the 'King's Friends', who let themselves be guided by the King's wishes. George had not only strengthened his hand in Parliament in the elections of 1761; he also had at his sole disposal the abundance of rewards and favours which loomed large in the hopes and wishes of many members. When Rockingham asked George for a peerage for one of his followers he spoke to deaf ears. Could it be expected that a man as stubborn as George would consent to the repeal of an Act to which he had only just signified his assent, particularly when this repeal was based on constitutional arguments which he could not but consider an encroachment upon the plenitude of his own royal power? In October, 1765, the insecurity of the ministry was quite unexpectedly and dangerously intensified a few months after it had come into being by the death of Cumberland at the early age of forty-five, for it now lacked its most effective advocate with the King. Men whose fortunes and strength of principle made them immune from royal pressure and court influence could obviously not count on any personal sympathy from George.

Rockingham was too honest to conceal from himself the weakness of his ministry. He was, moreover, quite clear in his own mind where he could best find support. There had been times when he had been in touch with Pitt on political matters. He now showed Pitt a mark of his goodwill by bringing his protégé, Pratt, the Lord Chief Justice of Common Pleas into the Lords as Lord Camden and giving a well-paid post to James Grenville, the only one of the brothers who still stood by Pitt. In foreign policy, too, he took the line which Pitt favoured by working for an understanding with Prussia. Several members of his ministry were pressing him with growing insistence to call in the most popular statesman and the greatest parliamentary orator. Again and again attempts were made to induce Pitt to come in. Old Newcastle now showed that he could bring himself to sacrifice his much-ridiculed ambition to the cause by formally offering to give up his post, should Pitt prove unwilling to sit in the same ministry with him. But Pitt still contrived to find some pretexts for withholding his acceptance, or else made conditions with which no self-respecting man could comply, asking, for example, that Rockingham should make way for Temple at the Treasury. In this connection it was already more than evident that Temple's attitude to the burning question of the day—America—was the same as his brother George's, that is, diametrically opposed to Pitt's as well as Rockingham's. Pitt's proposal must therefore have seemed to Rockingham not only a deliberate slight but also a threat to his policy.

None the less, at the instigation of those of his colleagues who backed Pitt, he persevered in his efforts with him and even urged the King to intervene personally and invite Pitt to an audience, since Pitt had declared during the negotiations that he would only join the administration with the King's full and cordial confidence. But George refused in a letter to Rockingham (9th January, 1766). He knew as well as Rockingham that Pitt's entry would appreciably strengthen the administration. But did he really want this? A weak administration suited his book far better than a strong one which could stand on its own legs and, if need be, defy him.

How thorny a problem was the repeal of the Stamp Act was shown when Parliament reassembled in the middle of January, 1766. Rockingham, if one may believe Burke's classic speech on the taxation of America, had already decided to abolish the Stamp Act. Of course, to do this he first had to win over his own Cabinet, and here opinions were at first very divided. He had also apprised Pitt of his intention in advance by inviting him to a confidential exchange of views. But the Speech from the Throne contented itself with general references to the intention of settling the point at issue not by a forcible oppression of the Americans but by peaceful means. At once a heated debate developed. Pitt was by now so obsessed with the importance of the question that he quitted his self-imposed retirement and suddenly left the country for London. With calculated unexpectedness he appeared in the House in the middle of the debate. Of course, everyone expected the man, by whom 'America had been conquered in Germany', to intervene in the discussion. Nor was this expectation disappointed, and his speech gave striking proof that if he wished he was still well able to take over the leadership, but also that, however much he might incline to this course, he could make it very difficult for others to work with him. With capricious emphasis he underlined his special position *vis-à-vis* the government as well as the opposition. He complimented the ministers on their unexceptionable characters, but he explicitly withheld his confidence from them with the odd phrase that confidence was 'a plant of slow growth in an aged bosom' (he was only 58 years old). Nor did he deny himself the pleasure of a veiled attack on Newcastle, although he knew that the Duke was prepared to sacrifice office to secure his collaboration.

But when he went on to deal with the real point at issue, he could not have been more clear and businesslike. He roundly condemned the Stamp Act. The arguments he advanced were, it must be admitted, somewhat singular and little calculated to win endorsement all round from the opponents of the Act. King and Parliament, he said, were sovereign and supreme over the colonies in every circumstance of government and legislation. But taxation was no part of the governing or legislative power. In justifying this strange assertion he quoted as his precedent the fact that taxes in England were a voluntary gift and grant of the Commons alone as representatives of the British taxpayers. But the American colonists were not represented in the Commons, he went on. Parliament could properly bind them by its laws, by its regulations and restrictions in trade, navigation and manufactures, but it might not take their money out of their pockets without their consent.

Almost every sentence of this argument was faulty or at least open to question. George Grenville at once replied to his brother-in-law, and, being vastly his superior in expert knowledge of financial and constitutional affairs, he showed how untenable an argument it was, and all Pitt could say to this hardly came to any more than that he drew his ideas of freedom from the vital powers of the British constitution. On the other hand, his rejection of Grenville's reproach that the seditious spirit of the colonies owed its birth to factions in the Commons was all the more triumphant. Pitt boldly shouldered the reproach and flung down a defiant trump card: 'I rejoice that America has resisted. Three millions of people so dead to all the feelings of liberty, as voluntarily to submit to be slaves, would have been fit instruments to make slaves of the rest.' Without ambiguity or hesitation he demanded the total and immediate repeal of the Stamp Act. Two million pounds, he said, was the sum which trade with America brought to Great Britain every year; it was a miserable financial policy which would jeopardize this sum for a peppercorn. And here he hit the nail on the head.

Whatever one may think about some of their arguments, these speeches of Pitt's were historic. He was the first to come out into the open and demand the repeal of the Stamp Act. Admittedly he did not go about it quite straightforwardly. He knew that Rockingham planned it. He himself had been asked at Rockingham's instance to give his views on it. Despite this he boldly maintained in his speech that he had been 'unconsulted'—obviously to secure for himself the credit of being the only begetter of the repeal.[1] Rockingham did nothing to dispel this false impression. On the contrary, on the day after this debate he once more asked the King to bring into the Cabinet this man, who had again demonstrated his overpowering influence on the Commons. But the King made difficulties and once again Pitt cast round for pretexts for saying 'No'.

If Pitt's dramatic entrance on the scene had cleared the air, Rockingham was left with the no less difficult task of translating the political theory into legislative action. His own Cabinet was not so united that he could operate safely; the King had made sure that some of those who sat in it listened to him more than to the prime minister, notably that intriguer of a Lord Chancellor, Northington, an old Leicester House man, who had already belonged to Grenville's Cabinet. But the greatest difficulties were made by the King himself. On the one hand he told Rockingham that he approved of the repeal of the Act. On the other, he gave all his followers to understand that he was against it and would raise no objections if they wished to vote against it. Apparently he feared that implementing the Stamp Act by force would occasion disorders in America with which he would be unable to cope, and the responsibility for which he was unwilling to shoulder. If the ministers relieved him of this responsibility by repealing the Act, well and good. Such a success, however, was not to be a source of strength to them; on the contrary, they were to live in constant fear that he would set his janissaries on them. On some pretext or other he evaded all Rockingham's attempts to bring him to support the administration's policy by exercising the customary pressure on these men, particularly by dismissing from their positions at court those who voted against the administration. Rockingham saw George's duplicity quite clearly, but was powerless.

[1] It is not altogether free from doubt whether Pitt used the word 'unconsulted', or 'unconcerted and unconnected'. The speech has come down to us with variant readings. (Basil Williams, II, 189, note 1). But there can be no doubt that the whole tenor of Pitt's remarks on his position *vis-à-vis* the ministry tended towards conveying the impression that not a whisper of what the ministry proposed to do had reached his ears. The disingenuousness of his statement remains the same, therefore, whichever reading one accepts.

One may assume that consideration of the mood and attitude of the King played a part in determining the course which the administration finally took. They proposed the unconditional repeal of the Stamp Act, but linked this up with a bill declaratory of Parliament's unrestricted right to legislate for the colonies and people of America on any subject whatever. The right of taxation was essentially included in it but was not mentioned in so many words. In the face of other ministers Rockingham had prudently managed to preserve this omission. In view of George's disinclination to forgo any right or claim, the ministry had reason to hope that such a solemn declaration would make it easier for him to give his assent to the repeal of the Stamp Act. Beyond a doubt this declaration also expressed the view of the overwhelming majority in Parliament, particularly the law officers. About this time Blackstone's celebrated commentary on the laws of England began to appear, and amid general approbation from the legal profession had made a classical maxim of the doctrine of the sovereignty of the 'King in Parliament'. Blackstone himself sat in the Commons where he championed his doctrine. Among the legal lights only Lord Camden (Pratt), who had imbued Pitt with his ideas, took up a position of his own. He pleaded in the Lords that there could be no taxation without representation, but was, by common consent, decisively defeated by Lord Mansfield. In the Commons Burke supported the Declaratory Bill by arguing that Parliament had a dual function: one was to rule Great Britain herself, the other, as the Parliament of the whole Empire, to supervise the local parliaments in the colonies and to make good any of their omissions. Pitt sharply attacked the bill in the Commons; he drew a distinction between internal taxes levied for the purpose of raising a revenue, which were inadmissible, and external duties imposed for the regulation of trade, which might, therefore, be fixed by Parliament. But he was almost entirely alone. Only ten votes were cast against the bill.

But public interest was now focussed on the question whether the repeal of the Stamp Act would pass through Parliament. For here very considerable interests were at stake. Nor was Parliament alone in paying the keenest attention to the debates to which Pitt contributed weighty speeches. He attacked Grenville and his fiscal policy most violently, but when Grenville rose to reply, Pitt left the House. Grenville took this as a personal slight hardly in keeping with the family peace which had been patched up shortly before. A stiff exchange of letters followed, in which Pitt excused his conduct on the grounds of his poor state of health. In the course of the debate Pitt had occasion to congratulate a very promising newcomer. This was Burke, newly elected to Parliament, who, from his very first speeches, as his personal friend and political opponent Dr. Johnson wrote, at once gained more reputation than perhaps any man at his first appearance ever gained before. On 21st February, 1766, the crucial debate took place in the Commons. With the King's attitude what it was, no one could predict the outcome. An excited crowd surged up to the doors of the House, with the London merchants, who felt that their very livelihood was in the balance, much in evidence. Pitt spoke calmly and moderately for the Bill but emphasized categorically that any future resistance on the part of the Americans was not to be tolerated. In such a case he would press for the most vigorous measures; England should then employ every man and every ship to break their resistance. Such words as these could not fail to sound most sweetly in the King's ears.

The debate was conducted with such pertinacity on both sides that the division could not be taken until the small hours after one o'clock. The administration triumphed with the unexpectedly high majority of 275 to 167 votes. But when the doors of the House were thrown open and the expectant crowd heard the welcome result, it was Pitt to whom they offered the most impressive homage. All bared their heads as the well-known figure came out, and in their hundreds they escorted him home.

A messenger brought Hester news of the great victory and she at once sent post haste a few lines to her dear husband. 'Joy to you, my dear love. The joy of thousands is yours, under Heaven, who has crowned your endeavours with such happy success. May the Almighty give to mine and to the general prayers, that you may wake without any increased gout . . .' 'Happy indeed', ran Pitt's answer, 'was the scene of this glorious morning . . . when the sun of liberty shone once more benignly upon a country too long benighted. My dear love, not all the applauding joy which the hearts of animated gratitude, saved from despair and bankruptcy, uttered in the lobby, could touch me in any degree like the tender and lively delight, which breathes in your warm and affectionate note.' In these hours of the most joyful exhilaration Pitt struck the simple, natural note so often missing in his letters.

Among the Grenvilles, it is true, the jubilant Hester was a figure apart. George was hissed by the crowd which paid homage to his brother-in-law, and Temple opposed the repeal in the Lords and even signed the protest against it.

The news of the withdrawal of the hated Stamp Act caused the utmost enthusiasm in the American colonies; once again it seemed as if peace and friendship between them and the home country would revive. Nor did it look as if the Declaratory Act would greatly affect this mood, however much it was at variance with the theory of the right of the colonies to representation. Perhaps, too, it would have remained innocuous if the question had not been stirred up again within a short time. No one could foresee that this would be done by a Cabinet with Pitt as its formal leader. But what could be foreseen was that if this matter were to come to a head, the Americans would use the arguments with which Pitt had entered the parliamentary lists to do battle with the right of taxation.

For the moment Rockingham and his friends could enjoy the consciousness of having done their country a great service, but this did nothing to strengthen their position, least of all with the King. He, who had formerly treated any opposition as a revolt, had permitted his friends to vote against his own government. Among Newcastle's papers was found a comprehensive list of 'King's Friends' who had voted against the repeal of the Stamp Act. The occupants of all possible offices, beginning with the War Ministry, appear on this list. As for the Lords, the list contained no less than five 'Lords of the Bedchamber', that is, peers from the King's immediate personal entourage. Not a hair of any one of them was touched. Rockingham could be in no doubt that at the first opportunity the King would now turn against him once the storm over the Stamp Acts had been weathered.

But in spite of everything the King's manoeuvres would have had no prospect of success had not the man whom the masses thought of as the representative of the people's interests against court intrigues come to his aid. Rockingham gauged the situation quite accurately when, a few days after his victory in the Commons, he entrusted a friend of Pitt's with a message to him. He suggested that Pitt should come to a conference with himself and two colleagues who were firm supporters of Pitt. At this conference an attempt was to be made to fix up a ministry with Pitt himself at the head, which they would then jointly propose to the King. To this Pitt returned an answer which could not have been different if George had dictated it himself. His respect and duty to the King, he had Rockingham informed, indispensably forbade him to discuss plans of that kind without His Majesty's express commands. All that Rockingham could conclude from this servile answer was that the Great Commoner expected more for himself from the King's favour than from collaboration with men who not only professed the same political principles as he did but had also shown that—as Burke put it— they were 'attached in office to every principle they had maintained in opposition'.

The crisis was brought to a head by the Duke of Grafton, who was a Secretary of State in the Rockingham Cabinet and relinquished his office at the end of April because Pitt would not come in. He declared in the Lords that if Pitt were to join the administration he was ready to take up the spade and the pick-axe and dig in the trenches. Rockingham could find only a weak substitute in the young Duke of Richmond, Lord Holland's brother-in-law. None the less he succeeded in making general warrants illegal, thus wresting a dangerous weapon from the caprice of the executive. Then the treacherous Northington dealt his colleagues a mortal blow: either of his own accord, or else at George's instigation, he picked some quarrel with them and declared that he would no longer attend any cabinet meetings.

George now felt that the time was ripe for ridding himself of the irksome Whigs. Significantly it was Northington who was given the job of establishing contact with Pitt. Through Northington he invited Pitt to an audience at which, he said, he wished to discuss with him the formation of a new ministry. Pitt's answer, dripping with loyalty, servility even, shows that he had been waiting for the invitation and had based his whole policy on this expectation. 'Penetrated with the deepest sense of

L

your Majesty's boundless goodness to me, and with a heart
overflowing with duty and zeal for the honour and happiness
of the most gracious and benign Sovereign . . .' Thus begins the
letter of England's greatest citizen at this new turning point in
his life.

Macaulay, in one of his brilliant essays on Chatham, has laid
at Pitt's door the grave reproach that he had wantonly destroyed
the government provided by the Whig party and played the
King's game. Nor can this fact be in dispute. Had he joined
the ministry he could have so strengthened it that it could have
coped with all intrigues and opposition. Certainly the blame for
the fact that this did not come about cannot be laid to the
charge of Rockingham and his friends. Later historians who
admire Pitt have tried to rebut Macaulay's indictment by
stressing the differences which divided Pitt and Rockingham
on many questions. It is true that they did not see eye to eye over
the Declaratory Act. But this measure had been passed and was
no longer a subject of dispute. Any collaboration between
independently-minded politicians would be quite impossible if
controversy over points which had been settled was never
allowed to die down. What was immediately important was
simply that parliament should make no unreasonable or
dangerous use of the authority it had acquired, and no administration would be better able to prevent this than one in which
Pitt worked together with the Whigs led by Rockingham.

But, above all else, the only man entitled to overthrow an
administration is one who can replace it by a better. And that
Pitt was unable to do this was to be most strikingly demonstrated by the utter fiasco of the Chatham ministry.

CHAPTER XI

THE FIASCO OF THE
CHATHAM MINISTRY

SINCE giving up his post as Secretary of State in the autumn
of 1761, Pitt had lived for the most part on his estate at
Hayes, in Kent, which he had bought in 1756. The place
was far enough from London to let him enjoy the peace of a
country life and withdraw whenever he wished from contemporary politics, and yet near enough to allow him to reach
Westminster in a few hours. With the annual pension of £3,000
which George had settled on him he could have lived a comfortable and carefree life had not his extravagance and weakness for sumptuous display, particularly his mania for building,
repeatedly driven him into financial straits. But his luck held.
An unexpected legacy came to him in 1765 for the second time
in his life. An old country gentleman, Sir William Pynsent, who
had voted against the Peace of Utrecht half a century before
and had never been able to stomach it since, heard in Pitt's
struggle against the Peace of Paris an echo of the campaigns of
his own youth, and he showed his appreciation by making Pitt
his heir. The principal part of the bequest was the rich estate
of Burton Pynsent in Somerset, which brought in £3,000 a year
and gave Pitt a magnificent country seat with a park and farm-
land attached. In the years which followed he often went here
to live; of course, this place too had to be converted to his taste
and according to his own fancy, and once more he treated the
question of expense like a *grand seigneur*. He now liked to style
himself a 'Somersetshire by-stander', but only, of course, when
any call to action was unwelcome. On other occasions he could
write that though he was *buried* deep in Somersetshire, he was
not *dead*.

The Pitt family now boasted five children, three boys and
two girls, all born between 1755 and 1761. They were the apples
of their parents' eyes, and the constant topic of the letters they
wrote each other. Both father and mother gave their undivided
attention to bringing them up. The father pinned his highest

hopes on his second son, William, while he was still quite a youngster; William, born in 1759, was a far brighter child than any of his brothers and sisters, including his elder brother, John (born in 1756), and he shared all his father's interests with boyish enthusiasm. In the letter to Hester dated 22nd February, 1766, in which Pitt rejoiced over the repeal of the Stamp Act, he did not omit an affectionate reference to his children: 'Loves to the sweet babes, patriotic or not; though I hope impetuous William is not behind in feelings of that kind.'

But dearly as Pitt loved his children, he could not bear the noise that children always make. More and more a morbid nervousness of all noise was taking hold of him. This went so far that he had a private wing built which was out of bounds to the children. Eccentricities such as this showed that he suffered from other disorders besides gout, which even in these less hectic years returned again and again to plague him, forcing him to spend months at a time taking the waters at Bath in search of relief.

§

Pitt was in Bath when he received the King's letter of July 7th, which he rightly construed as a summons to form a Cabinet. '. . . I shall hasten to London as fast as I possibly can . . .' he declared in his reply of July 8th. And, in fact, he did set out with the utmost despatch as soon as ever he could, covering the intervening distance at a speed which at once filled Hester with the deepest anxiety when she heard about it. This anxiety was by no means unjustified. Pitt was not equal to the strain of the journey and fell ill on the day he reached London. And thus the very first day bears the imprint of the disaster in which his ministry was to end. He was still able to talk with the King on July 12th, and receive the commission to form a Cabinet. But three days later he was seized by a fever and had to retire hastily to a friend's house in Hampstead, still at that time quite a rural district, in order to escape the heat of the London summer. Here the fever at first abated but a stormy discussion with his brother-in-law, Temple, brought it on again.

As on all previous occasions, Pitt invited Temple to join his ministry. An invitation like this must needs sound rather surprising coming from a man who always stressed that in his eyes measures, not men, were what mattered. For Temple, just like his brother George, was sharply opposed to the repeal of the Stamp Act, and indeed, to Pitt's whole American policy. And so it is impossible to see how in practice the two men could ever have hit it off, if Temple had accepted Pitt's invitation. Was it, perhaps, merely a gesture of courtesy on Pitt's part, one which he could not well avoid making in view of their former political connection and his debt of gratitude towards Temple? If this were so, obviously Pitt ought to have welcomed a refusal which extricated him from an embarrassing position. Yet it was clear that exactly the opposite was true.

Temple discussed his reasons for refusing in letters to his brother George and his sister, Lady Chatham. In these he complained that Pitt would not allow him to bring his own friends along with him into the ministry and had, moreover, insisted on filling it with the people with whom he, Temple, essentially differed on many accounts, more especially during the last session—an obvious reference to American affairs. Had he joined the ministry, he said, he would have been a great cipher at the head of the Treasury, surrounded with other ciphers of a different complexion, all named by Mr. Pitt. '. . . I would not', he concluded, *go in like a child to come out like a fool.*

Wounded vanity cries out in every line of these letters. Temple considered his own political standing entitled him to bargain with Pitt as one equal with another. That Pitt denied him this equality, and claimed the sole right to determine who should make up the ministry, was in Temple's eyes a piece of presumption to which he would in no circumstances defer. However much he put himself in the wrong by it, it must be recognized that there was some real substance in his complaint. For what he was getting at was that Pitt's touchstone in choosing his Cabinet was not an agreement on policy among its members, nor the weight or capacity of the individuals concerned, but their readiness to bow to his will. This is much the same complaint as that Burke laid to the charge of this Cabinet some years later in his celebrated speech on American taxation (April 19th, 1774). Pitt, he said, had 'made an administration so checkered and speckled; he put together a piece of joinery so crossly indented and whimsically dove-tailed; a cabinet so variously inlaid; such a piece of diversified mosaic; such a

tesselated pavement without cement; here a bit of black stone
and there a bit of white; patriots and courtiers; King's Friends
and republicans; Whigs and Tories; treacherous friends and
open enemies; that it was indeed a very curious show, but
utterly unsafe to touch and unsure to stand on'.

Burke's luxuriant and picturesque rhetoric points to a basic,
fault not only in the way Pitt set about forming a ministry but
in his political methods in general. He was at one with the
King in his endeavour to destroy the existing parties. For the
King this did make sense, even if very dangerous sense; he
wanted, by destroying the parties, to destroy the centres where
political will was born, because then, of necessity, his own will
would alone command the field, thanks to his constitutional
position and the means of bribery and favouritism at the
Crown's disposal, by which he himself could create a personal
following at any time. But if, on the other hand, a solitary
statesman, who could at any time be dismissed, managed to
break up the parties, he created only a chaos or a vacuum,
indeed he threatened the very existence of Parliament, which
cannot live without the cut and thrust of debate, except in the
special conditions of a national crisis, where the country's need
welds all the parties together. An administration which is
united not by community of principles but solely by submission
to its leader can only consist of minds which 'wheel into line like
sergeants on parade', as Bismarck demanded of his ambassadors. But ministers like this will scurry and scamper pell-mell,
like ants in an upturned ant-hill, if the will-power which has
bound them together gives out. Such was the fate which actually
befell this ministry.

It is vain to scan the ranks of those summoned by Pitt in
search of a single point of policy on which they were of one
mind. Just as vain is it to look for outstanding political capacity
and experience in any of them. The Earl of Shelburne, who was
appointed Secretary of State for the Southern Department, had,
it is true, a head for politics, but he was a mere twenty-eight
years old and until then had only controlled the destinies of the
Board of Trade, an office of secondary importance, for a few
brief months. Once a friend of Bute's and Henry Fox's, he had
broken with each of them in turn. For some years he had been
an out-and-out supporter of Pitt, declining an invitation to join

the Rockingham ministry because Pitt did not sit in it. In American affairs at least his policy was plainly charted: he was against the Stamp Act and against the right of Parliament to tax America. Thus his attitude was the same as that of Camden, whom Pitt now made Lord Chancellor. Another young aristocrat, the thirty-one-year-old Duke of Grafton, a descendant of the line started by a son of Charles II and Barbara Villiers, became First Lord of the Treasury and formal head of the Cabinet. He, too, was so uncompromising a supporter of Pitt that he had broken up the Rockingham ministry on his account. But he lacked experience and—what was to be of fateful consequence for himself and his country—character. He had possessed insight enough to struggle to the utmost of his ability against accepting an office to which he knew he was not equal, and had yielded only in the face of Chatham's threat to relinquish the whole project otherwise. In the Commons the new administration was represented by two ministers, General Conway as Secretary of State, and Charles Townshend at the Exchequer. Pitt took over Conway from the Rockingham ministry. He was a gallant officer, but in politics hardly more than a well-meaning amateur. Charles Townshend possessed the most brilliant talents and could hold the Commons utterly spellbound by his eloquence. But he was unprincipled and, above all, as moody and capricious as a pampered beauty; no one could predict on any one day what he would be about on the morrow, or, indeed, where he would land up at the end of one of his spirited and witty speeches.

But Pitt could maintain that all this was of no importance since to a man these ministers were to be nothing more than his tools. Indeed he treated them quite openly more as secretaries than as colleagues. A few days after the ministry's formation, the Prussian Ambassador reported how Pitt, immediately after being received by the King, held a levée of his own in the antechamber. He gathered his ministers around him and handed each of them a small slip of paper, with which the gentlemen withdrew into a corner like schoolboys whom their master has given some work to do. The Ambassador labelled the incident a symptom of the subordination in which Pitt kept his ministers, to whom he issued his orders like a general addressing his subordinates. So Temple had been quite right when he envisaged ciphers which were to be affixed to one single numeral. One can understand Grafton's lament that Pitt never condescended to explain the broad aims of his policy to the Cabinet.

For himself Pitt did not choose the office traditionally linked with the leadership of the administration; he first offered the Treasury to Temple and then installed Grafton there. He himself took the office of Lord Privy Seal, the very post that Newcastle had taken over in the Rockingham ministry to underline the fact that he was simply the grey-headed counsellor to his younger colleagues.

But Pitt crowned all these errors by letting himself be created Earl of Chatham and leaving the Commons, where he had laid the foundations of his fame and popularity and where the roots of his power lay, for the Lords. That by doing this he sacrificed his popularity at one blow, even in the City which, until now, had stood by him through thick and thin, is perhaps not in itself the most important thing. What is, rather, more significant is that he had not learned the lesson which Walpole had mastered and demonstrated a generation earlier—that Britain's parliamentary government can only be conducted from the Commons. The English people showed an instinctive grasp of this principle when they dubbed Pitt the Great Commoner, and they stood by this principle by withdrawing their confidence from Pitt for voluntarily giving up his seat in the Commons. Broadly speaking, it must be said that at every point where Walpole had furthered Britain's constitutional development Pitt took a big step back. Walpole falls short of Pitt in genius to just the same extent as he excels him in clear, statesmanlike vision. The country's later constitutional development, which has made England a political model for Europe, followed the lines laid down by Walpole. But Pitt smoothed the path for George III's experiment in personal government which interrupted and seriously threatened constitutional development. He persuaded himself that he possessed George's entire confidence and could therefore count on the blind obedience not only of the ministers but of Parliament as well. Such was his misreading of the King and of the critical constitutional problem too.

To be sure, one could defend Pitt's acceptance of an earldom on the grounds that his shattered health would no longer sustain the exhausting activity of the Commons with their long sittings, which often went on far into the night. This argument meets in retrospect the objection raised by Temple the year before that his system was not sound. But, after all, Pitt himself had long been well aware of this brake upon his parliamentary activity; he should have thought of it before refusing Rockingham's invitation to join the government.

But Pitt cannot be properly sized up without taking into account the attraction he found in the proud title of 'Earl'. Pomp and circumstance made up the very air he breathed. His way of life was that of a *grand seigneur*, driving four in hand with a retinue of liveried lackeys trailing along behind him, and he felt he must mingle as an equal with the great noble families into which he had married.

Quite apart from all these serious blunders which Pitt made in forming his ministry, it still seems reasonably clear that it had but scant prospects of great achievements or long life, even if Pitt himself had remained free from serious illness. But as things turned out he was not able to keep up even a pretence of leading it for more than a few months. At Christmas, 1766, he left London to take the cure for his gout at Bath. Throughout the whole of his subsequent formal tenure of office only once again, in March 1767, did he return to the seat of government, and even then he was for the most part confined to his bed, having after a few days to retreat afresh to the solitude of Hampstead. Even during the few months before Christmas, which can be regarded as his effective period of administration, the ministry was already cracking at all its joints. A slight which one of the Whigs left over from the Rockingham ministry suffered at his hands led to the resignation of almost all the rest. If George rejoiced at this, one can well understand it. If Chatham accepted it with equanimity, then it only shows that in overestimating himself he had already lost touch with realities. He filled the posts which had fallen vacant with Tories and followers of Bute, among them Jenkinson (later Lord Liverpool), once Bute's very adroit and very formidable secretary and the real leader of the 'King's Friends' in the Commons. This, too, was very much after George's own heart; but by doing this Pitt put paid to the last chance that the ministry would go forward along lines of his own choosing.

The brief duration of Chatham's effective leadership of the ministry made it impossible for him to carry out a programme. But it was long enough to bring him several defeats, for instance in foreign policy. He at once set to work on the programme he had laid down in advance: concluding a treaty with Prussia. He knew that Frederick had spoken of him with appreciation during the war and had been indignant at his fall from power. He believed that he still possessed Frederick's confidence and he counted on his outstretched hand being grasped at once. But here his judgement of Frederick was completely at fault. True, Frederick still considered Pitt the only English minister who was a real politician. But in view of the frequent ministerial re-shufflings under George III, he had serious doubts about the duration of Pitt's ministry; he had obviously heard from his London representatives of the bad impression which Pitt's elevation to the peerage had made, and he told the British ambassador bluntly that he was afraid Pitt had done himself a lot of harm by it. But probably this difficulty could have been surmounted if Frederick had at all favoured the view that an alliance with England would benefit Prussia. In 1764, however, he had concluded an alliance with the Czarina Catherine in order to take his place at the imminent partition of Poland. This, he believed, made him strong enough to sit back quietly and await developments. On the other hand, he feared that an alliance with England would lead to a renewed *rapprochement* between France and Austria, such as he had faced after the Westminster Convention of 1756. So he brushed aside the feelers from London. Chatham was forced to admit to himself that even his own reappearance on the scene was not sufficient to divert foreign policy from the course initiated by the Peace of Paris.

Another problem which the Seven Years' War had brought to a head was India, and this also became acute during the Chatham administration. Clive's victories over the French and their allies had so extended its frontiers that the East India Company was changing its character. It was no longer predominantly a trading venture but had become the ruler of vast territories and millions of people. The question was whether Britain should leave things as they were or should herself take over the administration of this huge colonial empire. Earlier on

Clive himself had brought the point to Chatham's notice. It might be thought that it would be in keeping with Chatham's active temperament if he had taken up a question like this with vigour and had settled it conclusively. But instead he simply gave a display of irresolution, hesitation and nerveless fumbling.

Certainly the problem was knotty enough. Enormous political and financial interests were involved. A decision against the Company was bound to antagonize the City, where most of the shareholders were installed and wielded influence. If the Indian revenues were to be allowed to pour in to the Crown, then that might mean a dangerous increase in its power and influence. The more serious and tangled the problem, the more imperative the need for a clear, bold lead from the foremost statesman of the day. But although Chatham quite saw the outstanding importance of the question, he shied away from taking any initiative. He wanted the matter to be debated and decided by Parliament and to take part in the deliberations purely as a private member. He assigned the ministers no higher task than the prevention of unreasonable or high-handed decisions. He explained this to Clive's agent in Bath in October 1766, at a time, that is, when he was still active and his authority had not yet been impaired. If, to all intents and purposes, he thus early shelved his responsibility in a matter which he well knew to be of the greatest national concern, it is not surprising that later, as he degenerated more and more into a mere figurehead, he allowed every minister to act on his own responsibility; with the result that the most active and unscrupulous of them all, and the most influential Commoner among them, Charles Townshend, took things into his own hands and brought about a solution which was really no solution at all but a mere expedient, which clashed with every single idea which Chatham had on the subject.

Charles Townshend had at first taken much persuading before accepting Pitt's offer of the Exchequer. He had long ago grown used to being offered a post by every prime minister of whatever persuasion, not only because he belonged to one of the greatest Whig families—he was a kinsman of Newcastle and a grandson of the Townshend who for years had shared power with Walpole—but because he was really a very talented man. He had ideas and could put them forward in such a way that the House hung on his lips as if spellbound. He had succeeded Holland as Paymaster-General and had not the least desire to exchange this attractive office, which brought him in seven thousand pounds a year, for the much more exacting post at the Exchequer, where he would have to make do with a paltry two thousand five hundred. When he subsequently allowed himself to be talked round, he was at first so powerfully influenced by Chatham's personality that he confessed that he now realized for the first time what a very much greater man Chatham was than he and all the others.

But this impression very quickly faded away when he noticed how far Chatham fell short of giving the lead required. He had never concealed the fact that on the American issue he stood far closer to George Grenville than to Pitt, and if Pitt, despite this, had no qualms over giving him the Exchequer, Townshend in his turn had none about pursuing a financial policy in America which suited his own ideas. He cannot be reproached with having deceived anyone about his views and intentions; still less can Chatham be excused on the score of being in the dark about Townshend's plans. As early as the end of January, 1767, Townshend had told Parliament that he was planning taxes for America and that in principle he was in agreement with the Stamp Act; on this occasion he openly attacked Chatham's pet theory by calling the distinction between internal and external taxation an absurd one. Shelburne, who supported a policy completely opposed to this in all respects, at once gave Chatham a detailed report of the rebellion of his Chancellor of the Exchequer and appealed to him for help. But Chatham's answer contained only touching complaints about the difficulties mounting up on both sides of the Atlantic and never a word of decision or reproof for Townshend. Time and again Shelburne sued for aid, always in vain. Then, at the end of February, the administration suffered a heavy defeat in Parliament. The former Chancellor of the Exchequer in the Rockingham Cabinet, which had recently fallen, moved a resolution to reduce the land tax. Townshend opposed it, but so halfheartedly that the motion was adopted by a majority. This was said to have been the first time since the revolution that a ministry had been defeated on a money bill.

Now at last Chatham pulled himself together. He had left

Bath in the middle of February but had only got as far as Marlborough, where he took to his bed in a hostelry while his lackeys in their blue and silver liveries swarmed over the town and set passing travellers agape. He now continued his journey and arrived in London early in March. The gout had not yet left him; whether his condition was really so bad that he could not even obey a summons from the King to visit him at once cannot be determined. At all events, he put off his first audience until March 12th. In the meantime he had cast about for a fresh Chancellor of the Exchequer. Among others he had offered the post to Lord North, who, as George III's confidant and prime minister, was later to bear the chief responsibility for the American War. But North had declined and another politician had followed his example. What did Chatham do then? He folded his arms and did nothing. He, who at the historic meeting of October 2nd, 1761, had cast in the teeth of his colleagues the declaration, 'I will be responsible for nothing that I do not direct,' now kept in office a Chancellor who openly proposed to flout the Pitt policy on the most important question of the day.

On the same day that Chatham had his first audience of George, a Cabinet meeting took place at which Townshend boldly flung down the gauntlet to his opponents; his colleagues he threatened point blank with open opposition if they did not do what he wanted. Grafton and Shelburne, in a state of some agitation at the way things had gone at the meeting, gave Chatham, who had not been present, an account of the proceedings. Shelburne believed he had found the key to Townshend's attitude when he heard that North had himself told Townshend how he had refused the post. 'It appears to me,' he wrote, 'quite impossible that Mr. Townshend can mean to go on in the King's service.' He could hardly urge Chatham more plainly to show the dissident Chancellor the door. But Chatham declared that he was too ill to do anything and left London for Hampstead, where he immediately took to his bed once more. Thenceforth he completely relinquished all ministerial activity. This was bad enough, but what was worse still was that he did not at the same time vacate the office which he no longer administered, but held it for a full eighteen months longer.

Here is the nadir of Chatham's career. What a tragedy that

the man who had said of himself: 'I am sure I can save this country, and nobody else can,' whom King and people had with one voice summoned to the head of affairs, could now no longer exercise his power but had to withdraw into the sickroom, broken in body and mind! There can be no doubt that Chatham was seriously ill. To all appearances the gout had now affected his internal organs and even attacked the brain. His penchant for solitude assumed the most morbid forms. At the end of May, 1767, a most urgent letter from the King induced Chatham to receive Grafton in his Hampstead sickroom. The Duke was utterly staggered by the spectacle of complete collapse which met his eyes. Chatham's nerves and mind were affected to a shocking degree. He obviously suffered severely from being compelled to conduct a serious interview and Grafton had to rest content with a few scraps of extremely general advice which were of very little help to him. A few months later, in July, 1767, Chatham's condition was described by an apparently well-informed correspondent of George Grenville's in these terms: 'He sits most part of the day leaning his head down upon his hands, which are rested on the table. Lady Chatham does not continue generally in the room; if he wants anything, he knocks with his stick; he says little, even to her, if she comes in; and is so averse to speaking, that he commonly intimates his desire to be left alone by some signal rather than by any expression. The physicians, however, say there is nothing in his disorder which he may not recover, but do not pretend to say there is any prospect of its being soon.'

Again one asks oneself: why did he not lay down his office then? One may concede that at times his mind was so completely clouded over that he was not even able to realize for himself how impossible his position was. But this was not continuously the case. Without a doubt he enjoyed at least an occasional lucid moment when he knew how things stood with him. Grafton, Shelburne and the King asked him again and again for decisions on urgent matters. The answer normally took the form of a note written by Hester in which Chatham lamented, with emphasis, his illness and complete inability to deal with any state affairs. But it became known in London that at times his mind was quite clear and brisk. An architect, whom Grafton had sent out to Hayes in the summer of 1768 to

discuss a few alterations to be made there, related that Chatham
had shown him round and discussed everything with the most
lively interest and complete good sense. What was even more
significant was that when he went out to Hayes a second time,
and was taken to task by Lady Chatham for presuming to give
such a wrong impression of her husband's mental state, she herself had to admit that at times he was quite well.

Moreover, Chatham must have realized full well that,
politics apart, he was not even performing his very minor duties
as Lord Privy Seal. In January, 1768, a matter arose which
demanded his attention, and when Chatham refused to take
official action on the grounds of his illness the peer concerned
threatened to ventilate the question in the Lords. This would,
of course, have been very unpleasant for the other ministers.
But instead of seizing this chance and finally laying down his
office, Chatham allowed a highly complicated expedient to be
adopted by which his seal was handed over to a commission of
three which functioned in his stead. After this official act the
seal had to be brought back to Chatham in March by the Lord
Chancellor and half-a-dozen members of the Privy Council—
and he accepted it!

All that is known of Chatham's state of health in these
unhappy eighteen months points forcibly to the conclusion that
at times he was well able to realize how impossible, how un-
justifiable it was for him to remain in office. Even if he did not
read all the letters written to him from London, he cannot have
been ignorant all the time that a policy was being pursued there
which sheltered under his name but was bringing discredit upon
it. Chatham must have recognized quite clearly that the
ministry, which still bore his name, was gradually undergoing a
transformation which was radically altering its character. At
the end of 1767 Bedford's followers had entered the ministry as
a united band, occupied two of the most important Cabinet
posts and thanks to their unity were gaining decisive influence.
This was utterly at variance with Chatham's policy of breaking
up the parties, for not only were the 'Bedford Whigs' a recognized party, but they were also a positive prototype of the kind
of party which Chatham most strenuously warred against.
Personal interest far more than political agreement bound
them together, and their political aims, in so far as they had

any, were the exact opposite of Chatham's, especially where America was concerned. Yet Chatham clung to his post and permitted such people as Lord Weymouth and the parliamentary adventurer Rigby to shelter behind his name. A man in his position and with his great past could choose between only two alternatives. Either he could intervene, cast out the men who were acting against his interest and settle his own policy, or, if this were not possible for mental and physical reasons, he could resign.

Since he took neither course he cannot be absolved of responsibility for what his ministry did. This applies most strongly to the taxes which Townshend imposed upon goods exported to America, particularly tea, taxes which were to be collected by British Customs officials in American ports (June, 1767). This was the most disastrous step which a British administration and a British parliament could take, for at one blow it destroyed all Rockingham had achieved by the repeal of the Stamp Act. Of course it is very much open to question whether the secession of the American colonies could have been prevented in the long run in any case. But the only possible way of preventing it would have been by inspiring the Americans with confidence in the justice and fairness of British policy, as Rockingham had tried to do in accord with Pitt. But a zig-zag policy, which gives today what it withheld yesterday and takes it away again tomorrow, must inevitably lurch into catastrophe. Chatham, and Chatham alone, made this zig-zag policy possible. He it was who overthrew the Rockingham Cabinet which was acting on the right lines. He it was who formed the new Cabinet which took the wrong turning, and he it was who did nothing to restrain the Cabinet which bore his name from persevering in the paths of error.

A comparison of the irresolution of which he gave signs even before this crowning illness and, on the other hand, of the rapidity with which he recovered after he had at last gone out of office in October, 1768, clearly points to the conclusion that there was a still closer interaction between office and illness: the feeling of not being equal to the problems of office aggravated his illness—and the illness had to serve him as an excuse for avoiding decisions to which he could not brace himself. This seems a far cry from his great, historic achievements. But one set of qualities is needed to tackle the specific problem set by a war with vigour, verve and inspiration: quite a different set is needed for framing one's own policy by choosing from among several possible solutions the one which promises to pay the highest dividends. That Chatham's *forte* did not lie here had already been indicated by his inconsistency in the days before he became a secretary of state. Perhaps, none the less, in those earlier days of better health he might have been able to fix on a policy of his own, but from 1766 to 1768, during which time he reached the age of sixty, he was certainly incapable of it.

What is tragic, painful even, about all this is that Chatham did not recognize his own limitations, drugged as he was by the fumes of the incense which the public burned before him. One may wonder—but not determine—how much his irresponsible clinging to office was due to the large salary involved, which he could not do without because of his extravagant way of living. Even here pathological symptoms appear. He had, for example, sold his Hayes estate in order to develop Burton Pynsent. But as early as the following year he was gripped by an uncontrollable urge to get it back, although this plunged him into incalculable expense. Even when the buyer, who had in the meantime poured many thousands of pounds into it, offered to let him live there, this did not satisfy him.

On October 12th, 1768, Chatham asked Grafton to carry his resignation to the King. The immediate occasion of this was that Grafton wished to drop Shelburne, the one remaining minister who could be considered as representing Chatham's point of view. Grafton would have liked to talk the matter over with Chatham in person and to this end he went to Hayes, but he had to rest content with seeing Hester, who could only tell him that her husband did not agree to Shelburne's dismissal. But at this interview Grafton had at least been able to make the comment that he had no further hope of Chatham's taking part in the business of the administration. Chatham's answer was his request to resign, and from this he could not be dissuaded, even by a personal letter from the King.

George had every reason for wanting the administration to continue in the form it had assumed during the last year and a half. More than any other single factor, it had brought him nearer his goal of governing the country himself. What could

M

be more congenial to him than an administration sporting the name of the most eminent statesman in the land but really controlled solely by the King? Who could defy him in a Cabinet containing no man of independent weight—Charles Townshend having died in September, 1767—and where every man's hand was against his neighbour? The majority of the ministry now consisted of 'King's Friends', including North, who had entered upon Townshend's inheritance, and Bedford's followers, who were accustomed to think only of their own jobs. If this administration could enjoy a permanent majority in Parliament, then George had accomplished the mission which his mother had constantly dinned into him when a child with her cry of 'George, be a King!' The power of the King would then once more be as strong as in the days of James II, and the British crown would bid fair to achieve a position analogous to that of the German monarchy under the Kaiser prior to 1918.

Such were the fruits of the Chatham ministry.

CHAPTER XII

THE MIDDLESEX ELECTION

I N the spring of 1768, when the administration could still boast the name of Chatham, there had been a general election. The outcome was well calculated to warm George's heart, and fill him with confidence that he would never be without a majority in Parliament while he used methods which he himself damned as corruption as long as they were wielded by Newcastle, methods to which he now took no exception. If there was anything at all to distinguish his tactics from Newcastle's, it was only that his own were even more blatant and shameless. Never were constituencies bartered more unscrupulously than in the election of 1768. Army contractors, bloated with war profits, and East Indian adventurers who had piled up fortunes knew of no better investment for their capital than a seat in the Commons, which offered such golden prospects of advancement. These gentlemen were not exactly weighed down by political principles, which would have been only an encumbrance under a régime which had outlawed the parties. It was enough to be one of the 'King's Friends' and to vote as Jenkinson or North directed. Newcastle, now an old man of 75, had defended the seats of his friends in the Rockingham group with all his former verve and so much organizing skill that they were roughly in their old position. It was his last election. A few months later death put a term to a life which was certainly not as useless and undignified as it has often been depicted to posterity.

Among the new members there were two of whom George was to hear a great deal more. One was the nineteen-year-old Charles James Fox, and the other a figure from the past, John Wilkes.

The hero of the *North Briton* Number 45 and the focus of so much controversy had never really settled down to exile in France. When Grafton, who had formerly been one of his supporters and had visited him in the Tower, became a minister, Wilkes turned to him in 1766, begging him to let the past be forgotten and grant him a pardon. Grafton had placed the letter before Chatham, who had advised him to do nothing. This advice was neither prudent nor courageous. The sensible course would have been to spike Wilkes's guns by pardoning him, but that would have meant struggling to penetrate the thick skull of His Majesty and Chatham did not want the matter to go as far as that. So Grafton had given Wilkes an evasive answer, and Wilkes had gone back to Paris. And now, in 1768, he came to England, determined to become as sharp a thorn in the side of those who had left him in the lurch as he possibly could. He had to reckon with the risk of being indicted for his old offences. But he took the chance. He stood for a seat in the City and, unsuccessful there, transferred his candidature to Middlesex, one of the few constituencies where there were independent voters and a real election. It was at once plain that during his years of exile his popularity with the masses had not abated a jot. The old battle-cry of 'Wilkes and Liberty!' rang out again, and a slip of paper marked 'Number 45' was the only ticket of admission to the polls at Brentford. Wilkes triumphed by a large majority over his ministerial opponents, and on the night of his victory all who were anxious not to have their windows smashed by the mob had to illuminate their houses. The London glaziers rubbed their hands: had not this Middlesex election brought them more business in a single night than all the Indian victories put together?

Proof of Wilkes's return to the status of a popular hero was given when the legal machine, halting and creaking, was set in motion against him. He had to contrive, despite his followers, who were all for putting him at the head of a triumphal procession, to make his way to prison by stealth. His popularity was still further increased, if this were possible, by the sentence passed on him by Mansfield, which deprived him of his freedom for twenty-two months and made him pay a fine of one thousand pounds for two literary productions now more than five years old. Small wonder that the masses looked on Wilkes as a martyr, sacrificed to the malice of the King and—inseparable from him in the eyes of the people—of Bute.

George had, in fact, already shown that he would contribute to enhancing Wilkes' political importance as much as possible. As a member of Parliament Wilkes could certainly not prove a danger to the administration, which had so large a majority that the loss of one vote was of no moment at all. Wilkes carried no great weight as a speaker and the applause of the Commons would doubtless be very much more half-hearted than that of the public. Moreover, a man accustomed to live by begging and borrowing could hardly in the long run play a big rôle in the House. Any counsellor with an ounce of political wisdom would have advised George to disregard the member for Middlesex. But the position of a minister was not yet one which entitled its holder to give the King advice, but one in which he obediently received the King's orders and carried them out. A few weeks after Wilkes had been returned, George gave North, who led the Commons, the express command to have the member for Middlesex expelled from the House.

And this was done. For various reasons some months were to elapse before the motion was debated, long enough, in any event, for wiser counsels to have prevailed. But George stopped his ears to them and so, in consequence, did his 'friends'. On February 3rd, 1769, the Commons decided on the expulsion of Wilkes by 219 votes to 137, after a debate in which the injustice of this step was pointed out not only by Burke but by George Grenville as well. Grenville, who had led the first persecution of Wilkes, now made a speech which did him all honour, attacking both the legality and the political wisdom of this thinly-veiled act of revenge on the part of the King.

The issue thus turned on something more than John Wilkes himself; it touched the right of electors freely to choose their members, indeed, the very constitution itself. The next move lay with the electors of Middlesex, and they were quite ready to show George that they could be as obstinate as he and would not let themselves be imposed on even by the House of Commons, should it stoop to become the obsequious tool of a king's caprice. The wealthiest and most prominent electors took the lead and proposed that Wilkes should be re-elected, and no one even ventured to stand as a candidate against him. Naturally, the House again expelled the new member and, equally naturally, the people of Middlesex re-elected him. After this game had been repeated several times, the ministers induced a Colonel Luttrell to enter the lists as a candidate against Wilkes and go through with it. Wilkes defeated him by 1143 votes to

196. But the administration now moved a resolution to declare Luttrell duly elected, and the Commons adopted the motion by 197 votes to 143. This resolution at least had the merit of originality. The right of the Commons to exclude a member as unsuitable was theoretically unchallenged, ridiculous and odious as it was in practice in the Wilkes case. But the right to declare a man elected who was not elected had never been claimed by the House nor could it make such a claim without striking at the very roots of the constitution. 'The arbitrary appointment of Mr. Luttrell invades the foundation of the laws themselves, as it manifestly transfers the right of legislation from those whom the people have chosen to those whom they have rejected. With a succession of such appointments we may soon see a House of Commons collected, in the choice of which the other towns and counties of England will have as little share as the devoted county of Middlesex.' Thus wrote the most widely-read pamphleteer of the day who concealed his identity under the name of Junius.

The Letters of Junius owe some part of the sensational interest which they enjoyed in their own day, and for some years afterwards, to the impenetrable mystery in which their author contrived to envelop himself. 'Stat nominis umbra' was the motto with which he prefaced his letters, and later generations have put their minds to solving the riddle of the name covered by this shadow. Although no entirely convincing proof has ever been given, it is now generally accepted that *Junius* was Philip Francis, who occupied a post in the War Office at the time, and was later celebrated for the obstinate and spirited campaign which, as a member of the East India Company's Council in Bengal, he waged against Warren Hastings, the Governor-General. But it would be a mistake to use this insoluble mystery to explain away the effectiveness of *The Letters of Junius*, for this was mainly due to the way they expressed, with reckless audacity and in most highly polished style, what thousands felt and thought. It must be admitted that the mysterious author had a predilection for appealing to the baser instincts. His readers' appetite for scandal could find no more piquant food than the malicious and envenomed invective which *Junius* hurled not only against the ministers' and courtiers' public lives, but against their private lives as well. In this branch of the pamphleteer's art he was a past master. Grafton, for example, never recovered throughout his life from the wounds which *Junius's* deadly thrusts dealt to his reputation. Such personal excesses make *Junius's* writings just as little to the taste of later historians as they were attractive to many of his contemporaries. But it would be unjust to forget, amid these shortcomings, the sureness of aim and the trenchancy with which he defended the British constitution against its most dangerous foes, not least against the King himself, and elevated the battles of the day to the dignity of a struggle for principles.

The Middlesex electors refused to put up with the representative who had been foisted upon them, and sent Parliament a barbed petition and remonstrance. It came up for discussion on May 8th, 1769, in the Commons. The most distinguished and eloquent lawyers now employed all their skill. Burke shattered the government spokesman with the full force of his mighty rhetoric and the profusion of his political ideas. Even though the opposition were defeated on the division, intellectual and oratorical superiority seemed unquestionably to lie with them. Then a black-haired, dark-eyed young fellow of twenty got up to measure his skill with Edmund Burke and his brilliant legal allies, and as he ended his speech amid the rapt attention of the House, friend and foe alike agreed that the ministers had found a parliamentary champion who could try conclusions with the greatest and most experienced speakers in the House.

This young man, scarcely more than a boy, was Holland's second surviving son, Charles James Fox. His father had found him astonishingly mature even as a young child. He clung to him with an almost idolatrous love as can be seen in every one of his letters. Charles was barely three when his father wrote to his mother: 'I dined at home today, *tête-à-tête* with Charles, intending to do business; but he has found me pleasanter employment. . . .' Next day he wrote again, 'I grow immoderately fond of him'. The more doubtful side to his affection was that it made Holland completely incapable of opposing the child in any whim or misbehaviour. This powerlessness is best illustrated by the well-known story of his reply to Charles when the boy expressed a wish to destroy a valuable watch, 'Well! If you must, I suppose you must,' answered the weak father. Henry Fox had no inkling of the wisdom of the saw: 'It is a precious thing for a man to have worn chains in his youth.' His mother lost all authority over him as a teacher when Charles, at the age of six, caught her out making a mistake in Roman history.

Charles grew up in the most beautiful surroundings in Holland House and its fascinating park. Since 1762 the family had spent every summer at a seaside property which Henry Fox had acquired—Kingsgate on the cliffs of the North Foreland, where later Margate and Ramsgate developed. Of course, Charles went to Eton, like his father before him. He was accompanied there by a tutor, the Rev. Dr. Francis, father of the Philip Francis who is now believed to have written *The Letters of Junius*. Charles was at Eton from his ninth to his fourteenth year. With his great talent he rapidly learned all that Eton had to teach him, particularly the classics. For this he was grateful to his old school throughout his life, and even when a man of fifty he wrote that only those who had been at Eton could have a correct notion of Greek, or even Latin, metre. Personally, too, this was a happy period in his life. His liveliness and irresistible charm made him a favourite with his schoolfellows.

In these years, from 1758 to 1763, Henry Fox was accumulating his riches as Paymaster, and soon after that Charles was to taste of the adversity which overtook his father. In the spring of 1763 came the catastrophe which put a premature end to the political career of Henry Fox, or Lord Holland as he had since become. When, to assuage his bitter disappointment, he set out on his travels, he yearned for the company of his favourite son, and Charles, obedient to his father's wishes, left Eton before his school days were really finished and his character moulded. This was perhaps the greatest misfortune of his outwardly happy youth. Travel on the Continent meant visiting a city like Paris with all its seductive pleasures, and fashionable spas where the gilded youth and the hardened *roués* of Western Europe foregathered. In particular it involved nights of gaming at the faro-tables where grizzled sinners plucked green youths. The boy plunged into this whirl, and his doting father filled and refilled his purse with gold so that he might amuse himself to his heart's content. Here Holland should have taken warning from his experience with his eldest son, Stephen, already an inveterate gambler, whom his father had constantly to prise from the clutches of his creditors.

None the less, it is a proof of Charles being sound at the core that after the untimely distractions of the summer he was able to return to Eton. But it is understandable that Eton would hardly suit him now. None the less he seems to have applied himself to his books with a will once more, and the Headmaster was extremely anxious that he should not be absent on Speech Day, when the school wished to parade his powers of elocution. It is typical of the unusual relationship between father and son that Charles felt constrained to make a formal apology to his father for not wishing to interrupt his schooling again. 'I am convinced you will willingly consent to spend six weeks less agreeably, to make me a much better scholar than I should otherwise be, which is a glory you know I very much desire.' Holland did actually visit Eton on Speech Day to hear his Charles speak, and the boy made use of his holidays to scamper off to Parliament as often as possible, where he followed closely all he could still learn of the art of speaking. 'Charles', wrote Holland to his wife, 'will hardly come from the House of Commons before I am in bed.'

In the autumn of 1764 he went up to Oxford. There, too, it was regrettable that well-to-do young men gambled heavily, and again and again Charles let himself be drawn into the vortex, often as he had vowed to shun cards and the dice-box. For all that, he took his studies in deadly earnest. Besides the classics he studied mathematics and French. It is not surprising that, wishing to get a thorough grounding in the language, he should go to Paris for a few months and there slip back into the old life. Even then he must have been a remarkable young man. No less a personage than David Hume, the great philosopher and historian, who was at that time Secretary to the British Embassy in Paris, took notice of the sixteen-year-old boy. He referred with approval to his knowledge, his force of mind and his manly way of thinking, but added with a sigh that he feared the dissipation of Parisian life 'might check his ardour after useful knowledge and lose, in all appearance, a very great acquisition to the public'.

If it was possible to make yet another blunder in Charles Fox's upbringing, then this was to take him away from Oxford before he had completed his studies there. He enjoyed life at this ancient seat of learning not only because here, as everywhere, friends and admirers clustered round him on all sides, but even more because the development of his mental powers in serious work made him happy. A few years of work like this would have given him the maturity, the education and the knowledge which his unusual gifts deserved, and would have given his character enough strength for him to plunge without danger into the main stream of life.

But once again his father's blind love upset his peaceful development. In the spring of 1766 Charles, a bare seventeen, left Oxford for good and wandered round the Continent for over two years. He spent some months in Nice as company for his sick father, who always perked up when his darling boy was at his side with his wit, his gaiety, his conversation. From Nice he went to Genoa, Bologna, Florence, Rome and above all to Paris again. Wherever he went all doors were open to this distinguished, wealthy, talented and open-handed young Englishman; he moved in both the best and the worst circles, and poured out huge sums in buying stylish and extravagant clothes and even more in gambling. True, even in these wild years of lighthearted prodigality he knew more solemn hours when he buried himself with enthusiasm and discrimination in the beauties of the Italian poets, in Ariosto and Dante, and learned the languages of the countries in which he scattered his money. But none the less it was a thoroughly bad preparation for a young man who was to return home from these travels and step straight into his place in his country's Senate.

Nor was his political grounding much better: as a devoted son he sat at his father's feet. But what could Holland teach an impressionable young man, whose soul burned with a flame as likely to consume as to give light? The older Holland grew, the more of a cynic he became, greeting political ideals and principles with nothing more than a satanic grin. By the end of his days he had sunk to be a devotee of naked and unadulterated power. In July, 1767, he had his last audience with George III, whom he implored—as unsuccessfully as ever—to make him an earl. He took this opportunity of preaching to George the brutal doctrine of using ruthlessly all the means the Crown possessed to punish and reward in order to build up a compliant Parliament against which no opposition would have any prospect of success —to a certain extent the practice which he himself had followed at the Peace of Paris and made into a system of government. Then, he said, the King could make any of his lords-in-waiting a minister. These cheerless words of wisdom the studious Charles must also have heard from his father's lips. What a long road he was to travel before he became the inspired and inspiring prophet of freedom and the inalienable rights of man!

What his father told him about the politicians of the day, too, was hardly calculated to give him the right lead. The only politician of whom Holland still approved was Bute, a failure like himself. George Grenville, whom he had never been able to tolerate, he now loathed. That he had not a good word to say for his old rival, Chatham, who had now overtaken him on the social ladder, goes without saying. But even more than the members of the old families, he hated the *parvenus* who presumed to raise themselves by audacious newspaper articles and on the shoulders of the mob. That Wilkes should stand for Middlesex, where he himself resided, he regarded as an offence in his nostrils. Holland House became Luttrell's headquarters, and Stephen Fox, Holland's eldest son, insisted on proposing Luttrell to the Brentford voters from the hustings. Stephen was elected to Parliament at the same time as his brother, and there also he championed the Luttrell cause. Thus too was Charles's standpoint fixed for him.

History does not record what striking or bewildering arguments Charles Fox advanced for a bad cause. All that is known is that he made a great impression and was recognized on all sides as a debater of the first order. Holland wrote in high glee: 'I am told (and I willingly believe it), Charles Fox spoke extremely well. It was all off-hand, all argumentative, in reply to Mr. Burke and Mr. Wedderburn . . . I hear it spoke of by everybody as a most extraordinary thing. . . .'

Certainly this sensational success owed much to the staggering self-confidence with which the young orator attacked the seasoned gladiators of the parliamentary arena. It was the self-confidence of a youth who had grown up in the conviction that he 'belonged' to the families which considered that it was their vocation and their privilege to rule the country.

CHAPTER XIII

CHATHAM AND THE WHIG OPPOSITION.
CHARLES FOX'S YOUTHFUL FEATS

A STILL greater sensation than the debut of the precocious
newcomer in the political arena was caused some weeks
later by the reappearance of a belaurelled old gladiator
whom everyone had considered a spent force. 'You desired me
to write, if I knew anything particular. How particular will
content you?' wrote Horace Walpole on July 7th, 1769,
'. . . Come, would the apparition of my Lord Chatham satisfy
you? Don't be frightened; it was not his ghost. He, he himself
in propriâ personâ, . . . walked into the King's levée this morning,
and was in the Closet twenty minutes after the levée. . . .'

Chatham had recovered with astonishing rapidity after
finally casting off the burden and responsibility of office.
Hard on his recovery in November, 1768, followed a reconciliation with his brother-in-law, Temple, which also included the
other brother-in-law, George Grenville. Politically this was
of no small significance, for Temple in particular was keenly
interested in the Wilkes affair. Presumably, the conversations
of the brothers-in-law dwelt largely upon the conduct of the
ministers whom Pitt had himself appointed and who were left
over from his Cabinet, in particular Grafton and Camden, the
Lord Chancellor. Grafton, who had once broken up the
Rockingham Cabinet in order to bring in Pitt as the leader,
had been asked by the outgoing Pitt to remain at his post, and
he was now the head of the ministry responsible for damaging
the constitution; *Junius* saw to it that his personal responsibility
was not forgotten. Camden, Pitt's old friend and protégé, if not
altogether free from inward misgivings, had quietly remained
in the Cabinet which persecuted Wilkes, even though he owed
his popularity to the judgements he had pronounced in Wilkes's
favour. He now hastened to call on his old leader and assure
him that at heart he was still the same as ever. Chatham would
have nothing more to do with Grafton, and did not even give a
thought to how much he himself was responsible for Grafton's

becoming a minister and sticking to the post. When Chatham appeared at the Palace in July, everyone was struck by the forbidding coldness with which he returned the salutation of the man who was now prime minister.

And then, in the royal presence, Chatham showed the King himself that he had a different man to deal with. Gone was that languishing servility with which—or so his enemies jeered—'he used to bow so low, you could see the tip of his hooked nose between his legs'. Even Burke was mistaken in supposing that Chatham had once more talked some 'pompous, creeping . . . ambiguous matter, in the true Chathamic style'. No, this time he was quite outspoken and far from obliging. He told the King that in three crucial matters—Wilkes, America and India—his ministers were following the wrong course and that he must reserve the right to oppose their policy in the Lords, even though it was far from his wish ever again to hold office. George had now been warned, but he was far too convinced of his own superior royal wisdom ever to listen to a warning, least of all from a man whom in his heart of hearts he hated and believed he no longer needed.

But when Chatham spoke in the new session of Parliament on January 9th, 1770, George was to learn that Chatham was still a force to be reckoned with. He attacked the administration's American policy and moved an amendment to the Address, implying that the motion of the Commons on the representation of Middlesex was unconstitutional. In his most lofty vein he invoked Magna Carta and held up the 'iron barons' who had wrested it from John as a pattern to the 'silken barons' of the day. He condemned the arbitrary power of the Commons as being equally detestable as that of a king. The defeat of Chatham's amendment was a foregone conclusion. But what was that compared with the fact that the Lord Chancellor himself had got up and confessed that he shared Chatham's view, and that he repudiated as unconstitutional the policy of the administration to which he had hitherto belonged and still did belong even as he spoke? Often, he said, he had hung down his head in Council and disapproved by his looks those steps which he knew his avowed opposition could not prevent; but the time had come when he must speak out.

Of course, this speech of Camden's condemned not only his

colleagues but himself as well. It is the very acme of dereliction of duty if a Lord Chancellor lets unconstitutional Cabinet decisions pass in silence without resigning; it was scarcely decent to attack his own colleagues in public without first laying down his office. But this did not lessen the shattering effect of his words. Of course, everyone realized that Camden would now have to be dismissed, and Shelburne tried to make capital out of his imminent removal by exclaiming that he hoped 'there would not be found in the kingdom a wretch so base and mean-spirited as to accept the Seals on the conditions on which they were offered'.

As things turned out it proved extremely difficult for George and his ministers to replace Camden by anybody who would not cut too miserable a figure in an office of such weight and dignity. For the leading legal lights were almost all ranged on the side of the opposition. The ministers' choice fell on Charles Yorke, son of the former Lord Chancellor Hardwicke; he possessed all the necessary qualities and was consumed with the ambition to be the second Lord Chancellor in the Yorke family. But, like his brother, he belonged to the Rockingham faction, which was in opposition. For days he wavered between the promptings of party loyalty and the siren voice of his own ambition. After he had formally refused the Great Seal, he was at last persuaded to say 'yes' by George himself, who conveyed the threat that if he now refused he would never make him Lord Chancellor. In pronouncing his assent he pronounced his own death sentence. The reproaches of his brothers and the voice of his own conscience gave him no peace. Three days later he was dead. By his own hand? That is one of those questions which will probably never be answered with any certainty.

As might be expected, Yorke's death made a great stir, and when, a few days later, Grafton announced his own resignation many believed that the whole ministry would inevitably break up and that the opposition's day had now dawned. But George had no intention of giving ground. He now found a man after his own heart to be prime minister. This was Lord North, Chancellor of the Exchequer. He was promoted First Lord of the Treasury on January 28th, 1770, and kept the post until March, 1782. If the importance of an administration could be measured by mere length of days, then North could take his place beside Walpole and the younger Pitt. But the duration of North's ministry is not to be explained by his own personal importance but by his subservience to the King's orders. He did not look upon himself as the King's political counsellor, who could only remain in office as long as the King took his advice, but as a tool for executing the King's policy, even when he himself considered it mistaken. It is true that in the closing years of his ministry he repeatedly asked George to release him because he had recognized that, particularly in his American policy, the King was following a course which was fatally wrong. But George said 'No' and North stayed on. This, in fine, was the very prime minister the King needed for his system of government, and it is not surprising that he valued and esteemed this man most highly, the more especially as he possessed many outstanding qualities for his office. He was an experienced administrator and financier and a most deft and witty debater, with a distinct flair for handling and leading the Commons without ever losing his temper; indeed, under the heaviest thunderbolts of his eloquent adversaries, he could peacefully doze off while to right and left his two legal paladins, the chameleon Wedderburn and the bulldog Thurlow, kept watch. Personally North was a man of inviolable integrity. But, of course, all this cannot save him from the condemnation of history, which cannot but see in him one of the most disastrous ministers England has ever had.

For some time the administration was to be faced by a united opposition. Chatham had even brought himself to pay Rockingham a visit which led to a reconciliation. On the other hand, he could bank on the support of the Grenvilles and their following. The three brothers-in-law saw eye to eye over the most urgent questions of policy and worked together. However, George Grenville's activity came to an early end. On November 13th, 1770, death snatched him away, a bare fifty-nine years old. He had wound up his political career with a measure which shows his positive virtues in the best light. In the spring of 1770 he safely piloted through a bill which withdrew the right to try election petitions from a committee of the whole House and transferred it to a standing committee pledged to impartiality. This ended the abuse which allowed the parliamentary majority of the day unscrupulously to use these petitions to swell its own ranks at the opposition's expense. This was a beginning, however modest, of the parliamentary reform so urgently needed.

A far bolder step in this direction was proposed by Chatham on January 22nd, 1770, in a speech in the Lords. No knowledgeable person could contradict him when he called the boroughs the rotten parts of the constitution. But he warned against the operation which appeared the obvious measure, an amputation, because it might prove fatal to the whole constitution. He proposed increasing by one the number of representatives of each county, for it was in the counties and the great cities that the strength and vigour of the constitution resided.

It is not surprising that proposals like these found no answering echo from the party in power. But neither did they draw the plaudits of the Whigs who looked to Rockingham as their leader. In this year, 1770, when Chatham first broached the question of the franchise in Parliament, Burke published his pamphlet *Thoughts on the Cause of the Present Discontents*. It is rightly considered one of England's most significant political documents, and, after the lapse of more than a century, it is still readable, so packed is it with observations of lasting worth and with an acute analysis of contemporary grievances set out in powerful, rich and virile language. For example, Burke there explained the nature of a party better, and recognized its importance to the life of a state more clearly than had anyone before his day. But when he came to talk about the reform of the constitution itself, Burke was sceptical, cautious and ineffectual. 'Every project of a material change in a government so complicated as ours . . . is a matter full of difficulties; in which a considerate man will not be too ready to decide; . . . or an honest man too ready to promise.' For Burke had an almost idolatrous reverence for the British constitution and this—for all his sincere love of liberty and free institutions—gives his political thought a conservative cast. That this constitution was riddled with anomalies which could not be defended in the light of pure reason is not a defect in Burke's eyes, for his mistrust of the ability of the human mind to frame a satisfactory constitution on logical lines is one of the main pillars of his own political theory.

It is not surprising that Chatham was dissatisfied with

Burke's pamphlet. True, in a letter to Rockingham he calls it well intended, but he says that it has done much hurt to the common cause. He cannot find in it any 'large and comprehensive views' and he obviously fears that it will prove an obstacle to the union of all the opposition's forces—or, as he puts it, of *all* who will not be slaves—against the desperate designs of the Court. Quite possibly Chatham was a little nettled by the criticism Burke had applied to his favourite maxim: 'Not men but measures.' He had, said Burke, added this maxim to those which are as current as copper coin, and about as valuable; it was 'a sort of charm, by which many people get loose from every honourable engagement'. But even apart from this, Chatham was hardly the man to appraise the originality and depth of Burke's ideas.

The energy with which Chatham flung himself into this campaign against George and his compliant ministers is quite amazing. He spoke in the Lords on no fewer than fifteen occasions during 1770, a feat of which no one who had seen him in the dismal days of his ministry would have believed him capable. The King now called him a 'trumpet of sedition'. At first he did not taste success; the royal janissaries held too closely together for that, and so it is hardly necessary to go deeply into the details of these parliamentary proceedings.

But one chain of events is indeed worthy of note, for out of them there gradually developed the struggle for the freedom of the press.

In December, 1769, *Junius* had launched into the world his most audacious attack—a letter to George himself. It bristled with innuendoes and offensive allusions, and ended up by pointing out that the crown which the House of Hanover had acquired by one revolution might be lost by another. Rockingham called the letter 'a very animated and able performance, but rather too much of a flagellation'. As things turned out this excessive sharpness did in fact make the letter misfire and even caused a reaction in the King's favour.

George himself can hardly be blamed for demanding legal action on this letter. But if he had foreseen what a hornet's nest he would stir up, he would probably have thought twice about it. Under English law press prosecutions go before a jury, and thus it came about that Woodfall, the printer of the letter—

N

Junius was, as usual, unidentified and could not be arrested—appeared before a City jury. The judge was Mansfield, who had good reason to suppose that they would acquit the accused. He therefore made it clear to them at the outset that they had to decide simply and solely whether the accused had published or sold the writing complained of. On the other hand it was a point of law whether the writing was a defamatory libel, and consequently a point to be decided by the judge alone.

This doctrine of Mansfield's was not new. Judges had already held this view before. But it was by no means generally accepted. Many lawyers, Camden, for example, held the entirely opposite view that the question whether a publication in the press was a libel was something for the jury to decide. But one thing was clear at the outset: if Mansfield's doctrine found general acceptance, one of the stoutest bastions of the freedom of the press was overthrown. The London jury parried this attack by the learned judge by giving a verdict of 'Guilty of printing and publishing only'. With this word 'only' they put paid to all likelihood of Woodfall's being sentenced, and he was able to leave the court a free man.

The problem of deciding between the respective functions of judge and jury was a legal one, but it carried so many political implications with it that it had to come up for discussion in both Houses as soon as Parliament reassembled in December, 1770. In the Lords, Chatham set upon his lifelong foe with a fulminating speech in which he denounced Mansfield's doctrine as 'contrary to law, repugnant to practice and injurious to the dearest liberties of the people'. So firmly did he stand by this view that he contemptuously brushed aside as small-minded a Whig proposal to end the controversy by passing a new law. In the Commons a group of prominent lawyers fought for the rights of juries, among them the sly Scot, Wedderburn, who a few weeks later was to betray his party and sell himself to the King as Solicitor-General. But Charles Fox was undismayed at this formidable array of big-wigs, and what he lacked in legal equipment he made up for by the wealth of his ideas and the irresistible torrent of his eloquence.

Even at this early date he was able to speak from the government front bench. In a few weeks he had made himself so indispensable to the ministers that North pressed the King to give him one of the minor offices with which an ambitious politician usually started his career. George resisted this. He had always had a low opinion of Charles's father and he strongly disapproved of the private life of this young man who spent his nights at the gaming-tables and squandered his father's money by the fistful. For George had all the private virtues of a steady, respectable, God-fearing paterfamilias, and also had his share of the allied feelings of disgust and disapproval at the rakes who strayed from the paths of virtue. And Charles Fox certainly gave him grounds enough for disapproval. But North was inclined to close his eyes to all this as long as the young man's excesses did not impair the astonishing talents which he displayed in the van of the parliamentary battle amid the jubilation of the ministerial party and even, at times, the approval of the opposition. And when, in February, 1770, he even succeeded in sweeping the formidable Wedderburn from the saddle in his own tilt-yard, George had to yield to his minister's insistence and appoint Charles Fox a Junior Lord of the Admiralty. He was just twenty-one and on the Continent would still have been a minor in the eyes of the law. Holland was in the seventh heaven over this success of his favourite son, and Lady Holland wrote from Nice: 'I hope Lord North has courage and resolution. Charles being connected with him pleases me mightily. I have formed a very high opinion of his lordship, and my Charles will, I dare say, inspire him with courage.' Courage—Charles possessed enough and to spare, but it was not very long before he gave his exalted leader such a taste of it as North could not stomach in the long run.

The position which Fox had already gained among the speakers in the House was clearly shown in the debate on the powers of juries by the fact that it was Burke who replied to him. Burke's political thought was, of course, greatly superior to Charles', but in the highly important art of winning the 'ear of the House' the young Lord of the Admiralty had already far outdistanced him. The only interest of the arguments which he then advanced is that they contradict completely everything he said and did later, for it was Fox who, twenty-two years afterwards, put through a measure which confirmed juries in the functions which Mansfield had denied them, and so preserved the freedom of the press.

One of the principal and most important duties of a free press is conscientious reporting, and in a constitutional state what topic could have a better claim to be reported than the proceedings of Parliament? True, that ancient privilege which forbade the publication of parliamentary speeches still existed, but the English have a knack of stopping the sins of the fathers being visited on the children by letting a law become dormant once it has outlived its usefulness. So for years no one had stirred up this privilege and the press had been allowed to bring out more or less accurate reports, provided it took the precaution of practising a subterfuge which even the most simple-minded could see through.

But George III's Parliament had an uneasy conscience, and the King had based his whole system on sharing the control of its members with no one else, least of all with a despised but by no means innocuous public opinion. But what would happen if Chatham declaimed massive indictments from such a platform, and *Junius* revelled in retailing to the public, word for word when possible, the ill-advised or careless remarks of those whom he hated most? Obviously there would then be certain consequences. The time had passed for winking an indulgent eye while the law was being flouted. And so the Lords barred their doors to all strangers when Chatham spoke, and the Commons reminded all printers of its privilege in the most solemn terms, and thus threatened every publisher with the most ruthless persecution.

It was not political considerations alone which induced printers and reporters to take up this challenge. A good part of their livelihood was at stake if they could no longer inform their readers how Ch . . . . m had spoken in the Roman Senate or F . x and B . . . e in the City Council of Lilliput. But they were also conscious of fighting for a high political principle against an odious or despicable enemy. Most of the printing presses were to be found in that part of London which was already by common consent the economic hub of the Empire—the City. For years the City folk had been in opposition to the King, and they enjoyed time-honoured privileges through which they could make their opposition effective. The Lord Mayor and aldermen of the City had repeatedly exercised their right to lay their grievances before the King in person, and their coaches were cheered on by long lines of enthusiastic citizens whenever they passed the old city gate at Temple Bar to drive into Westminster to the royal palace. At one of these audiences the Lord Mayor, Beckford, an energetic supporter of Pitt, had replied to a testy rebuff at the King's hands with a vigorous speech which amounted to this: the King did not wish to hear the truth—the very reproach which was voiced by Johann Jacoby and hurled at Frederick William IV of Prussia in 1848. The only difference was that for decades afterwards Jacoby was blamed by German historians for his 'tactlessness', whereas Beckford's words were engraved by the citizens of London beneath the statue erected to his memory in their own Guild-hall, and Chatham praised him, saying that on this never-to-be-forgotten day the spirit of Old England had spoken through him.

The City had yet other old, well-established privileges, as befitted a town which had sent a representative as far back as 1215 to brush shoulders with the barons on the meadow at Runnymede when they wrested Magna Carta from King John. Why, even the King himself had to wait at Temple Bar until the Lord Mayor gave him the keys of the City. Finally, they enjoyed their own jurisdiction which they exercised through magistrates elected by the citizens. With such rights and privileges it was quite feasible to launch a campaign even against King and Parliament if only a man could be found to organize it. As events now showed, such a man was to be found.

The London printers continued to publish accounts of the proceedings of Parliament, and the outraged legislators thundered in the Commons against the impudence of the reporters. In the end something decisive simply had to be done. On March 13th, 1771, the House decided to call to the bar some half a dozen printers who had infringed its privilege. It had taken a day and night sitting and no fewer than twenty-three divisions to carry this motion against a tough minority. Putting the motion into effect was the job of the Speaker, and so he sent out his messengers to force those printers, who had not appeared voluntarily, to come in. The officers were to come back—but not in triumph.

A comic curtain-raiser preceded the main drama. One of the accused arranged for a fellow-printer to arrest him and thus earn the fifty pounds offered by Royal Proclamation to anyone apprehending a peccant printer. Captor and captive then made their way to the Guildhall, where an alderman sat in readiness to hear them. The alderman pronounced the arrest unlawful, set the prisoner free and bound the captor over to appear at the next quarter sessions to answer a charge of assault and unlawful imprisonment, which did not prevent him from claiming his fifty pounds from the Treasury. Then the alderman despatched a well-worded letter to the Secretary of State, pointing out that the warrant was illegal and a violation of the chartered privileges of a citizen of the metropolis of His Majesty's dominions. The Secretary of State—it was once more George Grenville's former colleague, Lord Halifax—must have turned pale when he saw the alderman's signature. It was 'John Wilkes'.

In April, 1770, Wilkes had left the prison where he had had almost two years to reflect on his misdeeds. It had not been exactly a severe ordeal. Prison discipline had not yet been developed into a science, and it held few terrors for a prisoner with distinguished and beneficient patrons. While Wilkes's aristocratic Whig friends supplied him regularly and unstintingly with money, his admirers from far and near sent him all the luxuries which a gentleman of taste could wish to find on his table. Even in America enthusiastic votaries remembered this martyr in the cause of liberty, and sent him enough tobacco for his pipe never to go out. But of all his followers none held him in such regard as did the Londoners; they made him an alderman while he was still the King's prisoner. Thus he was on the spot at the right moment to organize the campaign against the Commons, which had deprived him of his seat as an M.P. and had foisted an unwelcome representative on those who had voted for him.

Even George took fright when he saw this accursed name at the foot of the City's memorial. This was not his usual reaction, for, on the contrary, personal courage was undeniably one of his distinctive qualities, and it is only regrettable that it was not used in a better cause. But he now strongly advised his minister to have nothing whatever to do with Wilkes. This individual, he had at last discovered, was below the notice of the House.

Meanwhile matters took their inevitable course. One of the

Speaker's messengers had the misfortune to find a printer, one Miller, at home. He arrested him. Miller at once called a City constable, who promptly appeared upon the scene and invited him to take the Speaker's messenger in charge for unlawful imprisonment. This was duly done and Miller, the messenger and the constable, accompanied by friends and neighbours, appeared before Crosby, the Lord Mayor, as the magistrate competent to decide their case. Crosby, too, was on the spot, supported by Alderman Oliver and Alderman—Wilkes. With all due formalities the Bench pronounced that the Speaker's messenger, who had intended to arrest a man belonging to the City without having his authority backed by a warrant issued by a City magistrate, must answer a charge of assault and unlawful imprisonment. This judgement was communicated in due form and order to the Commons. Both Crosby and Oliver were members of the Commons, and in the eyes of the Londoners Wilkes was still the rightful representative for Middlesex.

George saw very clearly that this challenge was really aimed at him even though it was addressed to the Commons. He at once instructed North to have Crosby and Oliver committed to the Tower; otherwise, he maintained, the Constitution was lost. North was more realistic in weighing up the chances in a conflict with the capital of the Empire, a conflict in which at the very best there was no credit to be gained. But he was powerless in the face of George's pretorian guard in the Commons which followed out the wishes of the King if the minister boggled. Once again Charles Fox distinguished himself by the impetuosity with which he galloped into the fray, inciting the members to make a spirited defence of their power, which, he said, was recognized by the people of England, against the three City magistrates who had had the impudence to dispute it. It was a case, he said, of defending the admirable Constitution of England against those who abhorred and detested it. It was Fox as much as anybody whom North had to thank if the House flouted his wishes and resolved to call the three City men to account.

Wilkes refused to attend on the ground that he would appear only in that place to which, as member for Middlesex, he had a right, and at that moment no one, not even Charles Fox, had the courage to argue the point with him. But the Lord Mayor and Oliver obeyed the summons, and the way things turned out at once showed North how well-founded his fears had been. The route along which the coaches of Crosby and Oliver passed from the Guildhall to Westminster teemed with thousands upon thousands of London citizens of all classes who acclaimed them as supporters of the people's liberties. The same spectacle was repeated a few days later when they again drove to Parliament to hear the decision reached by their fellow M.P.s. Tightly-packed crowds which seemed capable of anything surrounded the House, while inside were enacted proceedings which showed neither judicial dignity nor political wisdom. If once again Charles Fox was one of the most fiery members present, he could at least plead on this occasion that the violence which was threatening at the very doors of the House had made his blood boil, so that his impassioned appeal to the gentlemen of England not to be intimidated by the mob appeared less artificial. 'I pay no regard whatever to the voice of the people . . . their business is to choose us,' he exclaimed. 'It is our business . . . to maintain the independency of Parliament; whether it is attacked by the people or by the Crown is a matter of little consequence. . . .' His vehemence attracted the virulent hatred of the crowd, and he could congratulate himself that in one of the scuffles which ensued he escaped with nothing worse than a torn coat and a tumble in the mud. North, who was unlucky enough to be mistaken for him, barely escaped with his life, it is said.

What could it profit the House to consign Crosby and Oliver to the Tower? It only enshrined them the more firmly as the idols of their fellow-citizens, who sent them everything they could possibly wish for in prison. Inevitably there was a bigger stir still when half a dozen of the noblest in the land, led by Rockingham and accompanied by Burke, appeared at the Tower to pay the prisoners a state visit. After a few weeks they had to be released after all, to return to their Guildhall amid a triumphal procession which any king might envy them. More important still, the battle for the freedom of parliamentary reporting had been fought and won. After these scenes no member ever again succeeded in talking of privilege if his speeches appeared in print, and no printer ever bothered his head about a ban which was dead, even if not officially buried.

There came a time when even Charles Fox paid tribute to

and exulted in this victory for the freedom of the press. But first a few years were still to come in which he was prominent among the enemies of all agitations for liberty. It was astonishing what dazzling arguments this young man could assemble for the most wrong-headed causes; indeed, the more wrong-headed they were, the more he sparkled. It was on one of these occasions that Horace Walpole called him the 'phenomenon of the age'. But thankful as the administration was to have the services of such a matador, there always lingered a slight feeling of uncertainty. A virtuoso, so conscious of his own virtuosity, might at any moment take it into his head to play a little piece to music of his own. He did, on occasion, show signs of such independence in the cause of religious toleration and the reform of the barbaric criminal code. But even so it was an unpleasant surprise for the prime minister when on February 20th, 1772, Fox announced his resignation from the post which had been given him two years earlier. This impulsive decision was partly prompted by the usual grievances which a self-confident subordinate so often has against a minister who is his official superior. But the reason which tipped the scale and was thrust well into the foreground by Fox, was the distaste he felt for a government bill which he wished to be free to speak and vote against.

This bill was an extremely personal affair of the King's. George was galled by the marriages which two of his brothers had contracted behind his back. In 1766 the Duke of Gloucester had secretly married Lord Waldegrave's widow. His brother Henry, created Duke of Cumberland, whose scandalous exploits constantly supplied fresh food for London gossip, had found himself compelled to marry another widow, the sister of none other than the gallant Colonel Luttrell who could pride himself on representing Middlesex in Parliament. Understandable as George's motives were, the methods by which he proposed to tackle the problem were equally open to criticism. No descendant of George II was to be allowed to marry without the permission of the reigning monarch; only when Fox's resignation had increased the administration's difficulties was the ban restricted to princes and princesses of the blood royal who had not yet attained the age of twenty-six.

It is characteristic of the nature and composition of the

Parliament of the day that its passions were roused by a topic in which a democratic age would find it hard to summon up more than a languid interest. Fox was not only determined to oppose the King's proposal with all his might; he considered the matter important enough to sacrifice his office, and even perhaps his political career to it. His strongest motives were personal ones. His mother had run away from home to marry his father, and so he saw himself as the knight-errant of all true lovers thwarted by a father or a guardian. He remained true to family tradition by attacking the Royal Marriage Bill just as passionately as his father had opposed Hardwicke's Clandestine Marriage Bill. For did not the blood of two royal families flow in his veins? There was the Stuart blood of Charles II and the Bourbon blood of Henry IV, whose daughter had been Charles II's mother. But this was not all. Had not George himself, who now came out as the champion of royal blood not marrying beneath itself, paid his addresses a decade earlier to Sarah Lennox, his mother's sister, who had inspired his own first stirrings of affection? Fox had not forgotten that George had let his love take second place to the orders given him by the Princess of Wales and Bute. And so Charles Fox raised the standard of revolt, and once again electrified the House with the wealth of arguments with which he went into battle and the acuteness of the logic with which he gravelled the legal satellites of the King. But he could do nothing to stop the passage of the Bill.

He went further than this: he introduced a bill for the repeal of Hardwicke's Clandestine Marriage Act. In content this is today devoid of all interest. But all the more interest attaches to an account of this sortie given by no less a person than Horace Walpole. For several years past Walpole had ceased to sit in Parliament nor had he been seen there since. But all he had heard about Fox's parliamentary and oratorical address had so whetted his curiosity that he went to this sitting just to hear the young man for himself. Charles had spent the previous day at Newmarket, where he had lost some thousand pounds; he then sat up drinking all night and came to the House without having so much as seen his bed. He was so completely un-prepared that he had not even drawn up his bill. If Walpole was impressed by the grace and logic of the speech in which Fox introduced the bill, he was amazed by the subsequent speech Fox made in reply to his critics, including the prime minister and Burke. While these were speaking, Charles had been running about the House, pausing here and there to hob-nob with a member. But then he 'rose with amazing spirit and memory; answered both Lord North and Burke, ridiculed the arguments of the former and confuted those of the latter with a shrewdness that . . . as much exceeded [that of] his father in embracing all the arguments of his antagonists, as he did in his manner and delivery. . . . Charles Fox had great facility of delivery; his words flowed rapidly, but he had nothing of Burke's variety of language or correctness, nor his method. Yet his arguments were far more shrewd.' Walpole sums up his judgement thus: 'This was genius—was almost inspiration.' Walpole, who had heard all the great speakers of the last three decades, was a competent judge, and this tribute of his carries weight. But genius which leads to carelessness and laziness brings the greatest dangers in its train. And how seriously does it threaten a young man who devotes himself to drinking and dicing right up to the morning when he is to introduce an important bill!

For the moment, however, it seemed as if he could not put a foot wrong. As he was astute enough to confine his opposition to this one field, North soon renewed his endeavours to tempt him back into the ministerial camp. With great difficulty and at considerable expense to the public purse a vacancy was created among the Lords Commissioners of the Treasury, and the post was given to Fox. But this new career in office lasted only from December, 1772, to February, 1774. The successes of this ambitious young man had gone to his head, and he was certainly in no awe of his chief. Finding that North lacked something of the old dash, he felt it his duty to gather into his own hands the conduct of policy in Parliament. When finally he made an attempt, in the course of a fresh conflict between the Commons and one of its alleged detractors, to force the prime minister into a course which he manifestly and with good reason found repugnant, North's patience was at length ex-hausted. The King's had run out some time before. Now as ever, he could not stomach this young ne'er-do-well, and his dislike was in no wise tempered by Fox's amazing gifts, but only strengthened. So George urged North to rid himself of a subordinate who jibbed at every rein and who must become as contemptible as he was odious. On February 24th an usher of the House delivered Charles Fox a note from North which informed him of his dismissal in a few dry words.

Charles was not surprised. He had already confided to his friends that he would congratulate North on his spirit if he could bring himself to turn him out. But if Fox had imagined that this was a mere question of a brief holiday from office, then he was very much mistaken. This time the game really was played out!

Shortly before this his private affairs, too, had passed through a serious crisis. In these years of his early successes and youthful fame he had led the life of a man of fashion whose personal magnetism made him the centre of a circle of friends ready for any sacrifice and any folly, a man whose inexhaustible credit was only exceeded by his lightheartedness and his bad luck at the gaming tables and the race track. His credit was largely based upon the belief that he would one day inherit the vast riches of his father, although he was only the second son, for his elder brother, Stephen, was delicate and had no children. But in the autumn of 1773 a son was born to Stephen, and in a trice all calculations were upset. At once all the money-lenders whom Charles had kept quiet by the promise of high rates of interest swooped down on him now that he had no possible hope of ever being able to pay them back their capital. A catastrophe seemed inevitable, and this would have involved all the other scions of leading families, who had not hesitated for a second to stand surety for their adored Charles. But could Holland sit idly by and see the life and career of his favourite son blasted even as they blossomed? He loved money and in the decisive years of his life he had sacrificed his prospects of political greatness to it. But he loved his son even more, and so he gave instructions for one hundred thousand pounds of his fortune to be realized to cover Charles's debts. But even this huge sum was not enough. Before the debts were fully discharged, Holland had to sacrifice one hundred and forty thousand pounds. Fabulous as his talents were the sums which Charles had run through in a few short years.

But now he was deeply disturbed by the knowledge that he had brought upon his beloved parents this great distress with which his mother upbraided him in reproachful letters. He had only a short time to show them his contrition. Holland, who had borne the heavy blow with philosophic calm, died on July 1st, 1774. His wife followed him to the grave only twenty-three days later. Before 1774 was out Stephen Fox, now the second Lord Holland, had also died. His title descended to the boy who, as the third Lord Holland and the master of Holland House, propagated the tradition of his uncle Charles in the nineteenth century.

Charles Fox had now reached the crossroads in his life. Where was his path to take him now? His intimates knew full well that he did not spend all his time at gambling, drinking or in the clubs. Even then his happiest hours were passed among his books—the classics, Shakespeare or some modern poet. He zealously pursued the study of history and amassed a rich store of knowledge into which he could dip at any time. Nor did he only keep company with young people who stood agape at his gifts and his knowledge, and boozed or gambled with him until the small hours. A man of the importance and intellectual pretensions of Edmund Burke allowed no political differences or parliamentary squabbles to prevent him from seeking the society of a young man whose outstanding qualities he had discerned behind a frivolous façade.

In this year, 1774, so critical for Fox, he had conferred on him the very highest intellectual distinction London had to offer. He was elected a member of that club which had gathered round Dr. Johnson, that society which was unique in being called 'The Club' without epithet or addition. Dr. Johnson was acknowledged to be the Great Cham of literature and the king of conversation. He was an inveterate Tory and at times even let out his pen on hire to the administration. But in his club he knew no party distinctions. He not only hailed Burke as a master of conversation in his own right, from whose store of ideas one could always learn something; he declared that anyone who by some chance or other fell into conversation with Burke for a few minutes must at once say: this is an extraordinary man. That Charles Fox was received into this circle at twenty-four showed that connoisseurs had discovered greater qualities in him than he had hitherto revealed to the world.

But it was of decisive importance in his political development that he won back his freedom of action before the American problem entered upon its most critical phase.

CHAPTER XIV

AMERICA. FOX IN OPPOSITION

A FEW weeks before Charles Fox's dismissal, news had reached London of a *coup de main* which has become world-famous as the 'Boston tea-party'. On December 16th, 1773, some citizens of Boston disguised as Red Indians had forced their way aboard three ships in the harbour which had cargoes of tea sent by the East India Company, and threw the tea into the sea.

This was a manifest revolt against the English laws. An import duty of a beggarly threepence a pound on tea was all that remained of the customs duties so confidently introduced by Charles Townshend. They had turned out such a fiasco that the Grafton ministry had already repealed the vast majority of them in May, 1769, retaining only the duty on tea, against the vote of Grafton and a strong minority in the Cabinet who were all for sweeping away every trace of these utterly ill-advised duties. The majority hardened their hearts and clung to the unhappy notion that this duty, the financial yield of which could never amount to anything at all considerable, ought to be maintained for the principle of the thing. As a result, the radical section of the American community in particular now hardened their hearts likewise over the principle of the thing, and refused to allow the import of English tea as long as the duty, which no one could possibly call a heavy burden, was not completely abolished. Seldom have smaller causes had greater effects. '. . . So paltry a sum as threepence in the eyes of a financier, so insignificant an article as tea in the eyes of a philosopher, have shaken the pillars of a commercial empire that circled the whole globe,' cried Burke in his speech on American taxation (April 19th, 1774), which, together with his speech on conciliation with America (March 22nd, 1775), still ranks today among the classics of English politics. In the controversy whether Parliament had a right to tax America, he soared higher in the second speech with the statesmanlike words: 'The question with me is not whether you have a right to render your people miserable, but whether it is not your interest to make them happy. It is not what a lawyer tells me I *may* do, but what humanity, reason and justice tell me I *ought* to do.' In the earlier speech he had already warned the House that undue emphasis on British sovereignty would at length teach the Americans to call that sovereignty itself in question: 'Nobody will be argued into slavery.' In his second speech he went even further and frankly admitted that it was not at all his wish that America's spirit should be wholly broken, for, he said, it was the spirit which had made the country. The Americans were descendants of Englishmen, and their idea of liberty was an English one. On this idea of liberty he adjured the House: 'These are ties, which though light as air are strong as links of iron. . . . Slavery they [the colonists] can have anywhere. . . . They may have it from Spain, they may have it from Prussia. But, until you become lost to all feeling of your true interest and your natural dignity, freedom they can have from none but you. . . . Magnanimity in politics is not seldom the truest wisdom, and a great empire and little minds go ill together.'

Was he perhaps alluding to the King in this final antithesis? Whether he was or not, it hits off George's policy so aptly that it might well be used as the heading for this chapter of English history. As soon as George heard of the incidents in Boston, he charged North with the task of taking punitive measures. He hopelessly misread the real meaning of what had happened in America, and deluded himself about the resistance which he might expect. He was only too ready to believe a general returned from overseas, who assured him that the Americans would be lions only so long as the British behaved like lambs, but that they would prove very meek the moment England took the resolute part. Being resolute amounted to four penal measures against Boston and the colony of Massachusetts which North brought forward one after the other. The first ordered the closing of the port of Boston and was intended to ruin the city's economy. The next revoked the provincial government of the colony, and so it went on.

All these bills went through in the face of a weak opposition. They undoubtedly reflected the mood of the country which was outraged by the open violence of the citizens of Boston. On this

occasion Charles Fox also spoke for the opposition; but he confined his attack to points of detail, and it was still too early to
speak of leadership being assumed by a man who but a short
while before had been sitting on the Treasury bench. But even
then he left no doubt as to where he stood on the American
issue. In the debate in which Burke delivered his great speech
on American taxation Fox also rose to explain that from no
fiscal viewpoint was the tea duty justified; but if it should be
preserved only for the purpose of keeping alive a contested
right, then its inevitable consequence would be to throw the
American colonies into such a turmoil that the conflict must
end in open rebellion.

If there was any man in England whose words were still
listened to by the Americans with respect and reverence even
in the most critical times, that man was Chatham. The laurels
he had won in the war against France were still fresh in the
minds of men across the seas—the rising town of Pittsburg, to
which they had given his name, reminded them of him. His
fight against the Stamp Act had enhanced his popularity all the
more since it was based on the very constitutional arguments
which they put forward themselves. Nobody could expect him
to excuse or palliate an act of violence such as the destruction
of the tea in Boston harbour; in a letter to Shelburne he termed
it 'certainly criminal' and demanded that Boston should make
reparation for it. But as a far-seeing statesman he at once condemned the government's excessive punitive measures, the evil
consequences of which he foresaw. He suspected the government, as he wrote in his letter, of wishing to take advantage of
the indiscretion of the Bostonians in order to crush the spirit of
liberty all over America. Had he written 'King' instead of
'government' he would have hit the nail on the head. But much
persuasion was necessary, particularly on the part of Shelburne,
before he decided to air his views in public.

The ministry recognized Chatham's particular importance
and standing by deferring the third reading in the Lords of the
last of the Penal Acts—which provided for the quartering of
troops in Boston—long enough for his health to permit him to
appear there. Chatham seems to have reckoned with the
possibility of a fresh summons from the King, and thus to have
framed his speech (May 27th, 1774) in such a way as not to

LORD CHATHAM

close this avenue. All the same, the speech criticized the misguided policy of the administration courageously and without reserve: instead of calling a few wrongdoers to account it was penalizing the whole body of the innocent inhabitants. 'I am an old man,' he cried, 'and would advise the noble lords in office to adopt a more gentle mode of governing America; for the day is not far distant when America may vie with these kingdoms not only in arms but in arts also. It is an established fact that the principal towns in America are learned and polite, and understand the constitution of the Empire as well as the noble lords who are now in office.' Chatham knew the spirit which had animated the Americans too well to persuade himself, as the King did, that they would ever submit to forcible suppression. 'There was no corner of the world', he cried to King and ministry, 'into which men of their free and enterprising spirit would not fly with alacrity, rather than submit to the slavish and tyrannical principles which prevailed. . . .' Of course, this warning too fell on deaf ears at Court, but the voice was heard in America.

There the response evoked by the penal laws fully bore out the prophecies of Chatham and the opposition. Not only was there no talk of compliance; if George and North had imagined that the movement was a purely local one restricted to Boston and Massachusetts, they were very soon undeceived. Once again their policy had the effect of welding the colonies into one and making Boston's cause America's. In the autumn of 1774, a congress of the colonies met once more, this time in Philadelphia. The majority, which included George Washington, still favoured an understanding with the mother country. But already, particularly in Massachusetts, a radical party had grown up which spoke openly of independence. Inevitably the policy pursued by Britain would very largely determine which side would gain the ascendancy in America. Of the votes and proceedings of this congress Chatham said that for solidity of reasoning and wisdom of conclusion, and taking into account the difficult circumstances, they were not outstripped by any other nation or body of men. However, accepting the demands of the congress would have meant a complete reversal of British policy. Such a retreat could not be expected either of George or his ministers, or of the old Parliament which reached the end

o

of its joyless existence in the autumn of 1774, or even of the new, which was just emerging from the polls.

George applied himself to managing an election with a zeal and expert knowledge unequalled even by the Prussian Land-rats of Bismarck's day. With the results he could, in general, be satisfied. True, the contingent of independent country gentle-men was strengthened, but as they were predominantly anti-American, he had no need to worry about this. But what was admittedly painful was that Wilkes was once again returned for Middlesex, and that throughout the length and breadth of the realm no one could screw up enough courage to stand against him. What was still more painful was that this time he could take his seat uncontested in the House. After all, the times were too serious for a minister to be so irresponsible as to conjure up a fresh Wilkes controversy.

Charles Fox had had a long search before finding a con-stituency in Malmesbury. By the ideas of the day it was ideal in two respects: the electorate was, to put it mildly, easily counted; were one to say that it comprised only a dozen voters one would not be guilty of more than a trifling exaggeration—there were actually thirteen. But on the other hand these thirteen good men and true had the right to return not one but two members to Westminster, and so as to hurt no one's feelings they chose one from the ministerial party and one from the opposition; the two gentlemen had, of course, come to a prior understanding between themselves. They supplemented each other admirably: the ministerial candidate's pockets were as full as Fox's were empty.

Fox now belonged beyond all question to the opposition. It may be assumed that his association with Burke did much to confirm him in this attitude. Did he not later, when they reached the parting of the ways, openly acknowledge that he had learned more from him alone than from all the others put together? In October, 1774, Burke received a letter from Fox which not only expressed his resolve to fight the ministry's American policy with all his might, but also revealed that he meant to work in close concert with Rockingham, even though it was only later that he joined that group. From the letter it can be seen even at this date that one of these fine days not Rockingham but Fox would be the real leader of the opposition.

It was, moreover, high time that a leader should appear, inspired with a powerful fighting spirit and, in addition, capable of rallying the various opposition groups round him. Chatham, who certainly did not lack fighting spirit, was becoming increasingly unable to fulfil the second condition. His innate tendency to tread a lone path was assuming more and more critical forms. When in 1775 he wished to introduce a bill abruptly demanding that the administration withdraw all troops from Boston, his main concern was not to rally as many votes as possible in advance for this somewhat extravagant proposal, but to keep it secret from the other opposition peers! He had obviously taken it into his head that a word from him would by itself have the power to carry the doubters along with him and force those in power to yield. As it turned out, his speech was once again a superb performance. His son William, who accompanied him to the House, was not alone in his enthusiasm, when he called it the most forcible speech that could be imagined: 'The matter and manner both were striking; far beyond what I can express.' Chatham placed the resistance of the Americans on a level with the English stand against Charles I's ship-money and arbitrary taxes in the seventeenth century. Both cases, he said, had involved the principle that no subject of the Crown shall be taxed but by his own consent. The glorious spirit of Whiggism animated three millions in America who were prepared to die in defence of their rights as freemen. Indeed he voiced the hope that the same flame glowed in the breast of every Whig in England. Here it can clearly be seen how definitely Chatham considered the American resistance as part and parcel of the party struggles of England's home politics.

Such being his frame of mind he had no hesitation in taking the American Benjamin Franklin into his confidence and discussing his latest parliamentary sortie with him. During the last year Franklin's position in London had suffered severely through the somewhat unscrupulous use he had made of the private correspondence between the Governor of Massachusetts and a friend in London. Wedderburn had taken this chance of making a fulminating attack on Franklin, which, though it won him a great oratorical triumph, cost England dear. For in America he had created the worst possible impression and he convinced Franklin, who until then had been working for a settlement, of the hopelessness of any effort in that direction. But the reputation for duplicity which had clung to Franklin ever since did not prevent Chatham from confiding to him in advance his plan for a reconciliation between England and her colonies nor from asking for his collaboration and criticism. But Franklin soon learned that Chatham's ideas on collaboration were somewhat singular, for when he visited him at Hayes to talk things over, he could spend several hours in his company and yet be unable to get in a single word. The old statesman spoke almost the whole time, and at the end Franklin had to return to his pocket unread more than half his notes criticizing the draft Bill, and console himself with the thought that there would still be time enough for discussion and amendment if Chatham's plan were to make further progress when it was put before Parliament. He was obviously somewhat sceptical about its prospects; and not without reason, for when Chatham brought forward his plan in a great speech on February 1st, 1775, the administration at once threw it out without even flattering him with a second reading.

This was his last attempt for a long time to ward off the approaching disaster. Infirm and disappointed, he withdrew from political life. For two years his voice was not raised, and hardly anyone believed that it ever would be heard again.

All the more clearly did Charles Fox's voice now ring out. In the newly-elected Commons he could, despite his five-and-twenty years, pass as an old hand. Obviously the new members would be interested to hear the man who had already roused up the last assembly and set it in motion when he was still a young man of twenty summers. If they were hoping that they would always get something worth hearing from him, they were certainly not disappointed. He spoke well in every important debate, and was always lively, skilful and original. There was not a single dull moment when the member for the thirteen electors of Malmesbury spoke, whether he delved deep into the difficulties of the American problem or pitted himself against the prime minister in person. Though personal invective is not the highest form of parliamentary eloquence, it appeals particularly to those who hear it and read it, and perhaps never so much as in the eighteenth century, which turned a far more

indulgent eye on the ethics of political warfare than did later
and more respectable periods. A reporter who would hesitate
to bore his readers with financial disquisitions, no matter how
important, never failed to inform them in minute detail when
two honourable gentlemen flung malicious innuendoes in each
other's face across the table in the House. How could he possibly
miss the chance of telling them how Fox, who but a year before
had been North's subordinate, told him to his very face on
January 27th, 1775, that he had no system or plan of conduct
and no knowledge of business? North had said again and again
with assumed modesty that he did not feel equal to his task.
Fox now exclaimed that this was a point on which he agreed
unreservedly with the minister, who was proving with every day
that passed how right he was in his self-criticism. It was his
incapacity which was to blame if the country was incensed and
on the point of being involved in a civil war. When North made
the obvious objection that Fox himself but a short while back
had clearly thought quite differently, Fox flared up still more,
reproached him with 'the most unexampled treachery and false-
hood' and was not to be silenced by repeated calls to order.
If he reproached North with his love of the emoluments of
office being the only thing that prevented him from drawing
the logical consequences from his consciousness of his own
incapacity, then he undoubtedly did him an injustice. North's
real motive was a mistaken sense of duty, which made him unwilling to leave his King in the lurch. But whatever North's
motives were, Fox was unquestionably right: at this highly
critical juncture England had no use for a prime minister who
was oppressed by a consciousness of his own inadequacy.

Such personal skirmishes were, of course, only a minor
accompaniment to a very serious political struggle in which
Fox at all events knew full well what was at stake, and to which
he applied far more than his astonishing readiness of speech
and skill in debate. He also studied and mastered every aspect
of the great issues and grave problems involved. This was
apparent, for example, a few weeks after the passage at arms
just mentioned, when he moved an amendment to the Address.
This amendment deplored the fact that the administration's
policy, instead of healing the unhappy differences between
Great Britain and America, tended rather to widen them still

further. His speech astonished even those who had already marvelled at him, for it disclosed qualities which he had so far given no proof of having. Among his hearers was one of the greatest historians of modern times. Edward Gibbon, author of the immortal *Decline and Fall of the Roman Empire*, had not been able to resist the temptation to dabble in politics as well, and got himself elected to the Commons in 1774. There he sat among the supporters of the ministry, to which, it is true, he merely gave his silent backing on the division. For, as he discovered in this debate, he lacked the courage to speak, and his well-rehearsed oration remained locked in his bosom. This deep personal disappointment no more prevented him than did his differing political views from recognizing that Fox, taking the whole vast compass of the question into account, had revealed powers for regular debate which neither his friends had hoped nor his enemies dreaded.

The effect of Fox's activity showed itself not only in the increase in the minority which voted for his motion, but still more in North's attempt to make concessions soon after. It was only a timid attempt, but even so it went much too far for the great mass of the politicians who still imagined that energetic measures would make the rebellious Americans see reason. North proposed that every colony which raised the necessary taxes by a resolution of its own representative assembly should be excused from submitting to taxation by the British Parliament. While the King's Friends, staggered by this unexpected turn of events, sat scowling, Fox rose to his feet and congratulated the British public on the change of attitude of its prime minister. Here, he declared, the blessing of a firm and spirited opposition was to be seen. Of course, he added, the minister in his attempt to reach two incompatible goals at once had fallen between two stools: his offer would not meet the Americans' demands and he had given umbrage to his own followers, as could be read from their faces. Fox was right on both counts. In the House North was lucky to escape defeat, and within a short time the mother country received the most unequivocal and tragic proofs of the mood of America.

Before matters reached this pass, North, scared by the frowns of his henchmen, had already returned to the system of compulsion and punitive measures against the colonists. In a

powerful speech Fox upbraided him with the inevitable consequences. These laws would have no other effect than to make
the last of the loyal Americans determined foes of the mother
country. If they, along with the rebels, were threatened with
death by starvation, they would join the rebellion in the conviction that its success alone could save them from famine and
ruin.

In the parliamentary battles of the spring of 1775 a new
Charles Fox emerged. This was no longer the youthful prodigy
who came into the House unbriefed and relied on his gifts of
improvisation, so certain was he that even as he spoke more
arguments would occur to him than to others who had spent
days preparing themselves in their libraries. This was Fox the
serious politician, who had gauged the gravity of the hour and
accepted the obligation to be the complete master of every
subject on which he spoke. It is true that with his glittering
talents he did not find this easy. It would be a great mistake to
think of Fox as a modern professional politician, whose conscientious discharge of his duties leaves him no time to enjoy
life. He was far, all too far, removed from this. The aristocrats,
who set their stamp on the Parliament of the eighteenth century,
did not see their rôle in this light at all. Even a patriotic Whig
would find a race at Newmarket at least as strong an attraction
as a debate, however important, at Westminster; often, indeed,
the race-course was the scene of what today would be called a
party conference. But unfortunately Fox pursued his life of
pleasure even further than most of his companions in dissipation. He still spent the best part of the night at the gaming
tables and he seldom went to bed before five in the morning.
His finances were usually in a sorry state, and more than once
the bailiffs stripped his house. Even his cherished books came
under the hammer. If Goethe is right in saying

> '*Adversaries, debts and women—*
> *No knight, alas, is rid of them*'

then Charles Fox was a true knight. Still more numerous than
his adversaries, indeed, were his friends. Seldom has any man
had such a wonderful gift for making friends and keeping them
as he. It goes without saying that he was the life and soul of
every company in which he moved. It was not simply his

animation, his wit, his gift of conversation and the rich treasures of his mind which gathered men around him; the underlying reason for his irresistible magnetism was the warmth of his heart and the strength of his feelings. He was always completely natural, and he could afford to be so because he had nothing to hide. He passed almost his whole life, except for brief intervals, in opposition. He hardly ever had a chance to bestow on his friends those gratifications which bulked so large in the political life of the day. But whoever got as far as calling himself a friend of Charles Fox remained true to him, even if it meant renouncing all hope of benefits to come. Uncontrolled and frivolous as was his private life at this stage of his serious political struggles, it constantly shows traits which lift him far above the world about him, and even today cannot but move anyone who reads his letters or the memoirs of his intimate circle.

§

He now ranked so highly as a politician that many eyes were bound to turn to him when the most shattering news came from America. At the end of May the first report of a bloody clash between the British army and the American militia reached London. On April 19th, 1775, the men of Massachusetts had set about an English detachment near Lexington and driven it back to Boston. The engagement had cost both sides dead and wounded. Thus, for the first time, blood had flowed. The guns had spoken. Civil war had broken out. The American revolution had begun in real earnest.

The facile optimism with which the ministers had so far cheered themselves was rudely shaken. George, on the other hand, could pride himself on having foreseen months earlier that things would reach this pass. 'I am not sorry,' he had written in the autumn of 1774, 'that the line of conduct seems now chalked out. . . . The New England governments are in a state of rebellion. Blows must decide whether they are to be subject to this country or independent.' Of the outcome George had no doubt. Nor was he alone in this. The great mass of the English thought the same as the King; their national pride would not for one moment permit the thought of England not triumphing over her colonists in the clash of arms. Could the army which the congress of the American colonies was trying to recruit from the rawest material, from untrained farmers and artisans, impose its will on the English? Or could this be done by Colonel Washington, whom the congress appointed as their commander-in-chief?

Only a very few people in England had any conception of the magnitude and the difficulty of the struggle which was now approaching. But among their number was to be found Chatham, as well as Fox and Burke. They knew only too well how inadequate were the men at the helm and how unbudgingly obstinate was the King who commanded them. When in one of the first of the Commons debates Wedderburn tried to console himself and his listeners for the initial setbacks by drawing a superficial analogy with the Seven Years' War, Fox knocked this specious argument out of his hand by recalling that the change in England's fortunes had only begun after the King had changed his ministry and summoned Pitt to power. 'But', he cried to the ministers with epigrammatic trenchancy, 'not Lord Chatham, not the Duke of Marlborough, no, not Alexander nor Caesar, had ever conquered so much territory as Lord North had lost in one campaign.'

Fox did not regard the war which had now broken out as a struggle against a foreign foe any more than Chatham did. Fox, too, thought of the American colonists as fellow-countrymen and brothers; more than that, they were up in arms against the same enemy as he himself was fighting. Nothing, in his view, had estranged the Americans from the mother country more than the feeling that the King would arbitrarily disregard their rights, and that the British Parliament would act as his willing tool in doing so. But Fox also knew that if George triumphed over the Americans, his triumph would also be assured in England. To use a modern term he regarded the American revolution as an 'ideological' war. The American ideology, however, was the Whigs' ideology and had its roots in the doctrines of their spiritual father, Locke. The methods which George used to wage this war against his colonists could only heighten Fox's distaste: he bought German mercenaries from their local sovereigns and tried to use these hirelings to subdue the Americans, who were claiming England's hard-won liberties as their own birthright.

Viewed in this light, not only does Fox's policy become understandable but so do his statements in confidential letters to his friends. When he learned that in September, 1774, a patrol of British troops had succeeded in taking a munition store from the Americans, he wrote in dismay to Burke: '. . . what a melancholy consideration for all thinking men, that no people, animated by what principle soever, can make a successful resistance to military discipline. . . . The introduction of great standing armies into Europe has, then, made all mankind irrecoverably slaves.' More characteristic still is the letter which he wrote to Rockingham when news came in of the heavy defeat of the Americans on Long Island, near New York, on August 27th, 1776: 'Above all, my dear Lord, I hope that it will be a point of honour among us all to support the American pretensions in adversity as much as we did in their prosperity, and that we shall never desert those who have acted *unsuccessfully* upon Whig principles, while we continue to profess our admiration of those who succeeded in the same principles in the year 1688.'

In this spirit Fox carried on his fight against King and ministry throughout the American revolution without ever flagging. It was a gruelling fight. In Parliament he was confronted by the majority who remained loyal to the administration, in serried ranks and far superior numbers. 'In this season and on America,' wrote Gibbon to a friend in May, 1775, 'the Archangel Gabriel would not be heard.' Popular opinion, too, was predominantly in favour of the war, at least as long as success attended the mother country; the only exceptions were the merchants whose trade was suffering severely from the conflict with the colonies. In such circumstances opposition must needs appear to be quite hopeless for years to come, and it is not surprising that many a member was inclined to mark his protest only by continued absence from parliamentary business. Rockingham and many of his friends were of this mind. They were great nobles with many other important interests, and believed they could make a better use of their time than by introducing motions in Parliament which were voted down without exception, and furthermore exposed them to evil gossip about their lack of patriotism. In October, 1777, Burke wrote to Fox agreeing that their friends had certain faults, 'intimately connected with . . . plentiful fortunes, assured rank and quiet homes. . . . They are, as you truly represent them, but indifferently qualified for storming a citadel.' From the very beginning Fox energetically contested every proposal which left the enemy in possession of the field. In the letter already mentioned, which he wrote to Rockingham on October 13th, 1776, after the British victory on Long Island, he said: 'A secession at present would be considered as a running away from the conquerors, and we should be thought to give up a cause which we think no longer tenable.' With the eye of a natural politician he saw that one can only awake and maintain belief in a cause by fighting for it undismayed and by making sacrifices for it. A fighter from birth, he was never so happy as when battle raged about him; his mind worked most quickly and his words went home most surely when his opponents' attacks rained down upon him and only a small band of steadfast friends supported him with their devotion and applause.

And so it followed automatically that he rose to become leader of the opposition, even though several years passed before he formally joined the Rockingham party. On the way in which he led his numerically weak forces judgement has been passed by a man who is qualified to judge as few others are— Edward Gibbon: 'Fox . . . in the conduct of a party approved himself equal to the conduct of an empire.' Thus wrote the great historian in his autobiography, as he looked back on these years in which, session after session, he regularly cast his vote for the North ministry, although he gradually came to realize that North's policy was disastrous. But that did not prevent him from forsaking the company of his party associates because of a strong preference for that of Charles Fox.

CHAPTER XV

CHATHAM'S END

Anxiously Chatham followed the course of events from his sickbed. How much he condemned the fratricidal struggles between the home country and the colonists is shown by his behaviour towards his eldest son, who had become an army officer and was serving with the British forces in America. In February, 1776, he made him resign his commission. Young Pitt was not the only British officer who declined to bear arms against his American brothers.

For the rest, Chatham had to deny himself all political activity. In July, 1776, by way of a political testament he gave his faithful attendant, Dr. Addington, a declaration that he persevered unshaken in the opinions he had always professed, and he here uttered the warning that he could foresee that France would exploit this war, waged by England against herself in America, to set her foot on English ground. About the same time the United States Congress in Philadelphia took a a step which showed the gathering momentum of events. On July 4th, 1776, Congress adopted the Declaration of Independence, in which Thomas Jefferson summed up in immortal phrases the new political doctrines of his country. By this declaration the colonies formally broke loose from the mother country and for this they made George III responsible, laying to his charge a whole catalogue of sins.

This was a step to which Chatham could never reconcile himself. To his dying breath he fought against this *fait accompli*. He could no longer endure his sickbed. In May, 1777, his health was so far restored that he could once more emerge and speak in the Lords again. He no longer commanded those ringing tones which in years past had struck terror into the hearts of all his opponents and reduced the boldest to silence. Painfully and low the words were forced from his mouth. But his ideas were as bold as ever. True, they were sombre ones. He saw the administration's policy as nothing but a series of blunders, and virtually demanded that they should resign before France took a hand in the game. To conquer America by force of arms he roundly dismissed as an impossibility. 'I might as well talk', he exclaimed, 'of driving them before me with this crutch!' But if that were so, could anyone, could Chatham himself, believe that the Americans would voluntarily renounce their newly-proclaimed independence? In any case George was not at all inclined to put it to· the test. Not only did he find Chatham's speech highly unseasonable, but he also wrote contemptuously that it contained nothing but specious words and malevolence, like most of the other productions of that extraordinary brain.

In the winter session Chatham was again on the scene, even though he had been in bed for weeks that summer after falling from his horse with a seizure. At the end of November he made a speech on the Address, reiterating his plea for peace with America and seeking to justify the hope that the sound section of the colonists would value the blessings of a union with the mother country more highly than untried independence. A few days later, however, news came from across the seas which made all such hopes chimerical: on October 17th, 1777, General Burgoyne had capitulated with a whole army at Saratoga. The catastrophe had been largely the fault of the London administration, particularly the Secretary of State for the Colonies, Lord George Germain (formerly known as Lord George Sackville). Chatham criticized the ministry in the Lords as sharply as did Fox in the Commons, where he treated the morals and politics of the woebegone crew to a dressing down of the first order. Another minister roused Chatham's ire even more than Germain; this was Lord Suffolk, who had dared to defend the use of Red Indians as British army auxiliaries against the Americans with the blasphemous argument that 'it was perfectly justifiable to use all the means that God and nature put into our hands.' 'I am astonished!' exclaimed the elder statesman, 'shocked! to hear such principles confessed—to hear them avowed in this House . . . principles equally unconstitutional, inhuman and unchristian!' And then, in his moral indignation, he rose to heights of oratory seldom surpassed even in his best years, which seem almost miraculous coming from an infirm old man. With all the fire of genuine emotion he described the appalling scenes of the Indian massacres and implored the bishops, the Lords Spiritual, to recall the doctrines of their faith and 'purify this House and this country from this sin'. This time no one could suspect him of straining for theatrical effect when he ended with the words: 'My Lords, I am old and weak, and at present unable to say more. . . . I could not have slept this night in my bed . . . without giving vent to my eternal abhorrence of such preposterous and enormous principles.'

One result of the capitulation at Saratoga Chatham foresaw with certainty: France would now find that the time was ripe for joining in the war. Again and again he implored the ministers to make ready for the struggle with France. His fears were only too well-founded. On February 6th, 1778, Louis XVI took the step, ultimately to prove so fateful for him and his empire, of concluding a treaty of alliance with the American rebels. Benjamin Franklin signed on behalf of his fellow-countrymen. At first the treaty was kept secret, but as early as February 17th Fox raised the subject in the Commons. Horace Walpole had heard about it from a cousin of his, and they had agreed to tell Fox so short a time before the sitting began that he alone would know the secret and could make the greatest political capital out of it. During this sitting North held forth to the House about a plan for conciliation with America which amounted to a complete reversal of his former policy. Not only were all measures of compulsion and punishment which he had so far put through to be repealed, but so also was the tea duty, the root of all the trouble. At once Fox was on his feet, congratulating himself and his friends upon the minister having come round to their way of thinking, and asking him whether it were not true that within the last ten days France had signed a treaty with the colonists. North was so thunderstruck that at first he did not trust himself to answer. Pressed by the opposition, he at last stammered that it was possible, likely even, but that so far he had no official information. A pitiful spectacle!

North did not need this incident to persuade him that he was a square peg in a round hole. For months he had asked, even begged, George to allow him to resign. But George had always treated this as an attempt at desertion and had flatly refused. Now, however, it penetrated even his thick skull that things could not go on like this, that something had to be done. North asked him to summon Chatham. That the victor of the Seven

Years' War, whom the people still worshipped as the embodiment of national prestige, would be an acquisition of extraordinary strength to His Majesty's administration, not even
George could deny. He was, therefore, prepared to accept him
as a minister (although in the same breath he called him 'that
perfidious man'), but only on condition that North remained
prime minister and Thurlow Lord Chancellor. For, in George's
eyes, more important than saving his country from disaster was
what he called his 'independency', which however was really
the preservation of his personal government. 'Having said this,'
he wrote to North in the middle of March, 1778, 'I will only
add, to put before your eyes my inmost thoughts, that no
advantage to this country nor personal danger can ever make
me address myself for assistance either to Lord Chatham or any
other branch of the opposition.' He added that he would rather
lose the crown he wore than bear the ignominy of possessing it
under their shackles. Such is the curse of personal government.

It is not surprising that negotiations under such auspices
should founder. Eden, North's confidant, spoke to Shelburne,
who represented Chatham. When Shelburne said that if
Chatham became a minister he must become a dictator, George
was beside himself with rage. Of course he was! If someone else
became dictator, there was an end to his personal government.

Eden also negotiated with Charles Fox. A few weeks before
Fox had happened to discuss his own future in a letter to a
friend, dated February 3rd, 1778. '. . . People flatter me that I
continue to gain, rather than lose, my credit as an orator; and
I am so convinced that this is all that I shall ever gain (unless I
chose to become the meanest of men), that I never think of any
other object of ambition. I am certainly ambitious by nature,
but I really have, or think I have, totally subdued that passion.
. . . Great reputation I think I may acquire and keep, great
situation I never can acquire, nor, if acquired, keep without
making sacrifices that I never will make.' He was now faced
by the problem of whether he should take over just such a high
office. All we know of his reactions is the other side's account,
which is perhaps not wholly reliable. But this much can be
gathered from it, that while Fox's attitude was reserved, he was
not in principle disinclined to accept. He made it clear that
although he belonged to no party grouping he would not come

in alone, but only in the company of friends of his who shared his views. On the other hand he described Germain as the one minister with whom he could not act on any account. One may gather from this that for all his hard words about North he would not in all circumstances have refused to work with him, a conclusion which goes a long way to explain the turn of events of five years later.

A still clearer light is thrown on Fox's attitude by a letter which he wrote to Rockingham in the following January. Rockingham had maintained an attitude of refusal *on principle* of all offers coming from the ministry. Fox sharply sketched the contrast presented by his own point of view. 'What you considered as a step of the most dangerous tendency to the Whig party, I looked upon as a most favourable opportunity for restoring it to that power and influence which I wish it to have as earnestly as you can do. . . . It has always been . . . my opinion that power (whether over a people or a king) obtained by gentle means, by the goodwill of the person to be governed, and, above all, by degrees rather than by a sudden exertion of strength, is in its nature more durable and firm than any advantage that can be obtained by contrary means. . . . You think you can best serve the country by continuing in a fruitless opposition; *I think it impossible to serve it at all but by coming into power,*[1] and go even so far as to think it irreconcilable with the duty of a public man to refuse it, if offered to him in a manner consistent with his private honour, and so as to enable him to form fair hopes of doing essential service.' These are not the words of a doctrinaire but of a practical politician who sees things as they really are. But at the time none of these principles was put to the test because this set of negotiations broke down completely.

It is idle to wonder whether Chatham could really have deflected the course of history if he had taken office again in the spring of 1778, for his days were now numbered. That seizure in 1777 had been a sign and a warning, even though he seemed to have recovered from it.

Once again he came out into the open to fight for his policy. The capitulation of Saratoga and the entry of France into the war had driven many English politicians to the conviction that there was only one way out of their tangled and dangerous

[1] My italics, E. E.

GEORGE III

situation: to recognise America's independence and to concentrate all resources on the war against France. In particular
this view was held by the leading Whigs, but Chatham found it
impossible to accept. He still thought of the Americans as
brothers-in-arms who had been his stout and willing helpers in
the days of his great successes. He might well think of the
British empire in America as his own creation. And so, to
recognize American independence seemed to him like lending
a hand in destroying his masterpiece. But, it might be asked,
how did he propose to prevent this, if England, as he suggested,
withdrew all her troops from America? Well, for him it was an
article of faith that England's American brothers would return
to their old attachment to the mother country once they were
convinced that she was treating them fairly.

Now, as he lay on his sickbed, he learned that the Duke of
Richmond, the most active of the Whig magnates, proposed to
submit a motion in the Lords which practically amounted to a
recognition of American independence. Richmond was the
brother of Charles Fox's mother and only fourteen years older
than his nephew. He had distinguished himself as an officer in
the Seven Years' War, had taken part in the peace negotiations
at Versailles and had been a Secretary of State for some
months in the Rockingham Cabinet. He opposed the King's
American policy in the Lords almost as pertinaciously as did
Fox in the Commons. Nothing was farther from his wishes than
to offend Chatham, by whose agreement and co-operation he
set the greatest store. On April 5th he wrote him a respectful
letter in which he tried to show that the difference between
their opinions was more apparent than real. But Chatham
replied somewhat stiffly that it was wide enough to make any
understanding out of the question, and announced that he
would appear in London on the following day.

This was April 7th, 1778, when Richmond's motion appeared
on the Lords' order paper. On that day Chatham, accompanied
by his three sons and his son-in-law, Lord Mahon, drove to
London. He was so weak that first he had to recover from the
exertions of the journey in one of the ante-rooms of the House
before entering the Chamber. When his face, furrowed by sickness and suffering, was glimpsed at the entrance, everyone,
friend and foe alike, was seized by the thought that England's

P

greatest son had summoned up his last remaining powers to give aid and counsel in England's gravest hour. The whole House rose in token of respect. His friends saw with concern how he was supported on either side by a member of his family, how he dragged himself painfully to his place and how under his wig little more was to be seen than his aquiline nose and his eyes, in which something of the old fire still burned.

Then, when he got up, his voice could hardly be heard at first. Clearly it was with the utmost difficulty that he managed to speak at all. Isolated phrases rather than complete sentences fell from his lips. Only now and again did he succeed in delivering himself of a connected argument, and then it almost seemed as if he were soaring to his old heights. Every loyal heart could not but be moved as he exclaimed: 'His Majesty succeeded to an empire as great in extent as its reputation was unsullied. Shall we tarnish the lustre of this nation by an ignominious surrender of its rights and fairest possessions?' 'My Lords, any state is better than despair,' he concluded. 'Let us at least make one effort; and if we must fall, let us fall like men.' With these words he sank back into his seat.

Richmond rose to make a reply which he sought to set forth in the most courteous and respectful terms. While he was speaking, the veteran statesman's uneasy movements showed that he wished to speak again. Richmond hastened to finish. With the greatest difficulty Chatham rose once more. But the next moment he collapsed, sinking down in a swoon. A great commotion arose in the House. Everyone pressed forward to help. Chatham's sons clustered round their unconscious father. He was carried into a nearby room and Addington was sent for at once. With his help the patient was so far restored as to be able to be sent home to Hayes two days later.

But his house welcomed a dying man. On May 11th, 1778, the heart of William Pitt, Earl of Chatham, beat for the last time. He was only seventy years old.

A sense of irreplaceable loss gripped the nation. In Parliament all strife died away to give place to an unanimous expression of grief and respect. Both Houses resolved that he should be buried in Westminster Abbey and that a monument to him should be erected there. Only one man did not agree: George III. '. . . This compliment . . . is rather an offensive measure to me personally,' grumbled the King, whose life's work had been to destroy Pitt's. What was it that Burke had said? 'A great empire and little minds go ill together.' But the petty spite of the man who wore the crown could not prevent the English people from burying their hero with all the pomp and ceremony demanded by the occasion, which would doubtless have gratified Chatham's own taste. Parliament gave a practical proof of its gratitude by a public grant of £20,000 for the payment of his debts and by settling an annuity of £4,000 on his heirs.

The City fathers, whom Pitt had always numbered among his warmest supporters, put up a cenotaph in the Guildhall which, as Burke's majestic and inspired inscription said, was intended to remind the citizens for ever 'that the means by which Providence raises a nation to greatness are the virtues infused into great men'.

Burke did not always speak of Chatham in so laudatory a tone. His confidential comments are often quite critical. He perceived a painful difference between Chatham as he really was and 'the ostensible public man'. Burke was not the only critic. A man who was Pitt's faithful follower for more than a decade said much the same; whatever one may think of Shelburne's character, there is no ground for considering that he was here actuated by any selfish motives. In the autobiography which he wrote in his maturity he called Pitt 'a complete artificial character' who was always acting a part and was incapable of friendship. In all the ten years in which he had been in continuous political relations with Pitt, he had never drunk so much as a glass of water in his house or had five minutes informal conversation with him. Indeed it is strange how few real friends Pitt possessed and how his friendships all broke up sooner or later. He seems to have confined all his warmer feelings to his immediate family, who returned his love in full measure. Thus his home life is the only relationship which has any human appeal to it, or brings one into close contact with him in any way.

It was inevitable that certain defects in his character should reduce his effectiveness in public life. Only a pedant would ever tax him with being consumed with burning ambition. But even a historian cannot brush aside the criticism that his need to assert himself frequently made co-operation with those of like mind difficult for him and played into the hands of their common enemy. Yet at the same time it must not be forgotten that he was a man who suffered severely from bad health. Even if things were perhaps not always quite so bad as he made them appear at the time, yet the will-power with which he overcame sickness and suffering often compels admiration. This is especially true of his closing years during the American troubles. Then it was that he fought with the fire and passion of a great patriot, sacrificing all his energies to wrestle with the misfortune which, as he saw with prophetic vision, would be brought upon his beloved country by the lust for power of a narrow-minded, thick-headed king and the servility and venality of his creatures.

The high noon of Pitt's life covers only a few years. But in those years he proved that he was a world figure of the type which powerfully determines the course of history in future generations. Then it was that he displayed all the qualities of a born leader of his people in the hour of need, which he himself turned into the hour of triumph. Perhaps the highest tribute one can pay to William Pitt is to affirm that he made good the bold words he uttered before entering upon his ministry: 'I am sure I can save this country, and nobody else can.'

CHAPTER XVI

CHARLES FOX'S
VICTORY OVER GEORGE III:
BEGINNINGS OF THE YOUNGER PITT

By this time Charles Fox had long ago risen above the family tradition of Holland House and had ceased to regard Chatham first and foremost as his father's rival and enemy. If some years back he had maintained in the face of Wedderburn that it had been Chatham's appointment which had turned the tide in the Seven Years' War, then this statement carried particular weight coming from the son of Henry Fox. On another occasion he had described Chatham as a 'venerable character whom I honour and revere', and he had called the House to witness that whenever his views differed from Chatham's he was moved by no early prejudice nor childish pique. He certainly felt to the full the loss which the nation had suffered by Chatham's death.

But it was in the nature of things that he should now be regarded as the real leader of the opposition, and that the hopes of all who yearned for an end to the King's personal government and to the American War should be centred on him. Although he had been sitting in Parliament long enough for it to be quite impossible to imagine it without him, he was still only thirty. Even now he was far removed from 'mature respectability and solvent morality'. But he was not simply the member most popular with friend and foe alike, whom everyone in the Commons called by his Christian name, and a welcome, indeed a lionised guest at the splendid country houses of the great nobles; though no Adonis, he stood in the highest favour with those witty and beautiful, gay and enthusiastic ladies at the centre of the glittering society of the 'Grand Whiggery' who smile down upon us from the masterpieces of Gainsborough and Reynolds.

Their acknowledged leader was the beautiful Duchess of Devonshire, Georgiana, the daughter of Earl Spencer. Her morals were not beyond reproach either, but what drew her to

Charles Fox was his idealism and the genuine camaraderie with which he treated her and other clever and witty women. What he himself thought about such women he expressed later in one of his great speeches on parliamentary reform (May 26th, 1797). Certainly, he said, no one had so far suggested the absurd idea of extending the elective suffrage to the female sex. 'And yet, justly respecting, as we must do, the mental powers, the acquirements, the discrimination and the talents of the women of England, ... knowing ... that they have interests as dear and as important as our own, it must be the genuine feeling of every gentleman who hears me, that all the superior classes of the female sex of England must be more capable of exercising the elective suffrage with deliberation and propriety, than the un-informed individuals of the lowest class of men to whom the advocates of universal suffrage would extend it.' Georgiana herself, at a time when Fox's political star was in eclipse, wrote to a friend of theirs: 'As I am sure you do not think that I, as a woman, ever was, could be, or am in love with Charles Fox, you will allow that in fervour, enthusiasm, and devotion I am a good friend. . . .' She also wrote: 'No, would I were a man, to unite my talents, my hopes, my fortune with Charles's, to make common cause and fall or rule with him. . . .' A man who could call forth such feelings and keep them alive for decades must have had something unusual, something unique about him. Nor was Georgiana the only person to think so.

In these years, Fox's political labours were sweetened by the feeling that they were not in vain. In Parliament the size of the opposition vote was increasing. Fox was tireless not only in debate but also in organizing and holding together the opposi-tion. He knew how to bestir the diffident and whip in the stragglers for a division; he had the knack of handling everyone in just the right way, of touching the string which would sound a responsive note.

Of course he regarded the struggle with France—soon to be joined by Spain and Holland—as being in quite a different category from the squabble with the Americans. This last he saw as a civil war; the other as a national war which fired his patriotic zeal. When the Franco-Spanish fleet appeared in the Channel and threatened the English coast, he hastened to Torbay so as not to miss the expected engagement. The seadogs in command of the warships were delighted to see among them this Westminster orator, whose name was a household word, and thanks to his frank and human bearing they were soon as full of enthusiasm for him as were his fellow members at Brooks's.

Fox saw clearly enough that the real foe he had to contend with was the King himself. George, too, looked on Fox as a personal enemy with whom he had to struggle for supremacy in his own kingdom. In this duel George had on his side all the open and secret influence which the Crown and its ministers wielded as controllers of the secret service money, as the fount of the most coveted titles, honours and dignities, and as principals in the financing of all state loans. Against him stood the continued run of failures in the war which was principally ascribed, and with good reason, to the incompetence and negligence of His Majesty's ministers, and also the intellectual and moral ascendancy of the opposition in Parliament which was increasingly backed by the mood of the country. It is inevitable that in a protracted war which achieves no successes the people should gradually turn from feelings of enthusiasm to sober reflection, and at length, to discontent. Quite apart from the heavy casualties, mounting taxes and an expanding national debt see to this. More especially when, as in the American War, calm reflection gives rise to misgivings about the justice of one's own cause and to something more than misgivings about the competence and worth of one's own government. The means by which popular feeling could find expression were, of course, far less developed in eighteenth century England than, shall we say, at the time of Cobden's Anti-Corn-Law League. But such few means as did exist were fully exploited for the first time by the opposition. It organized county and borough meetings; they were conducted by well-known members of Parliament, and they voiced their grievances in clearly-worded resolutions. Among other things they demanded electoral reform and the abolition of numerous sinecures which served no purpose but to swell the influence of the King, who used them to buy over members to vote in the 'right way'.

Fox took a vigorous, leading part in this movement. It was he who, on February 2nd, 1780, ran a meeting for the constituency

of Westminster in Westminster Hall itself, where more people
assembled than had ever before been seen gathered in one
place. This meeting not only adopted the usual resolutions but
gave political expression to its views even more clearly by
deciding to put up Charles Fox as its candidate at the next
election. And so a prospect opened up before him of representing, not the magnificent total of thirteen Malmesbury electors,
but a large London constituency where voters were numbered
by the thousand and elections were really contested. His whole
political outlook left him no alternative but to say 'Yes' to such
a summons, but his career was not really made any easier or
more comfortable by it.

This strong political movement of the winter of 1779-80
cleared the way for a parliamentary thrust at the very heart of
George's system. On April 6th, 1780, Dunning moved a
resolution in the Commons against the influence of the Crown.
Dunning belonged to the group centred around Shelburne,
who had placed a seat at his disposal; he was perhaps the most
capable and distinguished lawyer whom the opposition could
claim in the Commons. Chatham, who was, generally speaking,
no friend of the legal profession, had bestowed high praise on
Dunning: he said he was more than a lawyer, he was 'the law
itself'. Dunning contrived to draft his resolution in words which
impressed themselves on the memory of his own and later
generations. 'That it is the opinion of this Committee that the
influence of the Crown has increased, is increasing and ought
to be diminished.' This resolution was adopted by 233 votes to
215. When it is remembered that in the two Houses there sat
hundreds of men who depended on the Crown for their weal
or woe and well knew the care with which the King scanned
every division list, it can be seen that Parliament and freedom
of speech can set some limits even to a system of unscrupulous
bribery: all the golden arguments of the Treasury bench could
not wholly outweigh the political arguments of an opposition
backed by the feelings of the people.

The immediate effect of Dunning's resolution fell short of
what was hoped. There were various reasons for this, the most
important being the outbreak of disorders in London in June,
1780. These had nothing to do with the burning controversies
of the day but hinged on an attempt to take a modest step for-

ward towards religious toleration, one of the most attractive features of the Whig system. Sir George Saville, a most respected and enlightened figure among the Whig leaders, had managed to repeal the worst penal laws against the Catholics which had dragged on since the days of William III. A crazy fanatic, Lord George Gordon, whipped up rabid Protestants and the London mob against this supposed surrender of England to the Papacy by raising the battle-cry of 'No Popery!' For a whole week London was in the hands of the mob, where the rowdies, of course, gained more and more influence with every day that passed. Churches belonging to Catholics, even their private houses and especially their wine-cellars, were looted and fired; politicians like Burke, who were decried as friends of the Catholics, were threatened; and the gates of the prisons were broken down to swell the swarm of looters and incendiaries. The whole stark wretchedness of a metropolis with no regular police force became terribly plain to see. It was a situation in which the unflinching fortitude of George III could stand the test. He called in the military, who eventually restored order.

These riots had the effect which disorders and looting always have. Anyone with anything to lose rallied to the powers that be. The effect was hammered home by the ministerial press, which unblushingly accused opposition leaders of organizing and financing the outbreak in order to foment a revolution. This psychological situation was exploited politically by the King's surprise move of dissolving Parliament on September 1st, 1780. Organizing an election campaign suited his book far better than waging a war. The election brought back the ministerial majority to the Commons substantially unchanged. In Windsor, under the shadow of the castle, George did not disdain to pay personal calls on tradespeople who had a vote so as to make it clear to them, in his stuttering, abrupt way, that they would lose his custom if they even dreamed of voting for the Whig candidate, Admiral Keppel. Here he was successful, if only by sixteen votes. At Westminster, on the other hand, where he had his official residence, he had to swallow the bitter pill that 4878 electors plumped for Charles Fox as against the mere 4527 who supported the court candidate. But it had been a heated engagement in which Fox had to make innumerable addresses, visit countless voters, write letters and publish appeals in the newspapers before he could call the victory his own. At that time polling went on for days. Voting was of course done in public, and the candidates had to watch from day to day and from hour to hour how the scale tipped first this way and then that. To recompense Fox for his trials and torments, the electors carried him as the victor in triumph round the town, and their huzzas rang out most loudly in front of the palace. Whatever else one may say about eighteenth century elections, one can hardly complain that they were prosaic or colourless.

In this election William Pitt stood for Cambridge University. But the dons and country parsons who voted here had little inclination to be represented by a youth of twenty-one who had only just completed his studies. But with a name like Pitt it was not hard to find a more hospitable borough. The father of one of his undergraduate friends placed one of his eleven constituencies at his disposal, and so Pitt was enabled to enter the Commons on January 23rd, 1781, as member for Appleby, and he remained a member of the Commons for exactly twenty-five years, up to January 23rd, 1806, the last day of his life.

William Pitt the younger was born on May 28th, 1759, that is, in the year which was his father's *annus mirabilis*. (This makes him an exact contemporary of Friedrich Schiller, who died six months before him, while Fox's birth is parallel with Goethe's.) William, like Chatham, was a second son, and Henry, as well as Charles Fox, was a second son too; so incidentally was the man who set his seal on the coming age—Napoleon Bonaparte. This was fortunate for Charles Fox and William Pitt, since in this way they escaped having to enter the Lords when their fathers died. Chatham had recognized early on that his second son far excelled his elder brother in intellectual gifts, initiative and energy. He had given all his care to William's upbringing, and to what good effect is shown by the admission of Lady Caroline Fox: she compared young Pitt's good breeding very flatteringly with the behaviour of her own sons, and is even said to have seen in him at this early age a dangerous future rival to her Charles. After his own disagreeable experiences at Eton, Chatham preferred having his sons tutored privately at home to sending them to a public school. Here William's gifts matured unusually quickly, and when he was fifteen he went up to Cambridge. The boy's rapid strides are all the more remarkable when it is remembered that from his earliest days he was often ill for long periods at a stretch. His university studies, too, were often interrupted by illness. When they were over he kept his terms at Lincoln's Inn. He was also called to the Bar and practised as a barrister, but from the very outset he had his eyes on the political career for which his father had destined and prepared him.

His education equipped him admirably for many aspects of this career. Needless to say, it was grounded on a solid knowledge of the classical languages and the classics, and if throughout his life Pitt could embellish his speeches with, at times, most felicitously chosen quotations from them, this does not mean that he studied them to this end alone. He also mastered those branches of knowledge which are of immediate importance to the politician—history, law, and—not quite so comprehensible at that time—political economy. In 1776, that is, when Pitt was still studying at Cambridge, Adam Smith published his epoch-making *Wealth of Nations*, which shivered into fragments the mercantilist doctrines, dominant practically without dispute up till then, and demonstrated and praised the blessings of free trade. Pitt, when a minister in 1792, confessed himself a disciple of Adam Smith in his budget speech, and from this it is but a short step to deduce that he had studied Smith's book as an undergraduate. In any case he evinced an unmistakable and telling interest in economic, social and, above all, financial matters from the opening of his political career.

The course of Pitt's development shows that from the very outset he had fixed his eye steadily on his goal and subordinated all else to reaching it. He did not let himself be caught up by the giddy round of pleasure of the undergraduate life of the day. Perhaps it was not altogether good for his knowledge of men and his education in the art of social intercourse to have mingled so comparatively seldom in the gay and boisterous throng. But it was fortunate for him that he thereby escaped many of the temptations which had beckoned to young Charles Fox. But even William Pitt was not indifferent to the lure of play: when, however, he realized the dangers with which it threatened him he resolutely quitted the tables, never to return to them. If would have been a good thing for him if he had shown the same strength of mind towards the bottle, for port wine had a good deal to do with his early end.

Never, perhaps, has a young member so quickly won a place in the front rank as William Pitt. His maiden speech on February 26th, 1781, was an event. He spoke on a motion of Burke's for the reform of the Civil List and the abolition of sinecures, and showed that, even after this great orator and thinker had spoken, he could still find something new to say, and could formulate and present it with consummate skill. When Charles Fox was a very young man, his speeches, too, had caused a sensation. But Fox had impressed his listeners first and foremost by his mastery as a born debater and the effortless ease with which he developed his dazzling arguments. Pitt's first speech bore in greater measure the stamp of the statesman, and no one was more glad and ready to acknowledge this publicly than Charles Fox. It was far removed from his large-hearted nature to be jealous of this triumph of a newcomer, even if he were the son and heir of a man who had been for a lifetime his own father's successful rival. He congratulated young Pitt on his success in the most cordial terms and at once put him up for Brooks's, where he himself was the central figure and held his court. What could not have been achieved by lasting co-operation and alliance between these two brilliantly talented men, who complemented each other so admirably in so many respects? Nothing could have withstood them, least of all the King's personal government, as the declared foe of which Pitt also made his bow upon the parliamentary stage. But this is merely another of those unreal speculations which are as powerfully engaging to the fancy as they are idle. Fate willed it otherwise. It was the struggle between these two men which marked the succeeding decades and shaped Fox's life.

But no one could foretell the future at this date. With undaunted courage Fox set about winning in the new Parliament, as in the old, the self-same success that he had wrested from George by the surprise election result at Westminster. Once again he showed his complete mastery as a party leader and a speaker. His speeches are marked not only by debating skill, but by the vast, impressive grasp of the facts of politics with which he stripped all the weaknesses and subterfuges of the administration naked, and shed light on its blunders in the conduct of the war.

But heavier than the parliamentary blows with which Fox, Burke and Pitt battered the King's system were the military blows under which it reeled, thanks to General George Washington. On October 19th, 1781, a whole British army was forced to capitulate at Yorktown. At the end of November news of the catastrophe reached London. No intelligent man could now doubt that the attempt to subdue the American colonies by force of arms had completely and utterly failed. 'Blows must decide,' George III had written. They *had* decided —but not in his favour. True, George did not throw in his hand all the while that his band of parliamentary janissaries held together. It was another three months before they were scattered. Only on February 27th, 1782, were they transformed into a minority over a motion by General Conway, who called for an end to the war with America. Even so, George was for holding out. But now North had had quite enough. He insisted on resigning, or, as the King preferred to put it, he 'deserted'. Not even George's threat to lay aside the crown could dissuade him any longer. On March 20th he told Parliament that his resignation was a fact in a speech not unworthy of the historic moment.

A sigh of relief swept through the country. Dr. Johnson, that dyed-in-the-wool Tory, could not refrain from rejoicing at the fall of this ministry. 'Such a bunch of imbecility never disgraced a country. If they sent a messenger into the City to take up a printer, the messenger was taken up instead of the printer. . . . If they sent one army to the relief of another, the first army was defeated and taken before the second arrived. I will not say that what they did was always wrong; but it was always done at a wrong time.' What Johnson, in his loyalty to the Crown, did not put into words, thousands of others were feeling; not only was the ministry defeated but the King himself was beaten too. This American war had been *his* war, just as the Seven Years' War had been Chatham's. This was the bitter fruit which George's system of personal government had borne for the English people. Many might now recall Burke's words: 'A great empire and little minds go ill together.'

If any one figure in home politics can be regarded as George's

conqueror, it was Charles Fox. Some years before it had been
said—and again the voice is Johnson's: '. . . It was a doubt
whether the nation should be ruled by the sceptre of George III
or the tongue of Fox,' and it was Johnson who now rejoiced that
Fox had carried the day. By all the rules of the parliamentary
game the victor should now have taken the helm. But George,
too, knew very well who had beaten him, and if he had not been
able to bear Fox for many years past, he now loathed him as the
man who had crossed his path with such effect. He might
indeed swathe this hatred in the mantle of virtue, and trim it
with the virtuous abhorrence felt by a respectable paterfamilias for a gambler and contractor of debts. But everyone
knew the scandalous private life led by Lord Sandwich, the
Secretary of State, and by other gentlemen, who none the less
enjoyed the unclouded grace and favour of the puritanical
King, and everyone knew, too, the sliding scale which he adjusted to measure first the supporters and then the opponents of
his system.

George tried all possible dodges to avoid a ministry with Fox
as the brains of it. The opposition had previously been made up
of two groups; by far the larger of these, and the one to which
Fox belonged, looked to Rockingham as its leader. The smaller,
embracing all that remained of Chatham's following, now
clustered round Shelburne. The youngest and by far the most
important of their recruits was William Pitt. George turned to
Shelburne in order to avoid a Rockingham ministry, but Shelburne gave him the only answer possible in the circumstances—
that Rockingham alone had the power to form a ministry which
could face Parliament. Reluctantly George yielded. But he gave
Rockingham to understand in every way that he was not welcome as a minister. The marquis, however, was an old enough
hand to ignore these signs of royal disfavour. He formed an
administration out of both groups of Whigs.

A striking illustration of the nature of this coalition was the
way in which the two most important political posts, those of
the Secretaries of State, were filled by the most powerful man in
each group: Fox and Shelburne. The illogical division into a
northern and southern department was now at long last
abolished. Shelburne's office took in home affairs, Ireland and
the colonies, and Fox's, foreign affairs. This was a fundamental

step forward, out of which there gradually developed the two distinct departments, under the Home Secretary and Foreign Secretary, which exist today. Unfortunately it soon became plain at the peace negotiations that putting the colonies, that is America, under a department other than that of foreign affairs was leading to new, and in the end, to ominous difficulties. Outside these two offices, both groups, broadly speaking, were also represented fairly evenly in the Cabinet. But George succeeded in keeping one man in office belonging to neither of the two groups, who none the less in the true sense of the word represented the King himself: this was Thurlow, the Lord Chancellor. Rockingham had to make this concession in the interests of bringing the ministry into being, despite his unpleasant experience in his first Cabinet with Northington who had been Lord Chancellor and the King's confidant.

Apart from this, the greatest interest attaches to two men who did not get into the Cabinet: Burke and Pitt. Burke contented himself with the post of Paymaster-General, which did not carry Cabinet rank. His exclusion from the Cabinet has been put down to the aristocratic exclusiveness of the Whigs, but the real reasons probably lay more in certain personal shortcomings. No one can doubt, and Burke's aristocratic friends doubted it least of all, that in wealth of political ideas and profusion of political knowledge he towered above the average Cabinet minister. But he was sadly lacking in soundness of judgement, quiet tact and the ability to fit in. To this must be added a certain aura of political fortune-hunting which surrounded Burke's immediate circle even more than it did the man himself. A member of one of the accepted ruling families could get over this, but not an upstart of obscure antecedents. The most significant thing is that Burke himself never aspired to Cabinet rank, and, indeed, dismissed such a thought as absurd. He was quite content with the office which Rockingham gave him, and with the four thousand pounds it brought him in after he had himself rooted out the profitable abuses of the past with a true reformer's zeal.

Pitt thought and acted quite differently. Rockingham offered him a secondary post which seemed quite appropriate for a young man of two-and-twenty with only a single year's parliamentary experience. But Pitt declined. He had already stated quite gratuitously in Parliament some weeks before that he would never accept a subordinate post. At the time this declaration had caused laughter and headshakings. But it was made in all seriousness; if one thinks of later developments one can hardly doubt that Pitt had pondered the matter well and had deliberately announced his pretensions to all the world. Although he kept his promise by supporting the administration as a private member, this refusal determined the whole course of his later career.

But at first, indeed, Pitt and Fox were of one mind over one question which from the outset Pitt had made his own particular concern. This was the problem of electoral reform. Under the catchword 'reform' two different problems were discussed at that time. One was the so-called Economical Reform, which was directed against the King's underground influence in Parliament and planned to abolish sinecures and to regulate the civil list. Its most prominent spokesman was Burke, who was, moreover, able to carry out at least a part of his programme during his short period in office. But the reform movement had also turned its attention to the system by which the members themselves were elected. The first onslaught on the rotten parts of the constitution had already been delivered years before by Chatham: the popular movement of the winter of 1779 had in part taken up this reform, and Fox had already come out in support of far-reaching demands at the mass meeting in Westminster Hall. His uncle, the Duke of Richmond, called in the Lords for a uniform division of the constituencies and universal suffrage for adults. These were radical demands which sent a shiver down the spine of Burke, who idolized the British constitution. Pitt now took up electoral reform in the Commons. On May 7th he moved the setting up of a committee to examine the whole question. Fox supported the motion, and their joint forces succeeded in assembling a minority in favour which was only defeated by twenty votes. It was the best division which the friends of reform had ever achieved and the best they were to achieve for fifty years. It showed what Pitt and Fox could do when they worked in harness, and how much the country's progress was to be checked by their ceasing to be friends and moving into opposite camps.

One other problem came up which was not to be laid to rest

for a whole century—the Irish question. The system by which Ireland was governed was one of the strangest and most anomalous the wide world over. Ireland had her own parliament which sat in Dublin. But only the Protestant Irish were entitled to elect members to this assembly, and they made up only a tiny minority of the population. The Catholics, the overwhelming majority, had no rights at all. The administration was headed by the Lord-Lieutenant, an English viceroy appointed by the Cabinet in London. Also the Irish Parliament could only deliberate measures approved in advance by the Privy Council. And more than all this, the Parliament at Westminster could pass laws binding upon Ireland. In actual fact the Viceroy could only keep things running by a system of bribery which left the London example far behind.

The whole machine broke down when England was no longer able to maintain in Ireland the military forces needed to govern the country. This was one of the results of the American war, which compelled the ministry to reduce the Irish garrison to a few thousand men. Volunteer battalions organized themselves to defend the country against a French invasion. They became a power with which not only the enemy without but also the British administration had to reckon. They acted as backing for the very gifted parliamentary leaders of the Irish freedom movement, the most outstanding of whom was that great orator, Henry Grattan. He succeeded in uniting the volunteers and Irish politicians in a demand for legislative independence.

Such was the state of things when the new administration took over. Ireland came under Shelburne. He reached the conclusion that there was nothing for it but to meet the Irish demand. The Cabinet backed him, and the necessary bills were moved by Shelburne in the Lords and Fox in the Commons. Ireland became, legislatively and juridically, independent of Britain. But the hope that this had solved the problem soon proved a vain one.

Whenever Fox had to speak as a minister, he stood out head and shoulders above the rest of the new ministry. As early as the beginning of May, Horace Walpole wrote to a friend: 'He already shines as greatly in place as he did in opposition, though infinitely more difficult a task. He is now as indefatigable as he was idle. He has a perfect temper, and not only good humour

Q

but good nature; and, which is the first quality in a prime minister of a free country, has more commonsense than any man, with amazing parts that are neither ostentatious nor affected.' Horace paid him the highest compliment he could bestow by comparing him with his own father, Sir Robert Walpole.

The effect which Fox's eloquence had on an unbiassed foreigner can be seen from the travel letters which a young German, Carl Philipp Moritz, later celebrated as the author of the autobiographical novel *Anton Reiser* and as a friend of Goethe's, wrote from England at the time. When visiting Parliament he happened to hear Fox speak. 'Fox was sitting . . . not far from the table on which the gilt sceptre lay. He took his place so near it that he could reach it with his hand, and, thus placed, he gave it many a violent and hearty thump, either to aid, or to show, the energy with which he spoke. . . . It is impossible for me to describe with what fire and persuasive eloquence he spoke, and how the Speaker in the chair incessantly nodded approbation from beneath his solemn wig; and innumerable voices incessantly called out, "Hear him! hear him!" and when there was the least sign that he intended to leave off speaking, they no less vociferously exclaimed, "Go on!" and so he continued to speak in this manner for nearly two hours.'

Beyond a doubt Charles Fox was now well pleased to show what a man like himself aged thirty-three could do in a responsible post. His whole mode of life was changed. He was hardly ever to be seen at Brooks's, to the great disappointment of many members, who had hastily paid up their overdue subscriptions so as to bask in the sunshine of a minister's company. Never once during his term of office did he take a hand of cards; with great strength of mind he shook off the fetters of a passion which had done him such immeasurable harm. He devoted all his time and all his energy to his office. With the same astonishing rapidity with which he laid bare an opponent's weakness or produced a striking argument in debate, he now went to the root of the most complicated problems and put his finger on the key point when studying bulging files. The foreign diplomats who had to negotiate with him were delighted by his mastery of his material, and his accomplishment in the French language, as well as by his frankness, sincerity and irresistible friendliness. A memorandum of Fox's, written in French, which can be looked on as a programme for a foreign policy and was intended for Frederick of Prussia, made a great impression on him, without, however, bearing any fruit. Surely Fox would succeed in solving the great problem which awaited him as foreign minister—the problem of ending the war and making the peace?

The scene of the peace talks was Paris. Benjamin Franklin, the most distinguished and important representative of the American colonies, had been there for years. American affairs came under Shelburne, who, trading on the fact that he knew Franklin well from his London days, sent over a certain Oswald to invite him to an exchange of views on how peace might be restored. Oswald was sent with the knowledge and approval of the Cabinet. Franklin, too, declared himself ready to negotiate, but only if France took part in the talks; he suggested the French minister Vergennes to Oswald. When Oswald returned to London with his report, the Cabinet decided to follow up this line and open discussions with both powers. Shelburne was more than half inclined to take the French negotiations into his own hands as well. But, of course, Fox would not agree to this, and the Cabinet authorized him to send a suitable person on his own behalf for the talks with Vergennes. Fox chose one of his friends, the twenty-seven-year-old Thomas Grenville, a younger son of the author of the Stamp Act.

Although Oswald and Grenville got on tolerably well together, this arrangement was none the less disastrous. Even two cooks are enough to spoil the broth. This could only have been prevented if full confidence had existed between the two Secretaries of State. But that was out of the question. Fox had already said, soon after the formation of the ministry, that it consisted of two parts, one belonging to the public and the other to the King. His suspicions had obviously been roused by the way Shelburne let himself be used by the King to keep Rockingham at a distance from the throne. He was justified in this insofar as the King, for as long as the administration lasted, treated Shelburne as a minister of the same level of rank and influence as the head of the Cabinet, so that his leader's wishes only had a claim to be carried out if Shelburne approved them. It is highly significant that George wrote to Shelburne that he welcomed the sending of Oswald to Paris because it could not fail to be a useful check on that part of the negotiations which was in other hands, that is, of course, in Fox's.

In any case Shelburne already enjoyed the reputation of being an intriguer, which did not improve things at all. He was certainly an unusual type of man—and not altogether in a bad sense either. In political and more especially in economic questions he possessed an intellectual self-reliance which often raised him far above his contemporaries. He was the patron of freethinkers such as Morellet, the French encyclopedist, of Dr. Priestley, the English Dissenter, and of that relentless critic of everything traditional, Jeremy Bentham, the father of Philosophic Radicalism. Equally undeniable was his wide expert knowledge of both home and foreign policy. And yet, for all that, no one, except half-a-dozen followers, most of whom were for one reason or another under an obligation to him, would have anything to do with him. Nobody trusted him further than they could see him. His compliments rang false. Whoever was praised by him to his face, was quite prepared to be pulled to pieces remorselessly and viciously behind his back. His critics pointed out that he had fallen foul of all his temporary political allies. He was called a Jesuit or, in reference to an Italian Jesuit, who had been executed for his part in a murder plot, Malagrida. Few could find such a personality more antipathetic and distasteful than did Charles Fox, who—not infrequently to his own disadvantage—always bluntly said what he thought, quite apart from the mistrust which the recollection of his father's experiences with Shelburne must have aroused in him. His private letters during these months show how all the time he felt uneasy and intrigued against, and how it was almost always Shelburne on whom his suspicion lighted. But behind Shelburne he saw the King at work, plotting away. He guessed that the pair of them were working hand in glove to destroy the Cabinet. His one desire was to bring about peace before that happened, 'although I am convinced that in signing it I shall sign the end of this Ministry. *Faisons notre devoir, arrive qui pourra. . . .*' Thus he wrote on May 11th, 1782, to his friend, Fitzpatrick, who was at the same time Shelburne's brother-in-law.

Whether Shelburne was really intriguing in the way Fox

imagined is hard to determine. But Fox's worst fears seemed confirmed when he learned that Shelburne had kept his colleagues in the dark about a confidential note handed by Franklin to Oswald in which he suggested no less than the cession of Canada. Before this discovery could be taken up and thrashed out in public, a breach opened up over one of the fundamental questions of the peace negotiations. Fox demanded that the British government should recognize America's independence unconditionally without regard to the progress of the peace talks. When in one Cabinet meeting after another he failed to carry his point, he told his intimates that he was determined to resign.

Possibly, probably even, he could still have been dissuaded if the administration had not at this moment been struck by a catastrophe. On July 1st, 1782, Rockingham died at the early age of fifty-two. Although he was not a man of outstanding ability or impressive personality, his death was none the less an irreparable loss to his party and his cause, because he was a man of his word, of irreproachable purity of character, inspiring all who had any dealings with him with complete confidence. 'His virtues were his arts'; thus wrote Burke, who had recognized his weaknesses as well as his merits, giving epigrammatic brevity to the beautiful inscription which he dedicated to him. It is no accident that a true portrait of the aristocracy of eighteenth century England shows that at least one noble lord owed his career and his success to his excellent character.

Who was to succeed him? If weight in politics and the ability to lead had been the touchstone, then Fox must have gone to the head of the Cabinet. But in view of the King's hatred for him this was, of course, out of the question. Quite the contrary, in fact; George hastened to execute his long-planned coup against the Whigs and to summon Shelburne at once. The Rockingham Whigs protested against this. Their best political brain, if Fox was perforce left out of account, was Richmond. Unhappily Fox and his other party friends preferred the far less significant Duke of Portland to Richmond, though hardly anything could be said in Portland's favour but that he had a title. Fox went to the King and told him that the only man who could lead the Cabinet would be one who commanded the confidence of the dead prime minister's friends and that Shelburne did not possess that confidence. When the King ignored this, Fox resigned.

It has been a matter of controversy whether such conduct was constitutionally correct. The appointment of a prime minister, it has been argued, is a matter for the royal prerogative. To propose Portland as a successor to Rockingham has been termed an interference by an aristocratic clique with this prerogative of the King. But Fox himself has quite rightly summed up the situation in one of his speeches: if the King does indisputably possess the right to appoint the prime minister, every minister possesses just as indisputably the right to decide for himself whether he will go on serving under that prime minister or not. The right of the Crown to decide who is to be a new prime minister remains to this day as possibly the most important facet of the royal prerogative. But the King knows that in practice his choice is limited to the men who can form a cabinet and hold together a majority in the Commons. If on Gladstone's resignation Queen Victoria preferred Lord Rosebery to Sir William Harcourt, the then Chancellor of the Exchequer, or if when Bonar Law fell ill, George V preferred Baldwin to the far more brilliant Lord Curzon, they could only do so by assuming that the most important members of the existing Cabinet were or would be in agreement. This assumption was not valid in 1880 when Victoria, after the fall of Disraeli, wanted to summon Earl Granville to avoid appointing Gladstone, and in consequence, much against her will, she had to give up the idea.

Certainly it was not easy for Charles Fox to relinquish the post which had for the first time let him conduct higher policy in a responsible way and bring in the peace on which his heart was set. But he was convinced that a principle was at stake. It was not only that his mistrust of Shelburne made all fruitful co-operation with him impossible; above all he suspected him, as a confidant of the King, of being about to retrace the steps which the Whigs under his own leadership had taken in the struggle against the King's personal government and of betraying the fortress which he and his friends had at last taken by storm after such long, fierce battles. This suspicion, as we now know from the correspondence between George and Shelburne, was fully justified. The King was far from accepting his defeat as final. Even before Rockingham's death he was at work in secret on a recasting of the Cabinet which would give him back his 'independency', and in this Shelburne was his willing tool. Both were agreed that the most dangerous obstacle to their plans was Fox, and they were already pondering how they could pare his claws. George recommended that he should not be dismissed out of hand, but 'if Lord Shelburne accept the Head of the Treasury and is succeeded by Mr. Pitt' as Secretary of State, Fox might be driven to resign. On no account, preached George, should Shelburne be a party leader; rather must the administration be placed on a 'broad bottom', the old recipe, that is, which had proved itself so effective in the days of Chatham's ministry. How far Shelburne fell in with this is shown by his wanting to take Jenkinson, the experienced manager of the 'King's Friends', into his administration.

In the speech he made to justify his resignation to the Commons, Fox based his case on the plea that if he had stayed in office it might have been taken as a proof that the principle for which he had fought still continued to direct the ministry. '. . . He felt it to be indispensably necessary that he should come forward and ring the alarum bell, and tell this country that the principle on which they had, with due deliberation, formed this administration, was abandoned, and that the old system was to be revived, most probably with the old men, or indeed with any men that could be found.' This description of the plot which George had incubated and Shelburne had hatched was the bare truth of the matter.

But the success of Fox's manoeuvre was from the outset very much in doubt, because by no means all of his party associates followed his example. Richmond in particular not only refused to resign but exerted his whole influence to dissuade his friends from doing so. Among those who followed Fox were Shelburne's brother-in-law, Fitzpatrick, the Duke of Portland and Edmund Burke. It was generally assumed of Burke that he at least stiffened Fox's intransigence. He was a sworn enemy of Shelburne's, whom he considered utterly unprincipled, and he belaboured him in the House so viciously and personally that the excesses of his violence simply helped the victim of his attack.

In these circumstances it was easy for Shelburne to fill the gaps. The most sensational and by far the most momentous of the new appointments was that made to the Exchequer. On the day after Rockingham's death Fox had a conversation with Pitt and said he feared that the King's personal government would be revived, adding, 'They look to *you*; *without* you they cannot succeed. . . .' 'If they reckon on *me*,' answered Pitt, 'they may find themselves mistaken.' But Fox retailed the conversation to a friend with the remark 'I believe they will *not* be mistaken.' From his place as Secretary of State he had kept a close eye on this young member and had felt doubts as to where his path would lead him. He already took the view that Shelburne, in his attempt to restore the King's system, was counting on Pitt, and he could not altogether rid himself of the fear that Pitt's ambition might triumph over his integrity, especially if he were to be enticed by the hope of being the first. Fox's fears were justified; indeed, Pitt cannot have been sincere in his denial. For as early as June 30th Shelburne had written to George that a few days before he had had a conversation with Pitt with a view to a new arrangement, and that he believed he might be satisfied with the upshot. He now offered Pitt the Exchequer, and Pitt accepted it without hesitation. In the first debate on Fox's resignation, when Fox tried to justify the step he had taken by attacks on Shelburne, Pitt took the field against him in a way that must have driven home to Fox the fact that from then on Pitt and he were to be at war.

To a greater extent than either could foresee, the course of the lives of William Pitt and Charles James Fox was decided during these few weeks.

CHAPTER XVII

THE COALITION.
GEORGE III's VICTORY OVER
CHARLES FOX

Fox still had the game in his hands, at least to some extent. Shelburne had not got a majority in the Commons and knew it. So at the outset it was not altogether impossible that Fox's hour would yet come round again.

Shelburne's first and most important task was, of course, to conclude the peace. In the meantime England's position had improved somewhat in many of the theatres of war. Rodney's brilliant victory over the French fleet in the West Indies (April 12th, 1782) had saved Jamaica and cut the sea link between the allied powers of France and America. Gibraltar, the real war objective of the Spaniards, had withstood a year's siege, thanks to its heroic defence by General Eliott, and when in October, 1782, Howe's fleet managed to revictual the fortress, Spain had to abandon all hope and raise the siege. In France the war had led to a dislocation of her finances which in a few years made an early peace a necessity. America's war aims were achieved as soon as her independence was declared. None of the allies had much inclination to make sacrifices for the others; indeed, the French King's ministers discovered that it was by no means in their master's interests for the new American republic to grow too strong. So Shelburne and his envoys found a fairly wide readiness to make peace among all the enemy powers. The first to sign were the Americans (November 20th, 1782), and the preliminaries with France and Spain were signed at Versailles on January 20th, 1783.

The way the war had gone meant, of course, that these treaties were not advantageous to Britain. But a long and violent struggle over the extent of the concessions required raged both between King and Cabinet and within the Cabinet itself. On the cardinal question of whether American independence should be conceded unconditionally—as Fox had demanded from the outset—or only on condition that a general

peace was made between all the parties, there prevailed, even
after the signature, so little agreement that Shelburne and Pitt
made conflicting statements in the two Houses, and Pitt had to
endure a wigging from the King who could not learn from
experience. On the other hand, George was prepared to
exchange Gibraltar for other territorial acquisitions. Britain
owes it principally to the determination shown by Richmond
and Keppel that she kept this bastion of her Empire. The
antagonisms in the Cabinet over this and other questions
became so acute that Shelburne said to Grafton: '. . . As to Lord
Keppel, I should be happy to see him away from his Board.
The Duke of Richmond also must take the part he judges
proper. . . . But though it would be very unpleasant to me . . . to
differ from you, yet I must bear it, for I am resolved to stand by
the King.' And so things turned out just as Fox had prophesied
to his friends. Keppel and Grafton did in fact finally leave the
Cabinet, while Richmond stayed away from its meetings.
Thus the ministry was already moving towards its dissolution
before it was thrown out.

If Shelburne cast about him for a means of buttressing up his
position in Parliament, he could seek allies in two directions.
On the one hand there was North, last year's ministerial
casualty, whose following was estimated at 120, and on the
other Charles Fox, with some 90 reliable friends, while the
administration could count on 140 certain votes, the rest being
like shifting sands. One section of the Cabinet tended towards
the one side and the rest towards the other. The King of course
favoured a coalition with North. Shelburne first put out feelers
in this direction, but without success. Then he managed to get
George's permission for Pitt to try and bring Fox into the
ministry.

On February 11th, 1783, Fox and Pitt met. It was for both
of them a moment of decisive importance. If it led to an understanding, England lay at their feet, and there might then have
dawned an epoch of reforms which would have cleared away
much of the debris which was left for the nineteenth century
to remove. Fox was then thirty-four and Pitt twenty-four. Who
could have withstood this 'alliance of youth'?

The interview of February 11th did not however lead to an
understanding, but to a rupture. The conversation soon

worked round to the point on which Fox thought everything must hinge, considering all that had gone before—the position of Shelburne. He asked Pitt if Shelburne would lead the ministry when it had been recast. Pitt replied that he would. Upon Fox's retort that he could not sit in any administration of which Shelburne was the head, Pitt observed that, if this was so, further discussion was useless, 'as he did not come to betray Lord Shelburne.' After this there was nothing more to be said. Pitt and Fox had parted—for ever.

It is, of course, to Pitt's credit that he kept faith with the man on whose authority he had attended this interview. It is, however, strange that a few months later, when he had a ministry of his own to form, he completely forgot that such a person as Shelburne had ever existed.

What was to happen now? Obviously Shelburne had reached a dead end. Even counting those who would vote for *any* administration, his following did not run to a majority. A dissolution was unthinkable. Shelburne was too unpopular to venture on this, and the peace treaty hardly made a good election slogan. But Fox or North alone could count on a majority just as little as Shelburne could. Thus there had to be a combination of two groups against the third, and the only question was who could come to an arrangement with whom. In Shelburne's camp there was a former friend and colleague of North's, Dundas, the Lord Advocate of Scotland, a parliamentary bravo and political wire-puller with a wide range of accomplishments; on his own account he urgently desired a coalition between his former and his present chief, and for that reason he approached North with some eagerness. But on this occasion his tactics were unsuccessful. He insisted that North should not only *not* oppose the peace treaty but that he should even expressly give it his blessing, and threatened him, if he would not submit to this condition, with a coalition between Pitt and Fox which would squeeze him out and break up his party. The effect on North was the exact opposite of what was intended. Rather than yield to such pressure he was ready to try his luck and see whether he could not make an alliance with Fox. Such an alliance was especially urged by one of his sons, who was in close touch with a friend of Fox's. At this son's house North and Fox had a first meeting on February 14th. Both men had many insults and injuries to forget, nor could they see eye to eye on all matters of principle and practice. In particular the question of parliamentary reform had to remain open, so that each could speak and vote as he wished, but that was in any case the position in Fox's own camp. None of North's followers could attack electoral reform with more vehemence or more fundamental objections than Burke had already done on the floor of the House. But there was one point which Fox insisted in having cleared up right from the start: there must be no return to personal government by the King. In future, he told North, it must be quite out of the question for *the King to be his own minister*. To this North returned the clear-cut reply: 'If you mean there should not be a government by departments, I agree with you; I think it a very bad system. There should be one man or a Cabinet to govern the whole and direct every measure. . . . The appearance of power is all that a king of this country can have. . . .'

If his own ministry had itself been made up of departments, he said, he had neither desired nor introduced the system. Indeed these words of North's clearly paraphrase the constitutional conflict: since Chatham's illness in 1767 George had governed through departments by giving orders to the individual departmental ministers. This could only be prevented by the ministers receiving their instructions either from the prime minister or from the Cabinet, the decisions of which were their common decisions. It is roughly the same problem as the one which faced William II and Bismarck in 1890, when they were at odds about the Cabinet Order of 1852.

The result of the talks between Fox and North was a decision to join in opposing the Address which was to welcome the conclusion of peace. But the extent of this agreement obviously went further, for if joint opposition proved successful, the inescapable and logical upshot would be a combined administration.

This was how it was at once construed by the whole political world, and a hailstorm of the bitterest criticism lashed both the party leaders, when, in the Commons on February 17th, 1783, Fox and North acted in concert for the first time over a very carefully worded amendment to the Address. What! was the cry from all sides, does Fox dare to join forces with North, with whom year after year he has been at war to the knife, whom he has repeatedly attacked in the sharpest terms and branded as an enemy of his country! Could anyone fly more shamelessly in the face of his own past? What other motive can there be for such a political about-turn, if not an unbridled craving for the delights and sweets of office and a love of power? Even some of Fox's friends now joined his accusers. But in a debate on the peace treaty which soon followed, it was William Pitt, the Chancellor of the Exchequer, who attacked the new coalition most sharply and eloquently as a grave violation of political morality, and an ill-omened marriage which his blazing words called upon public opinion to condemn.

Fox defended himself against these attacks by pointing out that his quarrel with North had been caused by the American War, and this was now at an end. Therefore now was the time to put an end also to the animosity, the rancour and the feuds which the war had occasioned. 'It is not in my nature to bear malice or to live in ill will. My friendships are perpetual, my enmities are not so. *Amicitiae sempiternae, inimicitiae placabiles. . . .*' What had now brought him and North together, he said, was the necessity to remove a minister who was in his nature, habitudes and principles an enemy to the privileges of the people. He urged in his defence that his decision to resign rather than continue in office under Shelburne had been retrospectively justified by the resignations of his friends who at the time had been unwilling to follow him. 'But while I produce these as indisputable arguments in favour of the propriety of our resignation . . .' he continued, 'I shall not disavow my having an ambition to hold such a situation in office as may enable me to promote the interest of my country. . . . I flatter myself that I am not inadequate to the importance of such a situation; nor do I think that I gave, during the short time I held a respectable place in administration, any reason why I should not offer myself a candidate for a share in [a] new arrangement. . . .'

The coalition had a majority. The administration was defeated in division after division. True, they retained a majority in the Lords, but Shelburne realized that his cause was a lost one and resigned on February 24th. Pitt stated in Parliament that he was remaining at the Exchequer only until a successor had been found. But six weeks were to pass before this happened.

George, of course, was furious. That North, his confidant of twelve years' standing, had lent himself to an alliance with his worst enemy naturally filled him with indignation. In no circumstances would he ever again make Fox a minister. His political objections had been reinforced by some very cogent personal considerations. Between the King and his heir there existed the sharp antagonism traditional in the House of Hanover. This time it was all the more acute since the son's mode of life was poles apart from the father's. The Prince of Wales, now twenty-one, was gay and dissolute, gambled, piled up debts and indulged in expensive liaisons which were the talk of the town. And now the Prince had quite openly taken up with Charles Fox, a man with habits just as objectionable in the King's eyes, whom he of course blamed for his son's excesses—with how little justification can be seen from the later exploits of the future George IV. But it is certain that Fox had the same fascination over him as over so many other young people with whom the Prince mixed when Fox received them at his rooms of a morning in *déshabillé*. If the Prince told Fox the day he resigned that he considered him and his friends as his own party, then he was only following the tradition of his house that the heir to the throne was regularly to be found at the head of those whom the King detested with all his heart.

But it did not need this aggravating circumstance to rouse the King to the most violent opposition. The coalition struck at the very centre of his system. North and Fox had agreed on a Cabinet to be headed by the Duke of Portland. So they wished to dictate to him who was to be a minister and who was not, did they? Grinding his teeth, he had had to put up with North's being defeated, but none the less he had contrived that Rockingham should keep Thurlow, the Lord Chancellor, and the Shelburne group assured him of at least a certain degree of influence. But on this occasion Fox, who was well aware of Thurlow's intrigues, vetoed his appointment, and the coalition would not budge an inch.

First, with Shelburne's consent, George turned to Pitt. He was the only member of the fallen ministry whose prestige had risen. What a temptation for a man of twenty-four—to become prime minister of Great Britain! At first he was inclined to accept. But he asked for time to think it over, and after quiet reflection he decided that the task was not one he could carry through. It is characteristic that he did not even venture to propose dissolving Parliament. George thereupon made repeated attempts to win North over and separate him from Fox. But North remained true to his word and declined, even when George declared himself ready to summon the coalition ministers if only he were left free to appoint the prime minister for himself. Despite all the King's displeasure, North stuck to his guns: the only way out he maintained, was to summon Portland and accept his proposals. Only when all attempts to circumvent this had failed and the Commons showed visible signs of unrest, did George give way.

On April 2nd, 1783, the members of the new ministry were able to kiss hands in token of their taking office. A witty courtier who was present at the ceremony later said that the King's manner reminded him of a circus horse determined to throw the rider who was getting on it. The distinctive feature of the new ministry was the two Secretaries of State, Fox for foreign and North for home affairs. Portland was merely a figurehead. Most of the other members of the Cabinet were well-tried Whigs. Burke again became Paymaster-General, and Fitzpatrick, Fox's closest friend and a connection of Shelburne's, took over the War Office. A newcomer with a scintillating wit and a gift of the gab was Richard Sheridan, the most celebrated writer of comedies of the day; he was given a junior ministerial post. Politically the ministry had a strong Whig tinge, coloured by North and several of his followers. No one doubted that Fox was the real head of it. The leadership of the Commons devolved on him as well. That Pitt was not a member of the government is hardly surprising after what had gone before; no attempt seems to have been made even to invite him to come in. Richmond, too, was another missing figure; carefully handled, he might possibly have been won over, but he was put out of humour by an error of tactics and declined to come in. Finally, a man went over to the enemy's camp who was soon to play a part fraught with consequences for Fox: this was Lord Temple. As in their fathers' days, so too in the days of the younger Pitt and Fox there were three Grenville brothers on the political stage—three sons of George Grenville and cousins of William Pitt. One of them, Thomas, was a friend of Fox, who had sent him to the peace negotiations in Paris; he has become known to posterity as a collector of books, who bequeathed his large and valuable library to the British Museum. The eldest, who on the death of his uncle had inherited the title of Lord Temple, had been sent to Ireland as Lord-Lieutenant by Shelburne, and, when Shelburne fell, he laid down this office in high dudgeon. The youngest brother, William Grenville, had the greatest career in front of him; he was linked closely with Pitt, his cousin and contemporary, with whom he sat on the opposition benches in the Commons.

Of course, Fox was not deaf to the criticism levelled at his conduct. He said quite openly that nothing but success could justify the coalition. But he was confident of making a success of being a minister. A woman who knew him intimately and followed his career affectionately but not uncritically, his aunt Lady Sarah Lennox (now Sarah Napier), wrote at the time of the ministerial crisis: '. . . Nothing but a supernatural *power* could, I think, make Charles the *guide* of Administration in spite all the pains he takes to *mar* the genius that providence gave him. I am so far from thinking he seeks greatness, that I am sure greatness pursues him into gaming houses, etc., etc., and since the Fates have decreed him to be [Prime] Minister, can he avoid it? You will see he will never keep it, but it will always come back to him.'

Under the laws of the day, Fox, upon becoming a minister, had to stand at a bye-election in his constituency of Westminster. During his election address he was interrupted by shouts and jeers. But this was of little consequence. He was re-elected, no rival candidate venturing to stand against him.

§

Once he was back at his old post Fox again flung all his energies into foreign affairs. The first task, of course, was to conclude the definitive peace treaties. This was accomplished in September, 1783. But Fox can hardly have patted himself on the back over that. When all was said and done, he had only finished off what Shelburne had begun. It is most unlikely that he expected to win the applause or even so much as the support of the King in this field. George's one concern was to keep Fox at arm's length as much as possible. When the Secretary of

State offered to wait upon His Majesty to make a report, this was declined with the charming excuse that unnecessary discussions were not to His Majesty's taste. So that Fox might never forget what a petty and obstinate King he had to deal with, George harked back on every possible occasion to the Commons resolution which had overthrown the North ministry; that, he said, was the cause of all their troubles.

But great was the joy with which England's representatives abroad welcomed Fox's return to the control of foreign policy; they hoped that it would receive fresh impetus and buoyancy from him. And, indeed, Fox did try to take up the threads he was spinning before his resignation and find continental alliances to offset the preponderance of France. Once again his chief object in view was Frederick of Prussia, who, however, confined his reply to non-committal civilities.

In Parliament Fox could once more support Pitt when Pitt again brought in a motion on electoral reform. The kernel of this motion was a proposal to increase the number of seats for London and the counties. This followed the lines laid down by Chatham years before. Fox found no difficulty in falling in with it. He brought Pitt's proposal more up-to-date still by suggesting that rising industrial and commercial towns, such as Birmingham and Manchester, should also at long last be given representation. Pitt had taken occasion to attack isolated voices like Richmond's which called for universal suffrage. Fox labelled this idea a 'wild, extravagant doctrine', but he had already reminded the House that even such men as Locke, the great Whig philosopher, had speculated far beyond what was practicable, yet his speculations had ultimately borne good fruit. Of course, the united eloquence of Pitt and Fox was not in itself enough to make the House thirsty for reform. It rejected the motion by a two to one majority. The number of the champions of reform had not shrunk since the previous year, but those of the other side had been swollen by more than a hundred votes.

Fox employed the parliamentary recess, which lasted from July to November, in going thoroughly into the problem of India. Nothing much had been done towards solving it since Chatham held back in 1766. The East India Company remained not simply a trading monopoly but also the ruler of a

R

continent. Its dominion had been much extended during the recent war, and most credit for this goes to its energetic and successful Governor-General, Warren Hastings. But both in India and in England the methods of this strong and forceful man had met with fierce criticism. In India a member of his Council waged bitter war on him. This was Philip Francis, who is today considered to be the author of *The Letters of Junius*.

Francis had excellent connections, especially with the Whigs, and he saw to it that his complaints were loudly echoed in London. But the campaign against Hastings was not originally a party matter. Even under the North ministry, two parliamentary committees had been appointed to investigate conditions in India and the administration there, and one of them had Dundas as its chairman. The reports of these committees, particularly the one drawn up by Burke, are a mine of information on the India of those days. It was Dundas, too, who moved a resolution in the Commons in May, 1782, demanding the recall of Hastings because he had acted in a manner repugnant to the honour and policy of England. The Company's Court of Directors, its highest controlling body, agreed to this demand by deciding in favour of recall. But it was now seen that the Company's affairs were arranged in a way which Fox rightly described as anarchy. The shareholders, who had not been too badly out of pocket under the Hastings régime and had not the least interest either way in the treatment or maltreatment of the natives, reversed the directors' decision at their general meeting in October, 1782, and Hastings remained undisturbed in Calcutta.

It was patent that such anarchy could not go on indefinitely. Parliament had to step in and put things in order. No one was more firmly convinced of this than Burke. The picture which he had formed of the administrative practices of the Company during his zealous activity on the Select Committee revolted him, and his lively and inflammable imagination depicted the fate of the native population under this administration in the most horrific colours. For a man who revered the British constitution as an almost superhuman masterpiece, it went without saying that, when an Englishman took it upon himself to rule foreign peoples, he should govern them in the spirit of his own constitution and in accordance with British ethical standards.

That a British governor should think himself entitled to use the methods of an Oriental despot outraged his moral sense. Like all the Whigs, Burke had been a fervent and systematic champion of the Company's chartered rights earlier on. But when he learned how, under cover of their charter, they had allowed mismanagement to set in and spread its corrosion ever deeper, he had decided that the legislature was in duty bound to step forward and protect the tormented, plundered natives, and that even the Company's charter must take second place to this higher public interest. It was easy enough for Burke to inspire Fox with the same indignation and zeal for reform. As Secretary of State, Fox had to bring in the reform bill, the principles of which probably stemmed from Burke, and champion it before the Commons.

Fox knew very well that he had taken on a most difficult and hazardous task. He knew that he could reckon with resistance from the King. But it almost seemed as if this danger had been overcome: George raised no objection to the bill which the Cabinet submitted to him. He also agreed that the Speech from the Throne, which was to open the new session on November 11th, should include a reference to the situation in India calling for exertions to secure the happiness of the native inhabitants. Pitt, who obviously assumed that the ministry had not yet completed its plans and knew well enough how delicate and dangerous the problem was, at once got up and with the greatest emphasis called on the administration to bring in a reform bill without delay; he would not, he said, be satisfied with palliatives which only got over difficulties for the time being. He was demanding a vigorous and effectual plan, he exclaimed, suited to the magnitude, the importance and the alarming exigency of the case.

Fox was able to announce in reply that he would move for leave to introduce his India Bill as early as the following Tuesday. Besides this, he was at pains in his speech to stress the points on which he found himself in agreement with Pitt. But he went further still. A few days later he sent word to Pitt that he wished to discuss with him the ways and means of making a place for him in the administration. But Pitt brusquely waved aside this olive-branch. As his cousin Temple at once wrote in high feather to the King, he had immediately negatived the opening without even waiting for a fuller explanation. There is no doubt that George welcomed this piece of news and felt not the slightest twinge of conscience about being allied with the opponents of his own ministers.

Fox had spread his proposals over two bills. One proposed to vest the government of India in a board to be formed for the purpose. The other introduced a whole series of individual reforms which aimed in particular at tidying up the Company's finances, then in a hopeless state of confusion. One of his speeches in support of these measures shows how thoroughly he had gone into the formidable mass of material, and how amazingly skilful he was at mastering a highly complicated set of facts. Fox never claimed to be a financial expert. But this speech proves that it was well within his capacity to be one, and that he spared no pains whenever the matter in hand called for them. Incidentally, he too referred to Adam Smith, whose *Wealth of Nations* he called an excellent book.

The real bone of contention was the kind of Board to be set up. It was to consist of seven members who, according to the wording of the Act, were to be appointed by Parliament itself for a period of four years; thereafter they were to be appointed by the Crown. The real government of India was to be under their control and they were to be responsible to the Secretary of State and to Parliament. Under them was to be a council of eight assistants to deal with the Company's commercial concerns and activities.

These proposals aroused a real outcry. The opposition, with Pitt at its head, accused the administration of trying to get Indian patronage into their own hands. True, the members in opposition could not agree among themselves whether the measure would weaken or strengthen the influence of the Crown, but that it was a matter of patronage was their battle-cry to a man. Indeed this question of patronage stands in the forefront of eighteenth century political thought. The struggle between the King and the Whig aristocracy was looked upon— not least by the King himself—primarily as a struggle for patronage. With its help he had extended his influence on Parliament. In order to restrain the King's patronage Burke's economical reform sought to cut down sinecures. The Commons had patronage in mind when they voted for Dunning's famous resolution. Now the opposition was feverishly calculating how many hundreds of thousands of pounds the patronage involved in filling all the posts in India and in the Company's service was worth, and was maintaining that Fox and North were bent on misapplying it for the benefit of their own followers. That a man like Fox might be more concerned with the sufferings of the natives than with bestowing favours on his friends never dawned upon the ordinary politician, and those who did grasp it did not want to believe it.

However the question took on a quite special and arresting significance now that the State meant to intrude in a sphere hitherto reserved for the interests of private business. So long as patronage was confined to offices at court, in the State or in the Church, it was accepted as a traditional institution over which political forces might wrangle to their hearts' content. But if it was now to affect posts which had hitherto been the preserve of a trading company, then the whole matter assumed quite a different complexion. The English were a commercial people, economically more highly developed than other nations, and well they knew it. Thus they had an especially strong sense of the rights of contract and property. Could any rights be more firmly founded than a charter bestowed on a trading company by the King and confirmed by act of Parliament? Could legislation fly in the face of such a charter? The East India Company was far and away the most important of the chartered companies. Its shares were owned by innumerable merchants and capitalists, to whom they were all the more valuable since the unhappy turn the war had taken meant that they had lost almost half their capital in the other widely held investment —government stocks.

Fox frankly admitted to the House that his bill encroached upon rights protected by a charter, and he did not recoil from going to the very roots of the question. What is a charter? he cried. It is a trust made in return for some given benefit. Its continuance depends upon its being administered in such a way that the benefit is obtained. But the Company had criminally neglected the welfare of the natives which had been entrusted to it. 'What is the end of all government? Certainly the happiness of the governed. Others may hold other opinions, but this is mine, and I proclaim it. What are we to think of a govern-

ment whose good fortune is supposed to spring from the
calamities of its subjects, whose aggrandisement grows out of
the miseries of mankind? This is the kind of government
exercised under the East India Company. . . .' In these circumstances, he went on, legislative interference with the
charter was justified because it was necessary. 'But necessity
was said to be the plea of tyranny—it was also the plea of freedom. The Revolution which established the rights and liberties
of these kingdoms was undertaken and accomplished—nay,
was justified at the time—on the plea of necessity: a necessity
that superseded all law. . . .' Had not, he asked, the opposition
leaders, headed by Pitt, demanded a sweeping reform and
declined from the first to accept half measures? Fox made a
point of replying to every single one of his critics, and convinced non-party members that his aim was to root up the flagrant abuses and come to the aid of the afflicted. The same
heights were reached by Burke's impassioned speech, which
painted in stark colours the evils and injustices of the system up
to that moment, particularly the plundering of the natives by
the insatiable young officials sent out by the Company. 'Animated with all the avarice of age and all the impetuosity of
youth, they roll in one after another; wave after wave; and
there is nothing before the eyes of the natives but an endless,
hopeless prospect of new flights of birds of prey and passage,
with appetites continually renewing for a food that is continually wasting.' The speech culminated in a character sketch of
Fox, drawn with all the resources of Burke's inspired oratory
and mastery of style. Fox, he said, had set himself the task of
rescuing the greatest number of the human race that ever were
so grievously oppressed from the greatest tyranny that was ever
exercised: it was a blessing that this task had fallen to the lot of
abilities and dispositions equal to it.

In the Commons these speeches did not fall on deaf ears.
The coalition parties closed their ranks. The Bill was passed on
December 8th, 1783, by a two to one majority.

But there was still the other House to reckon with. How would
the Bill get on in the Lords? As a rule, any administration could
count on a majority in the Upper House, especially when it was
supported by such an overwhelming majority in the Commons.
There can be no doubt that the Lords would have passed the

India Bill if the King had given normal constitutional support to the draft which had been laid before the Commons with his concurrence. But George did just the opposite.

His thoughts kept returning to the question of where he could find an opening for ridding himself of his obnoxious ministers. On one occasion he had believed he was in sight of his goal: that was when Fox, led away by his attachment to the Prince of Wales, had got the Cabinet to sponsor a bill to settle a yearly income of a hundred thousand pounds upon the Prince. For a few days it looked as if the administration was on the point of being dismissed, but at the last moment the King shrank from the conflict. He saw that this sort of private quarrel between father and son hardly had the makings of a good election slogan for the campaign which would then perhaps be necessary. On the other hand, the Prince, to Fox's huge delight, agreed to an accommodation so that the incident could be closed by a decent compromise. This time, however, things were very different. Up and down the country the East India Company was organizing the opposition of those whose interests were threatened or were supposed to be threatened by Fox's bill. They had found a very active organizer in a man called Atkinson, who had made his pile during the war by supplying the army and navy with rum, and had been appointed one of the directors of the Company. Atkinson was in close touch with Jenkinson, the leader of the 'King's Friends', and he in turn kept the King secretly posted of all that was going on. From George's point of view the most important thing was that this opposition, being well provided with capital, was ready to put up money—and a lot of money—for a general election. George knew very well that there were two methods of winning over the borough patrons: money and honours. He himself could lay out the secret service monies and also the surplus from his civil list, which he had saved up for such purposes, provided he were certain beforehand that he had ministers who would back him up. But for the job in hand these resources of his were not enough. The case was altered, however, if Atkinson could tap the resources of the financial groups which clustered round the Company. Honours, promotions and titles George could supply. He had sealed off that source of power from the ministers; he did not even concede them the right to put forward the name

of one of their followers for a peerage. And so he was all the
more ready to place this cornucopia in the hands of the opposition.

None the less he wanted certainty before embarking on the
struggle. His manager at the last election had been John
Robinson, Senior Secretary to the Treasury during North's
ministry, and no one knew the tricks of the trade as well as
he. On December 3rd, that is while the bill was before the
Commons, Atkinson wrote to Robinson: 'Everything stands
prepared for the blow if a certain person has courage to strike
it. . . .' This 'certain person' now commissioned Robinson to find
out which seats could be snatched from the coalition in a fresh
election, assuming that there would be no lack of money and
honours forthcoming. Robinson thereupon drew up a list which
was fortunately preserved among his papers. It gives an insight,
unique of its kind, into the parliamentary life of the day.

In it Robinson wastes no time over sentimentalities, such as
the supposed popular indignation at the coalition's lack of
principles. He goes through the constituencies one after the
other, noting who has each in his pocket or has a decisive influence in it, how such-and-such a patron can be won over, how
much money will be needed to do it, who has to be 'seen' and so
forth. It won't be a very cheap business: it can't be done under
two hundred thousand pounds. But if this sum is forthcoming—
and Atkinson vouches for that—then at least 116 seats can be
wrested from the coalition and brought over to the new
administration to be formed by the King—and that is more
than enough to give a good majority. Robinson's calculation
was, of course, based on the assumption that the general
election would not be staged by Fox or North but by a ministry
which enjoyed the King's confidence, and could wield the
traditional weapons of royal influence and secret service
monies in the way George wished. So everything hinged on the
finding of a politician of enough repute and courage to head
this new administration and brave the infuriated coalition.
There was only one man who fulfilled these requirements:
William Pitt. In the spring he had held back. This time he
would certainly require guarantees of success, but these Robinson and Atkinson could now give him. On December 15th,
while the India Bill was before the Lords, Pitt met Robinson,

Atkinson and Dundas in the greatest secrecy at Dundas's house. The arguments and proofs they produced satisfied him. He agreed to obey the King's summons if Fox and North were dismissed.

At the same time George set his manoeuvre in train. His confederate was Pitt's cousin, Temple. Through him he conveyed secretly to all the peers who were approachable that His Majesty was opposed to his own administration's India Bill and that he would consider any peer who voted for it as an enemy. This stratagem was without question a flagrant violation of the obligations which the constitution imposed on the King. But— it was successful. On December 17th, that is, two days after Pitt's conference with Robinson, the bill was defeated in the Lords by 95 votes to 76. On the following day the King dismissed the two Secretaries of State, North and Fox, in the greatest haste and the rudest possible manner. Pitt was summoned and at once accepted. On December 19th, 1783, he became, at the age of twenty-four, prime minister and Chancellor of the Exchequer.

The Cabinet which Pitt formed was a weak one. Not even Temple sat in it. The noble lord had resentfully turned his back on Pitt when his demand for promotion in the peerage was not met. Shelburne, too, did not have a seat in the government. But that was not his doing; it was Pitt's, who obviously left him out on purpose. There were a number of reasons which might have kept him from burdening his already frail cockle-shell with the weight of Shelburne's unpopularity. Besides, his ministry could hardly make use of a man who had been found to be a very difficult colleague in every Cabinet he had sat in— a man who was quite capable of recalling his own far greater experience of the highest offices and citing it in the face of the youthful prime minister. But probably what finally decided Pitt was his fear that Shelburne might intrigue with the King, and even, if occasion demanded, against himself. At all events, this latest attitude of Pitt's towards Shelburne provides an interesting commentary on the events of July, 1782, and February, 1783.[1]

In the Cabinet proper Pitt was the only commoner. All the others were peers, among them Lord Thurlow who now re-

[1] See pages 237-8 and page 243.

sumed his place on the Woolsack. Outside the Cabinet, Richmond belonged to the ministry. Only two of Pitt's supporters really carried any weight in a debate in the Commons: Henry Dundas, who always lacked principles but never arguments, and William Grenville.

Such then, was the front which the administration, led by a prime minister of twenty-four, was setting up against an overwhelming majority and the most experienced and eloquent debaters of the day. The opposition tossed the catchword about that the welfare of the kingdom had been trusted to a schoolboy's care. Fox, Burke and their friends thundered against the abuse of royal power. But Fox must have known in his heart of hearts how insecure was his footing in Parliament if ever it were put to the test of a general election. He knew the forces which could be put into the field against him, and North must have known them better still. The only chance of avoiding a defeat was to prevent or delay the holding of an election and to overthrow Pitt before any such event. He adapted his tactics accordingly, but they forced him to use arguments about the constitution which were untenable. Pitt braved the storm with admirable courage and in the certain knowledge that his hour of triumph could not be long delayed. The longer the struggle lasted, the more Fox's majority dwindled. His followers fell away one after another, not because they disagreed with his leadership and policy, but because they could see bearing down on them unmistakable signs of what their fate would be at the polls if they did not make haste to line up with the King and the East India Company. On March 8th, 1784, Fox's majority had melted away to a single vote, and at this point Pitt dissolved Parliament. His henchmen had reported to him that they had made good use of the interval and were certain of gaining enough seats.

Robinson's calculations proved completely reliable. The administration took no less than 160 seats from the opposition. It was a land-slide! Two hundred years before, John Foxe, the divine, had set out in a book which was to be found in every pious household the fate of Mary Tudor's Protestant victims. With this in mind political wits now called those who littered the battlefield 'Fox's Martyrs'.

Pitt, it must be said, would only have regarded his triumph

as complete if he had had Fox in the bag as well. A struggle of unexampled violence and stubbornness ensued in the election at Westminster where Fox was standing. The royal palaces were in the constituency, and the King's influence was flung recklessly and unscrupulously into the balance. Two hundred and eighty Guardsmen were detailed to cast their votes for Fox's opponent. But in Westminster, too, stood the mansions of the great Whigs, and not only they themselves but, above all, their ladies campaigned with fiery zeal for Fox. The Westminster election has become famous not so much because Fox's political existence hung in the balance as because Georgiana, Duchess of Devonshire, canvassed for him from house to house, and it was said she did not even refuse to kiss a butcher who made his vote for Fox dependent on that favour. Once again the polling went on for days, and at first Fox had to endure all the anguish of a threatened defeat. But gradually his figures improved until, on the closing day, May 17th, 1784, a total of 6,234 votes had been cast for him while his rival polled only 5,998. At all events in this, his own constituency, no one could talk about popular feeling having turned against him. Moreover, his opponents had busily exposed every undesirable feature of his private life, so that he could say later that he was all the prouder of the outcome of this election since the voters had been fully alive to his private foibles.

But today, now that chapter and verse on the background of the 1784 election is known, one must be extremely sceptical of the view, formerly so widely held, that it was a punishment visited by the people upon those who fell from grace by forming the coalition. Dissatisfaction with the coalition may here and there have played a part, just as did the lustre of the name of Pitt and a sporting interest in his bold fight against numerical odds. Great harm was done to Fox by the savage cartoons with which the most gifted artists of the day flooded the country, distorting him most coarsely with brutal wit and jeering at him as a man puffed with ambition and thirsting for power. But what tipped the scale was the partnership between the King and a force new to politics which took the stage for the first time—the financial interests rallying around the 'established right' of the threatened charter. The East India Company and their political and commercial allies had put up the money, and the King granted no fewer than seventeen peerages to pay for promises of help in the election. To understand the difference between an election in the eighteenth century and one in the nineteenth or twentieth, it must be borne in mind that in this decisive election of 1784 four-fifths of the total seats were occupied without a proper contest; only about a hundred candidates had an opponent at all. In all the other cases, the matter was cut and dried by arrangement with the local bigwigs before there was any question of a poll.

But all this, of course, does not alter the fact that at this election Charles Fox had suffered a blow which affected his whole career. He lived for another twenty-two years and had to consume twenty-one of them in bitter and fruitless opposition. If he looked back on the two years between the formation of the Rockingham ministry in 1782 and his defeat in the spring elections of 1784, his thoughts must surely have dwelt upon the two steps by which he had believed he could shape the nation's destiny—his resignation from the ministry on Rockingham's death and his coalition with North to overthrow Shelburne. Could he square them with his own conscience? As far as his refusal to hold office under Shelburne went, he might fairly answer 'Yes'. But could he say the same of the coalition? It has often been stated that he could not, on the grounds that the nation was shocked to its depths by the coalition and so it turned away from him at the elections. We know today that the second part of this reasoning does not hold water. But also it is hard to believe that in those days political circles were so sensitive about coalitions between former opponents. The whole history of the preceding fifty years was one of a kaleidoscopic interchange of groupings. Anyone who was anybody at all was in alliance today with somebody whom he had fought against yesterday. Shelburne and Pitt were just as ready as Fox was to link up with North, and during the American War they had been quite as determined opponents of North as Fox had been. Dundas, who at that time had been North's active assistant, was now Pitt's right-hand man. The only difference was that Fox, who so often said what others only thought, had attacked North far more sharply and personally than they, and his enemies could now quote withering phrases from his speeches which stood out in stark contrast to his coalition. And, of course, these were very difficult to explain away. Fox hoped gradually to expunge this bad impression by an active policy when in office. But he was allowed no time for this once he had run up against all too powerful financial interests.

On the other hand, it must be remembered that during the abortive coalition negotiations in the spring of 1778 Fox had not named North among those with whom he was unwilling to sit in a ministry, and that his political and personal relations with North remained good from the time of his defeat right up to North's death. What is of more real weight is that North, in the course of the coalition negotiations of 1783, specifically came out against the King's political system, over which Fox previously attacked him. For in Fox's eyes that was the cardinal point, the thing which mattered above all else: to make the King's personal policy impossible. In this he was not only justified by England's past experience of this policy, he was also the champion of the political system which triumphed to England's benefit in the nineteenth century and might perhaps have triumphed fifty years earlier if Fox had not been defeated by Pitt and George III in 1784.

If, despite all this, anyone wishes to condemn Fox on moral grounds, he can hardly avoid applying the same standards to the conduct of George III and Pitt. That George acted treacherously is conceded by most historians. But what we now know shows beyond all doubt that it was with full knowledge and consent that Pitt supported him. Both sinned against the spirit of the British constitution. The intrigue for which they banded together can cut no better figure in the eyes of the moralist merely because it was brilliantly successful.

Yet Pitt is to be judged quite differently from the King. He did not lend himself to George as an accomplice to enable him to continue with his sterile and shortsighted policy. Nothing was further from Pitt's mind than to become the King's creature, as North had been for twelve years. He wanted to frame his own policy. For he—like Fox—felt he had the call and the ability to be a constructive statesman, able and willing to bring prosperity to his country. But—unlike Fox—he was granted two decades in which to be a leading statesman in the full sense of the word.

True, he had to pay the price for the way in which he came

to power and bow to the interests which helped him to do
so. How could the man, whom the East India Company had
helped into the saddle, proceed against them with such vigour
and effect as he had demanded of Fox on November 11th, 1783?
He had made his bow in politics as the courageous and enthusiastic protagonist of parliamentary reform. But how could
he now display an energy to match his beginnings and lay the
axe to the abuses in which the electoral system was rooted, after
basing his triumph and founding his power upon that very
system?

CHAPTER XVIII

PITT AS PEACE MINISTER

THE emergence of a new power in the land, predominantly
economic, as disclosed by the 1784 election, is a symptom
of the economic revolution which England underwent in
the second half of the eighteenth century. It is commonly called
the Industrial Revolution and very aptly, too, for it decided
that the interests of industry—and trade which marched with
it—were to be paramount, and that England was to grow not
simply into an industrial country but into the foremost industrial country in Europe. The years during which George III
disputed the mastery with the Whig aristocracy, and Pitt and
Fox crossed swords, saw the birth of the great inventions on
which modern industry is built. James Watt, who shares with
Adam Smith the distinction of being one of the two greatest
Scots of the age, discovered the principle of the modern steam
engine in 1765 and developed its practical use from 1774 onwards. Between 1760 and 1784 the processes for smelting iron
ore with coal, which transformed the natural mineral resources
of England and Wales into an asset of unprecedented worth,
were evolved. The inventions of Arkwright, Crompton, Cart-
wright and others, which made spinning and weaving a major
industry, fall between 1765 and 1790. The Englishman's head
for business proved equal to the new tasks. Men climbed into
prominence who united enterprise with the ability to organize
and control the process of the division of labour, so brilliantly
analysed by Adam Smith. The importance of communications,
so long neglected, was recognized; a network of good roads and
navigable canals criss-crossed the island, permitting the full use
of the matchless advantages offered by the sea, with its numerous ports at no point very far away.

Britain's population and financial strength increased under
the influence of this process at an unheard-of speed. Between
1760 and 1801, when the first official census was taken, the
population rose from six and three quarter millions to nine
millions, exports from fourteen and a half millions sterling to

thirty-four and a third millions and imports from nearly ten millions to more than twenty-eight millions. Imports of raw cotton, which in 1780 amounted to only four millions, had already reached fifty-six millions by 1800 and went on almost to double themselves in the next fifteen years. The figures for pig iron show very nearly as good a picture. And how important a development like this was bound to be to a country saddled again and again with huge new debts by three long wars in the space of half a century! The national debt (funded and unfunded), no more than one hundred and two millions in 1760, had swollen to two hundred and thirty-one millions in 1783, and the wars against France during the Revolution and under Napoleon added another six hundred and thirty millions. Only the massive boom in trade and industry enabled Britain to bear the gigantic burden.

Agriculture did not mark time during this period, but forged powerfully ahead. True, it was just like industry in having a social side which was black and grim. But the speed and scope of industrial development was naturally much greater, and this caused a radical shift of population and of the economic centre of gravity within the country. The population massed round the coal, iron and textile industries. Towns sprang up which had been sleepy little places, if they had been towns at all: Manchester, Birmingham, Sheffield, Leeds and more besides. London, however, retained its importance; indeed, it grew faster than any of the newer towns and became the centre of international finance. But many other places fell away. Of the numerous small towns which had enjoyed from time immemorial the right to return two members to Parliament, dozens could be offset in size by a single one of the new industrial towns which did not boast a single member. As has been seen, when the franchise was debated as far back as 1783 Fox had suggested giving these towns representation.

There was still time to deal with these and other political problems quietly and without much fuss and, perhaps, to solve them. Nobody could then know how brief this time was to be. A mere five years later and the face of the world was completely changed. In France the Revolution broke out and all problems—not only in France—took on a new complexion.

The events and effects of the Revolution mark a caesura in

Pitt's career in office. The years which lie before the caesura are the years of his real, constructive peace-time work.

His position during this period was as firm and secure as Walpole's had been in the early years, and his own father's in the closing years, of George II's reign. He could count unconditionally on the support of his King. For George III thought of Pitt above all else as the only man who could save him from a Fox ministry. Twice he had had the experience of seeing that dangerous spell-binder transform a parliamentary majority into a minority. And so a minister, who was a dab hand at keeping his majority together and could face Fox at least on equal terms, was someone George simply could not do without. This situation gave Pitt the whip-hand over the King, who had to allow him to pursue his own policy. Pitt was a real prime minister in the same sense as the great premiers of the nineteenth century, as a Peel or a Gladstone. He demanded and kept in his own hands the supreme direction of policy as a whole as well as that of individual departments. Government by the King through the departments, such as North, on his own confession, had tolerated, Pitt would not brook, and the King resigned himself to it. Pitt had no competition to fear from the departmental ministers. None of them could for a moment persuade even himself that he could hold a candle to the prime minister who was, moreover, his own Chancellor of the Exchequer. The only possible exception was Thurlow, the Lord Chancellor, and even he knew how much his political existence was bound up with Pitt's.

It is a perennial source of wonder how a man not yet twenty-five could reach such a position. It can partly be explained by the staggering self-confidence which marked him out from his first steps in politics—a height of self-assurance only credible in the son of the great statesman whose heir he felt he was. *Fortes creantur fortibus et bonis.* Success, of course, had strengthened this self-confidence, and every day during which he could rally round him such an overwhelming majority in battle with opponents like Fox, Burke and Sheridan, must have heightened it still more. No prime minister since Walpole had possessed such an admirable flair for handling and leading the Commons. The gift of parliamentary eloquence brimmed up in him in full measure. Fox, who knew how to appraise the merits even of an

s

opponent, said that, although he himself was never in want of words, Mr. Pitt was 'never without the very best words possible.' He had the particular gift of giving his followers the impression that whenever he acted he had weighed up the pros and cons to a nicety in advance and had reached his decisions with mature insight. If he lacked the fire and enthusiasm of Fox and kept his colleagues at a distance by his chilling reserve, all the more was he looked on as a man incapable of a rash act, a man one could serve under with every confidence.

That behind this glacial majesty some human weaknesses were lurking none the less could be seen from his attitude to Fox, at the very beginning of the new session. Fox had gained a majority in the Westminster election; the returning officer, however, had not done his duty and declared him elected but, in collusion with George and Pitt and without the least regard for justice, had ordered a scrutiny on the formal demand of Fox's defeated opponent. This was bound to take many months, if not years, during which Westminster would have been without a member and Fox would have been kept out of Parliament had he not found a pocket borough which gave him a seat. The Westminster voters laid their grievance before Parliament. Nothing would have been easier for Pitt than to recommend his followers to accept the petition, which would then have been certain to be granted unanimously. Politically, he had defeated Fox so heavily that it would have cost him nothing to be magnanimous personally. But he could not bring himself to do this. On the contrary, he sharply opposed the petition and thus caused eight months to be frittered away while the votes were checked; and even then nothing definite was arrived at. Fox and his friends, of course, raised the matter time and again, and in the debates Pitt, as a man, played a rôle which was far from matching his exalted political position. At last even the Commons, usually so docile, grew shamefaced and put an end to this cat-and-mouse business by rebelling against Pitt. The episode did Pitt no political harm, but many a member in the ministerial camp must have secretly asked himself whether Fox, now so fiercely persecuted, would himself ever have been capable of such pettiness and spite.

Pitt very soon tackled the task over which Fox had come to grief. As early as 1784 he piloted an East India Bill through

Parliament. In the light of what had gone before, it hardly needs saying that this measure was a compromise. It sought to further the country's interests as far as was possible without treading on the toes of the East India Company or doing over-much damage to their 'established rights'. It created a board of control to be formed by the King from members of the Privy Council, certain of whom had a seat *ex officio*. The filling of posts in India was left to the Company, but in such a way that for the really important offices, notably that of Governor-General, the royal assent was necessary. Fox criticized the bill on the grounds that the newly-created authorities were bound to be always at loggerheads among themselves. And, in fact, Pitt did find himself compelled a few years later to amend the Act in a way which bit somewhat deeper into the Company's rights. Apart from this, the Act remained in force up to the Indian Mutiny of 1857 without showing the flaws which its critics had every reason to predict. The English genius for compromise disposed of apparently insoluble difficulties. The nation's interests established themselves by their own weight, which made the leading member of the Board of Control develop gradually into the Secretary of State for India. None the less, it should not be forgotten that one of the greatest Viceroys of modern times, Lord Curzon, passed an absolutely damning judgement on the Act of 1784; in his view it could not have turned out worse if a committee 'assembled from the padded chambers of Bedlam' had drawn it up. Patronage, which, it had been claimed, was what the Whigs had been after in Fox's bill, was now of course exploited by the Tories, even if under the cover of the King's name. Pitt left this business to his ablest lieutenant, Dundas, who certainly had fewer scruples than Fox or any of his friends and here found the means of swelling his unbounded influence in his native Scotland.

Much of the success of Pitt's measure sprang from the fact that, as time went on, a new spirit animated the officials who worked in India itself. Among the many causes which combined to this end, the great state trial of the former Governor-General, Warren Hastings, stands out. Few trials in all history have been so often and so dramatically related as the proceedings against Warren Hastings, and Macaulay's essay has had the good fortune to live for more than a hundred years, although his conclusions have been largely rebutted by modern research.

The impeachment of Hastings was the doing of Burke, who was firmly convinced that Hastings was the author of inhuman crimes and a blot on the fair name of England. But none of Burke's compelling rhetoric would have succeeded in inducing the House to take proceedings, had not Pitt, to the surprise of his followers and opponents alike and to the indignation of the Company, suddenly signified his support. The reasons for his volte-face have never been completely cleared up, but it seems that a word from his idealistic friend, William Wilberforce, on whom Fox's indictment of Hastings had made a deep impression, tipped the scale.

The Commons now commissioned several of its members, all of them leading Whigs, as its managers to impeach the ex-Governor before the House of Lords as the highest court in the land. The proceedings were extraordinarily impressive but also extraordinarily long-drawn-out and expensive. The speeches delivered against Hastings by Burke, Fox and Sheridan were masterpieces of forensic rhetoric. But the hearings, constantly interrupted by parliamentary recesses, lasted from 1788 to 1795, that is, till a time when everything had changed, not least the relations between the managers, Fox and Burke. In the meantime legal costs and charges mounted to dizzy heights and brought Hastings to the brink of bankruptcy. His lawyers contrived by means of technical objections to deprive the prosecution of many important pieces of evidence, so that the acquittal which the Lords pronounced by a large majority is neither final nor convincing. But most historians who have since investigated Hastings' life and actions have reached the same conclusion.

It would, however, be a serious error to suppose that the campaign which Burke had waged along with Fox against Hastings had been misconceived, or a needless waste of energy, time and money. Even granted that Hastings personally suffered injustice, the system for which he stood did receive its deserts. It was an incalculable blessing for India and her peoples, just as it was for her rulers, that this system was placed in the dock before the whole world, and that Burke's powerful and colourful rhetoric and Fox's warm humanity threw the clearest and most searching light on the crimes and errors committed, even if it was perhaps unjust to lay them principally at Hastings' door; it was a blessing for India that the oppressed should not feel utterly forsaken nor the rulers feel able to sin unpunished and unseen.

In one of the debates which preceded the impeachment, Fox appealed to 'the laws of nature, not the statutes to be found in those books before us, or in any books, but those laws which are to be found in Europe, Africa and Asia—that are to be found amongst all mankind—those principles of equity and humanity implanted in our hearts.' These are words which fall strangely on the ears of politicians and legislators of a later day, like an excursion into the realms of poetry. But perhaps the world has become the poorer for no longer hearing such language, and it is only in the greatest crises of world history that now and then we still find, to our surprise, that words like these neither need apology nor lack effect.

After the reform of Indian administration came the turn of electoral reform at home, for it was with this question that Pitt's name has been linked since his first bow to the public. It was natural—for what else can one expect of any opposition—that the Whigs should display lively impatience and taunt the young prime minister with being lukewarm because he did not bring in a reform bill at once. But, in the spring of 1785, Pitt appeared before the House with a motion for the reform of parliamentary representation. True, it was a very cautious proposal. He wanted to disfranchise a mere thirty-six rotten boroughs and distribute the seventy-two seats thus vacated to the counties and some of the towns hitherto unrepresented. If this was in any case a step in the right direction, a further proposal of Pitt's which was bound up with it disclosed a highly questionable attitude. He wanted, quite simply, to buy the seats from the boroughs concerned. In other words, he treated the franchise as property with a cash value, and he believed he would merit a reputation for being particularly honest, because he openly acknowledged that constituencies were bought and sold for hard cash. In practice this amounts to treating parasitic growths as the essential core of the parent plant. How much more sublime and modern was the view which Fox advanced in his speech: 'He was uniformly of an opinion, which, though not a popular one, he was ready to aver, that the right of governing was not property

but a trust; and that whatever was given for constitutional purposes should be resumed when those purposes should no longer
be carried into effect.' It was this view of Fox's, and not Pitt's,
that was upheld half a century later when the Whigs put
through electoral reform in 1832.

But for all his objections Fox voted in favour of Pitt's resolution so as to help matters forward in any case—but in vain. For
only a minority of the government's supporters followed Pitt
into the division lobby. His resolution was defeated by a
majority of over 70. With that, reform was conclusively shelved
for more than a generation. Never again did Pitt touch this
cardinal question either before or after the French Revolution.
It would certainly be doing him an injustice to assume that he
was not entirely in earnest about it from the very outset. But it
would be no injustice to him to trace back this passivity to the
method by which he had won his victory at the election of 1784.

> '. . . a greater power
> *Now ruled him, punished in the shape he sinned,*
> *According to his doom.'*

Certainly it cannot be urged in Pitt's defence that no live
reform movement raised its head in the country or that the
collapse of his resolution was accepted without any stir. The
hall-mark of the real statesman is his ability to recognize what
his country needs before the broad masses of the people do.
That this reform was a very real want is shown by the far-
reaching developments sketched above in the broadest outline.
Certainly Pitt cannot be blamed for failing to foresee the French
Revolution, but he cannot be acquitted of responsibility for the
fact that the quickening of men's minds which it called forth in
England beat in vain against such grave and obvious abuses.

There was one field of law-making and administration in
which Pitt accomplished some really remarkable work, and
that was in the country's finances. They had, of course, been
dislocated by the American war, and to set them to rights was a
task of the first importance. Pitt was the very man for the job.
He had made a serious study of the subject. He had the broad,
clear, cool intelligence which as a rule showed him the right way
to go, and the energy and resolution to translate his ideas into
practice. He possessed in particular the ability, so valuable in a

Chancellor of the Exchequer, to expound and defend his fiscal policy plainly and impressively. He had the good fortune to be smiled on at the outset by the leading figures in economic and financial circles, who remembered the man who had saved them from Fox's India Bill. Still more in his favour was the upward swing which marks the whole of this period of England's economic history and which, once peace was restored, soared to the heights with elemental force.

The individual fiscal measures which Pitt put through have lost their interest today. It is worth recording that he had the courage to make a drastic cut in the tea duty in order to combat smuggling. His name will always be associated with setting up the sinking fund for the gradual discharge of the national debt. In 1786 he proposed to turn over a million pounds from the national revenue to an independent committee formed for the purpose. This fund, to be continuously increased by regular contributions, was to be kept separate from the ordinary budget and applied solely to liquidating national indebtedness. The original idea came from the Nonconformist preacher, Dr. Price, a man of great authority in economic—and particularly financial—questions; he believed that by applying the cumulative effect of compound interest he had found the philosopher's stone, the means of wiping out the burden of the national debt almost automatically, and at first Pitt himself seems to have believed this as well. Even if this was really an illusion, the idea of a sinking fund was a very sound one. The fund—which Fox, too, vigorously championed—completely fulfilled its purpose in times of peace and cancelled out several millions of the national debt. Then, when war broke out with France and inevitably swallowed up more than the yearly revenue, the sinking fund, which was formally kept going, became more and more of a fiction. But even then it was an influence for the good for several years more by preserving public confidence in Britain's financial position. In matters of finance and currency, hard to understand as they are, facts are often less important than appearances.

Pitt struck out along similar progressive paths in his commercial policy. He had learned from Adam Smith how great are the blessings which free trade brings to nations and he tried to put the master's precepts into practice. His first attempt, which concerned traffic between Great Britain and Ireland was unsuccessful. The Irish problem had not been solved even by the granting of legislative independence to Ireland. After a careful study of the question, Pitt believed he had hit on the solution by opening up an exchange of goods between the two countries, making it as far as possible unrestricted. In the spring of 1785 he laid a series of resolutions to this effect first before the Irish Parliament in Dublin and then before the British Parliament at Westminster. But while the Irish assembly approved them, on this side of St. George's Channel they ran into lively opposition. English industrialists feared ruinous competition from the cheaper Irish labour. Fox and his party became the spokesmen of these fears, and thus won back for a time the popularity they had lost in this quarter over the India Bill. Manchester prepared Fox a gala reception which would have been impossible a year earlier. True, the protectionist arguments were not the only ones he brought out against Pitt. Neither Pitt's parliamentary tactics nor his practical proposals were quite of the first water, and as the debates went on he was forced to modify his suggestions very considerably. Fox, on the other hand, once again proved himself a parliamentarian and debater of the top rank. The speed with which he picked holes in his opponent's latest proposals and tore them to shreds is amazing. But even if Pitt did at times come off second best in debate, he was still able to hold his majority together, so that in the end his proposals went through in their altered form.

But it was a Pyrrhic victory. For now the amended bill had to be debated again in Dublin and here the administration's majority had by this time so dwindled away that after the first division Pitt gave up the fight. Nor did he make any fresh attempt in the succeeding decade to master the Irish problem. A chance of bringing England and Ireland together was lost beyond recall. No one can say whether it would really have proved possible to lay the dust of the Irish problem for all time by doing what Pitt proposed. But the cause was important and pressing enough to risk trying. Fox is largely responsible for this failure, but Pitt also contributed his share by his high-and-mighty treatment of the opposition both in and out of Parliament.

Luckily for him he was able to wipe the slate almost clean in the following year by reaching a trade agreement with France; on both sides the duties on many goods were much reduced and simplified, while for others the most-favoured-nation clause was introduced (September 27th, 1786). This agreement, too, ran into opposition at home from business interests really or supposedly threatened, and once again Fox appointed himself their spokesman. Indeed, he went further by declaring France to be Britain's natural foe. Pitt rose above such prejudices with the fine words: 'To suppose that any nation could be unalterably the enemy of another was weak and childish. It had neither its foundation in the experience of nations nor in the history of man. It . . . supposed the existence of diabolical malice in the original frame of man.' A two-thirds majority in both Houses rewarded his pains, and in May, 1787, the agreement came into force. Pitt also tried to conclude similar treaties with other countries, such as Spain and Russia, but here he ran up against a blank wall.

As the above quotation from his speech shows, Pitt's efforts to conclude the French commercial treaty were part of a broader foreign policy. Before he came to the head of affairs Britain's international position was highly unsatisfactory; it could hardly be otherwise after she had lost a war. A defeated country has little to attract other powers, and so at first England was isolated. Before she could emerge from this isolation and go over to an active policy she had first to set her home finances to rights once more, and in this Pitt succeeded with astonishing speed. The government stocks, which had dropped to about 54 at the time of his taking office, had already risen to 73 in 1785 and climbed still higher after the trade treaty with France was signed. The initiative had come from the French minister, Vergennes. Pitt had followed it up, not least with the idea that he could in this way improve relations with France, for France did indeed at that time occupy a position of unusual influence in Europe. True, her stability at home in no wise matched the splendour of her position abroad. France's finances, too, had been upset by the American war, but she never found a Pitt to put them in order again. In France a fiscal reformer could not gain the position which Pitt enjoyed here thanks to the support which Parliament and the Crown gave him.

Pitt had taken as his foreign minister Lord Carmarthen, who

later became Duke of Leeds—a young aristocrat of pleasing gifts but limited administrative capacity. Pitt found himself more and more obliged to take a hand in foreign affairs and even at times, to draft the notes which the departmental minister merely signed.

The question which first induced Britain to pursue an active policy was that of Holland. Holland had long been racked by internal strife which had very important repercussions on foreign policy. The House of Orange, which for generations had occupied the post of Stadholder, was at daggers drawn with the 'Patriot' party, which wished to whittle down its privileges and influence. The antagonism had grown sharper during the American war, in which Holland had gone in on the side of France and had come off very badly. For this misfortune the 'Patriots' blamed the Stadholder, who was related by marriage to the English royal family, and they accused him of neglecting his duty by favouring the English cause. William V of Orange, who was Stadholder at the time, was an utter cipher. He was far outstripped in energy by his wife, a Prussian princess; she was by no means willing to be satisfied with the minor rôle which the 'Patriot' party was bent on giving her. She hoped to get support from her uncle, Frederick the Great. But the old King knew that the 'Patriot' party was backed by France and he had no great wish to fall foul of France. In any case, he already had enough to worry about with the projects of the Austrian emperor Joseph II, against whom he was forming the German League of Princes. Having succeeded in 1772, by the first partition of Poland, in extending his frontiers to the east at the expense of his defenceless neighbour, all he now wanted was to hold on to his gains and keep out of fresh conflicts.

If the alliance of the Dutch 'Patriot' party with the French caused Frederick to hold back, it gave England one more reason for following the activities of the party with concern and distaste. Her position on the map makes it one of Britain's primary interests to prevent any great power from getting a lodgement in the Netherlands as a base for threatening her coasts and cutting her communications with the Continent. But without allies she could not enter upon this struggle. And then, in 1786, Frederick the Great died. His successor, Frederick William II, was far too indolent and flighty to conduct an active and consistent foreign policy, and at first the cries of distress from his sister in Holland left him unmoved. But in the summer of 1787, she managed to goad a Dutch free corps belonging to the army of the 'Patriots' into an indiscretion which could be construed as a personal insult to a Hohenzollern princess. Touchy, like most weaklings, Frederick William took this incident as a slur on his own royal honour, and demanded satisfaction from the Dutch 'patriotic' government, but they, believing that they could bank on support from France, refused.

So far the British government had played a waiting game. It was Pitt himself who had got the Cabinet to adopt this policy in the face of the urgings of the very active minister at The Hague, James Harris (later Earl of Malmesbury). But now Pitt thought it was time to act. He himself took a hand and directed negotiations in Berlin and Paris. British diplomacy at last succeeded in instilling so much resolution into the King of Prussia, who had once more started to hum and haw, that on September 3rd, 1787, he sent the Dutch government an ultimatum. On September 13th Prussian troops crossed the frontier. The help from France on which the Dutch were counting failed to come. On October 10th, Amsterdam capitulated and the Prussian army's 'military promenade' was over.

The significant thing about the whole affair was that the French government let Prussia's intervention take place without making any serious attempt to interfere. This was due to a combination of domestic and foreign reasons, including the simultaneous outbreak of war between the Czarina Catherine II and the Turks. This moral defeat struck a heavy new blow at the French king's prestige. Pitt, whose policy Fox zealously supported on this occasion, went up in the esteem of his fellow-countrymen. He improved the shining hour by concluding a triple alliance with Prussia and Holland, where the Stadholder was once more in power (August 13th, 1788).

But a matter of far greater importance was to occupy Pitt, and Fox as well, for decades. Among the youthful friends and admirers who swarmed round Pitt was a pure soul fired by a fervent belief in God and full of active idealism; this was William Wilberforce, member for York. He came into close touch with a group of earnest, energetic men and women whose moral sense was outraged by the traffic in African slaves and the

horrors inseparable from it. The more Wilberforce busied himself with this cause, the firmer grew his conviction that there
was only one effective remedy for the evil—the complete and
utter abolition of the slave trade. Should he make it his life's
work? It was Pitt, the prime minister, to whom he put this
question. In the summer of 1787, under an old oak on Pitt's
estate there took place the conversation between the two friends
which decided the course of Wilberforce's life. Pitt urged him
to do so. Thenceforth Wilberforce worked unremittingly for
twenty years to rescue African negroes from a ghastly fate and
to remove the disgrace from England's fair name. In the spring
of 1788 everything was in readiness for this great question to be
raised in Parliament for the first time. Then Wilberforce fell so
seriously ill that his life was despaired of. Before he left London,
his last request to Pitt was to bring forward the motion on his
behalf. Pitt consented, wrote Wilberforce, 'with a warmth of
principle and friendship that have made me love him better
than I ever did before.'

On May 9th, 1788, the prime minister moved that at the
beginning of the next session the Commons should tackle the
question of the slave trade. Pitt forbore to define his own
attitude pending the findings of an official investigation. If this
was completely understandable in a minister who was aware
of the resistance he might expect in his own Cabinet, others
were able to express themselves more freely. No one who knew
the warm humanity of Charles Fox could doubt what his
attitude to such a question would be. He said that he had himself had the intention of bringing forward a motion like this,
but had forborne to do so when he heard that a follower of the
administration, whose purity of principles and sincere love for
the rights of humanity he knew, had the same intention.
Without mincing matters or making reservations, he stated it
to be his conviction that the slave trade 'ought not to be regulated but destroyed'. With these words he raised the banner
which he upheld until his dying day.

In this question, too, it was apparent once again how much
common ground there was between the two great opponents,
for Pitt championed the same view. Wilberforce, when fully
recovered, brought the question before the House in May, 1789,
in a great speech which combined balanced objectivity with

moral fervour and had the full approval and support of both Pitt and Fox. But their parties were by no means solidly in support of them. The leaders had to fight not only against well-organized vested interests but also against the English love of compromise solutions, and the aversion felt by very many members for radical interference with the rights of property. And so the struggle dragged on from year to year. It reached its climax on April 2nd, 1792. Fox made a rousing speech against the delaying tactics of Dundas, the Secretary of State. But the great event of the debate was Pitt's speech which far outshone any he had previously delivered. Morning was already breaking through the windows of the House when he drew to a close and, with superb inspiration, summed up his hope that the sun of civilization which now shone upon England might in future also lighten Africa's darkness in the lines of Virgil:

> '*Nos . . . primus equis Oriens afflavit anhelis,*
> *Illic sera rubens accendit lumina Vesper.*'

Fox was quite transported by this speech of his rival's, which he agreed was one of the most extraordinary displays of eloquence he had ever heard. But on the division Dundas won the day with his amendment to abolish the slave trade 'gradually'.

This result was partly due to the mighty events of the time in Paris which cast their shadow over England. It was by then the fourth year of the French Revolution which had become a source of increasing uneasiness to England, and, worse still, the bloody slave revolt in San Domingo seemed to counsel prudence. Then came the war, which killed all zeal for reform. By degrees even Pitt became uncertain and doubtful. From about 1797, his zeal cooled off, and what had been unattainable with his help became utterly impossible without it. But Fox did not flag. How in the end he brought his ship safe to port has still to be told.

In sketching the further progress of the slave question we have run on rather far ahead of some of the events of the time. Going back to 1788, we can see that five years of work by Pitt had considerably increased England's stability at home and prestige abroad. There can also be little doubt that his reputation in his own country had risen unusually high. Britain had grown used to looking on him as the arbiter of her destinies.

Then, quite suddenly, an episode occurred which seemed to put the whole of his position in question.

In November, 1788, the insanity, which had threatened George III for a time in 1765, attacked him again so violently and permanently that on this occasion his incapacity to rule was obvious. He had dreadful attacks of raving lunacy and was quite unconscious of himself or his surroundings. At first the doctors attending him believed the malady to be incurable. Beyond all doubt a regency was a necessity.

Now it is one of the peculiarities of England's unwritten constitution that the problem of a regency has never been clearly and systematically set forth. Precedents were the only things which legal experts could cite, and these dated from times and conditions long past and were capable of very varied interpretations. The Regency Act of 1766 did not apply because it only covered the period during which there was no heir to the throne capable of ruling. But by this time there was an heir. The Prince of Wales was twenty-six years old, and undoubtedly of an age to rule.

Yet the Prince was a problem in himself. Everyone knew not only that he was on bad enough terms with his father to live up to the settled tradition of the House of Hanover but also that he was a close friend of Fox's. No one doubted—and Pitt and Fox least of all—that his first act as King would be to dismiss Pitt and summon Fox. It is true that the Prince was a profligate and a spendthrift, whose debts Parliament had repeatedly been obliged to pay, but this could hardly have been urged against his worthiness and capacity to ascend a throne once graced by Charles II. But what was worse was that he had already given proof positive of his lack of self-control and of all sense of responsibility by secretly marrying a widow called Mrs. Fitzherbert in 1785; she was a Catholic and, by law, marriage to a Catholic made it impossible for the heir to ascend the throne. Only a very few people knew of the marriage, and Fox was not of their number. He had employed all his powers of persuasion to dissuade the Prince from any such union, and the Prince had had the unblushing effrontery flatly to deny it to him in writing. He had, indeed, gone further still. When, in the debate on the Prince's debts, a member had referred openly to the rumour of the secret marriage, the Prince gave Fox direct authority to discount the story as untrue and unfounded. Fox discharged this commission with that forthrightness which was all his own, only to learn later that he had been impudently deceived. This led to a breach—unfortunately only a temporary one. Not even a Fox was free from the weakness common to politicians of sacrificing moral scruples to ambition. He never brought himself to break clean away from the one man through whom he might hope to reach the goal of his political exertions and ambition.

Fox was in Italy when the news of the King's illness first became public. His friends at once sent a messenger to bring him home again with all possible haste. Just before this Fox had received word that his nephew, Lord Holland, was seriously ill. When he heard of the arrival of an express messenger he was violently alarmed because he thought that this meant that his nephew was dead. But then he promptly responded to his friends' summons and posted home at top speed. By the time he reached London he was very ill himself; it was quite a time before he could join in the struggle which had now flared up.

His attitude, no less than Pitt's, was determined in advance. Fox had to stake everything on getting the Prince made Regent as soon as possible. Pitt, on the other hand, had to do his best to stave this off as long as possible and, when that policy ceased to work, to hedge the regency round with so many restrictions and conditions that the Regent would be prevented as far as possible from abandoning his father's policy or altering it. He clutched at every straw of a hope that George III might recover. On this crucial question the doctors did not agree, and each party suspected those who took a view unfavourable to them of being prompted less by medical than by political considerations.

Thus the struggle over the regency question was essentially a struggle for power between Pitt and Fox. No one had any doubts about that, least of all the two rivals. A struggle like this is not usually conducted with the calm objectivity and sweet reasonableness of an academic discussion. So it is not surprising to find each party choosing the arguments which seemed best suited to meet its own ends, and not troubling over much whether they were fully in tune with its general policy. Fox maintained that the heir to the throne was Regent of right.

This argument would have sounded quite in order in the mouth of a constitutional lawyer on the Continent, but characteristically enough in England it brought down on Fox's head the most violent reproaches that he had deserted the principles of the Whigs and the Revolution. Pitt, on the other hand, particularly wanted to deny the Regent the right to create new peers. No one knew better than he how effective, how indispensable a counter this very prerogative was in a political trial of strength. Not only did he remember the part it had played in the election of 1784, but he himself had made use of it—and continued to do so as long as he held the reins of government—to a hitherto unknown extent for wooing or rewarding supporters. The Prince sent a letter—probably drafted by Sheridan —vehemently protesting against this restriction. How could one take from the representative of royal authority the power of rewarding services to the state? Was it intended that, in his person, an experiment should be made to ascertain with how small a portion of the kingly power England could be governed? Pitt's former rôle as champion of the power of the Crown certainly seems to have very little in common with these proposals.

The contrasting attitudes of the Parliaments of Westminster and Dublin shows how confused the whole question was. After a long struggle the English Parliament accepted Pitt's proposals. But the Irish Parliament utterly ignored them and declared the Prince of Wales to be the rightful Regent with full powers, and this in spite of all the despairing manoeuvres of the Viceroy, the Marquis of Buckingham (as Temple had lately become). It is impossible to tell what complications might not have sprung from this divergence if George III had not shaken off his bout of madness. On February 24th the Lord Chancellor was able to inform the Lords that the King had fully recovered. The crisis was over and everything remained as it had been before, except that Pitt had discovered the unreliability of Thurlow, his Lord Chancellor. The noble lord had scampered off to join the Prince when it looked as if his moment had come, and had deserted him just as quickly when he gathered that King George would again become capable of ruling. A few years later Pitt got rid of this shifty colleague.

During the crisis Fox had confidently reckoned that within

CHARLES FOX

a short time he would have the reins in his hands. The Whigs had already been busy drawing up lists of the new ministry, and rivalry for certain posts had already sprung up. The ambitious politician, who believes he has reached the goal of his heart's desire and is harassed by the uneasy feeling that the fruits of his toil may escape him, easily exposes himself to criticism and mockery, particularly from those who have themselves been spared such ordeals. Now it turned out that all the excitement had been for nothing, and the lists of ministers had to be put away for use on some future occasion—which was never to arise. Charles Fox had to resign himself to remaining what he had been for the last five years—the leader of an impotent opposition who was still listened to with pleasure and respect by the House but was always in a minority on every division except when he happened to find himself in agreement with his luckier rivals. He was now nearly forty and in the noon-tide of his life. He had sat in Parliament for twenty years and all this time, except for short intervals, he had had to chew the bitter cud of opposition. But his verve and enthusiasm had not declined, nor had his enjoyment of life. Solid in the bourgeois sense he had never been. His finances were in the same hope-less disorder as ever. But at least he now had something like an establishment of his own.

Since his downfall in 1783 he had been living with Elizabeth Armistead. She could not boast an altogether blameless past, having passed through all sorts of hands. Among her dis-tinguished lovers even the Prince of Wales is mentioned. The portraits which Reynolds painted of her show that she was a beautiful woman. What drew Fox to her must have been far more than a fleeting infatuation, for their alliance lasted until his death. All this time no semblance of a shadow fell across her devotion to him. Most of Fox's friends and relatives treated her with the greatest respect, even before the association of some years was regularised by a formal marriage ceremony in 1795. Fox found his fullest happiness in this union, as is shown by scores of passages in his letters, particularly in those to his favourite relative, his nephew Henry, third Lord Holland. Much of his contentment was due to the fact that he now had a home he could call his own. St. Anne's Hill, a simple country house in Surrey, belonged to all appearances to Mrs. Armi-

T

stead; but it was Charles Fox's home in the fullest sense of the word. Here he spent every day that political business did not call him to London. Here he watched spring drawing on, saw the trees putting out their blossom and heard the birds sing. Here he buried himself in his beloved books or read them in the company of his life's partner. Here fate granted him not only the chance to be happy but also the knowledge that he was, and that he could call himself, a happy man.

How much poorer was William Pitt's private life. At times one almost feels that it was nearly completely engulfed by his public life. There is a price to pay if one becomes prime minister of a world empire at twenty-four and has to adopt a bearing and manner calculated to exact from one's seniors the respect due to the office. Shy by nature, Pitt early grew accustomed to keeping his colleagues and supporters at a respectful distance. Only a few of the friends of his youth knew that he could unbend with them in his leisure hours and remember to be young, particularly when he opened his heart in light or serious conversation with Wilberforce in his charming, comfortable house at Wimbledon. Far less delicate were the pleasures which that worldly schemer Dundas offered him when he was his guest—also at Wimbledon. Dundas set great store by a good cellar and Pitt by no means scorned the pleasures of the table. He was, and remained, more addicted to port than his weak health could stand. There is a well-known epigram about the after-effects this tippling sometimes had. The two of them entered the House in such a condition that Pitt muttered in his friend's ear:

'I cannot see the Speaker, Hal; can you?'

'Not see the Speaker? Hang it, I see two!' Dundas replied.

Certainly Pitt's contemporaries did not take such weaknesses too tragically, and if they compared Pitt's way of life as a whole with that of his rival, then the scales were tipped very decidedly against Fox. Yet if Pitt did avoid many of Fox's failings, it is true that he also missed many of his pleasures. Women played no part in Pitt's life, good or bad. In his later years one incident occurred which, by a slight stretch of imagination, could perhaps be invested with an amorous significance. He was turning over the idea of marrying Eleanor Eden, daughter of the diplomat Lord Auckland, but then suddenly withdrew on the plea that his circumstances forbade him to realize this plan. Information on this episode is too scanty to permit of any certain judgement. However, it is safe to conclude that it can hardly have been a very powerful inclination which drew him towards the young girl. And, in short, that is the only event in Pitt's private life on which any speculation is possible.

Certainly many of the friends who clustered round Fox were not really worthy of him. But there were also many men of intellect and character to bear witness to the irresistible charm which he always exercised. In later life Pitt hardly added a single friend to those of his youth. Besides, he had inherited his father's recklessness in money matters and his inability to keep his personal affairs in order. The man who for almost twenty years drew the handsome salary of a prime minister and, on top of this, enjoyed the lucrative office of Warden of the Cinque Ports from 1792 onwards, was a bankrupt while still living and deep in debt when he died.

CHAPTER XIX

THE FRENCH REVOLUTION

I T scarcely needs saying that the French Revolution cut deep into the lives of both Pitt and Fox. It was so much more than a revolution in France; it was a world event challenging the notice of every thinking man, an event producing effects which could be traced in all the countries of Europe. Nowhere is its world-wide significance more strikingly brought home than in the words which Hegel spoke as Prussian Royal Professor from his chair at Berlin a generation later. He hymned the outbreak of the revolution as a 'glorious dawn'. 'All thinking men have joined in celebrating this epoch. A spiritual enthusiasm has thrilled the world, as if only now the union of the Eternal with the Temporal has arrived.' When Hegel thus commemorated the days of his youth he was already the acknowledged spiritual head of European conservatism and the high priest of the Prussian monarchy.. How much more must feelings like these have fired such a man as Charles Fox, who could breathe no air but freedom and symbolized the liberal ideal before it had become a party programme? Small wonder that he hailed with joy the news that the Bastille had fallen. 'How much the greatest event it is that ever happened in the world, and how much the best!' he wrote to his friend Fitzpatrick. And yet, outside France, few men were harder hit by the Revolution than Fox. It cost him the friend whom he had looked up to as his mentor in politics, it shattered the party which he had held together with so much skill and enthusiasm, and it decided his destiny— to wander through the wilderness until his strength was broken and his end was near.

It was a misfortune not only for Fox but for England's political development as a whole that Edmund Burke, the most intellectually distinguished of all his comrades-in-arms, was deflected from his course by the Revolution.

When it was still only a few months old, and had not yet degenerated into the Reign of Terror, Burke had already turned away from it with a shudder. His world-famous *Reflec-*

tions on the Revolution in France was written as early as the spring of 1790, when the National Assembly in Paris was still striving to organize a constitutional monarchy. But even then the Assembly roused Burke's wildest anger, not merely because most of its members were provincial lawyers—and not men of birth and substance—but also because it was trying to frame a radically new constitution by the light of reason alone. Such a plan seemed stark lunacy to one who worshipped the British constitution with an almost religious fervour precisely because it had developed slowly down the centuries and often, apparently, by accident—who found its very oddities worthy of reverence because they were hallowed by history. Burke's protest could hardly fail to impress, because it was based on a coherent, well-weighed theory of the state and because it was cast in language of manly strength and dazzling richness. His description of the young Marie Antoinette is a literary jewel which no reader can forget, however wide of the mark it may be as a political argument. George III, who as a rule was not unduly addicted to literature, said it was 'a book which every gentleman ought to read'; and the gentlemen who followed his advice certainly had no reason to regret it. But it was only the few who read the book to enjoy the richness of its language and the profundity of its theory of the state. Most people read it as a defence of the existing order and an onslaught against all reforms which might undermine it. Here, too, was the reason why George was well pleased with this book from the pen of a man whom he had always numbered among his enemies, who had campaigned against his system root and branch, had sympathized with the American revolution and had prosecuted Warren Hastings with the fire and frenzy of a prophet.

Burke saw the French Revolution as a monstrous threat to everything he held most dear; he battled against it not only with the weapons of reason but far more with his passions, which had now cast off every fetter. He had always been in danger of being carried away by his own passionate nature. He now gave it full rein, all the more recklessly as the excesses of the Revolution and the Jacobin reign of terror seemed to bear out his sombre prophecies. The more hideously the flames spread across the Channel, the shriller did Burke's curses and lamentations ring out, the more dangerous did all reforms seem to him, the more radically did he preach his '*Quieta non movere!*' and the more recklessly did he press on as the spokesman and standard-bearer of uncompromising reaction.

Even religious toleration, though it was, after all, one of the cardinal principles of the Whigs and though Burke had fought doughtily for it in the past and had suffered for it at times, now found him amongst its opponents. For years Fox had battled against the old penal laws dating from Charles II's time, which debarred Dissenters from holding public office. He had no political reasons for showing the Dissenters any particular favour, for they had deserted the Whig party, to which they had belonged from time immemorial, to help Pitt into the saddle. But this could not damp Fox's ardour on so fundamental an issue. Previously Burke had always sided with Fox. But when in March, 1790, Fox again brought in his motion for the repeal of the Test Act, he was to find Burke getting up to say that as things were he could not support it, for the leaders of the Dissenters were party men with dangerous principles, or in other words, supporters of the French Revolution and democracy. A democratic speech made in the autumn of 1789 by one of their leaders, the highly respected Dr. Price, had been the first thing which urged Burke to take up his pen and write his *Reflections*. The effects of the surprising stand he had taken up showed themselves when the House divided. Whereas in May, 1789, there had been only twenty votes against the motion, in March, 1790, it was thrown out by a two-thirds majority. Fox had every reason to complain that this statement by the man who had given him his own political education had filled him with grief and shame, and to remind Burke of the experiences he himself had had with religious fanatics during the Gordon riots. Pitt, who had always opposed the motion on toleration, could not but rejoice at the rift between these two members of Parliament who had been linked together so closely and so long.

The French Revolution, and the interpretation placed on it by Burke, were to have an even more crucial effect on reform. It is true that the Revolution had breathed new life into the reform movement, which had slumbered for so long. But, quite understandably, the movement had now assumed a far more radical complexion. Men came to the fore who were proposing not to improve the constitution on existing lines, but to recast it completely, men who talked of universal suffrage and even, at times, of a republic. The most radical spokesman of this school was Thomas Paine, a man of little depth or education but with a keen intelligence and outstanding gifts as a journalist, who attacked established political institutions just as ruthlessly as he did established religion. His pamphlet, *The Rights of Man*, which was directed against Burke and called forth his most wrathful anathema, was distributed by the thousand, particularly among those classes who did not possess a vote. Burke saw this as a striking proof of the infectious and subversive effects of the Jacobin spirit, the rooting out of which he now regarded as his life's work.

The Whigs were, of course, very far removed from radicalism of this kind. But none the less they were unwilling to drop the cause of reform, which a young sprig of one of the old Whig families, who had become a close ally of Fox, now made his special business. This was Charles Grey, the very man who, as 'Lord Grey of the Reform Bill', piloted the measure through forty years later. When Grey raised the matter in the Commons in April, 1792, not only did Burke come out against him with impassioned fanaticism, but Pitt, whose former motions for reform Grey had cited, also refused to consider any sort of reform on the grounds that it was inopportune. He confessed he was afraid, at this moment, that if reform was agreed on by the House, the security of all the blessings the nation enjoyed would be shaken to the foundation. Fox countered this with the liberal argument that timely and judicious reform was the surest means of averting unrest. But this, of course, had no effect. Fear was the argument which carried the day, and reform was buried for a generation.

Despite this hostile trend, Fox did at least succeed in putting through a reform of *one* important point at the last moment. Since Mansfield's ruling in the Woodfall case, the judges had not relaxed their efforts to appropriate the right to make the real decision when libel actions against the press were heard, and to limit the jury's rôle to deciding whether or not the accused had *published* the statement complained of. The more numerous these actions grew, the more dangerous this tendency had become. No one had attacked the Mansfield doctrine in court more brilliantly or successfully than Thomas Erskine, one of the leading barristers and perhaps the greatest advocate of his day. He was a faithful henchman of Fox and now sat by his side in the Commons. If Erskine deserves the credit for having kept the question open in the law courts, it is to Fox's credit to have solved it in Parliament. In May, 1791, he introduced a bill to establish beyond all question the right of juries to decide the issue in all its implications, so that their verdict also determined whether what the accused had published amounted to a libel. The judge, as in other criminal cases, was to confine himself to directing the jury. To Pitt's credit it must be said that he was faithful to his father's example, and supported the bill. And so, after some difficulties, it got past both Houses and became law. It was a timely step. A little later a storm of reaction broke over England and threatened the freedom and reputation of anyone who flourished his pen against it. During this period English juries, with the help of doughty fighters like Erskine, proved themselves a bulwark of free speech. Without Fox's Act this would have been impossible. Thus the man, who once in the exuberance of youth had plunged head over heels into squabbles with the press, now became its greatest benefactor in his riper days.

In the early years of the French Revolution, Pitt's attitude towards it was very reserved. He was as far from the enthusiasm of Fox as he was from the crusading wrath of Burke. He viewed it principally in the light of foreign policy, and secretly welcomed the weakening of France by internal troubles and her consequent embarrassment in her dealings abroad. He banked successfully on her weakness when he fell out with Spain over Nootka Sound, a fishing settlement on the Pacific coast of North America, near what is today Vancouver. Here again he took matters into his own hands and insisted on an energetic policy, even at the risk of war. The fleet was strengthened and the notorious press-gangs were used to man the warships. England could face the prospect of war with Spain quite unmoved. But it would have been another story if France, faithful to the 'family compact', had gone to Spain's help. But Pitt reckoned on the impossibility of an understanding between the old Spain and the new France, and he proved to be right. Spain had to climb down and Pitt was able to pull off a diplomatic triumph, the full significance of which was only recognized by later generations when the tide of settlement had advanced right over Canada to the Pacific coast. Fox grasped the significance of this only very imperfectly and belaboured the treaty concluded by Pitt with unjustified severity.

But things turned out very differently in the following year, when Pitt's policy put England in danger of war with Russia. While the French Revolution was engaging the breathless attention of Europe, the three eastern monarchies—Russia, Austria and Prussia—turned their eyes towards the Poles, at whose expense they had already enriched themselves in the first partition of Poland. More than this, the Russian Czarina, Catherine II, and the Austrian Emperor, Joseph II, were also trying to advance their frontiers at the expense of Turkey. Out of this a combined Russian and Austrian war against Turkey had developed from 1787 onwards and dragged on for years with varying fortunes. Prussia tried to exploit this situation to further her own expansionist plans, particularly the acquisition of the Polish towns of Danzig and Thorn. The main aim of Pitt's efforts was to avoid a major European war and to reach a settlement without, however, abandoning England's treaty obligations towards Prussia. And indeed by a union of foresight and energy he successfully carried out this policy for a considerable time. Britain's prestige under his leadership had risen so high that his words were listened to with respect at almost all foreign courts. Thanks to Britain's influence, Austria and Prussia returned to the *status quo* (Convention of Reichenbach, July, 1790) and the new ruler of Austria, the Emperor Leopold II, made peace with Turkey. Pitt might well be satisfied with the success of his foreign policy.

But now he strayed from the paths of prudence and took a step liable to lead to incalculable consequences. After Austria had laid down her arms (Armistice of Giurgewo, September, 1790), Russia had still to make peace with the Porte. In its closing stages, the war had taken such a favourable turn for Russia that Turkey had to resign herself to ceding some areas round the Black Sea.

Considering the military position, Catherine's demands were not excessive. But she wanted to keep the district and town of Oczakow, a Black Sea fortress in the Bug-Dnieper delta which General Suvorov had taken for her by storm. This was too much for the Turks, and they were backed up by the British ministry, who, indeed, considered the ownership of Oczakow so important a question that they at once put a finger in the pie, demanding that the Czarina should be content with a return to the *status quo ante bellum*.

It is hard to see why Pitt set so much store by Oczakow, for he had in his possession the expert opinion of a Dutch admiral, who undoubtedly knew what he was talking about; from first-hand knowledge he reckoned that the value of Oczakow to the Turks was very small. The British ambassador at The Hague, Lord Auckland (formerly William Eden), one of the most distinguished British diplomats, sounded an urgent warning against plunging into difficulties on account of Oczakow. On the other hand, Pitt and his Minister for Foreign Affairs, the Duke of Leeds, seem to have been strongly influenced by the representations of Frederick William of Prussia, who was most eager to cause his eastern neighbour a palpable discomfiture and appealed for help from his British ally. Besides, the ministers believed that Russia was so exhausted by the lengthy war that the appearance of another opponent on the scene would at once make the Czarina acquiesce. On March 25th, 1791, Pitt and Leeds managed to get the Cabinet to endorse the despatch of a ten-day ultimatum to Catherine.

But Britain was not an absolute monarchy, like Russia or Prussia, where the wishes of the king and his ministers were the only factors in deciding on peace or war. To give the ultimatum weight, the armed forces had to be strengthened and Parliament alone could sanction the necessary expenditure. And so, at the same time as the ultimatum was despatched, Pitt presented the King's message to Parliament which told the Houses in a few not very informative words of the decision to strengthen the fleet in the interests of procuring peace between Russia and the Porte. On the next day, March 29th, Pitt moved an address of thanks. But even then he did not go as far as half way towards explaining the reasons for this dramatic departure, although the press at home and abroad was already buzzing with disquieting news. Obviously he did not take enough account of the dangers which faced him, and as a result he badly bungled his parliamentary tactics.

Of course, the opposition were not satisfied with such meagre information. Fox taxed Pitt with having 'enveloped himself in mystery and importance', but having explained nothing. With great seriousness and emphasis he opposed England's plunging into another war over an insignificant place like Oczakow with a great power like Russia, which on the contrary was England's natural ally. Burke enquired with some heat whether it could be the aim of British policy 'to bring Christian nations under the yoke of savage and inhuman infidels'. One is almost reminded of Gladstone's outcry ninety years later at the time of the 'Bulgarian atrocities'.

Once again Pitt did, it is true, secure a majority on the division, but it was very far from being its normal size: 135 members voted for the opposition, which was more than they had mustered for years. Worse still, Pitt had the feeling that even among those who had voted for his motion, there were many who had their hearts in the other camp and had only remained loyal to the administration on this occasion in the hope that somehow peace might still be preserved. He had to reckon on their going over to the opposition if the Czarina rejected the ultimatum and thus threw the onus of declaring war on England. Fox had obviously hit off the mood of the House—and the country—when he cried that Oczakow was not worth a war with Russia or—as he once said in a similar connection—'the hundredth part of a British life or the hundredth part of a British pound'. (A Bismarck would have spoken of the bones of a single British musketeer.) Pitt was not the last prime minister to discover that the English want to know in advance what they are going to fight for before they enter upon a war.

Pitt himself, in private conversation, described the opinion of the House as the deciding factor which persuaded him to change his diplomatic tactics. News from Berlin, where Frederick William was once more starting to waver, may also have had something to do with it. Even in Pitt's Cabinet itself there was a stiffening of resistance to a foolhardy policy which Grenville in particular opposed. Even the King had convinced himself how impossible it was to persuade the country to take part in such a war. As the upshot of the whole affair, Pitt sent off an express courier with orders that the ultimatum was not to be delivered, and the Duke of Leeds, who was not prepared to have anything to do with these weathercock gyrations, resigned on April 16th; he was succeeded by Grenville. Now, of course, Catherine got her way and kept Oczakow.

And so Pitt had suffered a heavy political and diplomatic defeat. As things are viewed nowadays, this is when he should have resigned. Nor was this idea completely absent from his mind, but he believed that out of loyalty to the King he ought not to back down. Of course, the opposition tried to exploit this defeat and in the spring of 1792, when Parliament reassembled, he had to submit patiently to some withering criticism. When Fox, speaking at great length, remorselessly reproached him with all his blunders, Pitt had his revenge by referring to the fact that Catherine had given a bust of Fox the place of honour in her palace between the busts of Cicero and Demosthenes. For Fox's sake it is to be hoped that he did not attach any exaggerated importance to this token of imperial favour, for a few years later, when his speeches about revolutionary France fell less pleasingly on her ears than had those about Oczakow, she consigned that bust to the remotest corner of her cellar to find what comfort it could from the proximity of Voltaire's. 'Those who cry "Hosannah!" today will be shouting "Crucify him!" tomorrow.'

During the debates on the Russo-Turkish war in the spring of 1791 Burke, as we have seen, had once again fought on Fox's side. But some eulogies of the new French constitution which Fox had allowed to slip into his speeches had irritated Burke so much that he decided on an open breach with Fox. On April 21st, Fox once again paid a call on him to discuss their differences of opinion and possibly to talk him into a milder frame of mind. Once again they entered the House together, as they had so often done before, the House where they had waged such a long and glorious struggle as comrades-in-arms. It was for the last time. On May 6th, 1791, Burke attacked Fox's point of view in public and with extreme severity. After Burke had rained down his anathemas upon the Revolution, Fox recalled how it was from Burke himself that he had learned that no revolt of a nation was caused without provocation. Even the defection of his former teacher, he said, would not bring him to abandon that opinion. Burke grew more and more angry. Any agreement between them, he exclaimed, was impossible. 'It certainly was indiscreet at his time of life to provoke enemies or give his friends occasion to desert him. Yet . . . he would risk all; and as public duty and public prudence taught him, with his last breath, exclaim: "Fly from the French constitution!" ' Fox whispered audibly that there was no loss of friendship. 'Yes, there was,' cried Burke. 'He knew the price of his conduct —he had done his duty at the price of his friend—their friendship was at an end.' So moved was Fox by this brusque parting that tears rolled down his cheeks when he rose to reply and his words were broken by sobs. Even his opponents were deeply moved and a hush of emotion settled on the assembly which was usually so animated.

But there was no going back. Burke stood squarely by what he had said. He was the last man to combine political antagonism with personal friendship. His passionate nature knew no half measures. All later attempts by Fox to renew their private bonds of affection he brushed roughly aside. Even on his deathbed he refused him a word of farewell. No, for the rest of his political career he moved heaven and earth to detach from Fox as many of his friends as possible, for in his eyes Fox now embodied the spirit of Jacobinism and it was on the destruction of this spirit that the ageing Burke spent his last breath.

The French Revolution and the friends of reform in England saw to it that he attained his goal. The Revolution did not come to a halt but became more and more radical. An accommodation with the French monarchy was obviously hopeless. This was shown in June, 1791, by the attempted flight of Louis XVI and Marie Antoinette, which failed so ignominiously at Varennes. The effect on the English was twofold. One section of the populace demanded radical reforms, particularly of the franchise. In this movement the Dissenters took a leading part. On the other hand, the section of the people which clung to the existing order of things, saw every reformer as a Jacobin and a revolutionary. This mood found inglorious expression in the summer of 1791 in a disturbance at Birmingham, where the mob, with the tacit consent of some town councillors, raised a cry of 'Church and King for ever!', looted the houses and chapels of the Dissenters and destroyed the library and irreplaceable laboratory of their leader, Dr. Priestley, the distinguished scientist.

In these circumstances it said much for the courage and idealism of some young Whig members of Parliament, with Charles Grey at their head, that in April, 1792, they formed an association to further the reform movement and styled it the 'Friends of the People'. Their programme was by no means radical. It embodied only two points: a more uniform representation of the people in Parliament and more frequent elections. But every organisation directed against the existing order of things was suspect in the highest degree, especially since the shoemaker Hardy had founded a 'Corresponding Society', which set out to organize the underdogs and sent delegations to the National Assembly in Paris. Fox had taken no part in founding the 'Friends of the People'. He had to bear it well in mind that a considerable section of his party at that particular moment would not hear of any reforms, and, as a good party leader, he had therefore to exercise restraint for as long as possible. But when Grey gave notice of his Reform Bill in Parliament and, as a result, was accused by Pitt of stirring up anarchy and confusion, Fox did not hesitate one moment longer to back up the measures energetically. It never occurred to him, as it did to Pitt, to repudiate in foul weather what he had preached in fair. But he could not blink the fact that his loyalty to his principles was bound to lose him a large part of his circle of friends. Portland, whom Fox had put at the head of his ministry in 1783, was urged by his intimates to drop him. Portland found it very hard to bring himself to do this, for he had a personal liking for Fox and could not resist his charm. But he had become as alarmed as the ministers, and Burke was preaching with the fervour of a fanatic: Break loose from Fox! At length Portland gave way. Pitt brought things to a head in May by issuing a proclamation against seditious writings which set up a system of espionage hitherto unknown in England. Grey and Fox taxed the ministry in round terms with using this proclamation to drive a wedge into the Whig party. Fox deplored having to set up in opposition to old friends who were so near to his heart. But he obeyed the voice of his conscience and came out publicly against the proclamation, which was just as publicly welcomed by several secessionist Whigs.

That made the breach inevitable. This separation from men with most of whom he had lived in close friendship since his youth was a bitter blow to Fox. Indeed, after his death, many of those who remained loyal to him to the end said that nothing in his whole life had affected him so deeply. On hearing of Fox's death, Lord Fitzwilliam, one of the friends of his youth who had broken with him at about this time, fainted and remained senseless for some time; he felt, wrote a woman admirer of Fox's, that his desertion had caused Charles perhaps the greatest pain he ever suffered.

Fox's following could now raise only about fifty votes at a division. To such depths had the once dominant Whig party sunk within a generation. What held this little handful of loyalists together in distress and danger was, first and foremost, their leader's personality. Almost every one of them clung to Fox with the deepest respect and highest pride. Offices and dignities which others shared out among themselves might be beyond their reach, but they could cluster round a man who made every hour spent in his company worth living. When he spoke, they knew that they would hear not only an excellent speech but also firm and unsullied principles which would not be sacrificed to any playing to the gallery. Most of these men were in the fortunate position of being members who were not dependent on the favour of the people. The Whig families still controlled enough constituencies to provide them with seats. Thus they were the very last people who had anything to look for from electoral reform. Their dogged support of it in spite of this showed that idealism was not yet dead among the ruling class of English politicians.

This policy required not only idealism, but courage too. For the reports which came crowding in from across the Channel stirred up such irritation in England against all who seemed to be flirting with French ideas that anyone who mentioned reform was looked upon as little better than a public enemy. But the little band ranged behind Fox braved all this, knowing that the cause for which they were fighting was no less vital for the future of the country than were the warlike activities which were soon to occupy all thoughts.

CHAPTER XX

THE OUTBREAK OF WAR AGAINST FRANCE

W HEN in the spring of 1792 Pitt shivered the Whig party into fragments with his proclamation against seditious writing, he had never even toyed with the idea of making war on the French Revolution. On the contrary, he cherished the belief that England had a long spell of peace ahead of her, and in his Budget speech of February, 1792, he ventured to make the signally mistaken prophecy that the situation in Europe fully entitled England to count on at least fifteen years of peace. Obviously he was banking on France's being so weakened by her internal troubles that for half a generation at least she could be disregarded as a major factor in politics.

He was not the only person to make this fundamental error. Leopold II of Austria and Frederick William II of Prussia thought the same and believed that in the face of their combined strength the French revolutionaries would have to climb down (Alliance of February 7th, 1792). Unluckily the Girondins, who held the reins in France at the time, imagined the exact opposite—that the youthful revolutionary impetus of France would blow down the rickety thrones of the old monarchies like a hurricane. On April 20th, 1792, they forced Louis XVI to declare war on Austria, and Prussia came in as Austria's ally. Leopold, who was a shrewd politician, had died on March 1st, 1792, and was succeeded by his son, Francis I, a young man of indifferent talents and weak character. Both Francis and Frederick William were, in their heart of hearts, thinking more about Poland than about France. But, convinced of their military superiority, they believed they would win such a quick victory in France that they could then turn to their Polish booty undisturbed. Completely misled by _émigrés_ about the prevailing mood in France, they imagined they could conduct this war as an 'ideological' one.

This error found its strongest, most characteristic and most disastrous utterance in the notorious manifesto of July 25th,

WILLIAM PITT THE YOUNGER

1792, to which the Duke of Brunswick, the Commander-in-Chief of the allied armies, set his name. This is the most crass expression of the policy of intervention, that is, the policy of a great power trying to interfere in the internal affairs of another people. The worst blunder of the manifesto was to draw a sharp distinction between the King of France and the French people. It threatened that Paris would be razed to the ground if a hair of the King's head were touched. The result was that the Parisians stormed the royal palace of the Tuileries, butchered the Swiss guard and took the King prisoner (August 10th, 1792). When the allied armies actually did seem to be nearing Paris, the fury of the populace was vented in butchery among the political prisoners, the September massacres, which claimed 1,100 victims and have been regarded as the most appalling outbreak of political fanaticism until our own age witnessed atrocities of such horror and on such a vast scale that the earlier ones seem almost trifling in comparison. But Brunswick never got as far as Paris. After the cannonade of Valmy (September 20th) he turned back, and Goethe, who had taken part in the operation in Champagne as one of the retinue of his Duke, Charles Augustus, could sit by the camp fire at night and sum up the significance of this event in the classic phrase: 'Here and now begins a new epoch in world history, and you can say that you were there.'

English politicians followed this dramatic development on the tiptoe of interest. Pitt and his Foreign Minister, Lord Grenville, had not even the least intention of joining in this war. But beyond all doubt their sympathies were on the side of the old monarchies; they wished Brunswick success with all their hearts. In contrast to this, Fox regarded any success on that side as a mortal blow to freedom and progress, little as he sympathized with the conduct and excesses of the French. He deplored the bloodshed of August 10th, but he recognized—and here his view is borne out by modern, non-party historical research—that in this crisis the French had been compelled to render harmless a king who was on the side of their enemies. For the September massacres, on the other hand, there was no excuse, he confided to his nephew, Lord Holland; they were 'the most heart-breaking event' for anyone who, like himself, was unalterably attached to the cause of liberty.

u

How right he was in this is shown by the effect which these events had on public opinion in England. Reaction now swept all before it. The administration could now propose what it liked in the way of repressive measures; not only did the public accept this without a murmur but greeted it with the loudest applause. The minority who were suspected of sympathizing, if not with France at least with French ideas, had to be careful to keep in the background for fear of provoking violent outbreaks of popular feeling. One straw in the wind was the fact that the twenty-two-year-old George Canning, who had belonged to the Whigs when an undergraduate, now joined Pitt, in whom he saw the champion of the monarchy against the Jacobin spirit.

Thus, in the second half of 1792, the English people were in a mood which made them receptive to the preaching of a crusade. The preacher, of course, was Burke. In his view it was now England's mission to lay low the dragon of the French Revolution with the lance of St. George, after the Emperor of Austria and the King of Prussia had failed in the quest. The absurd lengths to which he let his fanaticism carry him are shown by the melodramatic dagger scene which he staged in the Commons in December, 1792. During the debate on a bill for the regulation of aliens, designed by the administration to keep a check on foreign immigrants and opposed by Fox as a denial of the best traditions of England, Burke maintained that three thousand daggers had already been made at Birmingham to arm the projected revolution. In illustration of this statement he suddenly drew a dagger from his clothes and flung it to the floor of the House, crying: 'This is what you are to gain by an alliance with France!' The storms of the day must indeed have shaken the composure of a people schooled to self-control and understatement, to make them tolerate such a piece of pantomime!

Burke preached his crusade not so much to the public as to the ministry. He paid repeated calls on Pitt and Grenville or wrote them letters to make it clear with all the authority of an elder statesman that it was their moral and patriotic duty to declare war on France. But so long as Pitt believed that he could see no danger for Britain, he clung fast to his policy of peace and non-intervention. However, the more excited the displays of popular feeling became, and the further the French let themselves be swept away by their revolutionary ardour and their confidence in victory, the weaker his resistance grew.

After the withdrawal of the allied army from Valmy, the French forces thrust victoriously into the Austrian Netherlands (present-day Belgium). Dumouriez' victory at Jemappes (November 6th) made him master of these provinces. The King of Prussia played into his hands by conducting the war with France very negligently so as to be able to keep a close watch on his own interests in Poland. All the big words which the eastern monarchs had mouthed about the revolutionary peril and the rescue of the French King could not blind anyone to the fact that in reality their share of the spoils of Poland meant far more to them. But the French revolutionaries, particularly the Girondins, persuaded themselves that it was their ideals and the inspiration with which they fired their soldiers that had crowned their banners with victory. A few days after the victory at Jemappes, the Convention issued the degree of November 19th, which promised the help of France to all peoples who might rise against their 'tyrants'. If this were taken seriously, then here was the most violent intervention in the internal affairs of other countries which could be imagined. Apart from this, the occupation of Belgium by the French touched British policy on its tenderest spot, and the French rubbed salt in the wound by declaring the Scheldt open to navigation. Under international treaties, in which Britain had taken a most prominent part, this river had been closed in favour of the Dutch Republic, and the Dutch were Britain's allies. The French justified their action by invoking the laws of nature which, they held, took precedence over all formal treaties. On the laws of nature, too, speakers in the French Assembly based France's supposed claim to her 'natural frontiers', that is, the left bank of the Rhine.

These were indeed doctrines full of danger for the whole existing system of states. Had the Dutch government invoked the treaty of alliance and asked the British government for help, then undoubtedly Britain would have been in duty bound to declare war on France if need be. But no such call for help was given. At all costs the Dutch government wanted to avoid a war which would have had to be fought on Dutch soil, and still clung to the hope that it would be able to edge its way through international difficulties under cover of neutrality.

Then, on January 21st, 1793, came the execution of Louis XVI. The impression it made in England was immense. True, the English had once executed a king themselves, but they looked on that as a crime of Cromwell's which they were very chary of recalling. Their horror at the execution of Louis now united them; even Fox voiced it in the strongest terms. The government at once ordered Chauvelin, the French ambassador in London, to leave the country within a week. Ever since Louis had been deposed they had ceased to treat Chauvelin as the official representative of France, because his powers had originally been given him by the fallen monarch. This was a point on which Grenville's pedantry fastened with characteristic obstinacy. He considered that he was being very obliging if now and again he received Chauvelin unofficially and at his own request, and he was greatly concerned lest the Frenchman should use this fact to draw conclusions flattering to his diplomatic status. And yet Grenville wanted to keep the peace as long as possible. But by using a stiff and doctrinaire tone in his notes he contributed his share towards making this more and more impossible. Now that Louis had been done to death, Pitt and Grenville took the view that by this token every vestige of Chauvelin's official status and right to remain in England had disappeared.

Technically, it is true, this was not a declaration of war, but war was now inevitable and Pitt knew it, as can be seen from his speech of February 1st, 1793, when he gave Parliament a review of the political situation and called for a strengthening of the forces on land and sea. It was a capital speech, which gave an effective summary of all the French provocations and was calculated in masterly fashion to strengthen every Englishman's conviction that Britain had to wage a war that was both just and defensive. Undoubtedly the vast majority not only in Parliament but also in the country at large was in favour of this war and of Pitt, just as it had been behind his father and the Spanish war half a century before.

With the strength of despair Fox strove to stem the torrent. He did not conceal his disapproval of French intervention and

French atrocities. But he attacked the view that the one and only answer to them was war. He felt it must still be possible to negotiate and he demanded negotiations in order to avoid war. Above all, he maintained that Pitt had indicated no practical aim for which war was to be waged. No war was worse than one without a definite object; for it was impossible to tell when such a war would end. In this he was far more right than any of his hearers could have imagined. The war which was imminent lasted twenty-two years and neither Pitt nor Fox lived to see the end of it.

Yet the die was cast. The French government replied to the expulsion of its ambassador by declaring war on Britain and the Dutch Republic, to the delight of the King, who confided to Grenville his hope that this step by France would rouse in England such a spirit as would curb that unprincipled country whose aim was to destroy the foundations of every civilized state. Whatever his ministers might think, George III had no doubt that he was waging an 'ideological' war.

The controversy which Pitt and Fox fought out in Parliament in February, 1793, has remained a live issue ever since. Again and again historians have discussed whether the war with France was avoidable, whether it was a war of defence or intervention. The view which Fox, and after him the Whig tradition, championed up to the middle of the nineteenth century was that Pitt had plunged his country into a fateful and unnecessary war of intervention, but since then the argument has not generally been advanced in this form. Today nobody doubts that Pitt was really eager to keep the peace, even at a time when public opinion in England was already clamouring for war. But it is not so easy to say whether he did in fact do everything conceivable or expedient to preserve peace. After the 10th August and the storming of the Tuileries it is understandable that Pitt and Grenville should recall the British ambassador, who seemed to be in some personal danger, from Paris. Also it is still possible to sympathize with their disinclination to send out a new ambassador after the September massacres. But they must have realized that in this way they were denying themselves the use of an indispensable means of influencing events in Paris, and employing diplomacy to settle disputed matters which threatened peace. The stiff and haughty manner in which Pitt and Grenville refused to have any official dealings with the French ambassador, because they regarded him as not properly accredited since Louis XVI had been deposed, and were unwilling to recognize the new government, made the breach almost inevitable. Pitt thus forfeited his chance of convincing the French that his policy was by no means the same as that of the continental monarchies. We know today from a note which Grenville sent to St. Petersburg on December 29th, 1792, undoubtedly with Pitt's full agreement, that they were both fully alive to this distinction and would even have been ready to come to an understanding with a republican French government, provided it agreed to recall its troops to within its own borders and to stop its propaganda outside them. But of all this the French could know nothing. It was not until his speech of February 3rd, 1800, that Pitt made this note public, and Fox then gave it his approval. However, in view of the fever of revolutionary over-confidence prevailing in Paris, no one can prove that a note of this sort would have led to an understanding if it had been sent there. But neither can the possibility of its having had some effect, particularly on the more sober and accommodating politicians, be dismissed out of hand, and this justified Fox's insistence, as continuous as it was unpopular and fruitless, on the need for negotiations.

It will always be a matter of argument how far Pitt was actuated by considerations of foreign policy and how far he was an interventionist, affected by French internal politics. It is a truism nowadays to say that no English administration could stand idly by and watch a military power establish itself in the Netherlands, and here Grenville could fully justify himself, as against Chauvelin, by reference to a century-old tradition. However the French had agreed to evacuate Belgium on the conclusion of peace. It goes without saying that Pitt need not have accepted this offer as genuine currency without putting it to the test. But he would certainly have fastened upon this as a starting point for negotiations if the French government had not been a revolutionary one which he—like his King—regarded as a danger to all civilized countries. On January 24th Grenville wrote confidentially to the British ambassador at The Hague: '. . . I do not see how we can remain any longer *les bras croisés*, with a great force ready for action, that force avowedly meant against France, and the language and conduct of that power giving every day more instead of less ground of offence to us and all the world.'

To stress the importance which domestic events in France played in determining Pitt's policy does not by any means imply condemning it out of hand. Certainly the policy of intervention has not always been condemned with the same assurance. Opinion on the subject has ebbed and flowed during the last century and a half. The generation which has seen the greatest war of all time waged as an ideological struggle will take a view different from that of its forbears, in whose minds the idea of intervention was linked with the name of Metternich and the firm of Legitimacy. In his celebrated correspondence with Leopold von Gerlach, Bismarck, writing on Bonapartism, advanced the theory that sympathies and antipathies ought to play no part in foreign policy. But, quite apart from whether he always acted on this maxim, he attached a very significant limitation to it. 'Bonapartism is distinguished from the Republic by the fact that it has no need to propagate its principles of government by force.' On this showing Bismarck would not have disapproved of an interventionist war against revolutionary France, for not only did France follow a deliberately propagandist policy but she undoubtedly had success with her propaganda, though not perhaps as much as hostile governments ascribed to her. 'And all men must learn from the mouth of their cannon the propagation of their system in every part of the world': in these striking words did Pitt describe the methods of the French in his great speech of February 1st, 1793, and at least he did no injustice to Frenchmen of the stamp of Brissot and the Girondins.

In spite of everything, Pitt would probably have struggled more obdurately to keep the peace if he had had an exact idea of the size, difficulty and length of the struggle into which the English now plunged with patriotic fervour and confidence in victory. But then it is too much to demand prophetic gifts even of the most enlightened statesman. Pitt could not possibly have foreseen that within a few years a military genius would be thrown up in France who would raise her to the topmost pinnacle of her power and glory. Yet it is still fair to say that in two directions in particular Pitt gave way to fatal illusions. He imagined that France's internal disorder and more especially her financial dislocation would make a longish war impossible. He knew by experience what careful and systematic work had been needed to restore and strengthen England's finances, and he considered it inevitable that a state which only dragged along with depreciated *assignats* should collapse. He failed to grasp that the national democracy born in France amid such horror and anguish released forces which could not come into play under the *ancien régime*; that the opening up of political and military careers to all Frenchmen, regardless of birth, status or religion, brought to the fore fresh, talented men who in other countries—not excluding England—would hardly have risen above a subordinate post. Nor could he see that across the Channel a new national spirit was springing up which burst forth most powerfully in defence of the mother country, a spirit which accepted conscription—inconceivable in any other country at that time—and crushed every counter-revolutionary rising, even if it was backed by British gold. However, it is only fair to recall that all these problems were completely new ones, that previous experience provided no yardstick for measuring them, and that even Pitt's mind was not prepared for them. To this extent his task was much more difficult than his father's had been.

On the other hand, Pitt made the equally dangerous mistake of overestimating the determination and willingness of other nations, and particularly of the continental monarchies, to concentrate all their strength on the destruction of the common foe. He knew well enough the strong attraction which the spoils of Poland had for the rulers of Russia, Austria and Prussia; he knew the jealousy with which they watched each other; but he believed that in the face of a common danger and with the active aid of England all this would change. This may explain the grave mistake he made when he provoked a breach with France before reaching binding and adequate agreements with Austria and Prussia in the event of war.

As things turned out, Pitt had made a complete miscalculation. These two powers were quite as ready to outlaw the Revolution as they were to pocket English gold. But as far as manpower went, they provided the common cause with only such forces as they did not need for their own immediate selfish ends and only for as long as they did not need them themselves. The British were the only people who really took their fight against the Revolution seriously. So Pitt might weld together coalition after coalition; yet again and again one or other of the allies failed him if they thought it would suit their book to do so.

CHAPTER XXI

THE WAR YEARS

THUS fate decreed that William Pitt, like his father a generation before him, was to lead Britain in a war which embroiled all Europe. Once again it was 'Pitt's war' just as it had been 'Pitt's war' from 1757 to 1761. This was the general opinion not only in England but also among England's friends and foes in Europe. And so, inevitably, the question arises: does the son bear comparison with the father as a national war leader? Those who judge by results alone must at once answer in the negative, but even among those who have gone more fully into the matter, there is scarcely a single one who has reached a different conclusion. On the contrary, eminent historians headed by Macaulay have decided that Pitt was by no means equal to the task. Nearly a hundred years have passed since Macaulay pronounced this verdict, and since then the world has had two fearful examples of the unique, incomparable difficulties of a war fought by a coalition. In the first world war there was a good reason for the standing joke among British officers that Napoleon's successes were not so very remarkable, for after all he had only to fight against coalitions. If history is to commend Winston Churchill for the masterly skill with which he held a coalition together and brought it into united action in the face of all the difficulties and internal differences of the second world war, then history must deny this tribute to his predecessor, William Pitt.

However, a somewhat closer scrutiny of Pitt's allies at once makes it plain both that they could not be held together permanently by any art or policy, and also that Pitt and Pitt alone had to lead every coalition. First, in Russia there was the gifted but unreliable and self-seeking Czarina Catherine II, who exhorted all the monarchs to join in a rousing crusade against regicide France—an apt text upon the lips of the woman who had murdered her husband, Czar Peter III—for she hoped to gain time to gather in her booty in Poland and Turkey with less risk to herself; after her death on November 17th, 1796, there

was her son, Czar Paul I, lapsing deeper into madness year by
year, and cursed with unpredictable volatility and the per-
sistently wounded vanity of a despot. In Austria the insignificant,
narrow-browed Emperor Francis was under the influence of his
minister Thugut, who, it is true, possessed many of the qualities
of a statesman and above all a policy—a policy, however,
which was never comprehensive but always exclusively
Austrian and was as unfavourably affected by his incessant (if
quite understandable) mistrust of Prussia as by his constant fear
of being squeezed out by his blue-blooded rivals at court.
Lastly, there was Prussia, suddenly raised by the successes of
Frederick the Great to the status of a great power, though as yet
unready to act up to that status under two kings who had widely
differing qualities, but were alike in their inability to grasp the
problems of the age and to lead their country through such a
world crisis. The dissolute and spendthrift Frederick William II,
jerked this way and that by his mistresses and favourites, and
lacking in all the qualities of his famous uncle and predecessor,
except his bad faith, was succeeded in 1797 by his domestically
irreproachable and frugal son, Frederick William III, who was,
however, far too much of a blockhead to evolve a policy of his
own, and far too timid to embark on action of any kind before
it was too late. The confidential letters of British diplomats in
Berlin paint a sad picture of the weakness, confusion, poverty
of ideas and lack of decision at the court of both father and son.

To fuse these disruptive elements into a dynamic whole
would perhaps have been beyond the powers of even a more
gifted personality than Pitt's. But he was not cut out either by
personal qualities or by training to get on with characters so
foreign to his own or to sound exactly the right note to influence
them. The Grenville stiffness, which he had inherited from his
mother's side, was still more sharply stamped upon his cousin,
Lord Grenville, who handled the diplomatic correspondence.
Expert knowledge, an appetite for work, acumen and character—it certainly cannot be denied that Grenville had all these.
But the elasticity and flexibility of mind with which a skilled
diplomat rounds a dangerous corner were not given to him. He
had a very strong feeling for the honour of his King and
country, and he looked upon the knavish tricks and broken
pledges of his allies as nothing more nor less than wounds to

that honour. '. . . In the last resort', he wrote in a confidential letter to the Austrian ambassador, 'it is better to lay oneself open to certain disadvantages than to betray the fact that, when an opportunity offers, one cannot maintain the rank and the honour of one's country.' Certainly he often had reason to deplore the selfish and shortsighted policy of the allies, but he made things no better by wagging his forefinger at them and reading them moral homilies in the accents of a dominie. A man like this was incapable of taking the sting out of one of Czar Paul's despotic fits by a judicious sop to his vanity or of grasping the outstretched hand of the First Consul, Napoleon Bonaparte, in order to reach an understanding.

Two of Pitt's colleagues had his ear during these trying years, and Grenville was one of them. The other was Dundas, also a Secretary of State, who, though he possessed very considerable administrative gifts, had negligible abilities as a statesman. Dundas was for years the real war minister, whose job it was to equip military expeditions and to select their senior commanders in consultation with the King. But no great soldier's name survives to show that he knew how to find and use men of talent. Dundas and Grenville were the two colleagues with whom Pitt was in the habit of discussing his plans. As a rule the other members of the Cabinet would then be confronted with *faits accomplis* and—they accepted them. There was but little change when Pitt strengthened his Cabinet in 1794 by bringing in the 'Old Whigs' under the influence of Burke, with Portland at their head. One of them, Earl Spencer, the brother of the Duchess of Devonshire, went to the Admiralty, which Pitt took from his own brother, the incompetent Lord Chatham. The Admiralty was the only department which won fresh laurels. Once more the British navy proved itself the best in Europe, and naval heroes like Lord Howe, John Jervis (later Lord St. Vincent) and not least Horatio Nelson won immortal victories. Yet it must be admitted that England also had the navy to thank for her darkest hours. In the summer of 1797 a mutiny which broke out aboard several ships lying in home ports spread like wildfire, and for a few weeks left England almost defenceless when she was threatened by a hostile fleet. The mutiny was originally caused by atrocious abuses which the seamen had every right to complain of, such as brutal treatment, bad food and wretched pay. It is a grave reproach against the ministry that it did not make sure that these scandalous conditions were swept away in good time. When it is remembered that most of these seamen were 'pressed' into service in the most brutal manner, by being kidnapped from merchant vessels or snapped up in the street or even in their own homes, the real marvel is that they had not revolted before, and that they should have performed such brilliant feats in all the naval engagements both before and after the mutiny. One section of the mutineers did indeed show their patriotism during the disorders and sent a message to tell another group that their conduct was a 'scandal to the name of British seamen'. But in another section there is no doubt that revolutionary tendencies played their part; the ministry believed that these could be traced back to radical organisations in England, but in the end it was forced to conclude that there was no question of this. It needed a combination of energy, patience and readiness for reform to get the upper hand of the movement after six critical weeks.

The most that can be said in praise of Pitt is that throughout the changing fortunes of the war and the vicissitudes of politics he never lost heart. After each setback, with untiring zeal and unfailing patience he always rebuilt the coalitions with which he hoped to bend fate to his will and conquer the French Revolution. Again and again the goal seemed in sight and then it would vanish once more, obscured either by the negligence of an ally, or by a surprising rally on the enemy's part, or by the inadequacy of Britain's own efforts.

When England entered the war in 1793 she found herself automatically linked with Prussia and Austria, the two great powers which were already at war with France. With both of them, as well as with several other powers, Pitt concluded treaties of alliance in the course of the year. The military forces of the allies were so superior to those of France that her defeat was inevitable, provided that every ally did his duty. But there was no question of that. In January, 1793, Russia and Prussia had come to an agreement behind Austria's back on the second partition of Poland, and wrangling over this was far too important to all three monarchs for them ever to concentrate their forces against France. Prussia used the situation to hold a pistol to the head of her English ally. At the beginning of 1794 Frederick William declared that he would withdraw his troops from the French theatre—except those provided for by treaty— if he did not receive subsidies amounting to twenty million thalers in the shortest possible time. Pitt dipped into the national purse to prevent the defection of an ally of such importance in the field. In April a treaty was arranged which bound Prussia to keep an army of 62,000 men on the Lower Rhine, while England and Holland were to put up subsidies paid at regular intervals and amounting in all to £1,800,000. In vain did Fox warn against making payments like these to a king who anyone could see was unreliable. 'So infamous, indeed, had been the conduct of the King of Prussia,' he exclaimed, 'that it was impossible for any man of the least prudence to trust that court in any-thing. . . .' He was right. The treaty only led to mutual bicker-ings and suspicion. The English soon suspected Frederick William, and not without good reason, of using their money not in the French theatre but for his own purposes in Poland, and they stopped the payments. But Frederick William resolved all doubts at Basle in the spring of 1795 by concluding a separ-ate peace with the French Republic—supposedly his enemy to the death—giving her a free hand on the left bank of the Rhine and withdrawing from the war for good.

This was a few months after the third and final partition of Poland in January, 1795. Russia and Austria had reached a secret understanding over it, but had left Prussia a share of the spoils. In the same year Holland and Spain left the coalition as well. Holland in fact became an appendage of the French Republic, and Spain in the course of time even became her ally. England had only one ally of any military importance left, and that was Austria. She, it is true, had some fairly substantial successes to show at the outset. But in the spring of 1796, the twenty-six-year-old General Napoleon Bonaparte took over the command of the French army in Italy and led it from victory to victory in a campaign which has never since failed to arouse the admiration of experts. At the beginning of 1797 he had conquered the whole of Northern Italy. A few months later he and his troops were in the Austrian province of Carinthia. In April he made Austria conclude the preliminaries of Leoben, by which she ceded Belgium and the Rhine frontier, and also by far the greater part of her Italian possessions to France. In the definitive peace of Campo Formio, which Austria only concluded in October, she was partly compensated for these losses by the annexation of the old and hitherto independent republic of Venice, which Bonaparte had occupied on the flimsiest of pretexts and now offered to his former adversary on a platter. With this, Pitt's first coalition had reached its inglorious end.

What had England done in these five years of war? She had won battles at sea, destroyed French commerce and endured great sacrifices and losses to conquer colonies which could at least be used as good bargaining counters in peace talks. She had supported her allies with enormous sums of money, Austria having been guaranteed a big loan. Her military efforts on land, however, had produced trifling successes and even failures. Pitt, the father, had known how to concentrate superior forces at the decisive point on all occasions. Pitt, the son, had not the knack, and all too often allowed them to be frittered away to no purpose. After some initial successes the attempts to arouse and support counter-revolutionary movements on French soil all broke down in the end.

Pitt's attempts to exploit the internal antagonisms in France for his own ends certainly cannot be held against him. But inevitably they embroiled him in French domestic squabbles. In order to hold his own there with any success, he should have had a well-defined goal clearly in view and above all he should have reached agreement on it with his allies. The first was difficult, the second almost impossible. To do this, it was not enough simply to be an opponent of the Republic, for even its opponents were by no means united among themselves. If, for example, Pitt adopted the restoration of the Bourbons as his policy, this made nonsense of the policy of self-aggrandisement and compensation by seizing French territory, which the allies, England included, pursued as long as the war situation seemed to hold out hopes of its being a success. It would seem that Pitt had not grasped this problem in all its bearings and had not reached definite conclusions on it. To this extent it must be admitted that Fox was right when he attacked the ministry in one of his great speeches (May 10th, 1796): 'The great defect in the management of the war, however, has, in my opinion, been the want of a determinate object for which you have been contending.'

In contrast to this, Pitt held that revolutionary France was a mortal danger to England and to the whole of Europe because it did not recognize those laws and customs which had hitherto regulated the intercourse between nations and ought always to regulate them. He therefore declared it was impossible to make peace with a revolutionary government, whether moderate or terrorist; there would be no real basis on which to build a lasting peace. He kept on using this argument against people who urged him to negotiate with France, and these included not only Fox and his followers but at times Wilberforce, one of his own bosom friends, who shuddered at the unending bloodshed.

But how could the war possibly end when, the longer it went on, the more conspicuous became the absence of military successes, and France drove one ally after another out of the ring? Pitt, speaking as Chancellor of the Exchequer, had an answer to this which he offered Parliament again and again: France must collapse economically within a measurable time. Her finances were disordered beyond repair. She was still managing to limp along by means of robbery and confiscation. Even these barbaric makeshifts were soon bound to be exhausted. Her currency had depreciated to a small percentage of its nominal value. Nothing could stave off the collapse! What Pitt said about the finances of revolutionary France was completely accurate. But a witty *émigré* at Wilberforce's table blunted the point of Pitt's conclusions with this quip: 'I should like to know who was Chancellor of the Exchequer to Attila.' Pitt could not reconcile himself to the fact that a new age had dawned even in the financing of war. Perhaps it is fair to say that here the defects of his qualities were apparent. Conscientious, methodical application had made him the greatest financial expert among the politicians of his day, and for that very reason he could not understand the wild accountancy of the revolution, which, none the less, swept aside all difficulties.

But Pitt was not so infatuated with his theories as not to have tried to negotiate, in spite of everything, when Bonaparte's successes showed the dangers to which Austria in particular was exposed. In the autumn of 1796 he sent Sir James Harris, ennobled as Lord Malmesbury, to negotiate a peace with the

French Directory at Paris. This evoked a storm of anger from Burke who a short while before, when the Hastings trial was over, had retired from Parliament. He poured out his wrath in the third of his *Letters on a Regicide Peace*. Of course all the 'letters' contain many a brilliant page and much deep political insight, but, taken as a whole, they are merely a long-drawn-out jeremiad over a development which Burke feared and hated but did not understand. Pitt had already summed up his disapproval of Burke's views by saying that his 'rhapsodies' contained 'much to admire and nothing to agree with'. In any case, Burke could be quite easy in his mind about the negotiations which Malmesbury was conducting in Paris. They very soon broke down, partly because of the crass and clumsy methods of the Directory and partly because Pitt and Grenville were uncertain what to do, and neither saw clearly what they ought to offer nor followed a common policy agreed well in advance with their ally, Austria. Thus these negotiations bore out Fox's criticism of the great defect in the conduct of the war.

The negotiations which Pitt sponsored in the summer of 1797 at Lille, which were once again handled by Malmesbury, seemed rather more promising. In the spring Austria had signed the preliminaries of Leoben and thus had no longer the same claim to consideration as before. Pitt had arranged the talks with great difficulty in the face of the stubborn resistance of Grenville, who considered them humiliating and had the King's support in this. But Pitt could argue that the English people had shown a strong desire for peace, and that therefore the administration must at least make a gesture of willingness to reach an understanding. The chances this time were rather more favourable because not only was there an equally strong desire for peace among the French people but there was also a peace party in the Directory itself. Perhaps on this occasion success might have been achieved if the British government had lent speed and vigour to the negotiations. However, their delaying tactics gave the war party in the Directory time to rid themselves of their pacific colleagues by a *coup d'état* (September 4th, 18 Fructidor), for which Bonaparte sent the necessary military backing through an emissary. On September 17th Malmesbury received orders to leave Lille within twenty-four

x

hours. On October 17th the Austrians signed a definitive and separate peace at Campo Formio.

Ill-starred as was the course of the negotiations, there can be no doubt that Pitt was sincere in his strivings for peace. If Fox saw them as nothing more than an attempt of Pitt's to settle himself more firmly in the saddle by making a sham concession to the people's longing for peace, he certainly did him an injustice. Burke, the implacable enemy of all peace negotiations, did not live to see them fail; on July 9th, 1797, death cut short the life which could only have brought him fresh disappointments.

When Pitt arranged for the negotiations in Lille despite the opposition of the King and Grenville, he had already suffered a severe reverse in a field which was particularly his own. In February, 1797, the Cabinet, to prevent a run on the Bank of England, had been forced to issue an Order in Council freeing the Bank from the obligation to redeem its notes in gold. Up to that moment, thanks to his careful fiscal policy which was borne forward by a rising tide of prosperity, Pitt had always managed to find the money not only to arm England but also to subsidise her allies. Of course the national debt had risen tremendously as a result. Between 1793 and 1802 the funded debt increased by almost three hundred million pounds, from two hundred and thirty-four to five hundred and twenty-two millions. The increase in taxation aroused widespread discontent. Fears of a French invasion led to a run on the banks. Yet in spite of all this the financial strength of the country was by no means exhausted, and the monied interest continued to give Pitt its confidence, as could be seen whenever a loan was needed, even if raised in the form of a voluntary 'Loyalty Loan'. In the same way Parliament, which had recently been elected, backed up Pitt. When the suspension of cash payments was raised in the House, the opposition moved for an enquiry into the causes which had brought it on. But this was rejected by a three to one majority.

In the parliamentary arena Pitt was victorious and remained so, nor were his victories undeserved. The speeches he made to the Commons in defence of his policy in all its phases are most of them masterpieces. They bear the stamp of a master mind, of a born leader conscious of the overwhelming magnitude of his task. In majestic, rolling periods he conjured up before his listeners' eyes the lofty aims from which nothing could make him swerve, and he inspired them with real confidence that he had chosen and tested his path towards these goals with the most minute and scrupulous care. He knew how to give them a bird's eye view of a complicated diplomatic transaction, or an intricate question of fiscal policy, in language of unequalled clarity. Certainly it is easy enough to show self-confidence when backed by an overwhelming majority, but Pitt's confidence was rooted no less firmly in his ability to meet any opponent in debate on equal terms. Victory in the cut and thrust of debate is the very basis of every parliamentary success and parliamentary reputation, and Pitt used and mastered all the weapons of debate with consummate art. In particular his sarcasm was dreaded. Whenever he trounced one of his critics with biting, sarcastic sallies, his gleeful followers could relish the tonic feeling that he had not only proved himself right but also that he *was* right.

Of course, it was not so easy to get the better of Charles Fox. Small as was the number of friends he could muster in a division, whenever he rose to speak the whole House listened with attention as one argument reinforced another and passion and pathos lent wings to his words. Still, neither speaker could always be at the top of his form. More than once Fox let himself be tempted into making the mistake of blaming every single action taken by the ministry—as men in opposition are always prone to do—and Pitt was not always above exploiting popular prejudices in order to disparage his critic. But when the great, decisive problems which have exercised men ever since were in question—the problems which everyone must decide for himself even today—then the House witnessed a duel of dramatic, overpowering verve between intellects raised to the highest pitch. Not until the days when Gladstone and Disraeli came to grips was it to be treated to such another spectacle.

Wilberforce, who was wholly on Pitt's side personally, confessed none the less that when Pitt and Fox spoke against each other, the one who had the last word seemed to bear away the palm. Pitt himself—and he certainly did not suffer from false modesty—confided to his friends that, whenever he thought he had spoken better than usual, he had had the feeling that Fox

had surpassed himself in his reply. Neither the stiff and angular
figure of Pitt nor the plump and somewhat more than well-
covered and negligently-dressed Fox were attractive sights at
first glance. But they seemed transformed

> '*When round those forces which move mortal hearts,*
> *At once so fearful and familiar,*
> *The speaker's lips are playing gracefully.*'

When Mrs. Fox caught sight of Pitt she cried out what an
ugly man he was. But Charles replied that she should not say
that, as, if she had seen Pitt when he was speaking, she would
have found him handsome. A French friend of Pitt's said to him,
'I am greatly surprised that a country so moral as England can
submit to be governed by a man so wanting in private character as Fox. . . .' 'That', retorted Pitt, 'is because you have never
been under the wand of the magician.'

What gave Fox's speeches their particular drive and characteristic pathos was his grief at seeing his country moving forward along a bloody path which he thought could lead to
nothing but disaster. Of course, he too wanted Britain to be
saved from defeat. But he could not hope for any benefits from
a victory achieved in company with the ancient monarchies
at the expense of revolutionary France. Fox would certainly
not have felt at home in the Europe which emerged from the
decisions of the Congress of Vienna and was overshadowed by
the spirit of Metternich. But the Europe which would have
been created in his own day by the triumph of the military
powers of the *ancien régime* would certainly have worn a far
more ominous look. For then Europe had not learned the lesson
she was given after Austerlitz and Jena—that the only thing
which could shake off Napoleon's yoke was the drive for freedom by the common people. In the era after the Congress of
Vienna Pitt's most gifted pupil, Canning, gained the highest
popularity and won his place in history because his policy was
based on the recognition that Britain was fundamentally
different from the traditional monarchies of Europe. Fox had
already realized this fact a generation before, at a time when the
mocking wit of Canning's 'Anti-Jacobin' was still trying to
throw ridicule and contempt upon anyone who felt uneasy at
England being a brother-in-arms of the Czar of Russia or the

King of Prussia. Fox acted upon this perception of his at a time when all it brought him was a harvest of coarse caricatures which grinned at him from every bookseller's window in London.

Fox had good reason to fear that there would not be much left of the ancient liberties of England if she allied herself with absolute monarchs to win a victory over France. For he was filled with grief and bitterness by Pitt's repressive measures and the ravages which the counter-revolutionary spirit wreaked in England. This spirit was supposed to be directed against the Jacobins, but in reality it attacked anyone in Britain who championed reforms. As early as 1793, the first year of the war, prosecutions started in Scotland. Muir, a young Edinburgh lawyer of blameless reputation, who could be found guilty of nothing more than recommending Paine's *Rights of Man* as a book to be read, was sentenced to deportation to the criminal settlement at Botany Bay for no less than fourteen years. The judge who imposed this barbaric sentence had the effrontery to state from the bench: 'The promotion of that measure [the extension of the franchise], in the circumstances, was, of itself, sedition.' 'God help the people who have such judges!' cried Fox when he brought up this outrage for discussion in Parliament and pleaded for a pardon for Muir. But Pitt was inexorable: the thought that a respectable man, whom he could have saved, had to languish among common felons for years untold never lost him a night's rest.

Indeed, he went even further along the paths of persecution and oppression. In the spring of 1794 he suspended the Habeas Corpus Act, that bulwark erected with such toil to protect English liberty, which no one had extolled more forcefully than Chatham. Then, in England too, he had reform leaders like the shoemaker Hardy, the organizer of the 'Corresponding Society', and the renegade parson, Horne Tooke, brought to trial. Fortunately for them, Pitt overplayed his hand and had them charged with high treason, for, anti-revolutionary though the London jury was, they recoiled from passing sentence of death on their political opponents. They acquitted the men in the dock, whom Erskine defended with brilliant eloquence. Horne Tooke had the satisfaction of calling Pitt as a witness that ten years before the prime minister himself had made the very demand for which he was having others dragged into court. However, the acts of repression continued. In 1795 not only was the suspension of the Habeas Corpus Act renewed (it was only restored after Pitt's resignation in 1801), but a new law against 'Treasonable Practices' created new offences with excessive penalties, and a law against 'Seditious Meetings' made it almost impossible to hold public meetings of more than fifty persons. In 1799 there followed an Act which prohibited all political societies, and also repressive measures against the press.

All these bills were passed by great majorities in Parliament. What were alleged to be seditious activities playing into the hands of the national enemy were used to justify them. That such fears should emerge during a war with 'ideological' aims is not hard to understand today, but whether they were in fact well grounded is quite another matter. Historical research has shown that at the very least they must be described as highly exaggerated. Fox himself was firmly convinced that there was absolutely no truth in the assertion that a dangerous revolutionary movement existed in England, and thought that it had been trumped up by the administration to further its own political ends. Even before the outbreak of war at the opening of Parliament in December, 1792, the Speech from the Throne had maintained that 'a spirit of tumult and disorder . . . has shown itself in acts of riot and insurrection'. At that Fox, in words as emphatic as they were ineffectual, had demanded that the ministry should produce proofs of this statement. 'An insurrection! Where is it? Where has it reared its head? Good God! An insurrection in Great Britain! No wonder that the militia were called out. . . . But where is it? . . . I will take upon me to say, Sir, that it is not the notoriety of the insurrection which prevents . . . gentlemen from communicating to us the particulars, but their non-existence.' It goes without saying that the majority in Parliament ignored this speech. But in the country, too, there was such a mood of alarm that Fox had to defend his conduct in an open letter to his constituents. The English middle classes believed Pitt only too readily when, in 1794, he assured Parliament, solemnly but without the least proof, that there were people who 'would be most likely to congregate into an enormous torrent of insurrection, which would sweep away all the barriers of government, law and religion. . . .' And when the fear of a French invasion was rife and the sailors mutinied in the navy, which was the nation's pride, the average Englishman was inclined to see ghosts everywhere and to think that any harmless fellow-citizen who grumbled in a tavern was a Jacobin or a French agent.

Neither the hopelessness of his position in Parliament nor the fevered mood of the country did anything to quench the resolution and fire with which Fox plunged into the fray against this policy of repression. Let others, let even many of his own close friends, quake before the Jacobin bogy if they would; he stood firm and four-square in his belief that liberty was a boon, indispensable and irreplaceable. Each fresh attack only confirmed him in his resolve not only to praise it in fair weather but to uphold and defend it in darker days. 'Liberty is order, Liberty is strength!' 'If you mean to say that the mixed and balanced government of England is good only for holidays and sunshine, but that it is inapplicable to a day of distress and difficulty, say so!' he cried to the administration. This conviction was his guiding star in the struggle he put up step by step against each new measure of repression. Nobody could marshal a greater display of courage, a more disinterested spirit, a loftier ardour, a clearer statesmanlike insight, a purer patriotism, richer arguments or more striking wit than did Fox in the speeches which he flung into the battle against a Parliament that was hostile and yet at times divided against itself. He knew full well that skilled debaters on the other side of the House— and foremost among them Pitt himself—were on the watch to pierce any chinks in his armour that he might expose in the heat of the fray, and would not even shrink from twisting and distorting his words, while dozens of journalists and caricaturists made a business of maligning him as a dangerous Jacobin and enemy of his country. But this did not deter him from carrying his opposition to the furthest possible limits and even confessing in public that he believed in the doctrine that the people have a right to resist the destruction of their constitution. He said it was that right alone which the Hanoverian dynasty had to thank for the fact that it occupied the throne of England at that very moment; and he triumphantly confronted the prime minister with the argument that no one had paid more unreserved homage to the doctrine than had his great father, Lord

Chatham, who had cried out during the battle against the Stamp Act 'that he rejoiced the Americans had resisted'. Fox did not deny that the country was riddled with discontent, but declared it could not be stilled by making all expression of it punishable and thus stopping up an indispensable safety-valve. The only way that was likely to succeed—as he stressed again and again—was to probe to the roots of it and remove the grievances from which it sprang. The watchword must be reform, not tyranny! '. . . Show [the people] that liberty was as consistent with order as order with liberty. . . . His advice was only to render the number of the discontented as small as possible, by removing as many as possible of the causes of discontent. Let all civil distinctions on account of religious opinions be abolished. Let Dissenters find equal protection and equal encouragement. Let the rights of neutral nations also be respected, more especially the rights of America, so intimately connected with us by common language and common interest.' And on another occasion: 'Meet the evil; reform those who are adverse to your constitution by reforming its abuses; . . . reform the representation of the people in this House; keep your word with the public; tell them they may safely confide in your promise; proceed immediately to the abolition of that infernal traffic, the slave trade: show them the constitution of this country in its perfection: show them that it is favourable to the principles of liberty, and then your enemies will be so few that you indeed may despise them.' 'I know that liberty is the greatest blessing that mankind can enjoy, and peace the next. . . .'

Thus did Charles Fox proclaim and champion the pure doctrine of liberalism long before there was a Liberal party, even indeed before the word 'liberal' had entered the vocabulary of politics. Thus did he keep alive the belief in the blessings of political and religious liberty, a belief which set its stamp on British history in the next generation and spread out from England, to uplift and fire all free spirits throughout Europe. The fact that the Whigs did not remain a mere aristocratic group vanishing when the rule of the aristocracy sank into oblivion, but managed to develop into the forbears of the Liberal party, is a fact for which they have to thank Charles Fox and his struggle against the coercion, the intolerance and the political persecutions sponsored by Pitt and his Tory following. The speeches which Fox made in this campaign assure him of his place in history. They will not be forgotten as long as there are men who prize political liberty, personal liberty, liberty of belief, of speech and of political conviction, men whose hearts still thrill at Gottfried Keller's confession

> *'Praise be! A ringing word of freedom*
> *Among the free is still the coin.'*

It does not detract from Fox's reputation that for a time he broke off the fight as hopeless in the autumn of 1797. About this time Fox and a whole host of his friends, such as Grey, left the parliamentary battlefield without, however, giving up their seats. Secessions from Parliament are always a mistake, and Fox's was no exception. However, it is clear enough that after so many long years of utterly fruitless struggle he got no particular pleasure out of forcing divisions which became triumphs for Pitt whose position they strengthened, or making speeches which were travestied in the country at large as proof that he was a traitor to his King and country, or convincing himself day by day of his own impotence in the face of developments which his deepest convictions told him were sinister and pernicious. The thing that angered him most of all was to see a Parliament, under Pitt's influence, frustrate every single attempt he made to throw light on the seamy side of Pitt's policy and reject motions for the investigation of abuses and errors even when their existence could not be gainsaid. But things were vastly different from what they had been in 1776, when Fox was not prepared to take part in the secession planned by Rockingham during the American war. At that time the opposition had been far stronger numerically, and a change of heart by the non-party members of the House was much more within the bounds of possibility.

In May, 1797, the opposition brought forward a motion of Grey's for reforming the franchise as a final thrust. Fox himself wound up the debate with a great speech in which he announced his intention of devoting more of his time to his private pursuits in future because the House continued 'deaf and blind' to the ominous course of events. When once more a three to one majority voted against any reform, Fox and his friends bowed to the verdict and left the stage for a time. It was, as he often stressed, not so much a concerted decision as an identity of feeling among men with ideals and dislikes in common, who were, moreover, in the happy position of being able to lead active and agreeable lives even if they did stay away from the Palace of Westminster.

CHAPTER XXII

FOX IN RETIREMENT AND THE RISE OF BONAPARTE

'Tell me, dear friend, at which door may at last
Peace and freedom sanctuary sue?
In tempests the old century has passed:
Murder hails the coming of the new.'

THIS was the question and this the lament voiced at the turn of the eighteenth century by the German poet Schiller at Weimar, the little town grouped around its court which was living a peaceful life in the shelter of the Peace of Basle. After describing in magnificent lines how

'*Two gigantic nations strive together*
For the sole possession of the world,'

he ended by consoling himself with philosophic resignation:

'*The heart has hushed and solemn places; flee*
There for refuge from the daily throng.
Dreams are the only throne for liberty,
Beauty blossoms nowhere but in song.'

It was just such a retreat as this which had taken Charles Fox from the sound and fury of Parliament to the peaceful country house on St. Anne's Hill, and the beauty which blossoms in song raised him, as few mortal men are raised, above the misery of the times. Pitt and Dundas, Bonaparte and Talleyrand—all these were forgotten when he took up his beloved Homer and followed the 'god-like and much-enduring Odysseus' on his wanderings or listened to the greybearded Priam imploring Achilles for the body of his son Hector. And how Fox read his classics! How strongly their humane spirit took hold of him! He praised Antigone's answer to Creon as the most magnificent thing ever written. How closely he followed every refinement of phrase, every irregularity of metre, every doubtful interpolation! His correspondence with the learned philologist Wakefield shows that in knowledge and penetration he could try con-

clusions with any established scholar. But he by no means confined himself to the classics; he read anything beautiful and
worth reading in English, French, Italian and Spanish, and
gossiped about it in his letters to his nephew, Lord Holland,
who was as dear to him and as attached to him as a son. He also
tried his hand at some original composition. He planned to
write a history of England from the days of James II, and took
great pains over collecting reliable material and developing a
style free from rhetorical excrescences. But the fragment of his
literary remains which was published won him no more than
the applause of his own circle.

He was now free from material preoccupations. A group of
wealthy supporters, who not only worshipped him as a peerless
leader but loved him as an unfailing, affectionate and sympathetic friend, had clubbed together to pay his debts for him
and provide him with an annuity on which he could live in
comfort, if not in luxury. Fox had accepted this gift from his
friends with profound gratitude but without false modesty.
And so, with a heart set at ease, he could enjoy the happiness
given him by the loving care and devotion of his wife—for in
the meanwhile they had been married in due form—and by
the grounds and rural peace of St. Anne's Hill. He took a
strong and heartfelt delight in all these things, as can be seen—
to quote but one instance—from a letter he wrote in reply to an
invitation from his nephew to take part in an important debate
in the House. 'Never did a letter arrive in a worse time, my dear
young one, than yours this morning; a sweet westerly wind, a
beautiful sun, all the thorns and elms just budding, and the
nightingales just beginning to sing, though the blackbirds and
thrushes would have been quite sufficient, without the return
of those seceders, to have refuted any arguments in your letter.'

Can one blame a man, who almost from boyhood had led a
life of activity, incessant struggle and ceaseless excitement, for
being seized at about his fiftieth year by an irresistible urge to
taste the joys of a comfortable and contemplative existence?
The more this life delighted him, the more repellent did he find
the *strepitus fori*; at times he even showed signs of wanting to
make his retreat into private life irrevocable by giving up his
seat in the House.

Not, of course, that his interest in home and foreign politics ever flagged. The problems which they threw up he dealt with in his correspondence with his friends and intimates. Now and again he even attended the House to join in the debate on some bill to which his constituents attached special importance. Nor would his name have been Charles Fox had he not at once taken the field the moment any friend of his suffered an injustice. Early in 1798 the somewhat eccentric Duke of Norfolk was celebrating Fox's birthday at the Whig Club, and had first drunk a toast to him, and later proposed one in these words: 'The People, our Sovereign'. A toast like this smacked of revolution to the King and his ministers, and they took revenge on the dissident Duke by relieving him of his honorary post as Lord Lieutenant of the West Riding of Yorkshire. Fox promptly attended the next meeting of the Whig Club. He made a vigorous speech in support of the doctrine of the sovereignty of the people, ending up with the very toast which had cost the Duke his office. Pitt was beside himself. While fighting his repressive legislation in Parliament, the friends of reform had been well aware that one day these measures might be used against themselves. The letter which Pitt wrote under this provocation to Lord Grenville shows that such fears were not altogether unfounded. He asked him to consider whether Fox should not be summoned and publicly warned. '. . . If he offers a fresh insult at the next Whig Club, instead of gratifying him by an expulsion [from the House], to send him to the Tower for the remainder of the session. . . .' But the suggestion seems to have struck the other ministers as too dangerous a one, for it was not acted upon. It does, however, show not only the personal risks which were inseparable from opposition but also the lengths to which Pitt would go against a political opponent; this is in keeping with his spiteful attempt to prevent Fox from taking his seat for Westminster in 1784. But George III found another means of venting his anger upon his obdurate opponent. With his own royal hand he struck Fox's name off the list of the Privy Council of which he had been made a member in the normal constitutional way when he became a minister in 1782. George seems to have taken this childish action on his own initiative, for several years later Pitt is said to have reproached the King with the fact that he himself had advised against it at the time. Fox was quite unmoved by this loss of a well-earned title. The only practical consequence was that George was compelled to summon him afresh to the Privy Council, when he had no alternative but to make him a Secretary of State in 1806.

Meanwhile the interminable war dragged on year after year. For a time Britain and France faced each other alone, with neither able to do anything decisive against the other. The danger of a French invasion, which Fox was never prepared to believe in, did in fact grow more remote, without vanishing entirely, after General Bonaparte had examined the problem and had declared the undertaking hopeless. On the Continent, however, French power and influence were expanding further and further, and the English had to look on without being able to raise a finger. And then, in the spring of 1798, Bonaparte went over to the attack in a quite unexpected theatre. He set out on his expedition to Egypt, which was intended to open up the route to India. The knowledge that Britannia still ruled the waves was forced upon him. On August 1st, 1798, Nelson destroyed his fleet at Aboukir Bay, thus cutting his communications with metropolitan France.

England's naval victory at Aboukir is one of the factors which paved the way for the great Second Coalition against France. The incalculable Czar Paul I, who had at first been well-disposed towards the French republic, felt insulted because Napoleon had conquered Malta on his way to Egypt, for Paul looked on himself as the protector of the Order of the Knights of St. John, to whom the island had belonged. Austria had even more cause to go to war, since the irresistible progress of the French undermined her position in Italy and Germany. Pitt saw his chance: he offered both powers Britain's help. His clear-sighted action succeeded in bringing together the new coalition. His programme was to smash the revolutionary government in Paris, restore the Bourbons and put France back at her 1792 boundaries. But it was no easier than before to unite the ancient dynasties for a common purpose. It was December before an alliance with Russia was complete, and it was not until March of the following year that Austria declared war on France. On the other hand, all attempts to induce Prussia to come in foundered on the indecision of the King, the intrigues of his court and the old Prussian mistrust of Austria.

None the less, at first the coalition was victorious. The

Russian Marshal Suvorov won brilliant victories in Italy. England's own military achievements fell short of all reasonable expectations; her forces were criminally frittered away. True, the British soldier upheld his old reputation for matchless courage, but, generally speaking, at that time England's stock on land stood lower than ever before. Even at sea, for all the glorious victories of her naval heroes, her achievements could not win her the sympathies of Europe, for she ruthlessly ignored the rights of neutrals.

> '*The Briton's grasping polyp-arms reach out;*
> *See him, in his questing convoys, come*
> *To fence free Amphitrite's realm about,*
> *There to lord it as he does at home.*'

These lines of Schiller hit off to a nicety the mood prevailing on the Continent. This in particular was what Grenville could not help reading in the despatches from his envoys at Berlin.

By the autumn of 1799, the military and political position of the coalition had already deteriorated, while that of France was distinctly strengthened when Bonaparte, even though he did leave his army behind, succeeded in returning from Egypt to France in defiance of all the British fleets, and making himself master of the country on November 9th, by the *coup d'état* of 18 Brumaire. True, he was only the first among three consuls, but his personality and his prestige ensured that in reality his was the controlling hand. 'Bonaparte . . . thought it necessary to reform the government,' said Fox in his speech in the House on February 3rd, 1800, 'and he did reform it, just in the way in which a military man may be expected to carry on a reform— he seized on the whole authority to himself.' Fox called him an 'extraordinary man'. However, the British ministers were still far from recognizing the personal importance of the newcomer, and further still from making a precise estimate of the extra strength which his genius and irresistible energy were to give to France.

This lack of insight came out in an embarrassing way when on Christmas Day, 1799, the First Consul addressed a most skilfully worded letter to George III, proposing peace negotiations. Never did Pitt show himself less equal to his task than when confronted by this unexpected offer from Bonaparte.

Instead of rejoicing at the chance of ending a war which was now dragging on into its eighth year and had cost his country untold sacrifices, he and Grenville became much exercised over the fact that '*Sa Majesté très Corse*' had presumed to treat as an equal with His Britannic Majesty. Pitt himself made it his business to cast the British reply in such a form that Bonaparte could not bring himself to believe that he personally had received an answer at all. Instead of grasping with both hands this chance to show Britain's love of peace, instead of agreeing on the best terms possible, Pitt and Grenville sent Talleyrand, the French foreign minister, a note which lectured him from chilly heights and in the stiffest tones, saying that their King could only negotiate with a French government in which he had confidence and that the Consulate did not fulfil that condition. Worse still, they favoured him with the excellent advice that he ought to restore the Bourbon monarchy!

Indeed, if we did not know that William Pitt was undoubtedly a very important statesman and Grenville at the very least a conscientious and experienced politician, we should have to conclude that this note was drafted by political greenhorns. The ridiculous underestimate of Napoleon is not the most fatal part of it. But could anyone play Bonaparte's own game better than by writing such a note, especially if Pitt was right in suspecting that the First Consul's prime motive in sending his letter had been to buttress his still shaky position at home by proclaiming his love of peace? The behaviour of Pitt and Grenville was all the more irresponsible as it can have been no secret to them that the coalition was cracking in all its joints.

Pitt defended his policy in the Commons on February 3rd, 1800, with a great speech, the brilliant wording and sonorous periods of which cannot hide its lack of solid reasoning. Certainly it created an impression in the House when he summed up his position in Cicero's words: 'Cur igitur pacem nolo? Quia infida est, quia periculosa, quia esse non potest.' But all these pretexts and arguments were swept away like withered leaves before a gale when Fox rose to reply. In his rural retreat he had at first scarcely believed his ears when he learned that the ministers had given a flat refusal to Bonaparte's offer. 'Surely they must be quite mad,' he had written to his nephew. Fully conscious of the high importance of the matter, he let himself be persuaded to attend the House on this occasion. But he stipulated that he would stay in London for only two nights, and when an unforeseen postponement forced him to prolong his absence from St. Anne's Hill, he sat, as Lord Holland relates, silent and overcome, with tears stealing down his cheeks. But he showed not a trace of stupefaction when he entered the lists against Pitt and his war policy. Pitt had permitted himself the legitimate, but very impolitic, pleasure of painting Bonaparte in the blackest of colours. Not only did Fox hold up against him what a great mistake it is to throw mud at an opponent when there is no hope of removing or neutralising him, but he also had a far more accurate idea of the First Consul's importance, and was bold enough to compare him with Cromwell. Combining deep feeling with sharp, unanswerable logic, he gave unvarnished expression to his loathing of the war and showed how futile it was to restore the Bourbons by force. His speech reached a climax when he tore to shreds Pitt's absurd idea that England must first wait and see whether Bonaparte would prove himself. 'Gracious God, Sir! is war a state of probation? Is peace a rash system? Is it dangerous for nations to live in amity with each other? . . . Cannot this state of probation be as well undergone without adding to the catalogue of human suffering?' And then he demolished Pitt's phrase: 'We must pause' with such ironic force and passionate assault than even Pitt's henchmen could not but be stirred. However, they held together on the division. Only sixty-four, a mere handful, followed Fox. But, none the less, Pitt cannot have counted February 3rd, 1800, among his red-letter days.

A few months later, when Bonaparte defeated the Austrains decisively at Marengo on June 14th, even Pitt must have been a prey to doubts whether he had really been so very wise in spurning the hand which had been held out to him.

CHAPTER XXIII

IRELAND, THE CATHOLIC QUESTION AND PITT'S RESIGNATION

O NE great, original innovation of Pitt's has still to be mentioned. In 1799 he introduced a general tax on income. The huge expenses of the war had in the main been financed by loans, which were always well taken up it is true, but had to be issued on terms which laid progressively greater and greater burdens on future generations. Their success was a sign of the healthy financial state which the country enjoyed in spite of, and partly because of, the war. More recent experience has shown that a major war is often accompanied by economic prosperity and that a reaction only sets in when arms have been laid aside. Yet the extent to which England's everyday life remained untouched by the war is hardly credible to a later age. Jane Austen's masterpieces were written during the course of the great war, but the society which she describes, obviously with great fidelity, pursues its existence as if not a shot were being fired anywhere and the greatest interests were not daily at stake—except that the uniforms of young men embodied as officers in the militia add an occasional splash of colour to the scene.

The country's traditional system of taxation was far too much of an improvised patchwork and, on the other hand, far too closely adapted to the requirements of the ruling class for it ever to have yielded enough in taxes to meet the ever-increasing demands made by the war. After many unsuccessful attempts at filling the gap by increasing the old taxes, Pitt came to realize that a thoroughgoing reform was needed. He achieved this by means of a tax which levied a fixed percentage on *every* income from *all* sources. He set about matters as carefully as was possible with the rudimentary machinery then existing. After exhaustive investigations he computed that the total annual income of the population of Great Britain exceeded one hundred million pounds sterling. On this he imposed a tax of ten per cent. and reckoned on an annual yield of ten millions, a completely unheard-of sum of money by the standards of those days. That the actual yield fell considerably short of his estimate is no reflection on the basic merit of Pitt's scheme. What is important is that he induced the nation to shoulder a very considerable part of the cost of the war forthwith. For Pitt looked on the income tax purely as a war measure; he and his generation were very far from thinking that in normal times as well Englishmen should permit the Treasury to appropriate a part of their income as a regular thing.

If Pitt's financial moves blazed a path along which almost every country has since followed him, it must be said that his method of tackling the Irish problem has been hotly debated right up to the present day, and has created fresh problems which have busied and disturbed Britain for more than a century.

The legislative independence which England granted Ireland in 1782 under the influence of Fox and Shelburne, who were the Secretaries of State at that time, only brought intermittent calm. The main cause of discontent—the corruption and unrepresentative character of the Irish Parliament—had remained unchanged. The great mass of the Irish thought of it as no more than a clique, abusing its position by selling its support of government measures for personal profit which was dispensed by its rulers from Dublin Castle. Perhaps Fox, if he had stayed longer in office, would have pressed for a reform of the Irish Parliament, and a more equitable treatment of Ireland. Pitt, it is true, had made an abortive attempt to alleviate Ireland's economic miseries by the customs union with Britain, but he had done nothing very far-reaching on the constitutional and religious issues while there was still time. For here, too, the French Revolution had a distinct repercussion. It is easy to imagine the impression made by French ideas of equal rights for all religions upon a people virtually unrepresented in the parliament of its own country, the overwhelming majority of whom were deprived of their most important civil rights because they were Catholics.

Pitt saw that he had to make allowances for changing times, at least to the extent of putting pressure on the Irish government to introduce some reforms in 1793. But, here too, he stopped half way. Admittedly a whole series of legal restrictions and disabilities under which the Catholics suffered were removed, but the doors of Parliament were not flung open to them nor was Parliament itself reformed. If Pitt had entertained the hope that these feeble reforms would make the Irish loyal subjects of the King, he was completely disappointed. And yet never was Ireland's loyalty more necessary or more important than in this war, during which an insurgent Ireland could not fail to attract a French army of invasion like a magnet.

The prospects of Irish reform seemed to brighten when the Whigs who had deserted Fox joined Pitt's ministry. However much the Jacobin bogy and the crusade Burke was preaching had set them against reform in Britain, they were not yet so completely oblivious of Whig doctrines as to fail to recognize Ireland's need for reforms, particularly Catholic emancipation. It is significant that on entering the Cabinet they had demanded the Viceroyalty for one of their own men—Earl Fitzwilliam, nephew and heir of Rockingham, the former leader of the party.

And, indeed, early in 1795 Fitzwilliam went to Dublin as Viceroy. Never has the Irish people received a Viceroy with such high hopes, never has it greeted viceregal measures with such applause and never has it been so sorry to see one go as it was when Fitzwilliam was recalled by Pitt no later than March of the same year.

What had happened? Fitzwilliam had let it be clearly understood in Ireland that his programme was Catholic emancipation and that he considered as his friends those who had previously formed the opposition in the Irish parliament. Above all, he had relieved one of the most influential men in Dublin Castle of his office without previously agreeing on the step with the Cabinet in London. That Cabinet—Pitt, Grenville, but also Fitzwilliam's Whig friend, Portland—maintained that he had exceeded his specific instructions by doing this. As far as a judgement can be reached on the published documents, there is some substance to this charge. At least Fitzwilliam seems to have acted over-precipitately, even if he could urge in his own defence that he had to be guided by impressions received on the spot and that the picture these gave him was far more serious than any that could be dreamt of in London.

But, when all is said and done, the question of personal blame is only of passing significance. Historically the important thing is that Fitzwilliam had a policy and that Pitt and Grenville had none. Really the Cabinet wanted to make an omelette without breaking eggs. Pitt and Grenville had vision enough to grasp that a departure had to be made from the course so far pursued by Dublin Castle, but they wanted at all costs to avoid giving the impression of a change of front. Hence the exaggerated importance they attached to personalities and appointments. Besides, Grenville was apparently influenced, with disastrous results, by his brother, the Marquis of Buckingham (Lord Temple), who, since his own period as Lord Lieutenant in 1788, had been at daggers drawn with the group now smiled on by Fitzwilliam. Looking on the matter objectively, there can be hardly any doubt that Fitzwilliam's policy was the right one. Ireland could not go on in the same condition as before, as Fox showed in an illuminating speech in Parliament. The catastrophic results of Fitzwilliam's recall proved him completely right. It had really been the very last moment at which civil war and revolution could have been avoided by timely reforms. If it is the mark of a statesman to seize Time by the forelock and make full use of each opportunity before it vanishes for ever, then in this instance Pitt did not stand the test, whatever laurels he might win in his paper contests with Fitzwilliam.

The sequel was horrifying. Open rebellion and treason by the Irish, an alliance with the French, a bloody and barbarous crusade by the Catholics against their Protestant neighbours, and a no less bloody and barbarous suppression of the rising by brutal soldiery and an embittered Protestant militia. The years following 1795 are among the most tragic of the all too many tragic years in the history of the Emerald Isle. If the French had managed to land a strong army on Irish soil, Ireland would have dropped into their lap like ripe fruit. When Pitt heard in June, 1798, that Bonaparte and his expedition had sailed from Toulon, he surmised that he was making for Ireland. Perhaps it was a piece of luck for England that Egypt attracted the young general's fancy even more strongly.

The Irish rebellion and its consequences decided Pitt to make sweeping changes in Ireland's constitution. A constitution which neither secured an effective government nor satisfied the people could obviously not have survived in the long run. There were two possibilities: either to reform it root and branch or to

extinguish Irish independence once and for all. A century
before, points of difference between England and Scotland, two
kingdoms joined by a personal link, had been removed by
uniting them as the Kingdom of Great Britain (1707). At first
many Scots had not taken kindly to the Union, and there had
been two Stuart rebellions on Scottish soil. But in course of
time it had taken root, and people had long ago given up
arguing that it had not turned out a blessing for Scotland.
Might not the same thing be done for Ireland? Pitt had worked
for a Customs union earlier on, and obviously when he was
considering the plan of a union his first thought must have been
of its economic advantages. But the exigencies of the time had
made the purely political considerations become still more
important. Could the government of Great Britain sit quietly
back during a war of life and death and watch a neighbouring
island, with a population half as big as its own, conducting a
separate policy and lying open to the national enemy? Did not
the law of self-preservation make it imperative to rule there
with a power and authority equal to that maintained on
English soil?

But Pitt's ideas ranged even further afield. He was, of course,
much too astute and enlightened not to see that the treatment
given to the Irish Catholics was an anachronism, and that what
was called the 'Protestant Ascendancy' in a country which was
nine-tenths Catholic was a source of never-ending conflicts
and friction. But he feared that the complete emancipation of
the Catholics, which meant in particular their admission to
Parliament, would give them the ascendancy over the Protestants as long as there was a separate Irish Parliament. If, on the
other hand, the Irish sent their representatives to a general
British Parliament at Westminster, then the Catholics would
have to remain as a minority for ever and a day, a minority
which would never become a danger to the Protestant population or to Protestant interests. Hence Catholic emancipation
was to come after his plan of union.

Unfortunately the tactics he now adopted merely let him go
half way. Union could only be brought about by the British
and Irish Parliaments acting in concert. Only if the Parliament
in Dublin passed the same Union Bill as the Parliament in
Westminster could the union of the two kingdoms become law.

It went without saying that Pitt could rely on the Parliament at Westminster, but things were very different in Dublin. Feeling in Ireland was overwhelmingly *against* the union. A trial trip in 1799 ended in shipwreck. The Irish Lower House flung out the motion.

What was to be done? Everything hinged on getting Ireland into a frame of mind that was in favour of the union. To this end the ministry gave the Catholics to understand that they could count on the removal of their grievances if the union went through, This was not an official promise so precisely worded that the Catholics could have cited chapter and verse for it. It was more in the nature of unofficial hints sown broadcast by Lord Castlereagh, the new Chief Secretary in Ireland. But they were sufficient to rouse fresh hopes, and beyond a doubt they had their effect in certain circles. However, that in itself was not enough. Pitt did not contemplate dissolving the Irish Parliament; this could hardly have made any difference to the majority there, for most of the seats were in the hands of certain borough-mongers, whose first thoughts were for their own interests. Dublin Castle had an old custom of rounding up the majorities required by the government by bribing these borough magnates. Pitt now took the same course. Cornwallis, the Lord Lieutenant, and Castlereagh, the Chief Secretary, had to move heaven and earth to scrape together a majority. Titles were bestowed or promised; mere barons became earls; ordinary Irish peers were admitted to the more distinguished and influential ranks of the British peerage, and those in need of money received the necessary drafts or treasury notes. It was an unsavoury business, which made honest Cornwallis's gorge rise, while Castlereagh's cold arrogance readily became reconciled to the very worst. Not even Pitt's political admirers deny that one of his most important political achievements, one with which his name is for ever linked, was realized with the help of systematic, shameless corruption going far beyond anything previously known, even in Ireland. He seems to have felt just as few scruples over this as had Henry Fox when in 1762 he bought up a majority for the Peace of Paris against the elder Pitt, or as had Robinson and Atkinson when they pooled the funds of the King and the East India Company to give the younger Pitt a majority at the elections of 1784.

But just as Henry Fox came to grief soon after his triumph, so was Pitt to have a spell in the wilderness too. True, he put the union through. In March, 1800, it was passed by the Irish and immediately afterwards by the British Parliament. On August 1st it became law.

Pitt next wanted to tackle the second part of his programme, Catholic emancipation. So far he had thought it best not to commit himself officially so as to retain freedom of action in all directions. But, as Goethe's Prince of Orange knew, there are occasions when a wise man must be wise enough to be a fool. If Pitt had laid his cards on the table from the start, if he had not tried to promote the union until he had made what he was aiming at clear to his Cabinet and especially to the King, then undoubtedly both would have declared themselves in agreement. If Paris was worth a mass to Henry of Navarre, the Union with Ireland would have been worth Catholic emancipation to George III. But once he had the union in his pocket, he found he could develop the most sensitive religious conscience without the least risk. The majority of the Cabinet ranged themselves on the side of Pitt and Grenville when they laid their plan before him in September, 1800. But the dissenting minority included the minister traditionally known as the keeper of His Majesty's conscience—the Lord Chancellor, Lord Loughborough. This was the title assumed by Alexander Wedderburn, the man who had betrayed the Whigs in 1771 to become North's Solicitor-General, and since then had repeatedly shifted from one party to another.

This high-principled Chancellor not only betrayed Pitt's intentions to the King, but used the full force of his forensic eloquence to show him that Catholic emancipation conflicted with his coronation oath—at all times to maintain the Protestant reformed religion. Here was a theory very much to the taste of a strait-laced bigot like George III. True, it would be doing him no real injustice to assume that he knew enough of events leading up to the union to be quite well aware that Pitt was planning emancipation. But none of that had been official nor did he let it stand in his way: he dug in his heels over his coronation oath, reproached his minister with intending to do violence to his conscience and blocked emancipation with his complete and absolute veto. At the same time he had anything but a favourable opinion of the character of the 'keeper of his conscience'; when Wedderburn died some years later, his grateful sovereign pronounced his funeral oration by observing 'Then he has not left a greater knave behind him in my dominions'. At which the former Chancellor, Lord Thurlow, observed with good-natured *esprit de corps*, 'I perceive that His Majesty is quite sane at present'.

The crisis came into the open at the end of January, 1801, when Parliament was on the point of meeting. Once again George III produced the formula which he had used to throttle Fox's East India Bill in 1783: he openly stated that he would consider anyone who came out in favour of Catholic emancipation as a personal enemy. As a result, on February 1st, Pitt wrote him a letter announcing that he would resign his office if George persisted in his veto. George showed no signs of giving way, but got the Speaker, Henry Addington, son of the Addington who had been Chatham's doctor for many years, to become prime minister. Pitt himself had recommended Addington to the King as his successor and had promised Addington his support. On February 5th Pitt resigned. Along with him went Lord Grenville, who also considered Catholic emancipation a political necessity, as did Dundas, Lord Spencer and two other ministers. In the same way Cornwallis and Castlereagh, the two officials who had piloted the union through in Ireland, resigned as well.

So far everything had developed quite logically, but now occurred a strange interlude. Once again George had a fit of insanity—partly as a result of the excitement, partly as a result of an illness. For days his condition was extremely critical. However, on March 6th he was enough recovered to see members of his family. But what was the first use he made of his recovery? He sent his doctor to Pitt with the blunt message that Pitt was responsible for his illness. And now followed the strangest thing of all: Pitt gave the King—either verbally or in writing—a solemn promise that as long as George reigned he would never again raise the question of Catholic emancipation!

What can be made of these facts? No more need be said about the King's scruples of conscience. It may, however, be assumed that he would not have given such play to them if he had still found Pitt indispensable for keeping out a ministry led by Fox.

But Fox's secession had freed him from this anxiety; to this
extent the secession had justified itself from Fox's point of view.
Pitt's value in the King's eyes had fallen ever since Fox had
ceased to lead the opposition. In these circumstances a man like
Addington, who was the embodiment of mediocrity as a statesman and as an orator, was quite good enough for his purpose.
Granted, a war was still raging. Granted, foreign affairs were
at that moment as gloomy as they could well be. Since her
defeat at Marengo it was only a question of time before Austria
would conclude a separate peace with France. As for the
Russian alliance, things looked even blacker. Czar Paul I was
not only exasperated with his allies, but he threatened to found
a league of neutrality directed against England's conduct of the
war at sea. True, Paul's assassination on March 23rd, 1801, put
paid to that. But George must still have been ignorant of this as
he calmly dismissed Pitt, and appointed in his stead a man who
was simply a figure of fun when cast as the leader of a great
empire locked in a life and death struggle with Bonaparte.

Yet worst of all is the cunning with which George III exploited his mental disorder to extort from Pitt a promise to
abandon the Catholics. This shows that he was one of those
people who are popularly known as more knave than fool, and
that, when it suited his book, he was capable of combining the
most exquisite scruples with a complete lack of them.

On the other hand, this renunciation of Pitt's throws a
strange light on his own conduct. If he sent in his resignation
on February 5th, 1801, because he could not put through a
reform which he thought necessary as a statesman and to which
he was pledged as a man of honour, then nothing but respect
and praise can be given to his loyalty to his convictions. But
how can this be squared with the fact that on March 7th, 1801,
he undertook to shelve the self-same question for the rest of the
King's reign? After all, it was no less important on March 7th
than on February 5th, nor was he any the less pledged to it.
And yet he took up his offices again in 1804, this time not for
the purpose of settling the Catholic question but under a
promise to leave it entirely alone and with the intention of
opposing its solution. The glaring paradox cannot be explained
away by a reference to the King's illness between February 5th
and March 7th. Presumably it would not be doing justice to

Pitt's way of thinking to take up a strictly logical standpoint, and say that, where a reform which he is convinced is in the country's interest is in question, a responsible statesman ought to discount the conscientious scruples of a man who is obviously not a normal being. But why did he not avoid making any commitment by simply pointing out that he was no longer in office and therefore not in a position to carry through any measure against the King's will? And why did he say nothing of his renunciation to the colleagues who had resigned with him?

Pitt's contradictory and enigmatic behaviour drives one to the conclusion that the Catholic question, important as it was for him, was not the only reason for his resignation. Rather does a suspicion obtrude itself—one which many of his contemporaries were already putting into words—that the war situation and Pitt's grasp of the need for an early peace must at least have been partly responsible for his resigning. It is easy to understand his thinking that he was not the man to make this peace, especially after his rejection of Bonaparte's offer of the previous year.

Had the First Consul completed his 'probation' meanwhile? He had marched from victory to victory, from conquest to conquest, he had strengthened his position in his own country to an extraordinary degree, shattered hostile coalitions and handled the Czar so skilfully that he preferred Bonaparte to his former allies. Such, then, was the front presented by the man whom Pitt had attacked a year earlier in his great speech of February 3rd, 1800, calling him a perjurer, a usurper and a stranger in France. The idea of negotiating a peace with this man in this military situation could not possibly have held any attractions for Pitt.

And even if he could have got over the difficulty as far as he personally was concerned, he could foresee that his Cabinet would not have fallen into line behind him. Grenville, who filled the key post of Foreign Minister, was certainly not prepared to have any hand in a peace of the kind to be expected from a man in such a position as Bonaparte's.

If this assumption is correct, then Pitt's undertaking of March 7th to abandon the Catholic question can be explained by his desire to remove an obstacle which might have blocked his subsequent re-entry into the administration. And, in fact, once another minister had negotiated the peace, then Pitt would have been able and willing to take the reins of government once more. He could reckon on a majority welcoming this in both Houses. This would also explain why he was satisfied with a successor like Addington, whose inadequacy could hardly be a secret to him, and why he even agreed to give him unconditional support, a step which caused not only head-shakings but also mutterings among many of his own supporters.

It is true that on this showing Pitt's resignation appears less heroic than if it is put down solely to his resolve to stand or fall by Catholic emancipation. But Pitt is not the only statesman on whom power has exercised an irresistible fascination, and Catholic emancipation was not the only reform which he championed at first only to sacrifice later.

And so the union of Ireland with Britain remained Pitt's last important act. Neither the methods he used to put it through nor the manoeuvre which broke it off half finished make it a worthy climax to his historic administration. Whether it was a blessing for Ireland, whether it was a blessing for Britain will always remain a matter of controversy. It did not settle the Irish question. That remained a source of unrest until Gladstone made the vain attempt to solve it by Home Rule, and it then occupied the centre of attention in English politics for a generation. Even the setting up of the Irish Republic under the British Crown has not solved the problem, as time has shown.

CHAPTER XXIV

THE ADDINGTON INTERLUDE

WILLIAM Pitt could make good use of a breathing-space after being in office continuously for seventeen years, eight of which were war years. He was a young man of twenty-four, just down from the university, when he was called to the helm, and he was a mature and at times a thoroughly tired man of forty-two when he relinquished it. It had been apparent in 1798 that his nerves were no longer perfectly under control, when he fought a duel with pistols with a member of Parliament called Tierney who led the opposition during Fox's secession. The duel had been brought on by an incident in the House, and on that occasion Pitt had put himself in the wrong by his brusque disregard of the accepted forms; besides, every thinking man could not but feel that it showed little sense of responsiblity for the leading statesman to risk his life in such a childish way during a national crisis in which that life was regarded as indispensable. This time George III was justified in reading his prime minister a homily—that a public figure has no right only to think of what he owes to himself, but that he must also consider his duty to his country.

Pitt's health, never very robust, had repeatedly broken down of recent years. This was due not only to burdens of office, but also to private worries. His astonishing inability to keep his expenditure within the limits of what was nevertheless quite a large income, and to bring some sort of order into his personal finances, threatened him at times with the catastrophe of bankruptcy or executions in his house by bailiffs. Fortunately Pitt, as well as Fox, had friends who were ready to rally round him in a crisis. A few months after his resignation, which of course had added to his money troubles, a dozen of these friends clubbed together and raised close on twelve thousand pounds, with which his most pressing debts could be wiped out. However, he also had to sell his country seat which was the joy of his heart. His mother was still at Burton Pynsent, where his father had ended his days. She died on April 2nd, 1803, having survived her great husband by almost a quarter of a century.

True, the former prime minister did not lack a stately home. He remained Warden of the Cinque Ports, and as such had his official residence at Walmer Castle. Here he spent most of his time after his resignation. Here he busied himself organizing the local Volunteers, which were being raised everywhere to protect the country against the danger of invasion. But Walmer was also a welcome retreat when he wished to escape the necessity of defining his attitude on the political questions of the day. It was here that he took charge of his niece, Lady Hester Stanhope, on the death of his mother.

Hester was the daughter of Pitt's sister of the same name who had married Lord Mahon, later Lord Stanhope, a sprig of the famous Stanhope family. The mother had died early, and the father, an eccentric radical and amateur inventor, did everything he could to set his children against him. So Hester inherited eccentric propensities on both sides. These blossomed forth in her later life, which ended in a Lebanese oasis amid dreams of founding an oriental despotism. Moreover, she had also inherited the fiery Chatham spirit which made her a lively and attractive figure of a girl in her youth. In these years, while her eccentricity merely found expression in a most unconventional freedom of speech and comment, and while her love and gratitude towards her uncle and benefactor kept her egoism in check, she brought into Pitt's life a ray of cheerfulness, warmth and light which were otherwise unknown to him. Acting as hostess for a former and future prime minister suited her, and she played the part to perfection. Even if the guests could not always be certain that the lady of the house might not suddenly hurl at their heads some remark more original than flattering, yet they could be sure of being most hospitably received and brilliantly entertained. Pitt delighted in the company and conversation of his niece and felt at his ease in the atmosphere she created. She did not, however, do anything towards setting his finances to rights.

The guests at Walmer Castle sometimes included the new prime minister, 'The Doctor', as Addington was always called in recollection of his father's profession. He had been a friend of Pitt's ever since their schooldays. As Speaker of the House of

Commons he had turned out well, but no one had ever yet considered him a statesman. So malicious and witty a follower of Pitt's as Canning believed he was being as tolerant as anyone could possibly expect when he promised Pitt not to laugh at his successor! To make up for this he spread the rhyme about him:

> *'Pitt is to Addington*
> *As London to Paddington.'*

But even more charitable people could say nothing more in 'The Doctor's' favour than that he was a man of good character. There was not a man in his Cabinet who could have made up for their chief's lack of political capacity. Those of Pitt's former colleagues generally classed as incompetents had joined Addington. Pitt's elder brother, Lord Chatham, was one of them, and though this showed that the outgoing minister was not going to create difficulties for his successor, Chatham was not looked on as a political asset. Despite this, Addington's position in Parliament was not too bad: so many of those who sat in the lower House voted for any minister no matter how he shaped. On the other hand the opposition caused him no difficulties, because they did not want to clear the road for Pitt's return to power. '. . . Pitt was a bad minister; he is out— I am glad,' was Fox's epigrammatic comment in a letter to his friend, Charles Grey.

Fox soon had occasion to give active support to the new ministry. His prime and most urgent aim was and continued to be the restoration of peace. After Austria had concluded a separate peace with Bonaparte at Lunéville on February 9th, 1801, negotiations got under way between Britain and France as well. On October 1st the preliminaries were signed in London and these were used as the basis of the Peace of Amiens (March 25th, 1802). People on both sides of the Channel were weary of a war which had by then lasted eight years. The English, who acclaimed Addington as the peace-maker, took little interest in whether the peace turned out slightly better or slightly worse. In actual fact from England's point of view it was not at all satisfactory, but this could not be otherwise considering the military situation. Of all the overseas conquests made by the British fleet, Britain retained only Ceylon and Trinidad. Even Malta, which she had once more taken from

Bonaparte's forces, she undertook to give back again to the Order of St. John, and that under the guarantee of a neutral great power. If this settlement in itself bore no relation to the colossal expenditure England had incurred, the peace went further still: it meant giving up all the aims for which she had entered the war eight years before. The French Revolution was *not* overpowered, the Bourbon dynasty was *not* restored, Belgium had *not* been separated from France again and Holland had *not* been withdrawn from her influence. Even worse, in Italy and Germany the power and influence of France had increased beyond even the wildest dreams of the Girondins of 1793.

Thus Pitt and Grenville, who had led the English people into the war, had no reason to be satisfied with the results of their policy. However, at this point their paths diverged. Grenville sharply criticized the preliminary articles of peace in the Lords and voted against them. In the Commons Pitt made a determined speech in favour of ratification. It cannot have been easy for him to admit openly that the restoration of the French monarchy which he had wanted had been found unattainable. His argument that the concessions extracted by France were not really as considerable as they seemed at first blush sounded as unconvincing as his hopes for the future good conduct of the First Consul. But before Addington stepped into his shoes, Pitt had promised to support him with all his might, and Pitt was keeping his promise.

Fox's speech struck quite a different note. 'At no time, Sir, since I have had the honour of being a member of this House, did I ever give my vote with more heartfelt pleasure than I shall do on the present occasion in support of the preliminaries of peace between this country and the French Republic,' were his opening words. His subsequent review of the conduct of the war and the negotiations developed into an annihilating criticism of Pitt and his policy. What arguments could possibly be put up against him when he said that a peace as good as this, a better one even, could have been had a year earlier when Pitt brushed aside Bonaparte's outstretched hand, or when he reminded Pitt of the choice epithets which he had then showered on the very man he was now recommending to the House as a reliable party to a treaty? Fox likewise drew the most favourable picture he could of Bonaparte's intentions, but that at least was in keeping with the whole trend of his policy even if admittedly it betrayed no real foresight. The Commons, who had backed Pitt when he rejected peace with Bonaparte, came out unanimously for Addington who had concluded peace with him. And all England lit bonfires!

Alas, it was only a peace of very, very short duration. Fox took advantage of it: at last he could see for himself the land from which all these storms had blown up, the France which he had known so well in the days of the *ancien régime*. He set out with his wife at the end of July, 1802, and remained on French soil until the middle of November. It was more than a mere pretext when he said the object of his journey was to study the French archives for his historical work. He did, in fact, work very hard among the archives, but none the less his main purpose was to study the country and its leading men. He had himself presented to the First Consul at one of the official receptions in the Tuileries, and Bonaparte at once deluged him with a flood of the most flattering compliments. Fox, who did not like this approach, said very little in reply. Still, he accepted an invitation to dine with Bonaparte and had an exhaustive discussion with him, of which, however, no detailed account survives.

The conclusion of peace had put Pitt into a peculiar position. Even if he did not think it himself, at any rate his followers thought that the time had come for him to take the reins of government into his hands once more. Addington's success had not increased his personal prestige in the slightest. Men like Canning could hardly wait for him to give up his place to Pitt again. Pitt himself fully shared these wishes, but he felt that his promise bound him to support Addington. What tied his hands still more was that the King did not show the slightest inclination for a change of ministers; in his eyes a mediocrity like Addington was the ideal prime minister. Besides, Addington and his Cabinet were so diligent not only in securing Pitt's advice but also in following it, that in the name of decency Pitt could hardly do anything against them. An attempt by Pitt to form a coalition between Addington and his friends on the one side and Pitt's friends, particularly Grenville, on the other, ran up against the opposition of Grenville and even more that of

z

his brothers. Lord Buckingham made it clear to Grenville that it would be a heavy blow to his political reputation if he sat in a Cabinet with men whose views on the two cardinal questions of France and the Catholics were the complete opposite of his own. Grenville, it should be said, advocated a vigorous policy towards France, without wishing to bind himself to the provisions of the Treaty of Amiens.

But even the Addington Cabinet was unable to preserve this peace which it had itself concluded. Squabbles over carrying out the terms never ceased: Bonaparte accused the English of violating the obligations they had assumed, and the English replied in kind. Both sides had much justification for their complaints, but, while Bonaparte's temperament and military methods made him try to bluff and blackguard it out, the English ministers fell back on a policy of shuffling, temporizing and quibbling, though they lacked even the shrewdness and suppleness necessary for that. Finally the question of peace or war hung on the fate of Malta. The Addington Cabinet had decided not to hand it over, despite the provisions of the treaty, and it is fairly certain that here Pitt's counsels played a decisive part. At the same time the ministers conducted the negotiations in such a tone that Bonaparte exclaimed indignantly that they were treating him like a garrison which was being called upon to lay down its arms. In the middle of May, 1803, the British ambassador left Paris, and a few days later England once more declared war.

In the Commons Pitt came out in support of this decision with a speech which evoked a storm of applause from the kindled patriotism of the House and was praised by many as his greatest rhetorical performance. It was, however, so incompletely reported that posterity cannot verify this impression. Some idea of the tone of his speech may perhaps be gathered from Fox's reply. 'We have, indeed,' he said, turning to Pitt, 'heard some splendid philippics on this subject; philippics which Demosthenes himself, were he among us, would hear with pleasure, and possibly with envy; philippics which would lead us directly to battle, without regard to what may follow. But then comes the question: what shall we have to pay for them? What is the amount of the bill? I remember an old French proverb. . . . The author of [it] . . . tells us that, let things be ever so good, yet if they are dear, he has no pleasure in eating them—"*Le coût en ôte le goût*". Now so it is with me, when I hear the harangues of the right honourable gentleman in favour of war: I think the articles dressed up are exquisite, but that the cost spoils the relish. . . . In the beginning of the last war . . . there was no want of imagery, no want of figures of rhetoric, no want of the flowers of eloquence—eloquence seldom equalled and never surpassed by man, and all exerted to support the war. We know how that war ended, and the damp which was cast upon our ardour at the sight of the bill when it came to be paid. So now, when I hear all these fine and eloquent philippics, I cannot help recollecting what fruits such speeches have generally produced, and dreading the devastation and carnage which usually attend them.'

And so once more Pitt and Fox exemplify two types of rhetoric and two types of policy which are in conflict again and again throughout the history of mankind from the days of Thucydides. On the one side stands the powerful orator, who whips up national passions and sets every nerve a-tingle; on the other stands the scrupulous critic, who sees in his mind's eye a clear, distinct picture of all the misery which the unleashing of passions brings with it, who calls for prosaic negotiations when his hearers already believe that the fanfares of battle and the trumpets of victory are ringing in their ears. This time, as before, the critic was overborne; but the speech which Fox made, dissecting every single motive for war with penetrating analysis and complete expertise, rightly ranks as one of the greatest masterpieces of eloquence ever delivered in Parliament.

Again, the debate which Pitt and Fox opened in the Commons on May 24th, 1803, is one of those which has never been brought to a conclusion, but is still carried on by the historians of all nations. Was England the aggressor? Napoleon always maintained that it was England who made it impossible for him to follow a peaceful policy, and no less a man than Leopold von Ranke has undertaken to defend him against the reproach of being a 'beast of prey'. Today we know that the war which broke out in 1803 ended at Leipzig and Waterloo, and so we are inclined to consider the policy which led up to it as the right one from the English point of view. But in between there lay twelve years of bloodshed and eight years of Napoleonic victories, and not one of the causes which led to Napoleon's downfall was visible in 1803. From the viewpoint of the year 1803, it can indeed be seen that the spread of French or Napoleonic power had transformed the continent of Europe in a way that was very threatening to Britain, but that Britain was not in the right over the actual question of Malta which finally led to the war. Nor was Fox alone in criticizing the British government on this score; even Pitt's friend Wilberforce said in the debate: 'Malta is indeed a valuable possession, but the most valuable of all the possessions of this country is its good faith. . . . This, then, is my grand objection to the conduct of ministers, that by claiming the possession of Malta instead of its independence . . . they gave our inveterate enemy an opportunity of mis-stating our real views both to France and to Europe.'

But once war had broken out, there was no more delay or discussion. During the weeks of doubt which preceded the decision, Fox had written to his friends that if matters did come to war, even its most determined opponents would have nothing left but to support it 'in some sort'.

Whatever illusions he might cherish about Bonaparte's love of peace, he had no doubts about his energy and strength or purpose. The whole English people soon discovered the sort of enemy it had to deal with. When Bonaparte at once occupied Hanover, it is true that this disturbed the King more than his British subjects. But the news that he was assembling ships and troops at Boulogne in numbers never seen before was a rude awakening to all Englishmen, especially as they could not rid themselves of the fear that the Irish would receive a French army with open arms. In such a crisis the country's fate was in the hands of an Addington, and the very thought of this was enough to bring together men who till then had always been at loggerheads. No change could be expected from the King. Apart from his preference for Addington, he was always on the verge of insanity and frequently passed the border-line.

The only alternative to 'The Doctor' was William Pitt. All were agreed on this, and even Fox seems to have concurred. Still more was it the view and the wish of Lord Grenville, who had gradually assembled a considerable following. But Pitt himself went to work in a way which did not inspire confidence and made joint action impossible. Just as his father had done before him, he seemed to set great store upon reserving a special rôle for himself which marked him off from the rest of the opposition. But, as usually happens in such cases, the ministry felt aggrieved and reproached him with not keeping his word. A motion which Pitt introduced to emphasize his points of difference with both sides only showed the weakness of his position in Parliament. Only a mere handful of those who acclaimed him as long as he was in office followed him now.

In October, 1803, the situation was still further complicated by the fact that Grenville learned to his surprise of the pledge which Pitt had given the King on the Catholic question. Pitt's friend and former tutor, Bishop Tomline of Lincoln, told Grenville's sister about what had happened in March, 1801; the bishop made no secret of his opinion that Pitt had used his promise to try to keep in the saddle, and that this had been frustrated by Addington. Grenville later told Fox that Pitt had never breathed a word to him about his readiness to carry on the ministry while renouncing action on the Catholic question. Grenville appears to have written much the same thing in answer to his brother-in-law, who had passed on Tomline's disclosures, for the subsequent reply to Grenville praises his 'firm, manly and consistent conduct' and contrasts it with the 'shifting, undecided and fluctuating behaviour' of Pitt. For Grenville stood firm by the policy for which he had thrown up his post. The need to quieten the rebellious mood of Ireland, and to give as much strength as possible to the weak bonds of loyalty which linked at least a minority of the Irish Catholics with England, made the Catholic question, as Fox explained in his private letters, more urgent and pressing than ever.

And so it was natural enough that the Fox group and the Grenville group, which was called 'the new opposition', should draw closer to each other. Lord Grenville's brother Thomas, who had kept up his personal friendship with Fox despite the political estrangement which had cut across it, seems to have been particularly active in trying to reach an understanding. This came about in January, 1804.

Lord Grenville informed Pitt of the alliance in a detailed letter of January 31st, 1804. The two main reasons he gave for it were the need for an active opposition to a ministry patently inadequate and hence due to be removed, and the formation, after its fall, of a new ministry 'comprehending as large a proportion as possible of the weight, talents and character to be found in public men of all descriptions, and *without any exception*'.[1] These last words of Grenville's referred obliquely to Fox, and Pitt must have known it. True, Fox had declared that he himself was ready to waive all his own claims to a ministerial post, if only suitable places could be found in the Cabinet for his friends; he laid particular stress on Grey, whom he considered indispensable, as, indeed, the only statesman who could lead England in war. Pitt's answer to Grenville was very significant. In theory he agreed with both of the opposition's aims, but in practice he declined to take any hand in it on the hardly convincing grounds that this would have the very opposite effect to that intended: admittedly, he said, he could foresee that on the fall of the existing administration he might be summoned, but he would not then be in a position to form the 'comprehensive' government which he too desired.

Of course, the other party leaders could do nothing much with this. Fox, and even members of the Grenville group, put down Pitt's attitude to the fact that, while hankering after Addington's fall, in the event of it he wanted to commend himself on high by not having taken part in the opposition. Now, as always, George III looked upon opposition to his administration as opposition to himself. Pitt had been too closely bound up with this system ever to have attained to the modern constitutional view, which draws a clear distinction between the King and his government because it really puts the King above all parties. It can well be imagined that Fox's opinion of Pitt was not enhanced by these proceedings.

The next months saw a fairly close-knit opposition by the followers of Fox and Grenville. Pitt kept in touch with them but sorely tried their nerves by his vacillating and indecisive attitude. At last, however, he was brought face to face with a question on which he had no alternative but to fall in with the opposition. The Addington ministry was incapable of organizing the country's forces to defend it, and Fox and Grenville were at one in complaining of this. Nor indeed could it be denied that it was urgently necessary to do something about it.

[1] My italics, E. E.

When therefore on April 23rd, 1804, Fox raised the question of national defence and moved for a committee of the whole House to examine it, Pitt had to support the motion both on objective and personal grounds. This caused a great and painful sensation among the Cabinet. One of its younger members believed that there was no better way of parrying the blow than to revive the hackneyed song about the Fox-North coalition of 1783 and to issue warnings against a Fox-Pitt coalition. Fox was able to answer this by saying that he certainly acknowledged with pride the powerful aid given by Pitt, but that he had known in advance no more than any other man in the House what particular line Pitt meant to adopt on that day. He added, 'It is evident, indeed, that we fully concur in one particular opinion: we are perfectly agreed as to the weakness and incapacity of the present ministers.' It is safe to assume that most members were thinking the same. None the less, on the division Addington again had a majority, but it was so small (256 to 204) that he realized that *his* day was done.

Once more Pitt's day had dawned.

CHAPTER XXV

PITT'S SECOND MINISTRY AND HIS DEATH

I N the spring of 1804 George III had again been seized by one of his violent attacks of insanity. He had gradually recovered until he could display reasonably balanced behaviour and could grasp what was happening when Addington informed him of his decision to resign. Weak as were his mental powers, he was in fine fettle whenever it was a question of using his state of health to get his own way or of scotching anything which did not suit his book.

This was clear enough when he received Pitt, whom he now had to summon, at his first audience on May 7th, 1804. Pitt, who had brought down Addington with the help of Grenville and Fox, wished to propose an administration in which both of them could find a place, along with their most influential supporters. But George's feeble brain could not compass the idea that the country's plight called for a rallying of all forces. All he knew was that he had always hated that Mr. Fox and did not want him as his minister at any price. In the same way he clung to his coronation oath and insisted that Pitt should renew his promise to leave the Catholic question alone. On these points he was quite clear, definite and unequivocal. But arguments which he found unpalatable he simply ignored. Pitt afterwards confessed that he had never been so completely baffled by an interview with George as he was on this occasion.

Now it is certainly not easy to discuss things with a king who is always threatening to relapse into insanity if his wishes are crossed. Pitt found it particularly difficult, because he knew that if George went mad it would mean that the Prince of Wales would become Regent, and that would mean that Fox would be summoned. For once again in these last critical years the Prince had made it particularly plain that where politics were concerned Fox was the man for his money, even if their personal friendship had cooled off considerably. None the less, it is impossible to dismiss the suspicion that, if Pitt had put on a bolder front, he might after all have managed to secure Fox's appointment. For two years later, after Pitt's death, George agreed to this when Grenville insisted.

Pitt, however, accepted the King's instructions to form a Cabinet without Fox. George had at length agreed to the inclusion of a few of Fox's followers. Pitt submitted this proposal to Grenville, who now had to decide whether he should accept it and drop the programme which had brought the 'new opposition' together. He reserved his reply until he had had time to discuss the matter with his friends. Fox made things easier for Grenville by declaring at once that, as far as he himself was concerned, he was ready to renounce all thoughts of office and to support the new Cabinet just the same, provided that his more intimate friends were given important posts. These friends, however, proclaimed as one man that in no circumstances would they join a ministry from which their leader was barred. Grenville fully endorsed this attitude and wrote to Pitt declining to take part in his new ministry. In justification he repeated verbatim what he had written to him that January about the need for a 'comprehensive' government. Not only England but also all Europe would derive the greatest benefit from such an administration. 'We are certainly not ignorant of the difficulties which might have obstructed the final accomplishment of such an object. . . . But when in the very first instance all trial of it is precluded, and when this denial is made the condition of all subsequent arrangements, we cannot but feel that there are no motives of whatever description which could justify our taking an active part in the establishment of a system so adverse to our deliberate and declared opinions.'

If this last sentence was a hint to Pitt to make a fresh attack on the King's thick skull, it was neither taken nor acted upon. On the contrary, Pitt now hastened to form his ministry, although he had to pass over almost every man who could add talent or experience to it. The only one among the pillars of his old ministry to support him was Dundas, raised to the peerage as Lord Melville by Addington. Most of the other ministers equalled Addington's colleagues in mediocrity, and even from this source six men were taken over into the Pitt ministry. Perhaps, in view of the way he shaped later on, Castlereagh can be rated a little higher. Young Canning had to make do with an office which did not carry Cabinet rank.

This sort of Cabinet was not in the least what Pitt needed now, for the very reason that it burdened him with work which was much too heavy for his weakened powers. Lady Hester Stanhope, who kept house for him in Downing Street as well, described her uncle's daily round many years later, when she was living in voluntary exile in the Lebanese desert: 'Ah . . . what a life was his! Roused from his sleep (for he was a good sleeper) with a despatch from Lord Melville; then down to Windsor; then, if he had half an hour to spare, trying to swallow something: Mr. Adams with a paper, Mr. Long with another; then Mr. Rose: then, with a little bottle of cordial confection in his pocket, off to the House until three or four in the morning; then home to a hot supper for two or three hours more, to talk over what was to be done next day—and wine, and wine! Scarcely up next morning, when tat-tat-tat—twenty or thirty people one after another. . . . It was enough to kill a man—it was murder!'

All this weighed the more heavily on Pitt as he had lost the feeling of complete security which had steered him past every reef during his first ministry. At that time whenever he rose to speak in the Commons he could always be certain of mustering an overwhelming majority, however the battle might be going. That was all over now! His prestige had suffered severely during the years he had remained outside the government and had shown himself incapable of following a consistent line of policy. One group of his former followers was clustering round Addington, and an even stronger group had followed Grenville into opposition. In the summer of 1805 Fox, who knew the House as few others did, estimated that Pitt and Addington each had a following which was 60 strong, while he gave the opposition 150 members. On the other side of the picture, he described 180 as supporters of the Chancellor of the Exchequer for the time being, that is, as the ministerial party (and no mistake about it) which always votes with the Ayes whoever may be sitting in the Cabinet. Pitt himself considered his parliamentary position very precarious, as is shown by the fact that he invited Addington, whom he himself had ousted, to join his Cabinet at the end of 1804. At last Addington agreed and even allowed himself to be pushed up into the Lords. Although he was now called Lord Sidmouth, he was still known to politicians as 'The Doctor', as he had always been. However, he made conditions: at the time the most important was that he reserved his liberty to decide what his attitude should be towards Lord Melville (Henry Dundas).

For some time a storm had been threatening to burst over Melville's head. He was accused of having given his approval to the doings of his Under-Secretary of State, who had used £10,000 of public money for private speculation. A parliamentary committee had been set up, and its report was a crushing blow to Melville. Of course the opposition seized upon this damning material against an influential member of the Cabinet. Pitt tried at all cost to retain his old colleague, who was now at the Admiralty and the one efficient member of the Cabinet.

The matter came up for debate in the Commons on April 8th, 1805. Whitbread, one of Fox's supporters, moved a series of resolutions declaring Melville guilty of a gross violation of the law. Melville was called even more sharply to account in a loudly applauded speech by the twenty-five-year-old Lord Henry Petty, son of the Earl of Shelburne, lately further ennobled as Marquis of Lansdowne. The gulf between Fox and his old opponent had narrowed considerably since the outbreak of war with France in 1793, for Lansdowne had also been a determined opponent of the war. His son had rallied to Fox's banner in Parliament, and there let himself be fired with enthusiasm for the liberal ideas to which he remained faithful in later years as the third Lord Lansdowne. Thus it came about that the son of the man upon whose intrigues Fox's political career had once been shipwrecked became a powerful and important champion of the Fox tradition. He was one of the men who opened the doors of politics to Macaulay.

Pitt tried to save his colleague by moving the previous question. Fox spoke on the other side and reminded Pitt that he had begun his parliamentary career by implacably hunting down corruption. But the decisive blow fell when Pitt's friend Wilberforce rose to speak. He had always regarded Dundas as Pitt's evil genius and could not but see in him the man who had so far frustrated his own life's work, the abolition of the slave trade. It was not that, however, but higher motives which decided his attitude now. Speaking obviously from honest conviction, he said that Parliament would open a door to every species of corruption if it were to wink at so flagrant a case and let itself be misled by the specious arguments of the administration. When Wilberforce started speaking Pitt fixed his eyes on him with intense earnestness. When his opening sentences showed the line he was taking, Pitt sank back into his seat, a broken man. He realized that Melville's was a lost cause.

Curiously enough, when the division was taken, it turned out that both sides had the same number of votes—216. In this rare contingency the procedure of the Commons gives the Speaker the casting vote. Abbot, the Speaker, turned deathly pale as this grave and unusual responsibility was suddenly thrust upon him. There followed a pause during which Abbot marshalled his thoughts and the whole House hung on his words, tense and breathless. At last he gave his vote—*against* the ministry! A hurricane of cheering broke out on the opposition benches. But Pitt jammed his hat over his forehead to conceal the tears which trickled down his cheeks at this defeat. True, he did not resign as some of the shouts of his wilder opponents called on him to do. But it was a crushing blow not only to his political position but also to his nerves and health, all the more crushing as the main responsibility for the blow lay with his friend Wilberforce.

Addington's followers had voted for the criminal prosecution of Melville. This, of course, gave rise to difficulties between him and Pitt. He threatened to leave the ministry, but let himself be persuaded by Pitt to postpone matters until Parliament had adjourned for the recess. Not until July, 1805, was he really in earnest about it and he then resigned at the worst possible moment. 'The Doctor, Lord help him, is a great fool, and one whom experience cannot make wise,' was Fox's private opinion. But it seemed as if Fox himself would be affected by this step, for it was whispered on all sides that Pitt was about to offer the opposition a share in the government.

Fox had been anything but depressed when in May, 1804, Pitt had formed his ministry without him and Grenville. He confided to his nephew that nothing could have fallen out more to his mind. It revived and strengthened the party, he said, lowered Pitt's prestige and in particular lowered too 'the cause of *Royalism* (in the bad sense of the word)'. For he never for one moment forgot that the main aim of all his efforts was to destroy the power which George III had arrogated to himself. For this reason he attached the greatest importance to the opposition's showing itself strong, united and powerful—as he wrote to his nephew, obviously with an eye to a possible change of sovereign—so that if ever they should come into office it would be clear beyond all question that they had an existence of their own, and were not the mere creatures of the Crown. So when the rumours of an offer from Pitt bobbed up, Fox was very sceptical; for he could not believe that Pitt would be prepared to make the concessions which the opposition thought essential.

None the less, Pitt did in fact take a step in this direction. In the middle of September he went to Weymouth, where the King, alternating between madness and sanity and almost completely blind, was staying for the sake of his health. Pitt pointed out how precarious his position was in Parliament and declared for a 'comprehensive' ministry as the only feasible solution. He asked the King to approve his bringing in some leading members of the Fox and Grenville groups, but once again George abruptly refused. The lower the ebb to which his mental faculties in general had sunk, the more obstinately he clung to the few fixed ideas which were firmly lodged in his head. He would rather risk civil war than admit Fox into his councils, said this faithful servant of his people to an intimate of Pitt's. And yet Fox had publicly stated in a speech in the House (June 20th, 1805) that his own personal ambition would not stand in the way if it was now a question of replacing the existing inadequate administration by a 'comprehensive' one, or, as the phrase now had it, a 'ministry of all the talents'.

During the summer, to be sure, Fox had once more added a large item to his debit account by sinning against the other *idée fixe* of the King—his interpretation of the coronation oath. The Catholics had presented a petition to Parliament and Fox had given it his emphatic backing (May 14th, 1805). In so doing he had been at some pains to argue that the King's coronation oath was not in any way involved. But of course George would not hear of this. Pitt had turned down the petition as inopportune and the House had rejected it by a three to one majority.

Fox had been glad to take the lead on the Catholic question because he considered emancipation absolutely necessary and because he wanted the opposition to go into action over a matter of fundamental importance. But he cherished no illusions that it could possibly be settled while George III was on the throne. Indeed, he fully appreciated that a minister had to pay attention to the King's prejudices, and in a letter to Grenville before the ministerial crisis of April, 1804, he described it as conceivable that he himself might reach the same conclusion if he had *full* knowledge of *all* the attendant circumstances. But as he had not got into this embarrassing position, he felt himself free to act solely on his own conviction.

In time of war such incidents of home politics are dwarfed by foreign policy, significant as they may be for the personalities taking part in them and for an understanding of their characters. Once again the war had broken out, and it had gone on for a year when Pitt once more took over the administration. But so far it had produced no great military actions. England and France stood face to face like two wrestlers, each eager, but unable, to spring at the other's throat. Never until the year 1940 were the narrow seas separating England from Europe of such military and political importance as in 1804 and 1805. Despite the belligerent energy with which Bonaparte assembled his troops and ships at Boulogne, time and again he came to the conclusion that his forces were by no means powerful enough for the daring venture.

But Britain found it just as hard to confront Bonaparte on the Continent, although he probably suspected the British government of sponsoring attempts to assassinate him. In February, 1804, his police had uncovered a nest of conspirators, some of whom, such as General Pichegru, had secretly crossed from England in the summer of 1803. It is doubtful whether the English ministers really did know anything about this conspiracy, but Bonaparte cannot be blamed for having his suspicions. What was, however, much more serious was the step he took to bring it home to the Bourbons, who were undoubtedly at the bottom of the plot, that he was not to be trifled with. He could lay his hands on only one member of the Bourbon family, the young Duc d'Enghien, who was living close to the French frontier on the territory of Baden and was certainly more occupied with his own pleasure than with politics there; Bonaparte had him seized, and after a travesty of a trial by court-martial, shot. Effective as this action was—for thereafter all royalist plots against Bonaparte's life ceased—morally and legally it is still a murder and a violation of international law. It is no worse than the conduct of the Great Elector of Brandenburg, who, in 1670, had the Prussian Junker von Kalkstein treacherously kidnapped from Polish Warsaw, tortured and put to death. However, in the meantime more than a hundred years had elapsed during which men had become more sensitive about such brutal breaches of the law, and, apart from this, many people were still impressed by the special sanctity of royal blood. That point, to be sure, ought to have been made quite clear by the action taken by the kings themselves, but on this occasion the German princes and the German Reichstag showed how contemptible they really were: out of pure cowardice they did not dare to raise their voices against the activities of the First Consul, and left it to the Czar Alexander to protest against this criminal violation of the frontiers of the German Empire. It was the last and most shameful symptom of the utter decay of the Holy Roman Empire.

The most sensational consequence of these conspiracies was that Bonaparte was raised to the purple as the Emperor Napoleon (May 18th, 1804). Senate, army and people offered him the title and thus met his own wishes. It went without saying that this did not make him one whit the more popular with the crowned heads among whom he wished to be accepted. But even the ruler of Austria became reconciled to it in return for Napoleon's agreement to recognize him as Emperor of Austria, as it was clear that the days of the Holy Roman Empire were numbered.

Thus William Pitt and Napoleon I faced each other in the struggle which was to decide the fate not only of their own countries but also of Europe. At first, it is true, things did not appear in that light. Napoleon's army was still waiting at Boulogne and the great naval operation, which was to give him mastery of the Channel for at least twenty-four hours, somehow failed to come off. Then at the end of 1804 a new power, Spain, entered the war against England, but the English government had itself to thank for that in the first instance. It had ended a period of uncertainty by having the Spanish treasure ships seized on their voyage from South America, the only possible reply to which was for the Spaniards to declare war. These proceedings had by no means met with unmixed approval in England itself; Fox, in particular, wholeheartedly condemned them.

True, Napoleon saw to it that there was no lack of similar acts of violence. After he had had himself crowned King of Italy with the Iron Crown of Lombardy at Milan in May, 1805, he united the Ligurian Republic (Genoa) with France, and Parma and Piacenza with Italy. Austria could not stand idly by and watch this being done, however much the state of her finances and armaments made her need a long peace.

Before this Alexander I of Russia had reached the conclusion that such powers as were still independent would have to join forces to break France's ascendancy and resist her encroachments. Quite naturally his eye fell on the power which was in any case at war with France, and certainly England's capacity to draw him closer was enhanced by the fact that Pitt, the minister who had inspired both the coalitions, was once more at the helm. As it happened, Pitt, too, was at the time bending all his energies towards forming a great European coalition against Napoleon. His present aims, however, stood out in sharp contrast to his earlier ones. He had given up the idea of intervening in France's internal affairs: experience had taught him that this goal was unattainable. Moreover, by then the new order was so firmly rooted in France, and, what was more, under a new monarch, that even theoretically the demand for intervention could no longer be justified. Nor was there any longer any question of moving back the frontiers to where they had been in 1792. The left bank of the Rhine was now to be left to France; Pitt only wanted to throw up barriers in the north and the south against her further expansion. In Italy Austria was to take on the job. Belgium was to be given to Prussia to win her over to the coalition. Of course, Pitt did not trouble his head overmuch about the feelings of the people living in Belgium or Italy or the Germans on the left bank of the Rhine. Modern ideas of the right of self-determination and the principle of nationality were still far beyond his ken.

In his new coalition Pitt wished to unite Britain with the three old great powers, Russia, Austria and Prussia. It was an aim difficult of achievement. Even with the Czar, who in January, 1805, had sent a special envoy to London, agreement was reached only after long negotiations which were at times in serious danger of breaking down. The stumbling-block was Malta; the Czar demanded that it should be handed over to the Knights of St. John, but Pitt was obdurate. At the end of July the Czar finally gave way, since bigger things were at stake, as was shown by Napoleon's encroachments in Italy. It was harder still to get the Emperor of Austria to make up his mind, as he knew very well that his army still needed several months to get ready for action. Of course, the handsome subsidies which Pitt promised weighed the scale very heavily both in St. Petersburg and Vienna, but no agreement could be reached with Prussia. It was not only that Frederick William III was, as ever, incapable of making up his mind. Perhaps from his point of view a still greater factor was Hanover, which he would have pocketed only too gladly. It was impossible for Britain to offer him the hereditary lands of her King. But on the other hand Napoleon never let such considerations hamper him in the least. Pitt's counter-offer of Belgium was not half so attractive. The Czar's threat to march through Prussian territory was taken as an affront by the King of Prussia, and so it drove him much closer to the French camp.

Thus Pitt could only count on Austria and Russia when war broke out on the Continent in September, 1805. Napoleon had followed diplomatic developments with a sharp and suspicious eye and was at once ready to take up the gauntlet when Austria and Russia offered him an understanding on the basis of the Peace of Lunéville of 1801, which had meanwhile been completely overtaken by events. He had just heard from his admirals the highly disappointing news of the failure of the great naval operation he had planned. The invasion of England, which had by this time been threatening for two years, had to be abandoned for good. Thus was Napoleon released from a highly inconvenient, not to say humiliating, position, for it meant that he could now use the highly trained army at Boulogne for another large-scale task which fitted it better and was eminently suited to his own genius. With astonishing speed

2 A

he prepared his new plan of campaign and, before anyone in England knew what was happening, the army was on the march from Boulogne to Germany.

The war had thus changed its character at one stroke. Long-drawn-out stagnation gave way to one of the greatest dramas in the history of the world. Pitt looked to the outcome with his innate optimism, although he had only partially succeeded in forming the coalition he planned. He hoped that Austria and Russia, even without Prussia but with British help, would be a match for the Emperor of the French. Fox, on the other hand, was highly sceptical of the whole system of continental coalitions. He foresaw the defeat of Britain's continental allies, which, as he feared, had been forced into war before they were properly ready for it. 'The Austrians themselves admit . . .' he wrote on August 28th to Grey, 'there is nothing but a victory over the French army that can stop it from going directly to Vienna. . . . And if their first victory is not a decisive one, they must fight again and again; . . . if beaten in any one great battle, the enemy must be at Vienna.' How apt a prophecy! But what was the alternative? Fox apparently hoped that the war of stagnation between England and France, in which neither party could force a decision, must in the long run inevitably lead to peace negotiations. And who can say what course history would have taken if the battle of Trafalgar had been fought before the coalition was formed?

As things turned out, in any case Napoleon had every reason to be pleased with the course taken by the diplomatic negotiations. A quite unparalleled career of victory lay before him. As early as October 20th the Austrian general, Mack, had to capitulate at Ulm with an army of 60,000 men. A few weeks later the French occupied Vienna without resistance, and Napoleon and his army thrust on deeper into hostile territory to Brünn.

In the meantime, however, the British fleet had won a naval victory of incalculable importance. On October 21st, that is, at almost the same time as the capitulation of Ulm, Nelson defeated and destroyed the combined Franco-Spanish fleet at Trafalgar. Before putting to sea the great naval hero had paid a farewell visit to the prime minister. On this occasion Pitt had paid him a compliment which, as Nelson himself said, he would hardly have paid to a Prince of the Blood: he attended him from his room right down into the street and to the carriage which was waiting for him. It was a final compliment. Nelson met his death in the battle which made him immortal. Trafalgar is one of the decisive events of world history. The great victory not only made an invasion of England permanently impossible; it also laid the foundation of Britain's control of the seas which has lasted to the present day.

But what help was this naval victory at a moment when the decisive theatre had been shifted to the Continent? And then, suddenly, a reckless and high-handed action of Napoleon's seemed to offer hopes of a considerable extension of the coalition. To complete the encirclement of Ulm as quickly as possible he had made his regiments march through the territory of the Margravate of Anspach which was at that time a possession of the King of Prussia. According to the notions of national prestige prevailing in Berlin, this was a more important and decisive move than the fate of the Continent. The King was enraged with Napoleon. Czar Alexander took advantage of this frame of mind by appearing on a visit in Berlin on October 28th and making the King a further offer of an alliance. A touching scene at the grave of Frederick the Great seemed to announce that the fraternization had succeeded. In point of fact Frederick William did declare himself ready to join the coalition against Napoleon, but not at once and not without conditions! First he wanted to make an attempt at mediation, and only if this failed to take up arms. But in a secret clause he stipulated that Hanover was to fall to him as one of the spoils of victory.

This put Pitt in an extraordinarily difficult position. The Prussian army was so strong and—despite its failure in the revolutionary wars—its reputation was still great enough for people to believe that its entry into the war would tip the scales against Napoleon. On the other hand, Pitt could not expect his King to give away his old hereditary lands. In this dilemma he tried to temporize in the hope that in the meantime Napoleon would refuse Prussia's terms and so force her to come in.

In this situation it was obviously in the allies' interest for Count Haugwitz, who had been sent off to Napoleon by Frederick William, to use all possible despatch and for the

Austro-Russian army to hold back as long as possible and to avoid battle. Both did precisely the opposite! Haugwitz travelled so slowly and let himself be kept waiting so long by Napoleon that the moment for so much as putting forward his terms had slipped by. But Czar Alexander I was impatient to try conclusions in battle and attacked even before his own troops had been properly brought into position. Thus on December 2nd, 1805, Napoleon was enabled to win an unusually brilliant and decisive victory over the Russsians and Austrians at Austerlitz. In doing so not only did he extricate himself at one blow from a position which was not without its danger for him and win a reputation for being invincible; he also forced the Emperor of Austria to conclude a separate armistice and turn his back upon the coalition (Peace of Pressburg, December 26th, 1805).

However the victory of Austerlitz brought Napoleon yet another success. It freed him from the opponent whom he could not but see as the heart and soul of the enemy coalition: William Pitt was also a casualty of Austerlitz.

The first news of Mack's catastrophe at Ulm reached London at the beginning of November. It is typical of Pitt's optimism that at first he would give no credence to the bad news, but tried to cheer up those around him by assuring them that it was just a French fanfaronade. But on the next day he called on Lord Malmesbury, who knew some Dutch, with a Dutch newspaper which had just come in and asked him to translate the *communiqué*. Here it was set out in black and white, and was so clear and unambiguous that all illusions were dispelled. Pitt struggled to compose himself and put on a confident air in spite of everything, but Malmesbury, who had known him for years and could look behind the mask, saw clearly that he had received a blow from which he would never recover. Pitt assumed, he wrote, a manner and look which were not his own.

A few days later came the news of Trafalgar, which roused fresh hopes. Pitt was woken up to hear it and was so excited that his usual knack of going off to sleep again deserted him; he got up to work at his papers. Yet joy at the great victory was more than tempered by the death of Nelson. The English had grown used to looking on Nelson as an unfailing bringer of victory, and his death seemed too great a price to pay even for Trafalgar.

November 9th has from time immemorial been Lord Mayor's

Day, when he receives ministers and other public figures as guests of the City. When Pitt appeared he was received in triumph and the Lord Mayor toasted him as the 'saviour of Europe'. Pitt disclaimed this compliment in a reply of only two sentences: '. . . Europe is not to be saved by any single man. England has saved herself by her exertions, and will, as I trust, save Europe by her example.'

This is the shortest and finest speech Pitt ever made. It will live as long as England is able to preserve her place among the great powers of Europe, and it will remain a monument to Pitt's patriotism when most of his other struggles, successes and defeats are forgotten. It also marks an advance in political thought: it is an appeal less to the governments than to the peoples of Europe, on whose exertions, as history has shown, the fate of a continent actually depended.

Pitt and his Cabinet very understandably hoped for better news from the continental theatre, and the next session of Parliament, which had been fixed for the end of November, was postponed until the middle of January. Pitt's health was so bad that some rest and treatment seemed necessary, and on December 7th he went to Bath to which he had already paid many visits in search of relief, just like his father before him. Even so, there was no indication that he was dangerously ill. But this time the cure, which had usually done him good, proved ineffective. The old hereditary enemy, gout, for which Pitt's way of life had made too little allowance, this time attacked the stomach, where it was held to be particularly dangerous. But his physical sufferings were increased and complicated by the strain placed upon his nerves. What a state of tension he must have been kept in by the negotiations with the shifty and unpredictable court of Berlin, and still more by the military operations on the Continent, which were of such infinite importance to England and so entirely beyond the control of England's government!

Then came the shattering news of the defeat at Austerlitz. It has been related that Pitt heard the hoof-beats of the horse on which the courier came galloping from London. The courier brought in the despatch. Pitt tore it open, ran his eyes down it and turned pale, as if struck to the heart. He called for a glass of brandy, then for a map of Europe. After a short glance at it, he put it aside with the words: 'Roll up that map; it will not be wanted these ten years.'

This account, dramatized by Thomas Hardy in his *Dynasts*, does not stand up to close historical analysis. As often happens in such cases, it telescopes into a single moment events spaced over some length of time. But it reflects in a striking way the essential, the annihilating effect which the news of Austerlitz and the defection of Austria had upon Pitt. The European coalition which he had built up for his country with such zeal and with so many sacrifices had been smashed finally and irreparably on December 2nd, 1805. The break-up of this third coalition was more dreadful and disgraceful than that of its predecessors. They had at least held together for a few years, but this one lasted barely a few months. No thinking person could doubt that the King of Prussia would now consider discretion the better part of valour and turn to Napoleon. That man, of whom Pitt had spoken with contempt and harsh reproof a few years earlier when he had become First Consul, now gleamed in all the splendour of his crowning triumph.

Eventus tyrannus! Just as success is credited to the statesman who takes the lead even if luck has contributed more to it than merit, so too must he shoulder the blame even if others have made the fatal mistakes. The poet can lay the responsibility on the gods:

> '*The seed we leave within their hands reposing;*
> *The blossom—weal or woe—bides Time's disclosing.*'

A parliament and an opposition always fix on the man who has controlled the conduct of affairs and bears the political responsibility. In a few weeks Parliament had to reassemble. How was the prime minister to face Fox, who had always warned against continental coalitions and, as recently as June, just before the House dispersed, had asked to be enlightened as to where the journey led and what the administration had in mind? Would not all attacks be focussed on the person of Pitt, the only figure in a Cabinet of ciphers—to repeat a phrase coined about his father's ministry? What support could he get from the King, nowadays more often out of his right mind than in it, the King whose mental condition the very coffee-houses were discussing? Was not his fall inevitable? Was a career which had begun so triumphantly to end with such ignominy?

Seldom has a statesman's position been more desperate than was Pitt's about the turn of the year 1805–1806. A man of robust health could hardly have stood up to it; a sick man must inevitably break under the strain. The doctors now declared that it was pointless to continue the treatment, and on January 9th, 1806, Pitt set out on his journey home. His destination was a country house in Putney which he had rented a year before. When his niece Hester Stanhope saw him again she was aghast at the changes which had ravaged his features in the meanwhile.

The fact was, he was a dying man. He himself seems at first to have had no inkling of it, and even the doctors were still hopeful at the outset. But they watched with dismay as his powers steadily grew weaker and even short conversations with his colleagues utterly exhausted him. When Parliament reassembled on January 22nd it learned that the prime minister was too ill to appear, and the opposition postponed the attacks they had made ready. However Pitt had already left earthly cares behind him. His old tutor, Bishop Tomline, had prepared him for the approaching end. Pitt declined to receive the sacrament, but he prayed with Tomline and assured him that he had always striven to discharge his duties towards God and man.

The end came in the early hours of January 23rd, 1806, twenty-five years to a day since he had first taken his seat in Parliament. He had not yet completed his forty-seventh year. It was at just this age that Bismarck began his career as prime minister of Prussia.

§

At the news of Pitt's death all England mourned. Everyone, in whatever relation they stood to Pitt in politics, felt that England had lost one of her greatest sons, who was as much a victim of the war as Nelson had been. Grenville, who—apart from any ties of blood—had been so close to him for so long and in such stirring times, retired to his estate at Dropmore to devote himself to his grief in solitude. He exerted his whole influence on the opposition to urge restraint upon them and to induce them to agree to the mark of respect which was being planned by Pitt's friends.

On January 27th, these friends moved in the Commons that a statue be erected to Pitt in Westminster Abbey to perpetuate the memory of this 'excellent statesman'. Fox could not agree with such a description. It is an open question whether it would not have been more appropriate for him to have given at least his silent assent to this tribute to Pitt. In the nineteenth century it became the custom, whenever a leading statesman died, for even his lifelong opponents in Parliament to recognize and pay tribute to his importance and his merits. This fine custom has met with approval, and rightly so. However, when Gladstone forced himself to deliver a panegyric immediately after the death of Disraeli, his friend and admirer, Lord Acton, criticized him for sacrificing his principles. The great historian would certainly have appreciated the promptings of conscience which made Fox speak against the motion to honour Pitt. The way in which he discharged this difficult task deserves the highest praise. His speech was a model of tact and dignity. It could not but disarm even the most enthusiastic followers of Pitt, and convince them that the speaker was merely discharging a duty which was painful even to him and was going to the utmost limits that his conscience would allow in his appreciation of Pitt. Yet he had to deny him the name of an 'excellent statesman' because Pitt had misused his great gifts to preserve a system which spelt ruin for the country. In a struggle lasting more than twenty years Fox had seen his opponent as a champion of the King's personal government and he felt bound to protest against this even at the moment when they parted company for the last time.

Fox showed that he was far above all personal grudges by his willingness to agree that Pitt's debts should become a charge on the public funds. They came to more than £40,000. Fox was also prepared to make provision for Lady Hester Stanhope, but that proud lady declined to accept a favour from the man whom her uncle, now worshipped to the point of idolatry, had always looked on as his opponent and his rival.

William Pitt's mortal remains were interred in Westminster Abbey by the side of his great father. Wilberforce, who despite all the ups and downs of political life, had always preserved his personal friendship and attachment, expressed the feelings of many of the mourners when he wrote that the statue of the first William Pitt seemed to be looking down with consternation into the grave which was opened for his favourite son.

CHAPTER XXVI

FOX'S MINISTRY AND DEATH

SURELY Charles Fox must now become a minister. At first
the King tried to keep the rump of the existing ministry in
being. But the mediocrities of whom it was made up had
sense enough to see that they were not equal to the task of
governing the British Empire in an hour of crisis. They declined
with thanks. After this, all the King could do was to summon
Lord Grenville, who accepted the commission on conditon
that he might form a ministry from men of every political complexion, and that no one should be kept out of it. George made
one last attempt to exclude Fox, but gave way when Grenville
proved adamant.

And so the ministry followed the formula which Grenville
had laid down in his letter to Pitt of January 31st, 1804, and
has, in consequence, become known as 'the ministry of all
the talents'. Not, of course, that this implied that every one of
its members was a man of outstanding talent. Lord Sidmouth
(Addington), who was included as an earnest of the 'comprehensive' character of the new administration, remained as ever
a person of mediocre abilities. Most of the talent came from the
former opposition—Grey, for instance, who took over the
Admiralty, Erskine, who was made Lord Chancellor, and, of
course, Fox, who once more became Secretary of State for
Foreign Affairs.

What must have been the feelings of George III and Fox,
when Fox came to kiss the King's hands on receiving the Seals,
and they stood face to face? Certainly George grumbled that
now, after all, he was obliged to see this Mr. Fox in his inner
councils; but his dislike gradually abated as he got to know him
better, and in the end he seems to have felt that perhaps after all
Fox was not quite as bad as he had imagined. Fox, for his part,
can hardly have been able to suppress the thought that here
before him was the man who had prevented him from harvest-
ing the fruits of his life's work while they were still ripe. In
years he was, to be sure, far from being an old man yet, for he

was fifty-seven. But he had been in public life for thirty-seven years and, except for brief intervals, he had spent all these years in opposition. Such a length of time cannot but damp the most genuine enthusiasm and wear down the most ardent of men. Whenever his gaze roved along the ranks of his companions-in-arms and his opponents he could hardly avoid the sense of being almost a Nestor who had seen a generation of which they knew nothing. Where were they now, the men with whom he had crossed swords or had stood shoulder to shoulder during the American War? Both the Pitts, Burke, Gibbon, Shelburne, North, Wedderburn—all of them dead! The heroine of the Westminster election, the once captivating Duchess of Devonshire—now a blind, sick woman approaching her end, which came to her on March 30th. And he himself? Was he still the same man? Certainly he was in his ideas and his aspirations. But at times a deep depression settled on his soul, a herald of the illness which was so soon to snatch him away.

Fox had again taken on the Foreign Office, not only because at that moment it was the most important and the most difficult post, but above all because he hoped to restore peace, which had been his supreme aim for time out of mind. A strange chance enabled him at least to open negotiations with the French government.

Fox had only been in office a few weeks when a mysterious stranger sent in his name, declaring that he wished to communicate something of the utmost importance, which, however, he could only disclose to Fox in person. Fox granted him a private interview, and the stranger now confided to him that he was about to slip across to Paris to assassinate Napoleon. Everything was ready, he said; a house had been hired in Passy from which the attempt could be made with assured success and without risk.

At all events the Frenchman had believed that the famous champion of freedom would receive the murderer of a tyrant with delight, just as the youth of Athens celebrated Harmodius and Aristogeiton. How little did he know his Fox! Nothing was more repugnant to him than the principle that the end sanctifies the means. It disgusted him to think that his noble cause might be stained by murder. In his speech of May 24th, 1803, against the re-opening of the war, he had already referred to abortive attempts on Bonaparte's life when he exclaimed: '. . . The hostility of a great and generous nation gives no countenance to crimes, even against its worst enemies.' His actions as a minister bore out his words as leader of the opposition. He had the Frenchman arrested to prevent him from carrying out his sinister plot. But he did still more. He sent a communication to Talleyrand, the French minister for foreign affairs, informing him of the attempt which had been planned.

Talleyrand's answer begins: 'I have placed your Excellency's letter in the hands of His Majesty. His first words after reading it were: "I recognize here the principles of honour and virtue which have always distinguished Mr. Fox." ' After thanking Fox, Napoleon went on to profess that his own intentions were pacific and to refer to the unprofitable conflict between the two nations. Fox at once seized upon this and declared himself ready to enter into negotiations for a sure and lasting peace. But the subsequent correspondence shows that Napoleon was still very far from being really ready to reach an understanding. Napoleon's insincere diplomatic methods greatly disillusioned Fox. He was soon forced to realize that there was nothing for it but to continue the war and throw everything into the struggle.

Indeed, Fox was even obliged to extend the war and take on a fresh opponent, the King of Prussia. This conflict arose from the notorious mission on which the Prussian minister, Count Haugwitz, had been sent by his king in order to impose the conditions agreed with Russia upon the French Emperor by armed mediation. After Haugwitz—and his timorous and dishonest master is also to blame—had shirked delivering his ultimatum and had waited until Napoleon himself had snatched the decision into his own hands at Austerlitz, he had let himself be persuaded by the victorious emperor, who was quite clear what he was about, to conclude a treaty which stood in the most blatant contrast to his original commission. (Convention of Schönbrunn, December 15th, 1805). The clause of this treaty, by which Prussia received the electorate of Hanover from Napoleon's hands was bound to have a fatal effect on Prussia's relations with Britain. Instead of rejecting this disgraceful treaty as soon as it was laid before him, Frederick William III concluded the even more disgraceful treaty of Paris

on February 15th, 1806, which not only confirmed the annexation of Hanover but, in addition, laid down that Prussia was to
close the Prussian and Hanoverian ports to all English ships—
and all this despite the still binding pact with Russia, who was
allied to Britain! In his speech in the House on April 23rd Fox
justly described the policy of Prussia as 'a union of everything
that was contemptible in servility with everything that was
odious in rapacity.' But he also attacked the moral basis of the
Prussian policy of grab by solemnly protesting against the whole
principle of 'transferring the subjects of one prince to another
in the way of equivalents and under the pretext of convenience
and mutual accommodation', as if they were a herd of oxen or a
flock of sheep. Such a principle, he exclaimed, shook the foundations of all established government, and the existence of every
nation. Gladstone recurred to the same ideas in 1870 when he
protested against the separation of Alsace and Lorraine from
France against the wishes of their inhabitants.

Thus in his foreign policy Fox was unable to achieve what he
had at heart, just as he also had to give up all hopes of success
in dealing with the Catholic question. His views of this question remained entirely unchanged; but he saw quite as clearly
that for the time he had no possible hope of putting them into
effect, for his path was blocked both by the King and by the
majority in Parliament. For all his opposition towards the
King's personal government, he had told Grenville two years
earlier—as we have already seen—of his willingness to consider
the King's scruples to the extent of declaring that a temporary
postponement might be a subject of discussion. The view has,
indeed, been held that on entering the administration Fox gave
the King a promise similar to the one Pitt had given before him,
but this is more than doubtful. When in the following year the
King forced Grenville to resign by demanding that he and his
Cabinet should promise not to meddle any further with the
Catholic question, Grenville wrote to his brother, the Marquis
of Buckingham, on March 17th, 1807: 'We contracted no such
engagement when the government was formed—none such
was proposed—and if it had been proposed, I am very sure we
should not have acceded to it.' A letter which Fox, as Secretary
of State, wrote to one of the Catholic leaders points to the same
conclusion. In it he declares that he will speak and vote for

emancipation if it should be brought before the Commons by a petition from the Catholics. But—he urgently warns against presenting any such a petition. It could only result in a parliamentary defeat and the fall of the ministry. After the three to one majority which had rejected his motion the year before, there could be no doubt at all of defeat. Yet the ministry's position would have been all the more precarious as Sidmouth and his friends were now, as ever, out-and-out opponents of emancipation. Therefore, as Fox explains in this letter, the total result of such an attempt would have been the ministry's fall and its replacement by a new one from which the Catholics could not even have hoped for the removal of their less important grievances, a step which Fox was planning.

True as all this might be, Fox must have found it no less painful to shelve a reform which he thought not only justified but urgent, considering the state of Ireland and the threat from overseas. He may have comforted himself with the hope that he would tackle the question at some later date and carry it through in the face of all resistance. But fate willed it that this date should never come.

Fate had, in fact, only *one* success still in store for him. The abolition of the slave trade had made no further headway even during Pitt's second ministry. In 1804 the indefatigable Wilberforce had once more presented his motion and with the help of Pitt and Fox had got it through the Commons: 124 votes had been cast for it and only 49 against. At least the opponents of the slave trade thought they had attained their goal. However a great disappointment awaited them. The House of Lords rejected the motion after Pitt had refused to exert all his influence there in its favour. His Cabinet was split over this question just as his party was, and Pitt attached more importance to holding the party together than to freeing the slaves. When Wilberforce's motion came up again the following year for discussion in the Commons, Pitt failed to give his accustomed support and it fell through.

It was a tragedy for Wilberforce that the man, whose personal friend he remained to the last, was snatched away by death before he could lead Wilberforce's cause to victory. Throughout his whole political career he had been separated from Fox by party differences. As a pious Christian he took great exception to Charles Fox's way of life. In much the same way Fox could not forgive the apostle of slave emancipation for the political elasticity which must have appeared to him as 'servility' towards Pitt. But this had never for a moment made him falter in the determination which led him to support Wilberforce's motion year after year, nor in the warmth with which he praised the merits of his character.

Thus Wilberforce had no need to hesitate about entrusting his cause to the leading figure in the new administration. He called on Fox to talk matters over as frequently as he had in the past on Pitt. At first he felt a little uneasy about entering into such close relations with the politician whom he had fought against for more than two decades. However, he soon reached the stage of putting all his confidence in him. He found him personally 'quite rampant and playful as he was twenty-two years ago . . .' The pious Puritan could no more withstand Fox's freedom of spirit and warmth of heart than could the gay lords and ladies of the Whig aristocracy. Fox told him quite frankly that he would get the measure through the Commons, but that he feared a defeat in the Lords. Here, however, Grenville was at work, just as determined in his own sober fashion to wipe out the slave trade, and Fox managed to tie down the Prince of Wales to letting him have a free hand in the matter. True, the Cabinet included a few opponents such as Sidmouth, but Fox and Grenville had the great majority on their side and showed they were determined to exert the full influence of the ministry for the cause. They could rely on support from public opinion. The interested parties, who had carried on successful opposition for so long, lost heart when they were confronted by a ministry which was in earnest.

On June 10th, 1806, the resolution for the abolition of the slave trade was once again on the Commons' order paper. This time it was Fox himself who moved the resolution; he had asked Wilberforce to take it on as he had always done in the past, but he and his friends had entreated Fox to lead the way and bear the banner himself. Fox could not, of course, bring forward any new arguments upon a matter which had been discussed so often, but he spoke with all his old verve and with the confidence that this time success would not escape him. Turning to Pitt's friends, he reminded them that Pitt had never displayed his extraordinary eloquence with more brilliance or more ardour than in the service of this cause; his speeches on it, he said, would not easily be forgotten. Thus did he contrive in this great, humane endeavour to link his name in honourable association with that of his life-long opponent.

Once again it was clear that an administration which meant business could get its own way in Parliament. The House agreed to the motion by 114 votes to only 15, and in the Lords Grenville was victorious by 41 votes to 30. The decisive success had been gained! All that remained to be done was simply to put it into effect.

In his speech on June 10th Fox had cried: 'So fully am I impressed with the vast importance and necessity of attaining what will be the object of my motion this night, that *if, during the almost forty years that I have had the honour of a seat in Parliament, I had been so fortunate as to accomplish that, and that only, I should think I had done enough and could retire from public life with comfort and the conscious satisfaction that I had done my duty.*'

This sounded like a farewell. It was one. Neither Fox nor his hearers knew that never again would he speak in that House, the pride and ornament of which he had been for so long. Already the hand of death was upon him. Already the sands were running out.

Soon afterwards Charles Fox fell so seriously ill that he could no longer get to the House. The fact that his health had suffered did not escape the eyes of those who were closest to him. At the state funeral of Nelson in Westminster Abbey Lord Holland had noticed how the exertion had told on him more than ever before. Then he was struck by the fact that Fox was a prey to fits of depression, which until then had been quite foreign to his nature. The doctors advised him to take things easily, but he did not follow their advice until after he had piloted the slave trade measure through Parliament. Even then he still carried out his official duties and with his own hand wrote his memoranda, the clarity and technical mastery of which astonished the experts—but not for much longer. The gravity of his illness could not be mistaken: it was dropsy.

At first Fox hoped for a recovery which would permit him to resume his parliamentary duties. 'The Slave Trade and peace', he told his nephew, 'are two such glorious things, I can't give them up, even to you.' Grey suggested to him that he should retire to the Lords, but he would not hear of this; for, as he said that night, he had vowed in his youth that he would never wind up his political life with such an act of folly.

For a few short months the illness dragged on. Fox yearned for St. Anne's Hill where he had been so happy, but he was already too weak to risk the journey. The Duke of Devonshire put at his disposal the country house at Chiswick, where his father, Henry Fox, had been born. There he spent his last days. He could no longer walk, but at first he could still go round the garden in an invalid chair, before he was entirely confined to his bed. His wife tended him with touching devotion. Every day Lord Holland passed several hours reading or chatting to him. Neither his interest in politics nor his love of literature had declined. Indeed, a few days before his death Holland had to read him the eighth book of the *Aeneid*, and the sick man praised and repeated the finest lines with his old fire. Then the doctors had to operate, without however being able to give him lasting relief.

Now he knew that his end was near. His thoughts and his cares centred around the partner of his days who had been at his side for more than twenty years, and, both as mistress and as wedded wife, had never ceased to give him love and receive love of him again. By her and for her sake alone he let himself be persuaded to allow a clergyman to pray at his bedside. 'Towards the end,' related Holland, 'Mrs. Fox knelt on the bed and joined his hands, which he seemed faintly to close with a smile of ineffable goodness, such as can never be forgotten by those who witnessed it. Whatever it betokened, it was a smile of serenity and goodness, such as could have proceeded at that moment only from a disinterested and benevolent heart, from a being loving and beloved by all that surrounded and by all that approached him.'

On the evening of September 13th, 1806, he was released from his sufferings. His last words were to his wife: 'I die happy, but pity you.'

§

Thus, in the course of eight short months, death had robbed England of the two men who had dominated the foreground of her public life, and in the settled judgement of the country had stood out far above all other statesmen. No one, whatever his standing, could bear comparison with William Pitt or Charles Fox. A gap had been torn open which could only be filled after generations.

Neither of the two men left an heir. And so their death snaps asunder the chain, the first link of which had been forged when their fathers entered the Commons in 1735. For more than seventy years a Pitt and a Fox had had the ear of the House, had had the Commons or the Lords hanging on their words. Different in mind, ability, character and conviction though they were, Parliament could be proud of all four. All of them would have been thwarted in their development, their careers and their labours without that Parliament. Many were the defects and shortcomings of the Parliament of eighteenth-century England, yet it was not only the stage, but also the cradle of great men. Where else in the whole of Europe, before the French Revolution, was there a setting so favourable to the development of character and talent? Neither the courts of Versailles, Berlin nor Vienna can boast of bringing forward men to compare with the great English parliamentary figures of the time. Where else could a man who was hated by his King reach the top in spite of that, as Charles Fox did in the end? Even if Parliament was not representative of the broad masses of the people, it was none the less the tribune of free speech and the free clash of intellects. Even if it does fall short of the demands of abstract theory, all the same it did fulfil the one function which Britain required of it at this particular time and in these particular conditions. A day came when it was no longer equal to its task: if it then managed to adapt itself to the new age without revolution or a national convulsion, this was thanks to no man more than to Charles Fox, who sowed the seeds of the future and left behind him disciples to carry through the great reform.

It was the spirit of the two Pitts, both father and son, which triumphed over Napoleon at Waterloo. But the spirit which gave nineteenth century England her particular character and cast its spell upon so many free minds in all the countries of Europe was that of Charles Fox.

He himself, in his merits as in his shortcomings, was a man of

2B

his century, and perhaps it might be said that his death marks the close of the eighteenth century in England. But can the purpose which triumphed in nineteenth century England be more eloquently expressed than in the words which were heard on May 26th, 1797, when Fox entered the lists for a reform of Parliament?

'When we look at the democracies of the ancient world, we are compelled to acknowledge their oppressions to their dependencies, their horrible acts of injustice and of ingratitude to their own citizens; but they compel us also to admiration. . . . We are compelled to own that it gives a power of which no other form of government is capable. Why? Because it incorporates every man with the state; because it arouses everything that belongs to the soul as well as to the body of man; because it makes every individual feel that he is fighting for himself and not for another: that it is his own cause, his own safety, his own concern, his own dignity on the face of the earth . . . which he has to maintain. And accordingly we find that whatever may be objected to them on account of the turbulency of the passions which they engender, their short duration and their disgusting vices, they have exacted from the common suffrage of mankind the palm of strength and vigour.'

The appeal to the ancient world is pure eighteenth century. But the programme of ideas which Charles Fox proclaims points onward into the century which had just begun when he closed his eyes.

BIBLIOGRAPHICAL NOTE

DETAILED bibliographical references can be found in most English accounts of this epoch, particularly in volumes VI and VIII of the *Cambridge Modern History*, which admittedly date back to 1909 and 1904. Recent researches are largely dealt with in Sir Charles Grant Robertson's *England under the Hanoverians* (13th edition, 1944). Of the older accounts, Lecky's *History of England in the Eighteenth Century* (7 vols., 1892) is still worth reading. Wolfgang Michael's *Englische Geschichte im achtzehnten Jahrhundert* only goes up to 1742: the first volume, going up to 1718, has been issued in English (1936). The social background is sketched in G. M. Trevelyan's *English Social History* (1942), chapters XI to XVI.

T. W. Riker (1911) and Lord Ilchester, who has been able to draw on the Holland House Papers (1920), have both written two-volume biographies of Henry Fox. On the elder Pitt the most authoritative work is the two-volume biography of Basil Williams (1913); besides this there is Brian Tunstall's (1938). Lord Rosebery's *Chatham, His Early Life and Connections* (1910) only goes up to the threshold of the Seven Years' War. Macaulay's two essays on Chatham, thanks to his skill in presentation and his political penetration, have outlasted the criticism which has justly been levelled at many individual points in them. Of German historians, A. von Ruville has written a very profound and in places discerning biography in three volumes, which is unfortunately couched in a pedagogic style (1905, English translation 1907). There are detailed studies by D. A. Winstanley: *Lord Chatham and the Whig Opposition* (1912) and *Personal and Party Government* (1910). A selection of the correspondence left by Chatham was published in 1838–40 in four volumes. These are supplemented by the four volumes of the *Grenville Papers* (1852–3) and by the numerous letters, particularly of the Duke of Newcastle, which Philip Yorke has reprinted in his *Life and Correspondence of the Earl of Hardwicke* (3 vols., 1913).

Of other biographies, particular mention must be made of John Morley's *Walpole* (1889) and Basil Williams' *Carteret and Newcastle* (1943).

FOREIGN POLICY IN THE AGE OF CHATHAM

Sir Richard Lodge, *Great Britain and Prussia in the eighteenth century* (1923).

Reinhold Koser, *König Friedrich der Grosse* (2 vols., 1893, 1905) and *Politische Korrespondenz Friedrichs des Grossen* (1879–1920).

M. Immich, *Geschichte des europäischen Staatensystems von 1660 bis 1789* (1905).
Cambridge History of British Foreign Policy, vol. I (1922).
R. Waddington, *Louis XV et le renversement des alliances* (1896).
W. Windelband, *Die auswärtige Politik der Grossmächte in der Neuzeit, 1494–1919* (1922).

GEORGE III

His *Correspondence 1760–1783*, ed. Sir John Fortescue (1927–28). *Letters from George III to Lord Bute* (1939), with an interesting introduction by R. Sedgwick. The traditional view is critically examined by L. B. Namier in *The Structure of Politics at the Accession of George III* (2 vols., 1929), and *England in the Age of the American Revolution* (1930).

Charles Fox's youth has been portrayed in masterly fashion by Sir George Trevelyan in *The Early History of Charles James Fox* (1880), a gem among biographies. Unfortunately he has not continued the story of Fox's life in the same style, but has interwoven the biography with the history of the American Revolution: *The American Revolution* (1899–1907), and *George III and Charles Fox* (1912–14). Of numerous biographies which have appeared of recent years, that by John Drinkwater (1928) may be mentioned. Fox's parliamentary speeches were published in 1815 in six volumes. A selection of his correspondence is contained in Lord John Russell's *Memorials and Correspondence of Charles James Fox* (4 vols., 1853–7); see also Lord Holland's *Memoirs of the Whig Party* (2 vols., 1852–4).

The standard life of the younger Pitt is by J. Holland Rose (2 vols., 1911). A shorter biography has been published by Lord Rosebery (1891). Macaulay's essay can be found in the eighth to tenth editions of the *Encyclopaedia Britannica*, and there is a shortened and readjusted version in the eleventh edition; it has been separately reprinted on a number of occasions. The German biography by Felix Salomon (1906) only progressed as far as the outbreak of the war with France. A particularly important source for Pitt and his policy are the first seven volumes of the *Dropmore Papers* (Historical Manuscript Commission, 1892–1910), with excellent introductions by W. Fitzpatrick.

A recent publication on the American Revolution is John C. Miller, *Origins of the American Revolution* (1945).

For the election of 1784 see W. T. Laprade, *English Historical Review*, vol. 31 (April, 1916), and *American Historical Review*, vol. 18, page 254, as well as the *Parliamentary Papers of John Robinson* (Royal Historical Society, 1922), edited by Laprade.

On Burke there are biographies by John Morley (1867) and Sir Philip Magnus (1939); on Lord Shelburne, a biography by Lord Fitzmaurice (2 vols., 1912); on Wilberforce, one by Sir Reginald Coupland (Second edition, 1945); on Charles Grey, one by G. M. Trevelyan (1920).

FOREIGN POLICY SINCE THE OUTBREAK OF THE FRENCH REVOLUTION

H. von Sybel, *Geschichte der Revolutionszeit*, the third edition of which was translated as *History of the French Revolution* (4 vols., 1867–69).

A. Sorel, *L'Europe et la Révolution Française* (8 vols., 1885–1904).

A. Wahl, *Geschichte des europäischen Staatensystems im Zeitalter der französischen Revolution* (1912).

C. T. von Heigel, *Deutsche Geschichte vom Tode Friedrichs des Grossen* (2 vols., 1899, 1911).

H. Delbrück, *Weltgeschichte*, vol. IV (1925).

E. Bourgeois, *Manuel historique de la politique étrangère* (3 vols., 1892–1906).

R. W. Seton-Watson, *Britain in Europe, 1789–1914* (1937).

Lord Malmesbury, *Diaries and Correspondence* (4 vols., 1844).

SOCIAL LIFE

J. H. Jesse, *George Selwyn and his Contemporaries* (4 vols., 1843), and *George Selwyn, his Letters and his Life* (1899).

Marjorie Villiers, *The Grand Whiggery* (1939).

Iris Leveson-Gower, *The Face without a Frown: Georgiana, Duchess of Devonshire* (1944).

POLITICAL THOUGHT

Sir Leslie Stephen, *History of English Thought in the eighteenth century*, vol. II (3rd edition, 1902).

H. W. C. Davis, *The Age of Grey and Peel* (1929).

G. S. Veitch, *The Genesis of Parliamentary Reform* (1913).

NOTE ON THE TEXT

With some help from the author's original manuscript, all quotations and the key phrases of many passages have been checked against the earliest reliable printed renderings of the original sources, except that the bulk of the elder Pitt's speeches on American taxation in Chapter X are derived from Tunstall's composite versions of them in his fourteenth chapter. Nineteenth century rephrasings have been avoided, but for reasons advanced in the text Stanhope's version of the younger Pitt's last public speech is given, and not that printed in the *Sun* of November 12th, 1805, and reprinted by Professor A. Aspinall in *History*, Vol. XXXIII, Nos. 117 and 118 (1948). In a few passages the original English wording has replaced paraphrases designed by the author to eliminate difficulties of translation into German. All omissions are shown by dots; capital letters have been made to conform to the style of the rest of the book; punctuation has also been adjusted, but not to the complete exclusion of the semi-colon so dear to Edmund Burke. Thanks are due to the trustees and staff of the British Museum for all the facilities so generously provided; also to Miss C. Shaddick both for the help given and for the methods evolved by her in dealing with quotations and other matters stylistic and historical in the first nine chapters, methods which the publishers have found it wise to follow.

INDEX OF EVENTS

All dates are according to new style reckoning

INDEX OF PERSONS

Titles not mentioned in the text, or borne after 1806, are not given; successions to peerages are marked suc., *and creations* cr. *Foreign rulers are distinguished by the dates of their reigns*